Echoes of History

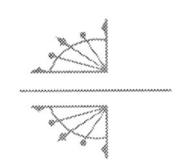

Echoes of History

Naxi Music in Modern China

HELEN REES

OXFORD
UNIVERSITY PRESS
2000

OXFORD
UNIVERSITY PRESS

Oxford   New York
Athens   Auckland   Bangkok   Bogotá   Buenos Aires   Calcutta
Cape Town   Chennai   Dar es Salaam   Delhi   Florence   Hong Kong   Istanbul
Karachi   Kuala Lumpur   Madrid   Melbourne   Mexico City   Mumbai
Nairobi   Paris   São Paulo   Shanghai   Singapore   Taipei   Tokyo   Toronto   Warsaw

and associated companies in
Berlin   Ibadan

Copyright © 2000 by Oxford University Press

Published by Oxford University Press, Inc.
198 Madison Avenue, New York, New York 10016

Oxford is a registered trademark of Oxford University Press

All rights reserved. No part of this publication may be reproduced,
stored in a retrieval system, or transmitted, in any form or by any means,
electronic, mechanical, photocopying, recording, or otherwise,
without the prior permission of Oxford University Press.

Publication of this book has been supported by generous grants from
the Chiang Ching-kuo Foundation for International Scholarly Exchange
and the Pacific Cultural Foundation.

Library of Congress Cataloging-in-Publication Data
Rees, Helen, 1964–
Echoes of history : Naxi music in modern China / Helen Rees.
p. cm.
Originally presented as the author's thesis.
Includes bibliographical references, discography, videography, and index.
ISBN 0-19-512949-0; ISBN 0-19-512950-4 (pbk.)
1. Naxi (Chinese people)—China—Li-chiang Na-hsi tsu tzu chih hsien—Music—History
and criticism.   2. Folk music—China—Li-chiang Na-hsi tsu tzu chih hsien—History and
criticism.   I. Title.
ML3746.7.Y8 R44   2000
781.62'95—dc21   99-054366

1 3 5 7 9 8 6 4 2
Printed in the United States of America
on acid-free paper

For the musicians of Lijiang

and all the many people who helped along the way

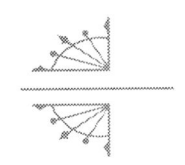

Acknowledgments

This study of Naxi music is primarily based on five periods of fieldwork in Yunnan Province, southwest China: an initial exploratory trip in May 1989; a ten-month period of research from September 1991 to July 1992; and follow-up visits in the summers of 1993, 1996, and 1998. Permission to conduct fieldwork was kindly granted by the governments of Yunnan Province, Lijiang Prefecture, Lijiang Naxi Autonomous County, and Chuxiong Yi Autonomous Prefecture. My first visit to Yunnan was undertaken while the recipient of a British Council/Chinese government postgraduate scholarship; the major period of fieldwork was funded by the President's Fellowship in Chinese Studies of the University of Pittsburgh; and the three summer trips were supported by a summer travel grant from the China Council of the University of Pittsburgh, a faculty development grant from New College of the University of South Florida, and a summer stipend from the National Endowment for the Humanities. Finally, a faculty research grant from the University of California, Los Angeles, has helped underwrite final revisions.

My work unit in China, the Yunnan Art Institute, assumed the administrative burdens connected with my visits, and I would like to thank Na Shihua and his staff for their efforts in this regard. The instructors assigned to me in Kunming, Guo Dalie, Huang Lin, Yang Fuquan, and Zhang Xingrong, were extremely helpful; similarly, my three instructors in Lijiang County, He Zhong, Xuan Ke, and Yang Zenglie, generously offered me the benefit of their expertise and experience, and greatly improved the standard of my work. In Chuxiong Prefecture, Xiong Wangping dealt efficiently with the red tape associated with my fieldwork and offered excellent academic guidance.

My greatest debt, of course, is to the many musicians of Lijiang County and other parts of Yunnan Province who welcomed me and took my interest in their music seriously. In Lijiang County, the Dongjing music groups of Baihua Village, Baisha Township, Dayan Town, and Jinshan Township all permitted me to record and document their activities and to join in their music-making. The leaders of each group who kindly welcomed me were, respectively, He Guowei and He Minda, He Huihan and Mu Shu, He Yi'an and Xuan Ke, and He Chenglin and Yang Jian. In addition, although I was not able to attend activities of the Changshui Village or Shigu Town ensembles, He Hongxing and He Yitian of Changshui and Zhao Yuxian of Shigu generously allowed long interviews. He Linghan, He Minda, He Zhong, Xuan Ke, and Zhang Longhan frequently accompanied me on interviews and interpreted between the Naxi and Chinese languages when necessary. Many musicians engaged in musics other than the Dongjing repertoire also allowed me to record and interview them. I wish to thank in particular He Fengxiang; He Heng; Wang Chaoxin; Yang Houkun; He Minda, He Zhong, Huang Erya, Li Xinmin, and the other personnel of the Lijiang Naxi Autonomous County Song and Dance Troupe; and Xi Hongyi, Wang Zhengwu, and the other members of the Dayan Town Xi'an Street Dianju Club. I would also like to put on record my gratitude to the many Dongjing musicians and local officials from other counties and cities in Yunnan who aided my work in their areas.

Many other people in China and Hong Kong offered me technical, academic, or moral support, including Ge Agan, Susan Kuyper, Lei Hong'an, Li Wei, Luo Ping, Tom Stanley, Suzanne Sterzer, Norman Track, and Zhao Hong. In particular, I wish to acknowledge the extraordinary lengths to which Wang Zhishan and his staff at the Lijiang County Library went to find the materials I needed and to provide a pleasant environment in which to work.

The Naxi musicians' tour of England in October 1995 was a huge success thanks to the organizing talents of Penny King, Rowan Pease, and Asian Music Circuit. He Jiaxiu, head of the propaganda department of the Lijiang Prefecture Communist Party Committee, accompanied the group and went out of his way to help smooth the course for all of us.

This book began life as a dissertation, and I could not have had a more supportive adviser or more constructive critic than Bell Yung. My other committee members, Akin Euba, Mary Lewis, Evelyn Rawski, and Deane Root, also contributed valuable suggestions from their very different standpoints. During the long process of revision and proofreading, I have benefited from the expertise and advice of Judith Boltz, Yan Bu, Nancy Guy, Laurel Isbister, Stephen Jones, Frank Kouwenhoven, Frederick Lau, Piet van der Loon, Stephen Miles, J. H. Kwabena Nketia, Timothy Rice, Dianne Roberts, Margaret Sarkissian, Antoinet Schimmelpenninck, Grace Tin-Yan Tam, Jocelyn Van Tuyl, Ben Wu, Bell Yung, and the four readers—Stevan Harrell, Joseph Lam, Charles McKhann, and Larry Witzleben. Pantelis Vassilakis produced the CD that accompanies this book, Miriam Gerberg created the camera-ready musical examples, Inne Choi is responsible for the map in the first chapter, and Jack Bishop for the maps in the third chapter. Maribeth Payne, Maureen Buja, and Cynthia Garver of Oxford University Press have efficiently shepherded the book through the editing and production process.

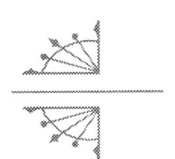

Contents

Romanization, Geography, Dynasties   xiii

1. Introduction   3
First Encounter   3
Research Methodology   6
Goals of This Book   6
Theoretical Issues   7

2. Ethnic Minorities and the Chinese State   10
Qing Policies in the Southwest   11
Republican Policies in the Southwest   13
Communist Minorities Policy   15
Communist Policy Toward Minority Performing Arts   19
The "Motif of the Music-making Minority"   23

3. The Naxi of Lijiang County   28
Who Are the Naxi?   28
Location and Population of Lijiang   30
Lijiang County and the Chinese State   32
Religion Among the Lijiang Naxi   35
Han Cultural Influence   37
Dongjing Associations of Yunnan   39
Dongjing Associations of Lijiang County   48

4. The Musical World of Republican Lijiang   54
Naxi Musics   55
Dongjing Music   68

Other Han-derived Musics　91
　　　Other Musics in Lijiang County　94
　　　The Demographics of Participation　94
　　　Music as a Barometer of Republican-era Lijiang Society　98

5. Dongjing Music and Local Interaction in Republican Lijiang　99

　　　Relationship Networks of the Dongjing Associations　100
　　　Transmission　104
　　　Regional Variation among Lijiang's Dongjing Associations　112
　　　Secular Groups and Social Interaction　114
　　　Summary　116

6. The Wider World Comes To Lijiang: The Musical Impact　118

　　　From the Moslem Uprising to the Civil War　119
　　　Liberation　121
　　　From the 1950s through the Cultural Revolution　122
　　　From the Death of Mao to the 1990s　133

7. The Dongjing Music Revival: Have Music, Will Travel　141

　　　The Beginning of the Revival　141
　　　The Tourist Concerts　147
　　　Lijiang's Dongjing Music on the Road　157
　　　Dongjing Music and Lijiang Society in the 1980s and 1990s　162
　　　Changes in the Dongjing Tradition　165

8. Representation and Ethnicity　170

　　　Names Attached to the Dongjing Tradition　171
　　　Representations from before 1949　174
　　　Representations from 1949 to the Cultural Revolution　176
　　　Representations since the Cultural Revolution　177
　　　Ethnicity　188
　　　Summary: Representation of Music in Lijiang　191

9. Conclusion　193

　　　From Dongjing Music to Naxi Ancient Music　193
　　　Minority Music and the Socialist State　194
　　　Theoretical Perspectives　196

Appendix A. Dongjing Scriptures of Lijiang County	199
Appendix B. Temple Interior for Dongjing Ceremonies in Dayan Town	203
Appendix C. Chinese Texts	208
Appendix D. Glossary of Chinese Characters	212
Notes	221
Bibliography	237
Discography	261
Videography	263
Recordings on Accompanying CD	265
Index	269

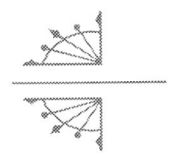

Romanization, Geography, Dynasties

Romanization

Romanization of Naxi terms in this book is according to Naxi Pinyin used in the People's Republic of China. The table here shows the conversion between Naxi Pinyin and the International Phonetic Alphabet. Note that Naxi has four tones. The high-level tone is indicated by placing the letter *l* at the end of the syllable, the low-level tone by placing the letter *q* at the end of the syllable, and the rising tone by placing the letter *f* at the end of the syllable. Syllables lacking any of these markers are pronounced in the mid-level tone.

Conversion table between Naxi Pinyin and the International Phonetic Alphabet (after McKhann 1992: 410).

PINYIN	IPA	PINYIN	IPA	PINYIN	IPA
b	p	q	tɕ'	iu	y
p	p'	jj	dʐ	ai	æ
bb	b	ni	ɲ	a	a
m	m	x	ɕ	o	o
f	f	zh	tʂ	u	u
d	t	ch	tʂ'	v	ʏ
t	t'	rh	dʐ̢	e	ə
dd	d	sh	ʂ	er	ər
n	n	r	ʐ̢	iai	iai
l	l	z	ts	ie	iə
g	k	c	ts'	ia	ia
k	k'	zz	dz	uai	uæ
gg	g	s	s	ua	ua
ng		ss	z	ue	uə
h	h	i	i	ee	ɯ
j	tɕ				

xiii

Romanization of Han Chinese names and terms is according to Hanyu Pinyin. Conversion charts between Hanyu Pinyin and the International Phonetic Alphabet are found in most Chinese-English dictionaries published in the People's Republic of China. The letters and combinations most confusing to non-Chinese speakers are the following:

c	like the *t's* in *it's*
q	like the *ch* of *cheap*
x	like the *sh* of *sheep*
z	like the *dz* of *adze*
j	like the *j* of *joust*
e	like the *er* in *her* (British pronunciation), except after *y* or *i*
ie, ye	like the *ye* of *yet*
i after z, c, or s	like "a weakly buzzing, syllabic z" (Ramsey 1987: 294)
i after ch, r, sh, zh	like "a syllabic American r" (Ramsey 1987: 294)
i after other consonants	like the *ea* in *mean*

Thus *Naxi* is pronounced "Na-shee" in Mandarin Chinese.

Yunnan has a rich variety of dialects of Mandarin, but to avoid confusion I have romanized all Chinese terms according to standard Hanyu Pinyin (except in a few places noted in the text). Those interested in Yunnanese Han dialects will find Gui 1990 to be a useful English-language source.

Quotations from authors who use different romanization systems are silently converted to Hanyu Pinyin. However, a few names better known by other romanizations (such as Canton, Taipei, and Hong Kong) are left in the customary form. Names of Chinese citizens residing in China are given in the usual Chinese order—surname first, given name last.

When quoting sources that use British English spelling, I convert silently to American spelling.

Political Geography

Chinese administrative divisions are complex and are redrawn and renamed frequently. As far as possible I have used those names and terms applicable to the time periods described. In general, post-1949 Chinese terms for geopolitical administrative divisions are translated according to the usage of the standard reference work *The Pinyin Chinese Dictionary* (Beijing: Commercial Press, 1979). The terms and explanations here are those relevant to this book; they by no means constitute an exhaustive list of administrative divisions:

sheng	province (the largest regional subdivision)
shi	city

diqu	prefecture (main subdivision within a province)
zhou	prefecture (main subdivision within a province)
xian	county (largest subdivision within a prefecture)
xiang	township (main rural subdivision within a county)
zhen	town (urban area within a county)
xingzheng cun	administrative village (in a township, several villages grouped together for administrative purposes)
ziran cun	natural village (lowest level of unit)

In this book I translate both kinds of *cun* as "village," since people rarely made the formal distinction in everyday conversation.

Dynasties and Republics

The main dynasties and republics mentioned in this book are:

Yuan	1271–1368
Ming	1368–1644
Qing	1644–1911
Republic of China	1912–1949 (ROC on Taiwan 1949–present)
People's Republic of China	1949–present

Echoes of History

1

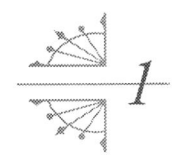

Introduction

> *"Echoes of history . . . ancient and graceful melodies"*
> (Sun Jiong, Yunnan Province China Overseas
> Tourism Company, 1996)

First Encounter

In spring 1989 I took an exploratory field trip to Yunnan Province, an ethnically diverse and spectacularly scenic area of southwest China. In early May I joined several other foreign students and tourists on a bumpy twenty-hour bus trip from Kunming, the provincial capital, to Lijiang, a county in the northwest of the province (see Figure 1.1). Known for its mountainous terrain (see Figure 1.2), the unspoiled traditional architecture of its county seat (see Figure 1.3), and the unusual culture of the local inhabitants, the Naxi ethnic minority (pronounced Na-shee in Mandarin Chinese), Lijiang had been opened to foreigners in 1985. By 1989 it was attracting several dozen foreign tourists a week, and a number of local ventures, especially restaurants, were beginning to cater to them. Also directed at the foreign visitors were bilingual Chinese-English advertisements for concerts of "traditional Naxi music," held a couple of times a week. Having heard in Kunming of a Lijiang "orchestra" of elderly men, I lost no time in finding my way through the maze of alleys to the picturesque old mansion in which the concerts took place. There, in the central stone courtyard, about forty chairs were set out for the audience, while the chairs and tables for the musicians were on the raised stone platform in front of the main hall. As the audience took their seats, sixteen or so mainly elderly men arrived in small groups and began selecting and tuning their instruments, which included bowed and plucked strings, flutes, a small double-reed pipe, and a variety of percussion. Eventually a lithe, middle-aged man stood up and addressed the audience in quite fluent English, introducing the music and musicians, and requesting us to buy the four *yuan*

FIGURE 1.1. Map of China, showing major cities and western provinces.

tickets in the intermission (at this time four yuan were a little less than U.S. $1). He explained that the music had originally been borrowed by the Naxi from the Han Chinese ethnic majority, and that before 1949 it had been used in religious rituals. It soon became obvious from the music played that evening (see CD Track 13) that the style, structure, and many of the instruments were very similar to those of the "silk and bamboo" (*sizhu*) instrumental ensemble music I was familiar with from Han culture in southeast China; moreover, the tune titles, and even the words of the few sung pieces, were in Han Chinese. Despite this, the English-speaking leader emphasized the Naxi ethnicity of the performers, and the Naxi "spirit" of the music—which he referred to as "Naxi Ancient Music" (*Naxi guyue* in Chinese). I immediately sought out a couple of Chinese-language descriptions of musical life in Lijiang, and discovered that this was in fact a very recent name for the music I had heard, coined only around 1980. It had historically been referred to as "Dongjing music" (*dongjing yinyue*), in recognition of its role as the auditory ingredient in ritual performances by Dongjing associations (*dongjinghui*).[1] These prestigious amateur musico-ritual associations were quintessentially Han Chinese in terms of deities worshiped, scriptures chanted and music played, and were widespread in Yunnan Province before 1949 among

FIGURE 1.2. The classic Lijiang view: across the Black Dragon Pool park to the Jade Dragon Snow Mountain, fall 1991.

FIGURE 1.3. Traditional houses and canal in Dayan Town, fall 1991.

the literati in both Han and some minority areas, including Lijiang. They blended Confucian, Taoist, and Buddhist elements in their beliefs and ritual, and had been renowned throughout Yunnan for their elegant music—the Lijiang variant of which, renamed Naxi Ancient Music, was now charming so many foreign visitors.

I was intrigued by the double anomaly inherent in the "Naxi Ancient Music" heard that evening: a musical repertoire that embodied potential contradictions of ethnic affiliation and appeared to have exchanged a traditionally religious character for a highly visible—and audible—role in the burgeoning tourist industry of Lijiang County. These apparent paradoxes induced me to return two years later to try to understand the mechanisms underlying their existence.

Research Methodology

I carried out my major fieldwork on Lijiang's Dongjing music between September 1991 and July 1992, and made return visits in the summers of 1993, 1996, and 1998. The technical musical aspects of the repertoire, its broader musical environment, and its history and extramusical context, were elicited through sound and video recording, photographic documentation, participant observation, and extensive interviews. I examined primary sources in the Lijiang County Library, Lijiang Prefecture Archive, Yunnan Province Library, and in private collections, and searched out existing Chinese scholarship, commercial recordings, newspaper articles, and travel guide write-ups on the subject. In addition, I made brief visits to several other counties and cities in Yunnan that have Dongjing music, and conducted fieldwork there for comparative purposes. This work in China was supplemented by library research at major collections in England and the United States.

Finally, in October 1995 I was engaged as guide and interpreter for a group of Lijiang musicians invited by the British concert promoter Asian Music Circuit to tour England for two weeks. Being actively, and exhaustingly, engaged in the tour, I was able to document the first-ever trip by these musicians outside China and to collect the ephemera associated with it.

Goals of This Book

China has seen incredibly rapid changes in political, economic, social, and cultural life in the last hundred years—changes that have affected and been witnessed by countless regional musics. While documentation of musical transformations has been relatively plentiful for high-profile genres of the Han-dominated center and east of China, less attention has been paid to the complex issues at play in the remote minority regions of the southwest.[2] Structured chronologically, this book focuses on the developmental trajectory traveled during the twentieth century by Lijiang's Dongjing music, a minority-performed genre for which there is an unusually plentiful body of historical evidence. It locates Lijiang's Dongjing music as one genre among many in the county's rich multiethnic musical culture, and describes its development against a broader local, provincial, and national cultural background.[3]

This study of Lijiang's Dongjing music raises both case-specific and wider concerns. At the most specific level, it offers narrative documentation of the extraordinary variety of uses to which this Han-derived music has been put in Naxi society, especially the huge changes in use and ideology in the twentieth century. Particular emphasis is laid on the music's widening level of recognition and significance. It has gone from being known at the county level in the late Qing and Republican eras (pre-1949), to regional and national recognition in the first forty years of the People's Republic, and to international exposure since tourist concerts began in 1988.

The range of activities, audiences, and changing worldviews to which this music has been exposed inevitably throws up a welter of diverse issues regarding class and ethnic consciousness, political ideology and individual agency, and ritual performativity and tourist reception. The appearance and relative importance of these issues vary as the chronological narrative wends its way through the changing backdrop of twentieth-century history; yet ultimately the interrelation of these apparently disparate elements becomes vital to explain the evolution of the tradition into the 1990s.

I call on all the issues outlined above to explain the role of Lijiang's Dongjing music in local social interaction, in which its Han characteristics in a Naxi setting have often been vital, and to contrast this with its recent role in Lijiang's outreach to the wider Chinese and international world, in which its Naxi-ness has been crucial. Particularly relevant to this theme is my discussion in Chapter 8 of changes in the perceived role of this music through the representations that local and non-local individuals have created as it has moved through its trajectory of widening geographical significance. I relate these changes to the Republican and Communist governments' ethnicity policies, which have been instrumental in defining relations between remote Lijiang and the central Chinese state, and which have had a strong impact on concepts of identity and cultural value among the local people and their visitors.

In addition, by looking at the overall musical landscape in Lijiang, I use the county as a case study of the interaction between national policies and local response since the institution of socialist-inspired cultural planning in 1949; I also draw attention to comparable or contrasting situations in other socialist countries.

Theoretical Issues

The immediate focus of this book is on a specific set of musical activities bounded by a limited space and time, and many of the conclusions drawn are particularly valuable to the study of cultural change and negotiation in a multiethnic socialist nation now opening to the outside world. But at a deeper level, it is worth considering two more general theoretical issues relevant to the cross-cultural study of music and its relationship to society. First, this case study of Lijiang's Dongjing music illustrates the fluidity of meaning attached to music, and suggests the validity and usefulness of music as a lens through which to examine society, social change, and historical events. Second, it moves beyond a view of music as merely a passive recipient of extramusical influences to a view of music as an active factor in the construction of identities and relationships—and as a cultural entity that may even dynamically affect the extra-musical environment.

Music, History, and Historical Witness

Musical phenomena are increasingly investigated for confirmation of, or clues to, a social order, social change, and historical events. This is in itself a facet of the much-vaunted ethnomusicological concern with the interaction between music and its context. Numerous studies attest to the use and function of music in helping create and maintain group identity and differentiation.[4] As for music as historical evidence, as early as 1940 American musicologist Charles Seeger titled an essay "Folk Music as a Source of Social History"; and since then scholars dealing with a variety of geocultural areas have demonstrated the value of musical evidence in historical and political research.[5] Such evidence frequently confirms what is already suspected, but it can also raise provocative questions and offer fresh avenues of inquiry: "an ethnomusicological study of a living music culture provides a multi-faceted and unique data base, which in its totality may well illuminate important aspects of a culture's history" (Shelemay 1980: 235).

Presented with a discipline whose conceptual thrust in the early days tended to emphasize society rather than the individual, and synchronicity rather than diachronicity (Rice 1987: 473, 475), ethnomusicologists have attempted in recent years to outline models that take account of the historical and individual dimensions to music. Timothy Rice explicitly addresses these issues in an influential article titled "Toward the Remodeling of Ethnomusicology" (1987), in which, inspired by a formulation of Clifford Geertz, he urges us to ask, "How do people historically construct, socially maintain and individually create and experience music?" (p. 473); he applies this interrogative model with particular elegance in a recent monograph on Bulgarian music (1994). Daniel Neuman, in the epilogue to an essay collection premised on the idea of the interaction between ethnomusicology and history, suggests three "paradigms" of such interaction: first, "reflexive music history . . . the history of music history"; second, "interpretive music history . . . in which music culture itself is the subject of history and the history is externally constructed and conducted . . . to make a point and present an argument"; and, third, "immanent music history," in which "music 'writes' or in some manner represents history: a history not so much of music itself as of its creators or consumers" (1991: 269).

The ideas offered by Rice and Neuman are particularly useful when applied to the musical situation in Lijiang this century, since a chronological treatment necessarily involves the writing of a history, the examination of histories already written and spoken, and, more subtly, of the representation of a history through musical performance. Both the way people write and speak about music and the sounds that issue when they perform it can offer clues to the general historian or ethnographer as to ethnic interaction, the degree of contact with the outside world, local events, and changing value systems. At the same time, Lijiang is sufficiently small and the protagonists sufficiently few for individuals to loom large in the oral histories constructed by living musicians. Some individuals to this day have an extraordinary impact on the direction the creation and experience of the music take, and thus too on its social maintenance and historical construction.

Music as Active Cultural Force

The simplest and commonest way to investigate the relationship between music and historical events or politics or society is to observe the effect of all these on music and music-making. However, the second general theoretical issue delineated above, the viewing of music as a frequently active rather than passive cultural phenomenon, takes inspiration from a suggestion by Nketia:

> Although it is the effect of all these [extramusical factors] on music and music making on which the ethnomusicologist focuses, now and then he may also look at the reverse, since influences are reciprocal. . . . For example, in a study of music and society, the scholar may observe not only the effect of social factors on music, but also the impact of music on society, individual behavior, consciousness of identity, and so forth. Similarly when studying music and politics, he may observe not only the impact of politics on music, but also how hierarchical structures or egalitarianism may be defined by the forms of organization and use of music. (1990: 88)

It is this bidirectional study of context that I apply to my investigation of Lijiang's Dongjing music as an active ingredient in the cultural interaction on China's southwestern frontier. A fuller appreciation of the extramusical factors at work certainly throws light on the surface anomalies of the repertoire today; but, in addition, the music itself may be seen to articulate certain aspects of its social, ethnic, and historical environment—and indeed sometimes to have a tangible impact on that environment.

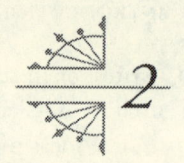

Ethnic Minorities and the Chinese State

The musical experience of the Naxi in the twentieth century has been shaped by disparate factors, one of the most important of which has been their position as an ethnic minority within the Chinese state. This chapter outlines the history of minority-state interaction in the southwest, and concludes by examining Communist policy toward minority performing arts—a vital subtext underlying many events in Lijiang in the post-1949 period.

Even very early Chinese historical records refer to ethnic groups considered different from the people constituting mainstream Chinese civilization; more than eight thousand groups are mentioned in literature spanning nearly three thousand years (Dreyer 1976: 7). Contact and conflict with these groups increased as the Chinese state expanded south and west and tried to maintain its northern border. Particularly dangerous were invaders from the north; indeed, several times in the last two thousand years dynasties established by northern peoples have ruled part or all of the territory considered to constitute China. The most recent of these "conquest dynasties" were the Mongolian Yuan (1260–1368) and the Manchu Qing (1644–1911). However, peoples to the west and southwest also threatened Chinese territory, including the Tibetans in the seventh century A.D., and the Nanzhao Kingdom, based in what is now Dali in Yunnan Province, in the ninth century A.D. (Backus 1981: 25–28, 105ff). Consequently, successive emperors faced the problem of how to deal with peoples on their borders. Each frontier presented unique challenges; the southwest was remarkable for the large numbers of disparate ethnic groups indigenous to the area.

Qing Policies in the Southwest (1644–1911)

As late as 1750, the majority of the population in China's far southwestern provinces of Yunnan and Guizhou was made up of indigenous peoples who were culturally quite distinct from mainstream Chinese civilization, and spoke various Tibeto-Burman, Tai, Miao-Yao, and Mon-Khmer languages. Nevertheless, immigration by settlers from eastern, northern, and central China was already well under way by this date: between 1253, when the Yuan conquered Dali in west-central Yunnan, and 1673, when the new Qing dynasty finally ousted Ming loyalists, soldiers sent in successive military campaigns to the region were left behind to colonize the frontiers, settling principally in fertile valleys and leaving the barren areas to the native inhabitants. Because Ming law required that military settlers take their families with them, it is likely that these immigrants numbered more than a million (Lee 1982: 287–289). Lee suggests that the settlers "introduced a deep and long-lasting cleavage in southwestern society" and altered the balance of power, providing "the coercive force that tied the southwest to China politically" (pp. 290–291). A further wave of immigration, involving about three million people, took place between about 1700 and 1850. During this period the government encouraged landless people to move to the southwest, offering them tax remissions, travel funds, and grants of seed and land. In addition, migrants included merchants, skilled craftsmen, and more than three hundred thousand miners who worked in the increasingly important copper, silver, and gold mines. By 1850, the Han Chinese, the majority ethnic group of China, had become a majority in the southwest (Lee 1982: 293–299).

Potential and actual resistance to the extension of the influence of the Chinese state in the southwest was met by a variety of ploys during the Qing dynasty. To secure the allegiance and loyalty of local ethnic groups, the court relied as far as possible on economical expedients familiar from Ming times (1368–1644), reserving more expensive military action for cases in which it could not be avoided. Perhaps the best-known method used was that commonly known as the *tusi* (native official) system. Of Yuan origins or before, but developed fully under the Ming, this system consisted of the Chinese court confirming a local notable as the rightful ruler of his people, exacting tribute, conferring an official Chinese title on him, and lending him moral support in local disputes. The arrangement frequently suited both sides: the local ruler bolstered his own position through outside support, while the Chinese court utilized the traditional local hierarchy to extend its own influence in peripheral areas. This form of indirect control has frequently been referred to as "using barbarians to rule barbarians" (*yiyi zhiyi*). The Qing followed the Ming in using the *tusi* system. Sometimes the Ming and Qing courts were actually able to extract military assistance from their native officials: in numerous cases from the sixteenth through the nineteenth centuries, the participation of troops under local rulers loyal to the court was vital in putting down insurgencies (Gong Yin 1985: 13–15).

Greater central government control, however, could generally be achieved only by replacing native officials with Chinese-appointed magistrates, and placing their domains under direct government rule. This process, known as "replacing the local and reverting to the mainstream" (*gaitu guiliu*), was attempted sporadically throughout the Ming dynasty and during the early Qing. From the Yongzheng reign (1723–1735) on, it was pursued more energetically: imperial policy increasingly aimed at undermining and eliminating native rulers, implementing direct Chinese rule, improving infrastructure, and exploiting the copper mines important to China's currency production (Smith 1970; Rowe 1994: 418). Lijiang, homeland of the Naxi, was typical in undergoing *gaitu guiliu* in 1723.

When absolutely necessary, Qing emperors sent armies to the southwest to impose imperial authority. In the late nineteenth century, government forces were eventually deployed in sufficient numbers to crush the massive "Miao rebellion" in Guizhou and the Moslem uprising in Yunnan, both of which lasted from the mid-1850s to 1873 (Jenks 1994; Jing 1986).

In addition to political and military means of tying indigenous populations to the Chinese state, cultural assimilation through public education was sporadically pursued in southwest China. Many indigenous customs found in parts of the southwest, such as cremation (e.g., among the Mosuo) and what were by Confucian standards immoral mingling of the sexes and immodest female attire (e.g., among the Miao), offended the sensibilities of educated Chinese officials. Schools were built with a view to "transformation by education" (*jiaohua*), based on the widely, though not universally, held belief that even "primitive" ethnic groups were educable in Confucian Chinese classics, rituals, and values.[1] It is estimated that about seventy-two prefectural and county schools, and thirty-three private academies, were founded in Yunnan during the Ming dynasty, of which about a fifth lasted into the Qing dynasty. The Qing began to pursue a public education initiative for remote aboriginal areas more enthusiastically in the eighteenth century; in 1725, for example, edicts ordered the establishment of schools for boys in all counties of Guizhou and Yunnan. Within Yunnan, ten public schools were founded between 1644 and 1704, ninety-one between 1704 and 1722, eighty-two between 1722 and 1732, and four hundred and sixty-five between 1733 and 1737 under the initiative spearheaded by the energetic Yunnan Provincial Treasurer Chen Hongmou (Rowe 1994: 425–426). Most of Chen's new schools were apparently still functioning in 1835. Nevertheless, despite the greatly increased successes of non-Han candidates in imperial exams following Chen's reforms, Nationalist educators in the twentieth century were still to deplore the low educational level of the minority inhabitants of the southwest, and the limited degree of sinicization achieved; Chen's education policies seem to have had uneven effects (Rowe 1994: 444–445). The Lijiang Naxi illustrate this situation well: despite a long history of Chinese-language schools, in 1933 only 7.8 percent of Lijiang's men and 0.26 percent of its women were literate in Chinese (Rock 1963: 29).

Overall Qing policy toward its ethnic minorities has been summed up as "a pluralistic form of integration that aimed at little more than control" (Dreyer 1976: 12). Though the increase in immigration from the interior of China to the southwest speeded a limited process of political control and acculturation, traditional indigenous languages, customs, religions, and social structures persist among many minority peoples to this day.

Republican Policies in the Southwest (1912–1949)

Under the Republican government, minority policies were to some extent a continuation of Qing methods, although they also foreshadowed the much more rigorous approach adopted by the Communist government since 1949. Sun Yat-Sen, leader of the revolution that overthrew the Qing dynasty in 1911 and established the Republic of China, favored assimilation, but still followed the precedent set by the Qianlong emperor (1736–1795) in recognizing five peoples of China: the Han (the majority group of China), Manchu, Mongolians, Tibetans, and Moslems (Gladney 1991: 83). Nevertheless, few special provisions were made for non-Han in most constitutional documents of the Republic, although equality of all citizens, regardless of race, was guaranteed as early as the *Provisional Constitution* of 1912. The *Constitutional Compact* of 1914 did affirm special treatment for Manchu, Mongolians, Tibetans, and Moslems, and some later documents mention some degree of self-government for Mongolia and Tibet (Pan 1945: 150, 177, 210, 232–233, 254). But it is the 1946 Constitution that implies greatest concern with other non-Han peoples and areas: the state offers legal protection to "the status of the various racial groups [*minzu*] in the border regions, and shall give special assistance in their local self-government work," with such areas as education, culture, communications, health, and land use especially targeted (Hoh 1946: 35). This late constitution, promulgated in the middle of a civil war that made its implementation extremely unlikely, is a step in the direction of its Communist-authored successors, which make a point of special provisions for ethnic minorities.

Despite their relative absence from constitutional and national policy documents, minority citizens were not ignored when the Nationalists were formulating policies for minority-dominated regions. In his discussion of Nationalist policy toward southwestern minorities David Deal identifies four main ideas that guided the Nationalist government's actions: race, border, self-determination, and assimilation. First, on the subject of race, he suggests that the Nationalists basically adhered to the traditional Chinese view of minority ethnic groups: they were not congenitally inferior and could become civilized through education and immersion in Chinese culture. Second, the Nationalists held that the "border area," which contained "border nationalities" (*bianjiang minzu*), peoples who had "a comparatively low level of civilization," constituted 60 percent of China's total area, and so was fair game for exploitation and development by the state. Third, "self-determination," a concept borrowed from the West, was conceived as applying only to the right of China to resist foreign intervention; it was not an invitation to minority groups to secede from the Chinese state. Fourth, assimilation was clearly the overriding ideal. Quoting mostly contemporary sources, Deal sums up Nationalist policy thus:

> Ethnic minority place-names were replaced with [Han] Chinese place-names . . . , minorities adopted [Han] Chinese surnames . . . , and Chinese officials in minority areas advocated the adoption of the [Han] Chinese language, wearing of Chinese dress, and intermarriage as a means of assimilation. . . . In 1928, the Ministry of the Interior sent a letter to the provincial governments of the southwestern provinces asking them to report on the efficacy of various methods used to "civilize" (*kaihua*) the tribes. Implicit in this concept of civilizing the aborigines is the idea that they must draw nearer to the Chinese norm. . . . There was, in sum, stress on the unity of China's nationalities under the Nationalists, and a desire to make the minorities aware that the best course for them to follow was to become part of a great Chinese nationality, rather than to cultivate a sense of ethnic loyalty. (1976: 32)

The effectiveness of the practical application of these principles was reminiscent of the Qing dynasty's attempts at control and assimilation. In southwest China, the de facto continuation of the much-criticized *tusi* (native official) system was symptomatic of the government's inability to control the administration in many minority areas. Minority enrollment in public schools, despite official encouragement, subsidies and adaptation to local conditions, remained very low. And many non-Han appear to have benefited relatively little from the economic boom enjoyed by the southwest during the Second World War (Deal 1976: 32–33); some even lost lands to the mainly Han refugees flooding in from eastern and central China (Dreyer 1976: 32).

A graphic foreign account of the hazards faced by travelers in Yunnan in the 1930s and 1940s from highway robbers, and of the independence of certain branches of the Yi (then pejoratively referred to as "Lolo"), underscores the lack of effective government control at a local level during this period (Goullart 1957: 5ff, 139ff). At the provincial level, the central government's ability to impose its will was similarly limited. From 1911 to 1928 Yunnan was ruled by Tang Jiyao, who was able by reason of the province's remote location and diversity of inhabitants to act with considerable independence. His successors Long Yun and Lu Han, both of Yi ethnicity, were willing to negotiate with the Communists rather than give unequivocal support to the Nationalists (Dreyer 1976: 29–30).

However, given the multiple problems facing the government of the Republic of China for most of its rule—most notably the plethora of independent warlords, the Japanese invasion, and the civil war with the Communists—it is not surprising that such policies as it did attempt to enact toward the southwestern minorities were generally ineffectual. It had neither the resources nor the political will to deal effectively with what was in the grand scheme of things a fairly minor problem.

Communist Minorities Policy (1930s to 1990s)

Today the government of the People's Republic of China extends official recognition to fifty-six *minzu*. This Chinese term is usually rendered in English-language government publications as "nationalities," so I shall follow this usage, with the caveat that it is closer, though not identical, to what we normally mean in English by "ethnic groups." The largest nationality is the Han, now making up about 92 percent of the population; fifty-five "minority nationalities" (*shaoshu minzu*) (also frequently translated "national minorities") account for the other 8 percent.[2]

From its earliest years the Chinese Communist Party took seriously the issue of the non-Han peoples of China. The *Resolution of the First All-China Congress of Soviets on the Question of National Minorities in China*, adopted by the Congress at Ruijin, Jiangxi, in November 1931, even appeared to provide for genuine self-determination as well as sympathy in the face of Han and foreign chauvinism and exploitation (Moseley 1966: 164). Later Communist documents never again went this far, but did offer many attractions to the national minorities. Unlike previous Chinese governments, the People's Republic does not overtly demand the cultural assimilation of its minority citizens, instead acknowledging the rights of recognized nationalities to diverse cultural identities, albeit within the unified socialist state. In 1949, the *Common Program of the Chinese People's Political Consultative Conference*, which laid the groundwork for subsequent constitutions, devoted a whole chapter to ethnic minorities. It guaranteed the equality of all nationalities within the People's Republic of China, regional autonomy in areas where national minorities were concentrated, and the freedom of minorities "to develop their dialects and languages, to preserve or reform their traditions, customs and religious beliefs." Indeed, "the People's government shall assist the masses of the people of all national minorities to develop their political, economic, cultural, and educational construction work" (quoted in Moseley 1966: 168–169). Similarly, in the preamble to the 1954 *Constitution of the People's Republic of China*, the state was enjoined to promote unity among nationalities while discouraging greater Han chauvinism and respecting the diversity of ethnic groups (Moseley 1966: 169).

To differing degrees these ideals have been written into each of the four constitutions promulgated by the People's Republic of China since 1949 (1954, 1975,

1978, and 1982). In practice, campaigns against minority distinctiveness and minority leaders were waged during extremist political movements such as the Anti-Rightist Campaign (1957), the Great Leap Forward (1958), and the Cultural Revolution (1966–1976); however, matters have improved considerably since the reforms of the late 1970s.

Greatest space is allotted to the national minorities in the 1982 constitution—sixteen articles out of a total of 138. It provides for considerable local freedom of jurisdiction in autonomous regions, including in cultural matters. The organs of self-government in such regions are enjoined to administer cultural affairs in their areas, "protecting and preserving the cultural heritage while striving for development and prosperity." Similar autonomy in economic and security affairs is allowed, and the use and development of minority languages, representation of nationalities at all levels of the People's Congresses, formation of the organs of self-government, and provision for the training of minority cadres are all guaranteed. In addition, the customary opposition both to parochial nationalisms and Han chauvinism is expressed. Importantly for many national minorities, freedom of religious belief is also mentioned (Hsieh 1986: 8–9).

How far these ideals are put into practice differs from area to area. Despite the emphasis on rooting out greater Han chauvinism, a certain Han paternalism is frequently apparent. Liu Shaoqi underlines the "higher political, economic and cultural level" of the Han, and urges the Han to extend economic and cultural assistance to the minorities, who "cannot immediately overcome their original economic and cultural backwardness simply by their own strength and in their present circumstances" (Liu 1954: 47). Official publications from the 1980s and 1990s still perpetuate a somewhat paternalistic approach. For example, one recent writer suggests that workers in minority affairs should seek to "raise the level of minority economics and cultural education, give leadership to and help the national minorities vigorously improve their standard of culture and science, raise their socially productive forces" (Wang Lianfang 1986: 19). Even where minority affairs are not the main subject, loaded adjectives often convey a similar impression. The Naxi, for instance, "while preserving their own national culture, also adopted in large measure the culture of advanced peoples (*xianjin minzu*), creating a warm and open national spirit which constantly forged ahead" (1991 preface to *Lijiang Fu Zhilüe* [1743]: 1). As with most countries with multiethnic populations, prejudice of one sort or another against ethnic minorities is often expressed by the majority group. I was warned against the Wa by Han who said they had unsanitary habits and inedible food, and it appears that some Han Chinese still fear the alleged use of poisons by the Miao (Diamond 1988: 1).

Furthermore, the creation of "autonomous" areas did not imply lack of oversight by the central government. Deal posits that while in the 1950s the peoples of the various autonomous areas in the southwest were indeed allowed some freedom to make administrative, financial, and security decisions for themselves, the influx of Communist Party, People's Liberation Army, and minority cadres in fact served to bind the minorities to the Chinese state more firmly than ever before. Similarly, the extension of state education to ever greater numbers of minority children was an effective means of inculcating government-approved values and, usually, Han Chinese language into non-Han citizens.[3] Zhou Enlai explicitly stated that a major goal of minority education was to train minority peoples in patriotism, to train minority cadres, and to overcome local nationalism (Deal 1976: 34–36). To this end, establishments such as the Central Nationalities University (*Zhongyang Minzu Daxue*) in Beijing and provincial equivalents such as the Yunnan Nationalities Institute (*Yunnan Minzu Xueyuan*) specialize in educating members of minority groups, who then return to their localities as government employees. Most scholars who have discussed Communist policy toward the national minorities point out the assumptions of Han superiority and expectation of political conformity that frame the overt encouragement of diversity (e.g., Harrell 1995b: 22–27). Dreyer sums it up neatly: "Policy toward minority nationalities under the Chinese People's Republic has been motivated by a desire to integrate the life patterns and institutions of these groups with those of China, both Han and Communist" (1976: 261).

The cornerstone of the Communist government's minorities policy is ethnic classification (*minzu shibie*). Each citizen of the People's Republic is assigned membership of one of the fifty-six "nationalities" legally recognized by the state. His or her affiliation is determined by descent (a child of a mixed marriage may elect to adopt the "nationality" of either parent), and is recorded on all official documents. Despite the neat appearance presented by government statistics, however, ethnic classification has often been a contentious business, and one with real political, economic, and social ramifications for the parties involved.

The Communist Chinese understanding of "nationality" (*minzu*) is based on Stalin's well-known definition of a nation as a "historically evolved, stable community of language, territory, economic life, and psychological make-up manifested in a community of culture" (1934: 8). The validity of Stalin's criteria for "scientific" classification has often been affirmed by Chinese theorists (e.g., Zhang Zhiyi [Moseley 1966: 34–35], and Xiong Xiyuan [1986], with some minor quibbles), although more recently it has also been critically reassessed. Acceptance of Stalin's criteria went hand-in-glove with acceptance of a linear theory of social evolution based on the writings of Morgan and Engels. According to this theory, humans progress from primitivism through slave, feudal, and capitalist stages, to the pinnacle of socialism; at the same time, their family structures progress from promiscuity to group marriage and matriliny, and eventually to patriliny and monogamy, the marriage arrangement endorsed by the socialist state.[4] Inevitably ethnologists working within these frameworks have tended to pin down the stage of evolution deemed to have been reached by non-Han peoples, whose different customs have often struck mainstream Chinese observers as backward and uncivilized, but could now be rationalized according to this schema.

In the early 1950s, it became vital for the new Communist government to identify and label its minorities, for, as renowned Chinese anthropologist Fei Hsiao Tung (a.k.a. Fei Xiaotong) notes:

> The People's Republic of China ... committed itself to ethnic equality as a basic tenet. But the principle would have been meaningless without proper recognition of existing nationalities. For how could a People's Congress allocate its seats to deputies from different nationalities without knowing what nationalities there were? And how could the nation effect regional autonomy for the nationalities without a clear idea of their geographical distribution? (1981: 60)

By 1955, more than four hundred self-identified ethnic groups had registered their names with the government, and beginning in 1953 government fieldworkers were sent out to determine the validity of the various claims. By early 1957, eleven nationalities had been recognized, including the Naxi in 1954; more continued to be added, until by 1979 the official tally was fifty-six—fifty-five minorities and the Han majority (Fei 1981: 60–61). National minority status carries with it some important benefits, such as representation in many political bodies; developmental aid to minority districts; often some degree of local autonomy; affirmative action in education; and frequently, since the 1970s, a more flexible application of the birth control policy. These benefits have encouraged many self-identified peoples to seek recognition; at the same time, the government has for obvious reasons wished to limit the proliferation of nationalities, preferring to classify many groups as branches of a larger nationality.

While the identity of a few groups such as the Koreans in the northeast was self-evident, it proved difficult to apply Stalin's four criteria with consistency. Consequently, gray areas in the classification system abound. Fei (1981) mentions certain groups that proved hard to classify; the "Miao" and "Yi" labels have both been shown to be problematic and far from monolithic (Diamond 1995; Harrell 1990); and the Ge, Mosuo, and Kucong resent being considered branches of, respectively, the Miao, the Naxi, and the Lahu (Cheung 1996; McKhann 1995; Gladney 1991: 296). Harrell cites the fascinating example of the Prmi people, who through historical accident ended up classified as Tibetan in Sichuan and as Pumi in Yunnan. Here, the curious classification appears to have been accepted by both the Prmi leaders and the ordinary people, and indeed to have influenced their own subjective identity (1996). Another quixotic case is that of the Bai of Yunnan: while many of them were largely acculturated to Han norms before 1949, when they were known as Minjia, they adopted the status of a national minority, with its attendant privileges and differentiation from the Han, quite enthusiastically thereafter (David Wu 1990). Harrell underlines the importance in China of the interplay among three sets of actors in minority classification: the ethnic group to be identified, their neighbors from whom they are differentiated, and the state. He suggests that "an identity is accepted if it does not contradict either strong primordial sentiments or cogent instrumentalist logics. When it does, the state's position being what it is, ethnic identity becomes a problem" (1990: 546).[5]

There are theoretical problems with this system of classification quite apart from those it sometimes causes in practice. Based on primordialist criteria and claiming a "scientific" rationale of implicitly timeless validity, the system promotes a situational ethnicity that is very much a product of the historical moment, manipulated for political and economic ends by both the ethnic groups involved and the government. Perhaps most seriously, the model it promotes is static: an ethnographic present created through the particular circumstances of the early years of the People's Republic is projected indefinitely into the future and the past, regardless of changes that may happen or have already happened. Aspects of class and gender and of the rural-urban divide, all of which are increasingly important in the post–Cultural Revolution era, are played down (Harrell 1995c). Hsieh points out a further theoretical problem if one views minority policy from a Marxist perspective, as Communist theorists do. Since classical Marxist theory maintains that eventually the nation will wither away, it is potentially opposed to freedom to express minority identity (1986: 15). The dangers inherent in this contradiction were indeed well illustrated by the disrespect shown for minority sensitivity especially during the Great Leap Forward (1958) and the Cultural Revolution (1966–1976) (Dreyer 1976: 164–171, 205–235). The best-known non-Han casualties of this latter period were probably the Tibetans; another example, which has produced enduring resentment, was the deliberate pollution in 1968 of Hui (Moslem) villages in Shadian, Yunnan Province, when pork was thrown into the wells (Gladney 1991: 137–138). At the same time, on the Yunnan-Sichuan border, Mosuo couples adhering to their traditional "walking marriage" (*zouhun*) relationships (in which each partner lives in his or her natal home, with the man visiting the woman at night, and any children being raised in their mother's house), were pressured into formal marriages; government officials had long found this institution offensive to their Confucian-inculcated proprieties (McKhann 1995: 43–44).

The Chinese government has acknowledged the damage done by left-wing extremism to both Han and minority groups; and in the more tolerant atmosphere of the 1980s and 1990s, many minority communities have been able to rebuild their places of worship, return to some traditional customs, and emphasize their ethnic identity.

Communist Policy Toward Minority Performing Arts

Although some minority traditions have been viewed with distaste as "objectionable customs" (*louxi*), and discouraged or forbidden at times by the Chinese state, the government has selectively showcased minority arts and cultural differences it deems acceptable—neatly summed up by Harrell as "things . . . that foster ethnic pride, but do not impede progress . . . festivals, costumes, and the inevitable dancing in a circle" (1995b: 27). The ideological framework for the encouragement of arts based on the people's own art forms, while combining artistic quality with a correct political viewpoint, was most famously set out in Mao Zedong's 1942 "Talks at the Yan'an Conference on Literature and Art" (McDougall 1980). Mao urged writers and artists to go among the masses for inspiration, and subsequently many revolutionary musical and dramatic works drew on folk genres, while cleansing them of any traditional religious or erotic content.[6] At the same time, prominent folk musicians were often elevated from low positions in society to high status as star performers, conservatory teachers, and cultural icons.[7] In the official worldview, folk arts of the people, Han and non-Han alike, were given new respect in the 1950s—even if the collection of folk music and dance was often intended less as an end in itself than to serve the needs of composers and arrangers, who were expected to use their formally honed skills to "improve" on the originals.[8]

The same basic principles and techniques have been applied to the national minorities, but with the addition of special policies tailored to their situation. As noted above, the successive constitutions of the People's Republic of China have guaranteed national minorities freedom to develop their culture, and often government help in doing so. The practical results of such policies have included employing experts to invent writing systems for minority languages that traditionally lacked them (Fu 1985); the publication of hundreds of books and articles on each of the recognized ethnic groups; the encouragement of literature and theater among ethnic minorities (Doležalová 1983; Mackerras 1996); the promotion of traditional minority "festivals" (defined memorably by McKhann as "annual rituals with the religious content largely extracted" [1995: 44]); and the creation of Soviet-style state-run song and dance troupes specializing in the collection, arrangement, and performance of minority music and dance traditions. The Central Nationalities Song and Dance Troupe (*Zhongyang minzu gewutuan*) was established in 1952 in Beijing and initially recruited some of its members by seeking out promising folk artists in minority areas. Many regional, provincial, and lower-level troupes were also set up in the 1950s, including the Xinjiang Cultural Troupe (1950), the Guangxi Zhuang Autonomous Region Song and Dance Troupe (1954), the Tibetan Autonomous Region Song and Dance Troupe (1958), and the Dehong Dai and Jingpo Autonomous Prefecture Song and Dance Troupe in Yunnan (1956) (Mackerras 1984: 213–214). Not surprisingly, such troupes tend to iron out aspects of their material, especially ritual or erotic, deemed unsuitable to the state's Communist and Han-dominated sensibilities.

Collection and arrangement of minority music and dance started early in the life of the People's Republic.[9] In 1951, the second issue of the fifth volume of *Huanan Gesheng* (Southern Chinese Song) described a song-collecting trip made by the Huanan Culture Troupe (*wen'gongdui*) and a visiting delegation from Beijing to minority areas of the southeastern province of Guangdong. Issues of *Renmin Yinyue* (People's Music) from the 1950s contain many articles and communications on minority music, including some on smaller groups such as the Naxi. The June 1951 issue offers several songs in praise of Chairman Mao and Liberation; they are described as minority folk songs. An intriguing cry for help came in 1953 from the Han composer Liu Tieshan, later leader of the Central Nationalities Song and Dance Troupe, who had been sent to collect minority musics in the southwest and to use them as the basis for his own compositions in praise of Party leaders and the new life of the minorities. He and his colleagues were obviously struggling with the problem of how to create "minority music": Should they stick to the "style" (*fengge*) of a single nationality? How could they resolve the use of Han language with minority musical style? And which language should they use when performing songs of one nationality to another? (Liu Tieshan 1953).

The tradition of national and provincial minority arts festivals also began before the Cultural Revolution. Part of the December 1964 issue of *Renmin Yinyue* is devoted to an exhaustive account of the first national festival of amateur (but nevertheless very much staged) minority performances (*Quanguo shaoshu minzu qunzhong yeyu yishu guanmo yanchu*). The report comes complete with photos of the performances, of the performers standing behind Mao Zedong, Zhou Enlai, and other top leaders, and with speeches and articles praising the revolutionary content and the united spirit of the nationalities involved. While minority cultural diversity was attacked during the Cultural Revolution, such festivals have proliferated at both national and provincial levels since the late 1970s.

At the same time, there have been obvious attempts to standardize the fluid world of minority culture in accordance with the categories and norms articulated by the state. In an amusing vignette, David Wu cites the efforts of nationalities affairs officials to standardize ethnic costumes:

> One local official of minority affairs was embarrassed during the author's visit to an Ewinki village in Inner Mongolia, for it was discovered that the women we met in a tent were in the wrong costumes. The official assured the visitors that sketches of the "correct" Ewinki costumes would soon be distributed to the villagers in this remote area so that they would not make the mistake of wearing another (Mongolian) nationality's clothing. (1990: 3)

Partial standardization of professionalized minority performing arts forms proceeds from the custom of sending promising minority performers to pursue a course of study at a national or provincial academy such as the Arts Department of the Central Nationalities University, the Shanghai Conservatory of Music, or the Yunnan Art Institute. There, usually taught by Han professors, the student learns the mainstream, Western-influenced, pan-Chinese conservatory style of playing, dancing, or singing.[10] He or she then introduces that ubiquitous national style and the associated Han and Western instruments to the state-sponsored regional performing troupes to which most such graduates are assigned. There are close parallels here with the Europeanized training of young Uzbek musicians at the Tashkent Conservatory (Slobin 1971; Levin 1979: 154) and of their Kazakh counterparts at the Alma-Ata Kurmangazy State Conservatory during the Soviet period (Muhambetova 1995: 76–77). Other forces tending toward standardization at the state-sponsored professional level in China include the adoption of simple Western functional harmony in many musical arrangements, Western equal temperament in preference to local tuning systems, and Western instruments, most frequently electric piano, cello, and double bass, to bolster indigenous instruments.[11] For festivals, the organizers will usually select a "representative" art form from each recognized ethnic group. Frequently such art forms become institutionalized; the Dai, for example, are inseparable in many people's imaginations from the peacock dance, the Miao from their *lusheng* (mouth organs with long projecting pipes), or the Naxi from their *dongba* dance. At the local, amateur level, however, such standardization is much less marked, and a great variety of forms persists. There is a marked disparity between ethnic image within the wider dominant culture and actual local practice within the minority cultures themselves.

In the field of music, dance, and other performing arts, a major source for post–Cultural Revolution policy toward the minorities is a speech made by Huang Zhen, minister of culture, at the All-China Minority Nationalities Performing Arts Festival of 1980 (Huang Zhen 1982, summarized in Mackerras 1984: 191). His five main points were as follows:

1. Bring back the cultural cadres, folk and other artists of the minority nationalities performing arts who were suppressed by the Gang of Four
2. "Let the minority nationalities enjoy full autonomy and power of initiative" in their performing arts "and be the real masters in their own house in culture"
3. Apply Party policy toward literature and the arts, encourage as much variety as possible, and preserve ethnic style and characteristics
4. "Do a good job in building the cultural enterprises of the minority nationality areas" and include the remote areas, emphasizing those art works with strong ethnic characteristics
5. Work in minority areas must promote unity, both between Han and minority workers in the performing arts, and among the various minority workers themselves.

A sixth aim was articulated by Vice Premier Yang Jingren (a member of the Hui minority) in his speech opening the festival: to salvage the cultural inheritance of the minorities (Mackerras 1984: 194).

These six points neatly summarize the perceived role of minority performing arts in China. On the one hand, they can spread state propaganda, both general and related to the unified patriotism of all nationalities. On the other hand, their encouragement is a showcase of the government's good faith in allowing cultural diversity, emphasizing the worth of non-Han heritages, and attempting to repair damage done to minority culture in the Cultural Revolution. The minorities' performing arts when properly cultivated and encouraged allow for a controlled, non-divisive expression of ethnic consciousness which accords with the state's ubiquitous description of itself as a "unified multinational socialist country" (*tongyi de duo minzu de shehuizhuyi guojia*).

The following example illustrates the use of the performing arts to this end. In February 1992 the Third China Art Festival was held in Kunming, Yunnan Province. The opening ceremony included a march by all fifty-six recognized ethnic groups through the streets of Kunming, with each group, in colorful costume, performing some representative music and dance form at designated spots along the route. Kunmingers packed the sidewalks to view the display of diversity that paraded past. The slogans that festooned the city, however, and which some of the performers carried, emphasized the necessity of pulling together for the good of socialist China as a whole. For example, "Let the arts serve the people and serve socialism" (*Wenyi wei renmin fuwu wei shehuizhuyi fuwu*); "Unite, flourish, progress" (*Tuanjie, fanrong, jinbu*); and on a bilingual billboard, "Display the achievements of national art exchange the essence of national culture and promote the national culture of socialism" (*Zhanshi minzu wenyi chengguo jiaoliu minzu youxiu wenhua fanrong shehuizhuyi minzu wenhua*). An official view of the function of the festival was offered shortly afterward in the *Beijing Review:*

> State Councillor Li Tieying, in his speech on behalf of the State Council, called the festival a grand cultural event, because it best demonstrates the vitality of all ethnic groups that work together to build socialism with Chinese characteristics under the leadership of the Communist Party.
>
> He said the festival would carry forward the fine tradition of Chinese culture, energize the nation, strengthen national unity, promote the national reform and open policy, boost the economy and advance socialist culture and ethics. ("Third China Art Festival Opens" 1992)

The "Motif of the Music-making Minority"

The special talents and achievements of minorities in the performing arts are keenly promoted in China—to such an extent that the foreign observer comes away with a strong sense of a kind of "domestic orientalism" at work, in which the minorities are presented as an exotic alternative to the more staid and sober Han. An awareness of this tendency is necessary to any examination of minority culture and its promotion to the outside world. There are, of course, some obvious parallels with situations outside China. In his polemical article "Representing African Music," Kofi Agawu examines a number of the assumptions which he feels underlie discussions by Western and African writers of African music. One of the most striking is what he terms "the motif of the music-making African" (1992: 248). He gives examples of the prevalence of this "motif" in both nineteenth- and twentieth-century writings and quotes a British account from 1830: "It would be as difficult to detach singing and dancing from the character of an African, as to change the color of his skin. I do not think he would live a single week in his country without participating in these his favorite amusements." Agawu criticizes the scholarly manifestation of this tendency, which he identifies even in recent works, as a "scholarly plot seeking difference between Africa and the West," and as one that is propped up by an essentialist view of that difference (pp. 249, 266).

Even a brief perusal of the representations of China's ethnic minorities in publications and in the media cannot but have an uncanny resonance for anyone who has read Agawu's work. The government's promotion of "festivals, costumes, and the inevitable dancing in a circle" (Harrell 1995b: 27) has certainly raised the profile of the minorities in the consciousness of citizens throughout China; but the stereotypical presentation of non-Han engaged in singing and dancing while wearing colorful costumes on the TV stage or in their home environment has in effect produced a "motif" similar to that described by Agawu: what one might call the "motif of the music-making minority."

This "motif" is confirmed both in print and in other media. One of the most common types of scholarly publication on Chinese music, both Han and minority, is the song or instrumental anthology. It does not take long to notice a certain style in the textual descriptions included in anthologies of minority music. For example, a random sampling from my bookshelves includes the following:

The Naxi—a people of song and dance.

The Uighurs are a nationality which is good at singing and dancing.

The brave Wa are always famous for their skill in singing and dancing.

Songs are an indispensable part of the life of the Dong people.[12]

And, for a more global approach, the compiler of an anthology of pieces from all fifty-five recognized minorities tells us, "The national minorities are good at singing and dancing" (Du 1993: 11).

Literature aimed at tourists takes much the same line. Describing the Chinese Ethnic Culture Park opened in 1994 in Beijing, the magazine *China Today* explains that it is "a showcase for the traditional architecture, folklore, performing arts, handicrafts and cuisine of China's ethnic minorities.... Every morning at nine, groups of singers and dancers wearing ethnic costumes from the park's different villages gather under the 'banyan trees' at the entrance to sing and dance in greeting for the first group of visitors" (Li Fugen 1995: 10–11).

The Splendid China theme park in Shenzhen Special Economic Zone near Hong Kong also displays several miniature minority villages for its visitors. The official brochure describes festival- and love-related music and dance activities for most of the minorities depicted. For example, "the whole village is located in a verdant and luxuriant wood of the tropics with green bamboos scattering all over the hills and slopes, and thus an extraordinary scenery of the Miao village is formed. When night is closing in, love songs are sung and reed-pipes are played, permeating with the style and feature of the Miao nationality" (Liu Chi Ping et al., n.d.: 109). The brochure paints similar scenes for the Dong, while the Bai and Buyi too are "good at singing and dancing" (pp. 101–108). The bilingual coffee-table book *Highlights of Minority Nationalities in Yunnan* emphasizes picturesque scenery, costumes, festivals, and music; the Naxi, for instance, "are all good singers and dancers. They would sing and dance round bonfires on the red-letter days" (Yunnan Sheng Renmin Zhengfu Waishi Ban'gongshi, n.d.: 46).

As Mackerras (1984: 202) and others have pointed out, a phrase consistently applied to the cultural identity of the national minorities is *neng'ge shanwu*, literally "can sing and are good at dancing." It is not, on the other hand, an epithet applied to the Han ethnic majority in China—despite the large amount of indigenous music making in many traditional Han villages, and the enthusiasm of urban Han youth for karaoke and disco dancing.[13] The strong association of singing and dancing with minorities was ironically demonstrated by the comment of a Hui (Moslem) ethnologist seeking to rebut the perception of Chinese Moslems as no different from the Han: "We Hui don't sing, we don't dance, but we're still ethnic!" (Gladney 1991: 98).

Film and television as well as the printed page tend to promote the image of colorful, exotic minorities ready to sing and dance at the drop of a hat, and indeed have done so since the 1950s. Discussing films from the pre–Cultural Revolution era, one Western scholar observes:

> Many ... minorities films ... blur the theme of class struggle by tending to glamorize the exotic. The southwest minorities in particular appear in these films not infrequently as "happy, smiling natives," more prone to drop axe and bow and burst into song than to take up arms against oppressors. Although film artists pay careful attention to the authenticity of costuming and customs, this type of presentation has pitfalls. A sort of "if it's three feathers, they must be Apache" syndrome arises as grinning Yi, Miao, Zhuang, Dai, Bai, and Dong dance across the screen. (Clark 1987: 21)

More recently, the ever more ubiquitous genre of television shows continues the same exoticist approach to minorities. By contrast, the Han, universally acknowledged in books and articles to be economically the most advanced ethnic group in China, and thus in the vanguard of national development, are almost always represented as "normal" and "un-exotic." To quote from an American scholar's observations about the four-hour 1991 New Year's program on Chinese TV:

> Even though only eight percent of [the Chinese] population is supposed to be minority . . . , fully one-half of the evening's programming is devoted to smiling minority dancers. . . . In striking resemblance to the "tribute" offerings of the ancient Chinese empires, the minorities performed, sang, and presented ritualized prostrations as they offered greetings to the studio audience, who appeared to be largely members of the Han majority. They appeared so, because the studio audience was uniformly . . . dressed in conservative suits with ties, Mao jackets, or other formal, dark "Western" attire, in marked contrast to the "colorful costumes" of the minority entertainers. [Han] entertainers and hosts exclusively wore Western-style suits and dresses. (Gladney 1994: 95–96)

Several other leitmotifs have been identified in the way minorities are presented to mainstream Chinese society. These include the genderizing of minorities as female; the characterization of many minority women, especially the Dai, as erotic, in contrast to staid Han women; and the depiction of minorities as close to nature (Gladney 1994, Schein 1997). Yet, while recent improvements in media and communications have allowed these images to be circulated more widely than ever before, they are hardly new. Norma Diamond's discussion of Chinese-authored "Miao albums" from the eighteenth to mid-twentieth centuries shows that illustrations of minority life home in on characteristics most alien to Confucian propriety and Han societal norms:[14]

> The recurrent theme for the Hua Miao is a scene showing several young men and women dancing to the pipes out in the wilderness. . . . In the volumes that present all eighty-two groups, at least ten emphasize the quarrelsome and dangerous nature of these peoples. . . . Another ten focus on sexual license. . . . Despite . . . lovely faces, [the women] fall short of the ideal. The pictures emphasize their large natural feet and the shamelessness of their dress. (Diamond 1995: 102–103)

Recent reappraisals by Chinese scholars of academic approaches to the "minority question" are complemented by a strong plea from ethnomusicologist Du Yaxiong to practice cultural relativism (*wenhua xiangduilun*) when doing fieldwork. He points out that, in the past, field reports contained many words such as "backward" (*luohou*), "primitive" (*yuanshi*), and "coarse" (*cucao*), which not only adversely influenced the quality of the scholarship based on such prejudices, but also caused serious offence; he urges his readers to eschew such prejudice, both to improve their own work and to assist in internationality unity (1994: 17). Despite the expression of this kind of sensitivity in some scholarly work, in the mid-1990s it remains the case that the presentation of China's ethnic minorities in print and on stage and television is usually still heavily informed by the exoticized "motif of the music-making minority."

The Naxi of Lijiang County

Who Are the Naxi?

The Naxi exemplify many of the characteristics of the minority-state relationship described in the last chapter. Officially recognized in 1954, they are regarded by most scholars as a branch of a western people termed "Qiang" in Chinese historical sources, and are thought to have migrated to northern Yunnan during the Han dynasty. Their language is generally assigned to the Yi branch of Tibeto-Burman (Kou, Wang, and He 1995: 12; McKhann 1992: 383; Ramsey 1987: 265). The 1990 population census of the People's Republic of China announced a grand total of 277,750 Naxi, of whom 265,450 lived in Yunnan Province, 8,595 in Sichuan Province, and 1,333 in southeast Tibet, with small numbers elsewhere. The greatest concentration of Naxi is in Lijiang County in northwest Yunnan, where slightly more than 180,000 were registered in 1990 (*Zhongguo 1990 Nian Renkou Pucha Ziliao*: 311; *Yunnan Cidian* 1993: 62). The nationality is a good example of a contested ethnic classification. It breaks down into two main subdivisions: the western group, by far the larger, living mainly in Lijiang, Weixi, and Zhongdian counties; and the much smaller eastern group, centered in the Yongning basin and Lugu Lake regions of Ninglang County, Yunnan, and in the adjacent area of Muli in Sichuan Province (see Figure 3.1). The western group self-identifies as Naxi, and is referred to as such by the eastern group and by outsiders; members of the eastern group call themselves Mosuo, Hli-khin, or Nari, and distinguish themselves from the western group, who refer to them as Mosuo or Luxi. The Mosuo have long sought official recognition as a nationality separate from the more numerous and politically more powerful western Naxi. They are certainly very different from the western Naxi: the languages are mutually

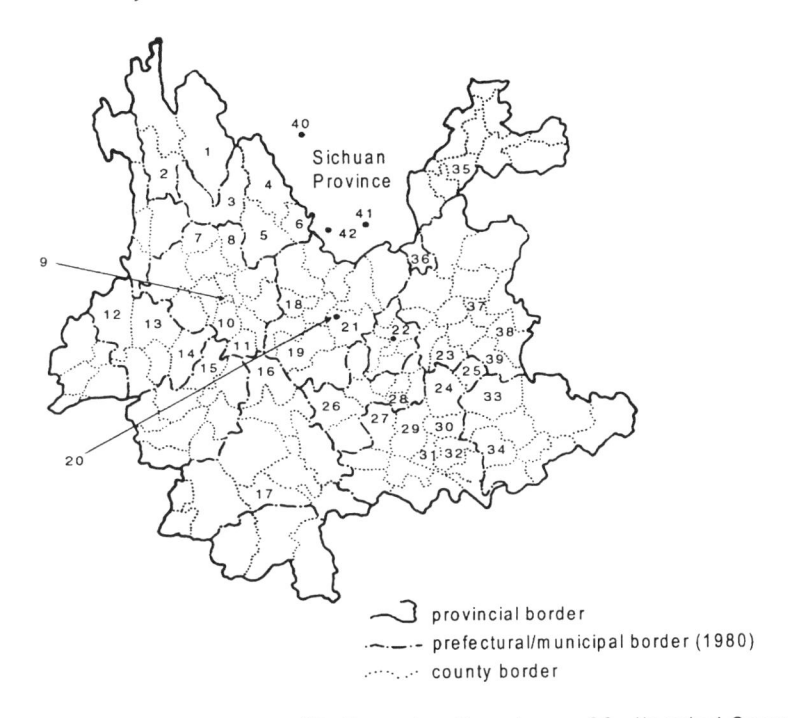

FIGURE 3.1. Map of Yunnan Province, showing counties, cities, and towns mentioned.

1. Zhongdian County
2. Weixi County
3. Lijiang County
4. Ninglang County
5. Yongsheng County
6. Huaping County
7. Jianchuan County
8. Heqing County
9. Xiaguan/Dali Old Town
10. Weishan County
11. Nanjian County
12. Tengchong County
13. Baoshan City
14. Changning County
15. Fengqing County
16. Jingdong County
17. Simao County
18. Yao'an County
19. Chuxiong City
20. Heijing Town
21. Lufeng County
22. Kunming City
23. Lu'nan County
24. Mile County
25. Luxi County
26. Xinping County
27. Shiping County
28. Tonghai County
29. Jianshui County
30. Kaiyuan City
31. Gejiu City
32. Mengzi County
33. Qiubei County
34. Wenshan County
35. Zhaotong City
36. Dongchuan City
37. Qujing City
38. Luoping County
39. Shizong County
40. Muli County
41. Huili County
42. Panzhihua City

unintelligible; Mosuo social organization includes both patrilineal and matrilineal descent, and duolocal "walking marriages" (*zouhun*) in place of Naxi patrilineal descent and virilocal marriage;[1] and though the Mosuo were traditionally devout adherents of Yellow Hat (Gelugpa) Buddhism, the western Naxi were much less committed to their several Red Hat (Karmapa) monasteries. Just as the Mosuo reject a Naxi identity, many western Naxi distance themselves from the Mosuo, describing them as culturally "backward" (*luohou*) and "chaotic" (*luan*) in their sexual practices. Confusing the issue, however, is the fact that before 1949 Chinese writers often referred to the western Naxi as "Mosuo" or "Moxie." Chinese ethnologists decided early on that the Mosuo and the western Naxi were closely related, with the Mosuo thought to represent an earlier phase on the Morganian evolutionary march from matrilineal to patrilineal society. Consequently, both groups are still officially classified as "Naxi." This umbrella term also includes a very small subgroup, the Lulu, who live in villages in the northeast and northwest of Lijiang County. The Lulu, however, appear perfectly happy to be classified as Naxi, and to have assimilated to and intermarried with the western Naxi (McKhann 1992: 371–378; McKhann 1995: 47–50; Chao 1995: 86–90).

This book focuses on the western Naxi, specifically those in Lijiang County; so from now on my use of the term "Naxi" will refer exclusively to the larger, western group.

Location and Population of Lijiang

Lijiang County is located in northwest Yunnan, six hundred kilometers from the provincial capital, Kunming. Until the institution of regular air service in 1995, travel between the two was by a twenty-hour bus-ride. The county as a whole covers 7,425 square kilometers, with the Jinsha River forming its northern boundary (see Figure 3.2). The altitude varies greatly, but the county town, Dayan Town (*Dayan Zhen*), and its surrounding plain lie at twenty-four hundred meters. The total population of Lijiang County is a little more than three hundred thousand; of these somewhat more than fifty thousand live in the county town, which functions as the political, cultural, and economic center not only of Lijiang County, but also of Lijiang Prefecture (*Lijiang Diqu*), with four counties under its jurisdiction (Tang and Jin 1988: 7–11, 16). Eighty-four percent of Lijiang County's population was engaged in agriculture in 1980 (Yunnan Sheng Cehuiju 1980).

Among the many ethnic groups living in Lijiang County, the Naxi are the most numerous and in 1990 constituted 57.9 percent of the population. The other major groups represented are the Han (17.8 percent), Bai (11.4 percent), and Lisu (8 percent), with smaller communities of Pumi, Yi, Tibetans, Miao, Hui, and Zhuang (*Yunnan Cidian*: 62). It is important to note that, though many Chinese and foreign scholars paint the history of minority-majority interaction in terms of a one-way assimilation by peripheral peoples to Han Chinese, state-encouraged cultural norms, Lijiang County offers ample evidence that such interaction was in fact a two-way phenomenon. Many residents of Dayan Town bear surnames other than the distinctive He and Mu which generally distinguish the Naxi. These people think of themselves as Naxi and are characterized as such by the state today; but they proudly preserve genealogical evidence that they are the descendants of military and artisan immigrants who came to Lijiang, often from Nanjing in eastern China, in the Ming and Qing dynasties.

A further dimension to the geographical and ethnic character of Lijiang County is that of internal topography. As many local residents told me, and foreign

THE NAXI OF LIJIANG COUNTY 31

FIGURE 3.2. Map of Lijiang County, showing places mentioned. Place names are those current in the 1990s. The following locations are approximately equivalent: Baihua (1990s) = Baima Li (pre-1949); Changshui (1990s) = Lasha Li (pre-1949); Jinshan (1990s) = Yinglie Li (pre-1949); Longquan (1990s) = Shuhe (pre-1949). To avoid cluttering the map, intracounty township boundaries are not shown.

observers have frequently noted, Dayan Town is considered the wealthiest, most sinicized part of the county, with other areas graded along a continuum:

> The rural lowland areas bordering the [Jinsha] River and Lijiang basin . . . are characterized as relatively less *hanhua* [sinicized] than the town. In these areas a combination of Chinese-influenced and Naxi rituals are performed. Naxi is usually spoken, although older men and virtually all villagers under forty-five understand and speak some Chinese. The inhabitants of these areas

are generally subsistence agriculturalists. The mountain villages to the north and northwest of the town are characterized as strongholds of "traditional Naxi culture." The mountain terrain and unsuitability of the land for wet rice agriculture have to some degree insulated these areas from Chinese influence. In the mountain villages, "Naxi" rituals and customs are practiced. Naxi is the primary language in these villages; only a few of the younger villagers understand any Chinese. The mountain villagers' subsistence is based on agriculture combined with transhumant pastoralism. (Chao 1995: 2–3)

Lijiang County and the Chinese State

Several Chinese-language sources from the Ming and Qing dynasties offer information on Lijiang's history, in particular on its relationship to the Chinese state.[2] One of the most important and comprehensive is the gazetteer of 1743 compiled by Guan Xuexuan, who took office as magistrate of Lijiang in 1736 (*Lijiang Fu Zhilüe*). While Guan's views were obviously those of an upright Confucian official, strongly colored by official state orthodoxy, his county history remains one of the most informative documents still extant. I quote part of it below in the translation by Rock. According to Guan, the Moxieman (presumably the Naxi) moved into Lijiang sometime during the Song dynasty (960–1279). They first expressed allegiance to the Mongols, and later transferred their loyalty to succeeding Chinese dynasties, ultimately accepting direct Chinese rule (*gaitu guiliu*) in 1723. Guan describes the process thus:

> In . . . 1252 the Mongols sent troops under Kublai Khan . . . to attack Dali. He led his troops . . . to Lijiang. As the Mongols respected the customs of the people wherever they went, the people turned to allegiance in all sincerity. They then established the civil office of Chahanzhang Guanmin Guan [Naxi prefect] in Lijiang. . . . In . . . 1382 . . . as Ade [the local ruler] was the first to submit to the [Ming] conquerors he was appointed magistrate and was given the surname Mu [subsequently distinctive as the family name of Lijiang's Naxi rulers]. . . . In . . . 1659 the territory of Yunnan was annexed to the Chinese Empire. . . . In 1723 [four prominent local leaders] . . . went to the provincial capital and applied for the appointment of Chinese officials. (Rock 1947: 59–62)

This resulted in the demotion of the Mu ruler to *tu tongpan* (native subprefect). Guan's account ends in 1743; an 1895 gazetteer follows Guan verbatim, adding only a couple of extra columns on later administrative changes (*Lijiang Fu Zhi*, 2: fols. 9b–10a). Rock himself brings Lijiang's history up to date for the first half of the twentieth century: "Today magistrates are still appointed by the Commissioner of the Interior, now called Minzheng Ting; the office of native subprefect still exists, but the present incumbent has neither voice nor power. He controls a few peasants on the land which he still possesses, but his holdings are being gradually reduced" (1947: 62).

Twentieth-century history, especially as it relates to the rise of Communism, is exhaustively presented in mainland Chinese sources. In 1936 the Communists passed through Lijiang on their Long March, and local Naxi assisted them in crossing the Jinsha River. The Naxi underground Communist worker Yang Shangzhi arrived in Lijiang in early 1947 as a schoolteacher and began to spread propaganda. Several other underground activists arrived in early 1948. By September 1948, there were more than twenty Party members in Lijiang, and by June 1949 more than three hundred. "Liberation" took place officially on 1 July 1949 (Lijiang Naxizu Zizhixian Gaikuang Bianxiezu 1986: 19–25).

Thereafter Lijiang participated in the many political movements that have swept the whole of China since 1949. The Russian resident Peter Goullart describes a number of fines, arrests, and executions of merchants and other disfavored elements in the immediate aftermath of the Communist victory, as well as the destruction of monasteries and temples. The general tenor of his account is confirmed by a local autobiography (Goullart 1957: 249–255; Track 1996: 67–73). Land reform was instituted in 1951, the first cooperatives in 1954; the Anti-Rightist campaign, which targeted intellectuals and cadres thought to be critical of the regime, began in 1957; and the Great Leap Forward of 1958 led to the well-known economic fiascos of the huge communes (Lijiang Naxizu Zizhixian Gaikuang Bianxiezu 1986: 66–75). In terms of nationalities policy, from the end of 1958 to early 1959, as in many other parts of China, "in Lijiang the mistake was made of instituting an 'anti-local nationalism' movement. This hurt a number of distinguished minority cadres, undermined the Party's policy of the unity and equality of nationalities, and seriously damaged the activism of minority nationality cadres" (Lijiang Naxixu Zizhixian Gaikuang Bianxiezu 1986: 75). In 1961, despite this setback, in line with the constitution's pledge of autonomy for areas with high concentrations of national minorities, Lijiang was renamed the Lijiang Naxi Autonomous County (*Lijiang Naxizu Zizhixian*).

From 1960 on, the central government moved away from its most extremist policies, with the massive communes broken up and the much smaller production team instated as the basic unit. Under these conditions, agricultural production improved in the early 1960s. The chaos of the Cultural Revolution (1966–1976), however, seriously damaged Lijiang's economy and culture and resulted in the destruction of many ancient landmarks and cultural artifacts. Following the establishment of more liberal policies in the late 1970s, Lijiang citizens who had been branded "rightists" or "local nationalist elements" twenty years previously were rehabilitated, as were many "landlords" and "rich peasants," two categories of people who had suffered discrimination since 1949. In economic terms, the government of Lijiang followed the national trend in experimenting with the "responsibility system," fixing agricultural output quotas for each household but reviving the free market for surplus produce. Grain production rose more than 36 percent between 1978 and 1982, and improvements were also seen in forestry, cattle rearing, and sideline industries. This was a boon to the 84 percent of the county's population primarily engaged in farming. In urban areas private enterprise was increasingly encouraged, so that privately owned shops now line the streets of the old part of the county town (Lijiang Naxixu Zizhixian Gaikuang Bianxiezu 1986: 75–81). Government statistics and comments from local people suggest that the availability of consumer goods, cash income, and the general standard of living for most Lijiang County residents have improved considerably since the end of the Cultural Revolution.[3]

In accordance with the nationwide policy of opening to the outside world, Lijiang County was declared open to foreigners in 1985 (Tang and Jin 1988: 5). Since then its magnificent mountainous scenery, unspoiled traditional architecture, and interesting minority culture have made it a mecca for foreign backpackers and, increasingly in the 1990s, for well-heeled domestic tourists, too. In October 1994, the Yunnan provincial government designated Lijiang a key city for tourism expansion. Air connections were instituted in 1995, a cable lift was under construction on the Jade Dragon Mountain by 1996, and by late 1996 more than ten foreign-funded firms and joint ventures had formally registered in Lijiang. In 1997 Dayan Town was included by UNESCO on its list of World Cultural Heritage sites. Local officials estimate that earnings from tourism will contribute more than half of Lijiang's annual revenue by 2010. The Lijiang Prefecture Tourism Bureau has tracked the explosion during the 1990s in "tourist days" and revenue. Although the figures may contain some inaccuracies, the general trend is clear. In 1990 visitors spent about 100,000 tourist days in Lijiang Prefecture and 16 million yuan; in 1995 they spent 900,000 tourist days and 230 million yuan, rising in 1997 to 1,600,000 tourist days and 800 million yuan; and in 1998, the year after designation as a World Heritage site, two million tourist days brought in 1,060 million yuan (in 1998 US$1 = 8.2 yuan). Many people in Dayan Town and the surrounding areas have benefited economically from the tourist influx, although poorer and remoter parts of Lijiang County and Lijiang Prefecture have not. Moreover, the sudden influx of huge numbers of tourists has resulted in many problems for local inhabitants, including rising prices, tensions between native and recently arrived entrepreneurs, tensions among local ethnic groups, commodification of local culture, and an increase in prostitution and drugs. Local residents and officials are considering how to maximize the benefits and minimize the problems resulting from the tourist boom (Kou Zhengling 1996: 21; McKhann 1999).

Religion Among the Lijiang Naxi

Before 1949

In its first few years, the Communist government succeeded in dismantling much of the highly diverse religious apparatus in place in Lijiang before 1949. Nevertheless, it is for one kind of religious professional that Lijiang has become famous: the indigenous *dongba* (priests), one of three types of ritual practitioners considered native to the Naxi. The other two are the lesser-known *sainii* (shamans) and *paq* (diviners).[4] McKhann characterizes the different roles of these specialists thus:

> Many . . . rituals seek to correct perceived imbalances in the state of the cosmos and in the relations of beings who dwell within it. Prior to the performance of such rituals, most notably those with a curing function, the source of imbalance must first be determined. Using a variety of methods, many of which (e.g., scapulamancy) appear to derive from neighboring cultures, this initial determination is the task of a diviner (*paq*). After divination has revealed the cause of the imbalance—usually the work of a malicious demon—one or more priests (*dongba*) are called in to perform the necessary corrective ritual. . . . In some instances they require the help of a shaman (*sainii*), whose particular talent lies in confronting the afflicting demon directly by journeying to that part of the cosmos where the demon dwells. (1992: 4)

It was not just the diviners, however, who borrowed from neighboring cultures: researchers have traced names of deities and certain rituals recorded in *dongba* texts to Tibetan Bön and Buddhist and Indian origins (McKhann 1992: 14–15).

The *dongba* have been the subject of much Chinese and Western scholarship over the last seventy years, largely because of their unique pictographic script. Both pictographic and phonetic systems of writing exist; neither can be dated with certainty, although origins of Song or earlier have been suggested for the pictographic, and Ming or early Qing for the phonetic (McKhann 1992: 8–9). These two forms of writing have been confined to *dongba* use, so that the vast majority of Naxi have no way of writing their own language; even the romanized system invented in the twentieth century has little currency. The pictographic system was in far more common use than the phonetic, and thousands of manuscripts recorded the religious ceremonies and lore of the *dongba*. *Dongba* studies is by far the most active branch of Naxi research today, and has resulted in dozens of publications both in Chinese and in Western languages.[5]

In addition to the three kinds of Naxi-speaking native religious specialists, before 1949 Lijiang County also was home to monasteries of both Tibetan and Chinese Buddhists (known colloquially in Chinese as *lama* and *heshang*, respectively). The five major Tibetan Buddhist monasteries in Lijiang were built in the Ming and Qing dynasties, and belonged to the Karmapa (Red Hat) sect. While monks were sometimes invited to perform funeral rituals by local inhabitants, Karmapa Buddhism does not seem to have had a strong hold on the Lijiang Naxi, and some of the monasteries were in decline in the early twentieth century (Rock 1947: 204–210; McKhann 1992: 375–376; Goullart 1957, ch. 10; Yang Qichang 1991). There were also many Chinese Buddhist temples in lowland areas of Lijiang; in the Republican era it was common for families to send a son to become a *lama* or *heshang* in order to avoid the military draft.

Other Han rituals were also practiced. Two of my elderly Naxi friends mentioned approximately ten families of Taoist priests (*daoshi*) resident in and around Dayan Town, whose livelihood depended on performing funerary and other rites for their neighbors (see also Li Jinchun 1986: 62–63). Also in Dayan Town, the county government observed the twice-yearly sacrifice to Confucius mandated by the Qing and Republican governments for the whole of China; the Qing dynasty protocol is set out in the local Lijiang gazetteers, and I met several elderly men who had taken part in the sacrifices in the early twentieth century.

Christianity was a much more recent import to Lijiang. Protestant missionaries first arrived in Lijiang in 1909; eventually missionaries from Holland, England, and Germany recruited more than a thousand local adherents of various ethnic groups at sites throughout Lijiang, including Dayan Town, Shigu, Judian, and Daju. The redoubtable Miss Scharten of the Dutch Pentacostal Mission seems to have become quite a fixture in Dayan Town by the 1930s (Xuan, n.d.; Reitlinger 1939: 116).

In addition to more institutionalized religious activities, Lijiang residents also observed important Han Chinese festivals, especially Spring Festival (*Chun Jie*) and Sweeping the Ancestors' Graves (*Qing Ming*). Furthermore, a number of private associations were active in Dayan Town. *Sainanzi hui* was a group of older male lay Buddhists, usually upper class but not celibate, who met on the first and fifteenth of each month for Buddhist sutra recitation (in Chinese) and vegetarian meals; they also organized prayer sessions at various temples during temple fairs, and sometimes accompanied monks to hold commemorative ceremonies on the first anniversary of a person's death. The *Mama hui* (religious women's associations) consisted of devout lay Buddhist women who held temple meetings on the first and fifteenth of each month, during which they recited Chinese-language sutras and ate vegetarian food. Also active were two other vegetarian and sutra recitation groups, which had both male and female members: *Fomindang* (People's Buddhist Party), and the *Bailanjiao* (White Lotus Sect). The White Lotus Sect was apparently of Taoist affiliation and engaged in séances (Chao 1995: 194–195, 254–261). The Confucian-oriented Dongjing associations (*dongjinghui*), societies of elite, well-educated males who met several times a year to honor the gods Wenchang and Guandi, are discussed in detail below.

After 1949

Although in theory the government of the People's Republic of China has always allowed freedom of religious belief, in practice the frequent discouragement and banning of religious activities are well known. In Lijiang, oral reports insist that the major *dongba* ceremony of the Sacrifice to Heaven was successfully stopped between about 1951 and 1986, while the shamanic practices of the *sainii* continued clandestinely in mountainous areas. In Dayan Town, Buddhist monks and celibate female devotees were encouraged or forced to marry; the leaders of the White Lotus Sect were executed, and the *Mama hui* were officially banned in 1958. Foreign missionaries were forced to leave after 1949; two of the five Karmapa monasteries were destroyed during the Cultural Revolution, the other three were badly damaged, and their monks were sent away (McKhann 1992: 36, 375; Chao 1995: 195, 255, 317–319). Oral history suggests that Taoist priests and Dongjing associations too were forced to cease practicing soon after 1949, and the Confucian sacrifice was discontinued throughout China at the establishment of the People's Republic.

With the onset of more liberal political policies since the late 1970s, some religious activities have revived. The Karmapa monasteries have been partially rebuilt, and a few monks have returned to maintain the buildings and grounds; they engage in few religious activities other than private worship, however, and their monasteries have become primarily tourist attractions. By 1991 two *Mama hui* had re-formed in Dayan Town, and a few foreigners observed *dongba* and *sainii* rituals in the late 1980s and early 1990s, mostly, but not exclusively, in mountainous areas of Lijiang. A community of more than a thousand Christians exists in the mountains above Shigu; they abstain from smoking and drinking alcohol, and meet on Sundays to read the Bible and sing hymns (McKhann 1992: 375; Chao 1995: 255; Xuan, n.d.). Nevertheless, the paucity of public religious activities around the county town contrasts with the situation in many other counties of Yunnan, where a vigorous religious revival is readily visible even in major urban areas near government compounds.[6]

Han Cultural Influence

The surveys above of the history and religious practices of the Lijiang Naxi indicate several centuries of continuous contact with the Han Chinese, especially among those Naxi living in urban and rural areas with good communications; and this has naturally led to substantial Han influence in culture and daily life. Today most Naxi inhabitants of Dayan Town, except elderly women, many of whom never attended school, speak passable to fluent Chinese as well as Naxi, and in the villages near the county town some middle-aged and elderly men as well as schoolchildren can communicate in Chinese. Even today, however, after the vigorous expansion of minority schooling under the People's Republic, Chinese language competence falls off sharply in remote rural and mountainous areas.[7]

Lijiang's ruling classes appear to have come to grips with Han Chinese culture quite early: in a recent anthology of Chinese-language poems by Naxi literati, the earliest example is by Mu Tai, who ruled in the late fifteenth century (Zhao Yintang 1985: 1). At about the same time, some Naxi also became proficient in Han Chinese-style calligraphy (Wang Zhihong 1991). Some sinicized habits trickled down to the ordinary people; for instance, shortly after the appointment of Chinese officials in 1723, some Lijiang Naxi began to change their funeral customs from the traditional cremation to Han-style earth burial (Li Jinchun 1986: 34). McKhann offers a good description of the mixture of Naxi and Han elements in funerals (1992: 263–289). As for Han-language education, private Confucian schools were established in Lijiang during the Yuan dynasty (1271–1368), and during the subsequent Ming dynasty (1368–1644) the Naxi ruling family set up private schools for male members of their Mu lineage. The eighteenth century saw a considerable expansion of schools, especially after the implementation of direct Chinese rule in 1723. Guan Xuexuan, the Chinese official responsible for the 1743 gazetteer, was influential in expanding Confucian education at this time: he initiated seventeen charitable schools in Lijiang, secured economic support for teachers' salaries, and decreed that officials should send their sons to school and get commoners to do the same. With twenty-two charitable schools in Lijiang Prefecture in 1736, thirty-one in 1895, and the continued presence of private schools, some local Naxi boys in the late Qing dynasty were receiving at least a few years of Han-language education (Hansen 1999: 29–32). In 1912, in accordance with the assimilationist goals of the new Republic, the county government organized a Chinese Language Society to teach Naxi men Chinese; members caught speaking Naxi were fined one copper coin (Track 1996: 141). Nevertheless, a census of Lijiang in 1933 registered only 5,340 men and 170 women as literate in Chinese, out of a total population of 132,582, implying that in the Republican era formal Han-language education had a rather limited impact (Rock 1963: 29).

As is often stated by local residents and outside observers, the greatest degree of Han cultural and linguistic influence among the Naxi tends to be among those living in and around Dayan Town. Local informants, historical documentation, and Peter Goullart's observations (1957) confirm that in the early twentieth century well-to-do Naxi men from this area routinely attended Chinese-language schools, participated in the state-sponsored Confucian sacrifices, intermarried with Han Chinese, and employed Taoist priests and Buddhist monks for religious services.[8] They also traveled on business not only all over Yunnan, but even to places as far away as Shanghai, Hong Kong, Lhasa, Burma, and India. Despite their sinicization and contact with the outside world, however, they continued to speak Naxi at home and to preserve many indigenous customs; Naxi women, for example, never suffered the custom of bound feet as did their Han Chinese sisters, and maintained a leading role in Lijiang's commercial life, much remarked upon by both Chinese and foreign visitors (Siguret 1937: 45–46; Goullart 1957: 94–96).

The presence of Han influence and its regional and class nature—greatest among the wealthier families in the political, cultural and economic center of Lijiang County, and along main trade routes—are of major importance to this book. Given the overtly assimilationist aims of the imperial and Republican governments, it plainly benefited the political and social elite of Lijiang to be conversant with Han Chinese language and customs, and thus to be able to accommodate to the norms of the Chinese state. Inevitably, there was a particular impetus for them to adopt Han-derived cultural institutions, among which the ritual-cum-musical-cum-social societies known as Dongjing associations (*dongjinghui*) were particularly visible.

Dongjing Associations of Yunnan

Prior to the Communist victory of 1949, most Han Chinese-dominated cities and counties of Yunnan Province, as well as a few minority areas such as Lijiang, were home to organizations called *dongjinghui* (Dongjing associations). Primarily the preserve of the educated male elite, these associations seem to have existed solely in southwest China, mainly in Yunnan. Their membership, usually of several dozen local worthies, met several times a year to perform rituals in tribute to a variety of Han Chinese deities, the most important of whom were Wenchang, patron god of the literati, and Guandi, god of war and wealth. Ceremonies lasted between one and seven days, and involved participants in the chanting and singing of scriptures in honor of the relevant god. Although the majority of association members were not professional religious specialists, associations nevertheless owned spectacular altar furnishings, multiple sets of scriptures and musical instruments, and other ritual paraphernalia. In addition, they frequently offered funeral services and other rites to their members, which overlapped with the work of professionals such as Taoist priests and Buddhist monks. Music was a major component in the rituals, and despite the fact that participants were musical amateurs, they were renowned for high standards, with each county or city having its own distinctive repertoire. Most associations used a variety of common Chinese bowed and plucked lutes, zithers, flutes, *suona* (shawms), and a plethora of percussion. They employed several modes of performance, including songs with heterophonic instrumental accompaniment, instrumental pieces, percussion patterns, unison chanting accompanied by percussion, and unaccompanied solo speech.

It appears that, before 1949, Dongjing associations existed in more than one hundred of Yunnan's 128 counties and cities, as well as in contiguous areas of

Sichuan and Guizhou provinces, and possibly in parts of northern Burma and Thailand settled by Yunnanese Han immigrants. Within Yunnan itself, while the Dongjing associations were primarily an activity of the Han Chinese, they have also been recorded for the Bai of Dali, the Naxi of Lijiang County, the Yi and Zhuang of Mengzi County, and the Mongols of Tonghai County (Wu Xueyuan 1990: 205–206; Huang Lin 1990: 16).

However, when the Communist government came to power in 1949, it discouraged religious activity, and in most parts of Yunnan speedily suppressed the Dongjing associations. This was primarily because such organizations were considered to be purveyors of "feudal superstition" (*fengjian mixin*); the fact that membership was frequently confined to the social elite was a further disadvantage. In many places the new government confiscated almost all the costly ritual paraphernalia, including musical instruments, scriptures, and other documentation; some of these objects have since turned up in museums, libraries, and archives. During left-wing extremist political movements in the 1950s and 1960s, many of the confiscated objects were destroyed, and some of the former association members were persecuted because of their previously high social status.

By the end of the Cultural Revolution, therefore, the Dongjing associations had been in abeyance for nearly thirty years, with most of their belongings destroyed or scattered and many of their members widely dispersed. However, by 1980, thanks to the gradually improving political climate, there was already an incipient revival of Dongjing associations in a few counties. While I have yet to see a comprehensive survey of the status of Dongjing associations and music in southwest China today, in the early and mid-1990s, I was able to visit active groups in sixteen counties and cities, and to gather detailed secondhand information on several more.[9] Dongjing associations that carried out a substantial complement of religious ritual existed at this time in at least the following areas: west and central Yunnan (Dali, Xiaguan, Chuxiong City, Lufeng, Weishan, and Nanjian counties, Baoshan City); south Yunnan (Tonghai, Jianshui, Kaiyuan, Mengzi, and Luxi counties); northwest Yunnan (Yongsheng, Heqing, and Jianchuan counties); and northeast Yunnan (Qujing City, rural areas). Groups that had revived only the music of their former local Dongjing association and played this mainly for secular entertainment were also plentiful, existing in west and central Yunnan (Kunming City, Tengchong County); south Yunnan (Shiping and Wenshan counties); northwest Yunnan (Lijiang County); and northeast Yunnan (Qujing City, urban area).[10]

Origins of the Dongjing Associations

The term *dongjinghui* is usually explained by informants as deriving from an abbreviation of the title of a major scripture. All the groups I encountered still used or had before 1949 used a version of the *Yuqing Wuji Zongzhen Wenchang Dadong Xianjing* (Transcendent Scripture of the Great Grotto of Wenchang). This full title, and variants upon it, are commonly reduced for convenience to *Dadong Xianjing*. The term for the associations which use this scripture as their main liturgical text is thus derived from the second and fourth syllables, with *hui*, "association," added to create a trisyllabic noun.

There is no question that nowadays *dongjinghui* is the term most commonly used in Chinese scholarship to refer to these groups. Not only is it the term favored in general articles, it is also used in local studies and anthologies. In addition, it is the generic term widely understood by local practitioners to designate their organizations, even though individual associations frequently have a specific name (e.g., *Zunsheng Hui* [Association for Honoring the Sage] in Dali, *Sanyuan Hui* [Three Origins Association] in Xiaguan).

Unfortunately, written and printed documentation from before 1949 is scarce,[11] but scattered evidence does suggest the term *dongjinghui* was in common use in both the late Qing dynasty and the Republican era. It occurs, for instance, in an inscription in the Wenchang Temple of Xin'ansuo, Mengzi County (now a school), dated 1843; in a copy of the *Transcendent Scripture of the Great Grotto of Wenchang* from Dacan, Weishan County, dated 1882; in a 1938 list of members of the Dongjing association of Dayan Town, Lijiang County (the *Yongbao Ping'an* [Eternal Assurance of Well-Being]); in some early-twentieth-century gazetteers;[12] and in several other publications from the Republican era, such as Zhao Yintang's vignettes of Lijiang (1984 [1948]: 154).

There is no agreement on how the Dongjing association phenomenon arose in Yunnan. However, Dali and Xiaguan, major cultural and communications centers just fourteen kilometers apart in west central Yunnan, are often cited as having the most longstanding associations. Documents surviving into the 1960s in Dali place the beginnings of the societies in the sixteenth century (Dali Shi Xiaguan Wenhuaguan 1990: 606–607).[13] Dali is unusual in that its Dongjing associations have been mentioned in at least four Western-language works. C.P. Fitzgerald appears to refer to these groups (1941: 108–110), although the description is so vague that it is not possible to be absolutely certain. A much clearer picture is given by Francis Hsu in his depiction of the response to the 1942 cholera epidemic in "West Town," a town of about eight thousand people under the jurisdiction of the district government of Dali, in which Dongjing associations performed scriptures asking for relief from the mounting death toll (Hsu 1943: 10; 1952: 17–19). In the 1980s, Kenneth Dean encountered the Dali "devotional societies" on a visit there (Kleeman 1988: 107). The associations of several other areas trace their origins either directly or indirectly to Dali, including those in Yongsheng County, Luxi County, and possibly Kunming.[14]

As for when Kunming, the provincial capital, may have instituted its Dongjing associations, Kunming musician Peng Youshan suggests the Ming dynasty (Zhang

Xingrong 1998: 412), while Kunming scholar Wu Xueyuan cites a "Record Book" (*Yizhibu*) of the Kunming *Baoshu Xue* association that mentions this group's successful prayers for rain in 1670 (1990: 207). Like Dali, Kunming is sometimes cited as a point of origin for Dongjing associations, for instance for those of the counties of Shiping and Qiubei (Liu Jiesheng 1991: 170; Yin 1991: 8–9).

Not all the regional associations, however, ascribe their origin to Dali or Kunming: many ascriptions are to outside Yunnan Province itself. In Wenshan County, the tradition is said to have started with an influx of settlers descended from soldiers from Nanjing, who were forced to settle in Jianshui County during Ming dynasty military campaigns and subsequently moved farther southeast to Wenshan (Wu Mingxian 1981: 1–2). Similarly, it is said in Weishan County that military settlers left behind after the campaign of Fu Youde in the late fourteenth century introduced their native customs by performing the *Transcendent Scripture of the Great Grotto of Wenchang* every year (Tang 1988: 6). Some Dongjing aficionados posit a deliberate introduction by travelers arriving or returning from eastern China, usually in the eighteenth or nineteenth centuries. This is the case in Jianshui County, Heijing Town in Lufeng County, and Xinping County.[15]

It is, of course, impossible to check the accuracy of these mostly oral histories. Furthermore, there is a serious problem in that few of them differentiate among the introduction of the scriptures used by the Dongjing associations, the music to which the scriptures were set, and the institution as a whole. Nevertheless, taken in aggregate, these traditions at least illustrate two popular perceptions of the Dongjing association tradition: first, its constituent parts originated outside Yunnan Province, mainly from the more developed, Han-dominated eastern side of China from which many of the Yunnan Han Chinese came; and second, Dali and Kunming, long political, economic, cultural, and communications hubs of Yunnan, were early strongholds of the Dongjing association movement.

Certain themes come through strongly in the textual and oral histories of the Dongjing associations. Often the late nineteenth century is viewed as a relatively vigorous time for the associations, once they had rebounded from the disastrous Moslem rebellion. In addition, oral evidence suggests that the last couple of years of the Qing dynasty and the entire Republican era were extremely fruitful for the founding of new Dongjing associations. For example, Tonghai County already had several conventional all-male associations by the late Republican period, but in 1947 added a real novelty: the first and only all-female association, the Guanyin Society (*Miaoshan Xue*), made up entirely of *xiuzhen guniang*, young women who had forsworn marriage (Zhang Jiaxun 1987: 130–131). Several aficionados of the Heijing Dongjing association went to Huili, in southern Sichuan Province, to teach the tradition in 1922 (Liu Yue 1991); at least three new associations were founded in the vicinity of Dali and Xiaguan in 1909 (Dali Shi Xiaguan Wenhuaguan 1990: 608–610); and at least five in Lijiang County between 1912 and 1949 (see chs. 4 and 5). In addition, many counties report the spread of associations to increasing numbers of villages throughout the nineteenth and early twentieth centuries, without being able to pinpoint exact dates. Overall, therefore, the picture for the pre-1949 period across Yunnan Province is one of thriving and increasingly numerous Dongjing associations.

Recruitment and Funding

The conventional wisdom is that the Dongjing associations before 1949 were the province of the literati, especially graduates of the national official examination system prior to its abolition in 1905 (Wu Xueyuan 1990: 207). The report on a 1962 government-sponsored research trip to several areas with previously strong associations reiterates this viewpoint, noting that before 1905 there was a preponderance of "intellectuals of the day" (*dangshi zhishi fenzi*), after which businessmen figured more prominently, together with some "musical enthusiasts" and "ordinary townsfolk." Major support, the report notes, was offered by "gentry" (*shishen*) and local officials (Zhou and Huang 1983 [1962]: 78).

The situation during the Republican era seems, in fact, to have been quite variable. Intellectual qualifications and social status were not always definitive requirements for entry to an association. The one necessary quality stressed in most groups I visited, urban or rural, was that the prospective recruit should be of good moral character. Ma Zhiqing, a former member of Xiaguan's Devotional Response Association (*Ganying Hui*), cited a propensity for gambling as a flaw that would disqualify an applicant. Informants in some areas did mention possession of *gongming* (official/scholarly achievement) as a necessary qualification for entry. However, not all Dongjing associations had such rigorous requirements. In He Family Village (He Jia Cun) near Heijing Town, Lufeng County—a village three hours' walk over a ridge of mountains from the nearest small town—any man before 1949 could join the association "as long as he was a good person," and there were even illiterate members, who could not take part in the singing and reading of scriptures, but played instruments. In Lijiang County, long-established associations in wealthy urban areas set high educational and social standards for their members, while newer associations and those in poorer or more rural areas were generally less exacting in their requirements. Many associations, however, did select their *huizhang* (association head) on the basis of *gongming*, or social and official standing and achievement, even if this was less important for ordinary members. In Xiaguan's Devotional Response Association, for instance, the head did not necessarily have to be able to take a skilled part in the ceremonies, but he had to have social distinction.[16]

Membership in associations often ran in families, and many people were able to offer evidence of extensive family connections with the Dongjing association of their area. He Yi'an, born in 1908, was the third generation in his family to join the association in Dayan Town, Lijiang County; Zhang Longhan, born in 1923, of the same group, was following in the footsteps of his father and eldest brother; and of the eighteen or so members active in the early 1990s in the Chuxiong City "Dongjing Music Association" (*Dongjing Yinyue Xiehui*), four were elderly brothers, and another four were grandfather, father, son, and grandfather's younger brother.

The occupations of former Dongjing association aficionados varied, but the membership commonly included businessmen, farmers, officials, teachers, and artisans. The vast majority of association members before 1949 were not religious professionals, although a few groups, such as those in Dayan Town and Chuxiong, allowed one or two Taoist priests to join.

Organizing a Dongjing association and running its multiday ceremonies was an expensive business. In Republican-era Lijiang County, for instance, the expenditure for a five-day gathering of the Dayan Town association was 120 silver dollars, covered by a combination of members' contributions and rent from corporately owned property; by way of comparison, at this time the Lijiang County Education Bureau paid primary school teachers fifteen silver dollars per semester (Track 1996: 123, 142). The authors of a 1962 fieldwork report note with characteristically disapproving vocabulary that "most [associations] had exploitative income from fixed capital in the form of land rent and interest from shops" (Zhou and Huang 1983 [1962]: 78). This corporate property was one reason for the antipathy of the socialist government toward the Dongjing associations, and it was invariably confiscated soon after 1949. Nevertheless, Zhou and Huang's depiction is unduly simplistic. While many long-established associations in wealthy areas (e.g., the urban areas of Chuxiong, Weishan County, Lijiang County, Xiaguan, and Jianshui County) owned shops, houses, or fields that they rented out to finance their ceremonies, this was only one source of income. Gifts of land or money from rich members or sponsors were apparently also quite common, and a few associations exacted entry fees from new recruits. However, newer or less well established groups in poorer areas did not necessarily have such resources: Lijiang County's Yinglie Li (today's Jinshan Township) association, established only in 1937, covered the expenses of each meeting by collecting small contributions from each participant.[17] In general, it was a point of honor not to use one's association to earn money. Several informants remarked that to do so would have been to descend to the level of Taoist priests, whom most seemed to despise.

Religious Affiliation

My Chinese colleagues were particularly interested in the religious or ideological affiliation of the Dongjing associations. Without exception the answer was that they were essentially Confucian in nature, even though most informants readily agreed that most of the deities worshiped and scriptures used were closely related to Taoism or Buddhism. This answer was also given to the researchers who visited several former associations in 1962, and clearly perplexed them: "the Dongjing associations are inseparable from feudal superstition. The members all say they believe in Confucianism, but they appear to have rather closer connections to Taoism" (Zhou and Huang 1983 [1962]: 79). In fact, though the main deities worshiped, Wenchang and Guandi, do have close connections with Taoism, these gods had also been incorporated into the state-approved pantheon, and were worshiped in this aspect by the respectable gentlemen of the Dongjing associations.

Each Dongjing association had its own roster of festivals celebrated, deities honored, and scriptures performed. The one common thread before 1949 for all the associations encountered was worship of Wenchang through the medium of the scripture associated with him, the *Wenchang Dadong Xianjing* (Transcendent Scripture of the Great Grotto of Wenchang). This scripture was performed on Wenchang's birthday, the third day of the second lunar month. Wenchang, popularly known to Westerners as the god of literature, also goes under the name Divine Lord of Zitong (*Zitong Dijun*), after the county in northern Sichuan Province in which his original cult center, Sevenfold Mountain (*Qiqu Shan*), is located. He seems to have originated as a serpent god worshiped for his ability to control thunder, but eventually became a national-level patron of the literati. In 1857 he reached the pinnacle of Confucian respectability, being placed on a par with Confucius and Guandi in the state sacrificial canon (Kleeman 1988: 1–5, 103; Mayers 1869–1870).[18] The *Transcendent Scripture of the Great Grotto of Wenchang* is a version of the *Dadong Zhenjing* (True Scripture of the Great Grotto), the major text of the *Shangqing* (Supreme Clarity) tradition in the Taoist Canon. The core of the text is a set of obscure Taoist stanzas that most of the Dongjing association members I met did not understand. Their respect for Wenchang was very much for his Confucian role as patron of the literati rather than for his Taoist and mystic connections, despite the abstruse Taoist scripture they chanted uncomprehendingly in his honor.[19]

Almost all associations in all counties also celebrated either one or both of the festivals of Guandi (the thirteenth of the fifth lunar month, and the twenty-fourth of the sixth lunar month). Long considered a god of war, protection, and wealth, Guandi was given imperial status (*di*) by the Ming in 1615 and, despite earlier associations with both Taoist and Buddhist temples, became an exemplar of Confucian morality. By 1853 he was raised to the same status in the official sacrifices (*sidian*) as Confucius. Under the Republican era Guandi continued to flourish, and he is one of the most popular Chinese deities today (Duara 1988a: 139, 1988b; Guo Songyi 1990; Mayers 1869–1870). A major Guandi scripture used by the Dongjing associations of Yunnan is the *Guansheng Dijun Jueshi Zhenjing* (Guandi Enlightenment Scripture). This scripture appears in the *Daozang Jiyao*

(Collected Essentials of the Taoist Canon), volume 23, under the title *Sanjie Fumo Guansheng Dijun Zhongxiao Zhongyi Zhenjing*. It centers on nineteen stanzas emphasizing the maintenance of health and fortune, and the avoidance of disaster, through the practice of traditional (Confucian) virtues. Dongjing association informants interpreted the scripture as a whole as promoting moral behavior.

Corporate ceremonies (*gonghui*) were also carried out by many Dongjing associations for the popular Buddhist goddess Guanyin on one or more of her festivals (the nineteenth of the second, sixth, and ninth lunar months). The main scripture associated with her was the famous *Lotus Sutra* (*Dacheng Miaofa Lianhua Jing* or similar titles). Some associations also performed the *Jade Emperor Scripture* (*Gaoshang Yuhuang Benhang Jijing* or similar titles) on the ninth of the first lunar month at the local Jade Emperor temple. Certain other gods and their festivals tended to be more localized in appeal.[20] Associations located in seats of county government or higher administrative centers were invited by the local authorities to provide music for the state-sponsored Confucian sacrifice during the Republican period, and probably during the Qing dynasty too. Since only educated men and boys could participate, this invitation certainly buttressed the claims of the more urban associations to membership in the literati.

In addition, all associations I visited would before 1949 perform funeral and memorial services for deceased members and deceased kin of members, and most would perform longevity ceremonies on members' sixtieth or other important birthdays. Two groups, those of He Jia Cun (He Family Village) near Heijing Town in Lufeng County, and Dayan Town in Lijiang, were also accustomed to perform new-house dedication rites (*anlong diantu*), which were normally the exclusive province of professional Taoist priests. The scriptures used for such services differed from those used for the gods' festivals. For example, in the village near Heijing, the *Shi Wang Jing* (Ten Kings Scripture) was traditionally used for memorial services, the *Xuehu Jing* (Lake of Blood Scripture) mainly for memorial services for women, and two different versions of the *Anlong Diantu Jing* (Dragon Pacification and Earth Settling Scripture) were used respectively for new houses and new graves.[21] A few associations reported taking part in ceremonies praying for rain.

Post–Cultural Revolution Recovery

Since the political liberalization of the late 1970s, a number of Dongjing associations in different parts of Yunnan have successfully revived their ritual and music. Doing this has required convincing local cultural cadres that they are respectable, politically innocuous folk organizations which infringe neither the spirit nor the letter of the law. In many counties the cadres readily approve their activities, and in a few cases, such as Lijiang and Luxi counties, have even offered financial support; for their part, members of a couple of groups were at pains to point out that they observed a strict rule of restricting services to their own members, not only because they traditionally have done so, but also because they wanted to be above any suspicion of engaging in "feudal superstitious activities" for profit. In most areas, funding for festivals now comes out of the pockets of individual members, since the groups' corporate property is long since gone; however, local, Taiwanese, and Chinese-American donors have also helped individual associations.[22]

A further difficulty is personnel: most former Dongjing association members were in their sixties and above by the mid-1980s, and a whole generation or more had missed out on traditional transmission. Some groups have successfully addressed this issue through formal training classes, through targeting energetic recent retirees, private entrepreneurs, and women for recruitment, or through drawing younger relatives of existing elderly members into the association. Other groups will probably die out within a few years through failure to recruit new blood. Retrieving lost scriptures, ritual paraphernalia, and musical instruments has also been a problem, solved in part by photocopying scriptures from groups that successfully hid them during the Cultural Revolution, buying or receiving donations of new items, and occasionally getting confiscated items returned.[23]

Considerable ingenuity has been applied to problems of political acceptance, economic stability, personnel maintenance, and equipment acquisition among the revived Dongjing associations. This goes too for those groups that have reformed, minus their ritual content, as essentially secular music organizations. The "ancient music association" (*guyuehui*) of Dayan Town, and "ancient music orchestras" (*guyuedui*) of other parts of Lijiang County are spectacular examples of this approach to the revival. None have resuscitated their ritual and religious content; instead, they have turned their music in a more secular direction, and one that has had unlooked-for implications for the county as a whole (Rees 1994: 117–127).

Performance of Scriptures

To understand the revived Dongjing ritual associations, and indeed the historical resonances of new secular Dongjing music groups such as those in Lijiang, it is vital to appreciate the audiovisual effect of Dongjing ritual performance, and thus its cultural affect. The performance of a scripture by an association requires the participants to recite and sing an entire text, from the first folio of the first fascicle to the last folio of the last fascicle, in a prescribed fashion. Each association has its own traditional way of dividing up the text for different modes of performance. The most complex mode of performance is reserved for rhyming stanzas, which are sung by the entire membership to the heterophonic accompaniment of the instrumental ensemble. Often these sung passages are rounded off by complex percussion patterns on drums, large cymbals, and other instruments.

Passages of commentary are generally declaimed unaccompanied by a solo reciter (*jiang* or *xuan*). The speaker exaggerates the natural speech tones of the Chinese language to produce a somewhat theatrical and highly inflected effect. Preparatory addresses to the gods and spells are commonly chanted by everyone present to the rhythm of more or less equidistant beats thumped out on the percussion instrument *muyu* (wooden fish). This mode of chanting, called *song*, appears to be less closely tied to speech tones than *jiang* or *xuan*, having instead one or more simple melodic formulae that are repeated many times. A different form of chanting, *du*, is used to read memorials to the gods. Actions without words, such as preparatory lighting of incense and presentation of offerings to the main altar, are accompanied by short pieces for the instrumental ensemble, once again playing in heterophony. [24]

The manner in which Dongjing association ceremonies are carried out is traditionally strictly prescribed, with regulations to ensure dignified performance of the liturgy. Occasionally these prescriptions are actually appended to a scripture belonging to an association, as with the third fascicle of the *Transcendent Scripture of the Great Grotto of Wenchang* of Dacan, Weishan County. According to this set of prescriptions from 1882, one should among other things show respect to the statues of the deities, maintain a pure heart and neat dress, and take care to play in tune.

All the many ceremonies I have witnessed in different parts of Yunnan have had one feature in common: movements are deliberate and intentionally dignified, while the participants wear long literatus jackets and gowns in somber colors (*shanzi magua*), display solemn facial expressions, and refrain from loud or facetious comments. There is a striking resemblance to the slow, dignified movements of the participants in traditional Confucian sacrifices. By contrast, the one Taoist funeral I attended in Yunnan featured a Taoist priest who wore bright blue and pink robes, and at one point led the mourners at such a rapid pace round the coffin and courtyard that several nearly fell over and started giggling. Visually, the spectacle offered by the Dongjing associations lends credence to their claim of Confucian affiliation and denial of affinity with professional Taoism.[25]

Dongjing Associations of Lijiang County

Origins of Lijiang's Dongjing Associations

As elsewhere in Yunnan, documentary evidence for Lijiang's associations is both partial and relatively recent. Major surviving sources include several scriptures preserved in the Lijiang County Library, with dates from 1903 to 1946; a privately owned scripture; privately owned hand-copied booklets of musical notation dating from between 1924 and the 1990s; a list of deceased members of Dayan Town's Dongjing association, *Moshi Bu Wang* (Never to Be Forgotten), from 1927; and a list of living members of the same group, titled *Yongbao Ping'an* (Eternal Assurance of Well-Being), from 1938.[26] There is also passing mention of the Dongjing associations in Naxi writer Zhao Yintang's local vignettes (1984 [1948]: 154), and a longer description in Peter Goullart's account of 1940s Lijiang (1957: 213–217).

While Zhao Yintang suggests that Lijiang's Dongjing associations date from the transition to direct Chinese rule (1723), she offers no evidence to support this assertion. The only surviving pre-1949 document to describe the history of any of the Lijiang associations is the preface to *Eternal Assurance of Well-Being*, translated below in its entirety. It was written by a prominent Naxi scholar-official and refers to the Dayan Town association.

> The god of Zitong appeared in the Jin dynasty [265–420 A.D.], and flourished under the Tang and Song dynasties [618–907, 960–1279 A.D.]. It is said that God commanded him to take charge of Wenchang's office and the records of human emoluments. At the beginning of the Yanyou period of the Yuan dynasty [1314], he was enfeoffed as "Divine Lord who supports the Yuan dynasty and civilizes, Wenchang who oversees emoluments." When the civil service examinations were selecting scholars [for office], scholars and officials all said that Wenchang held power over the examinations, and all the schools in the country established sacrifices to Wenchang. By the Qing dynasty temples were established to offer up sacrifice, and the rites were the same as in Confucius's temple. Lijiang was in the vanguard, taking the Dongjing scripture revised by the Divine Lord and assembling a Dongjing association to perform it. For a time the scholars were upright, the protocols were strict, the music was sonorous, and it flourished in a civilized fashion. The list of members' names was set out. On the cover of the book was written, "we hope for the help of the Divine Lord in the assurance of eternal well-being." It is impossible to trace the origins of the association. In 1806 our forebears re-organized the association, piously carrying out four festivals a year. During the Moslem rebellion of the Daoguang and Xianfeng reigns [1821–1851, 1851–1862], much of the association's ritual paraphernalia was lost; when peace was restored in the Tongzhi reign [1862–1875], relying on all the prominent gentlemen we succeeded in maintaining a revival. We also carried out the Guandi festivals, and the membership was even more energetic than before. The name-list was incomplete, so now [the association] has planned a new one, and entrusted myself, He Gengji, with the preface. From beginning to end I have collected information to carry out my responsibility. (He Gengji 1938)

The preface confirms the destruction of the Moslem rebellion and subsequent rebuilding mentioned by Dongjing association members from other parts of Yunnan. It also suggests a pre-1800 origin for the group, although how accurate

He Gengji's information was by 1938 is uncertain. All other information collected on this early period has been oral.

Several different versions of Dongjing association history circulate in the oral tradition. The forebears of leading Dayan Town association member He Yi'an (1908–1993) told him that around 1531 the ruler of the Lijiang Naxi, Mu Gong, sent envoys to the capital of China to learn "palace music" (*gongting yinyue*), which was introduced to Lijiang and became Lijiang's Dongjing music repertoire. Two other oral tales associate the introduction of Dongjing music to Lijiang with either the 1253 campaign of Kublai Khan in Yunnan, or else the 1381 campaign of Fu Youde, which resulted in the forced settlement of many soldiers in Yunnan, including musicians (Yang Zenglie 1990: 115–116). A fourth oral story comes from He Huihan (1914–1994), a former member of the Dongjing association of Baisha Township: according to his elders, an official born in Baisha, one Yang Bangwei, had learned the tradition in Bai-dominated Jianchuan County to the south of Lijiang, and introduced it to Lijiang sometime in the nineteenth century (interview, 3 June 1992). Both He Yi'an and He Huihan, however, cautioned that in the absence of documentary or other proof, their forebears' stories were mere hearsay.

What all these stories have in common is the attribution of Dongjing tradition to outside sources—Han, Mongol, or Bai. Nobody claims a local Naxi origin for the tradition. This has considerable resonance with the frequent invocation of outside origins for Dongjing ritual and music elsewhere in Yunnan.

Also similar to the situation in other parts of Yunnan was the expansion of Dongjing associations during the late Qing and Republican eras. By the end of the Qing dynasty (1911), there were at least five associations active in Lijiang: in Dayan Town, and in the more rural areas of Baisha, Shuhe, Lasha, and Gezi. During the Republican era these groups taught the Dongjing tradition to several new associations in the county. Detailed oral histories of the routes and means of transmission exist, and are examined in chapter 5 as a vital key to understanding the function of the Dongjing associations in local-level social interaction.

Festivals and Scriptures of Lijiang's Dongjing Associations

The festivals celebrated by the Dongjing associations of Lijiang County and the scriptures used for these occasions were paradigmatic for such associations anywhere in Yunnan. Within Lijiang County, they differed little among different groups.[27] The Dayan Town association celebrated four main festivals annually: Wenchang's birthday (*Wenchang Shengdan*), on the third day of the second lunar month; Wenchang's father's birthday (*Wenchang Fu Shengdan*), on the third day of the eighth lunar month; the festival celebrating the bravery of Guandi (*Dandao Hui*), on the thirteenth day of the fifth lunar month; and Guandi's birthday (*Guansheng Shengdan*), on the twenty-fourth day of the sixth lunar month. The scripture invariably used for the two Wenchang festivals was the *Transcendent Scripture of the Great Grotto of Wenchang*; that for the two Guandi festivals was the *Guandi Enlightenment Scripture*. Some of the other Dongjing associations in Lijiang County did not carry out the two Guandi festivals, reserving their attentions for just the two Wenchang festivals.

The *Guandi Enlightenment Scripture* is very much concerned with the promotion of traditional Confucian virtues such as filial piety, respect for heaven and human superiors, and trustworthiness; this emphasis is in tune with the appropriation of Guandi by the government and literary classes. The *Transcendent Scripture of the Great Grotto of Wenchang*, while focusing on abstruse Taoist concepts and spirits connected with *xiulian*, the practice of self-cultivation through meditative and physical exercises, is also associated with similar moral maxims, especially in the attached opening fascicle *Rite of Opening the Altar*. The organization and content of these two scriptures are set out in appendix A. Above all, both these Lijiang scriptures are part of the Dongjing mainstream, and indeed of the larger Han Chinese tradition of sacred texts.

In addition to the main four festivals of Wenchang and Guandi, Lijiang's Dongjing associations frequently performed other ceremonies. The Baisha association inserted a minor festival into its calendar: on the twentieth day of the first lunar month, when the Naxi god Sanduo was honored at his temple in Baisha, the local Dongjing association would assemble in the nearby Wenchang temple and perform the *Ershisi Xiaojing* (Classic of the Twenty-Four Exemplars of Filial Piety).[28] The ceremony lasted just one day. It is unclear why this particular scripture was chosen for the celebration, unless it was for its brevity compared with the Wenchang and Guandi scriptures, which could not be performed in a single day.

Private ceremonies were also common; among the most frequent were funerals for Dongjing association members or their relatives, at which the scripture *Classic of the Twenty-Four Exemplars of Filial Piety* was performed, and music was played for the ten offerings to the coffin (*lingqian gongyang*). Other private ceremonies included congratulations on an important birthday, often the sixtieth (*zhushou*), and wishing for a son (*qiuzi*). This latter was carried out using the final fascicle of Lijiang's version of the *Transcendent Scripture of the Great Grotto of Wenchang*, *The Wenchang Rite of Lighting a Lamp for Entreating Prosperity and Preserving Descendants*, and was usually slotted into the ritual at a major festival. A further private rite, that of *anlong diantu* (pacifying the dragon and settling the earth), was available to members of the Dayan Town association if they built a new house, although it was unknown among other Lijiang associations. A final commitment each year for the Dayan Town Dongjing association before 1949 was the state-sponsored Confucian sacrifice, for which the members were invited by the government to provide the music. In Lijiang County this usually took place twice a year, in the second and eighth lunar months.

In addition to all these formal ritual occasions, the Dayan Town Dongjing association also played occasionally for more secular public festivities—for instance, at the commercial Dragon Fair held in the local park in 1915 (Track 1996: 32). It was probably also this group that provided the background music for a Chrysanthemum Festival held in 1933 (Yang Zenglie 1991: 44). Some association members would also get together and play some of the most tuneful Dongjing melodies for fun. He Yi'an described to me how he would take an end-blown flute (*xiao*) over to a friend's house in the evenings to play; the same was true of association members at Yinglie Li (today's Jinshan Township). For the Dongjing association members, therefore, while the primary focus may have been on ritual performance, there was no bar to secular use of their instrumental pieces (*xiaodiao*) and accompanied songs (*dadiao*).

Dongjing Associations in Lijiang Society

Vibrantly active before their banning in 1949, Lijiang's Dongjing associations have not seen a ritual revival since then, although performance of their music has survived as a secular pastime. Nevertheless, it is clear that in the Republican era they were exemplars of a culturally Han Chinese, provincewide musico-ritual phenomenon, despite their Naxi membership. Participation in their activities meant participation in an elevated Chinese social ritual common to literati all over Yunnan, regardless of ethnic background; thus it was part of the public life of the educated Naxi gentleman.

The importance of education as a qualification for membership in long-established Dongjing associations such as those at Dayan Town, Baisha, and Shuhe was emphasized again and again by elderly informants. The Baisha association was even referred to by the local community as the "literatus association" (*wenren hui*). The Dayan Town group insisted that its recruits have official distinction (*gongming*) as well as good moral character (*daode*); in practice, only those from wealthy backgrounds with a high level of Han Chinese education were likely to be admitted. Other established associations too had fairly strict standards. In the 1920s, one highly accomplished young musician gained entry to the Lasha group despite relatively poor circumstances only because his uncle and teacher were members, and the group needed a good flautist. Generally in Lasha members were expected to have an education equivalent to that needed for the lowest civil service degree of the Qing dynasty (*xiucai*, equivalent to about nine years of study). A similar standard of education was expected at the Baima association established in 1923, although requirements seem to have been much less rigorous in the 1940s in the newly established associations of Jinshan and Shigu.[29]

As the next chapter demonstrates, even the soundworld of Lijiang's Dongjing associations proclaimed their allegiance to sophisticated Han culture, in sharp contradistinction to the Naxi musical world around them. Perhaps the last word on the social prestige attached to membership in a long-established association should be left to He Yi'an, a leading light in the Dayan Town group before 1949:

> [In the 1910s] my [primary school] teacher knew that I had a good family background so he agreed when my father asked if I could have leave to attend the Dongjing Society gatherings. Afterwards, my classmates envied me and asked me what we ate at the gatherings and how much of the sutras I remembered. Their questions encouraged and stimulated me to learn more; I was proud to be a member of the Dongjing Society. (Track 1996: 30–31)

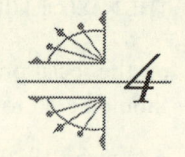

The Musical World of Republican Lijiang

"Each of the different kinds of barbarians has its own songs and leaping song-dances," says Guan Xuexuan, compiler of the eighteenth-century Lijiang gazetteer (*Lijiang Fu Zhilüe* 1991 [1743]: 208). Early-twentieth-century Lijiang also offered a wonderfully diverse soundscape, created through the interaction of a multitude of ethnic, religious, economic, political, and technological factors. There is much validity in the constantly repeated truism that, then as now, the opposite poles on a continuum from "Naxi" to "sinicized" are represented by remote mountainous villages at one end and Dayan Town at the other, with the lowland rural areas of the Lijiang basin and the banks of the Jinsha River coming somewhere in between. Yet within this common conceptual framework, there must remain room for shades of meaning and greater subtlety of distinction. There are, after all, ethnic groups in Lijiang other than the Naxi and Han; moreover, as McKhann argues from an examination of Naxi legends of interethnic contact, "the minorities of the Chinese periphery are in as much or more contact with neighboring minority groups as they are with the Han state" (1997: 2). Despite a tendency in much Chinese musicological writing to talk in terms of discrete categories of minority—"the Naxi," "the Pumi," "the Lisu"—the importance of interethnic musical contact and influence is widely recognized, especially for the spectacularly fragmented southwest (cf. Shi Xiao 1985; Liang Yu 1986). While for convenience I divide the musical types below mainly by ethnic origin, the importance of interethnic influence should not be forgotten. Furthermore, since music and dance mean little from dry descriptions on the printed page, I illustrate this chapter with recent photographs and recorded examples of the many pre-1949 musics that survive today, and recommend commercially available CDs and videos as supplements.

Naxi Musics

The Dongba and Sainii

Dongba, found before 1949 throughout Lijiang County and other Naxi areas, articulate three roles for their music: it is intended to please the spirits, to please people so that neither the audience nor the practitioner feels boredom or exhaustion in a long ceremony, and to summon ghosts for pacification and the expulsion of evil. As Lijiang scholar Yang Zenglie says, "People believe that when a *dongba* chants scriptures, his voice must be sonorous and pleasing to be heard by the spirits in heaven, the ancestors far away, men on earth, and ghosts in the underworld. Only then will his rites be efficacious" (1993: 104).

The core of the *dongba* musical repertoire is the tunes to which scriptures are chanted. There are about thirty types of melodies, with regional variants. Naxi musicologist Sangde Nuowa identifies five regional *dongba* traditions with distinctive melodic repertoires: the Baoshan tradition from northeast Lijiang; the Baidi tradition from the Sanba area of Zhongdian County; the Baisha tradition from the Lijiang basin around Dayan Town; the Tai'an/Ludian tradition from central and northwest Lijiang; and the Yongning tradition of the Mosuo *daba* from neighboring Ninglang County, who differ from the Lijiang *dongba* in not having written scriptures. Sangde Nuowa characterizes the melodies and singing style of the Baisha *dongba* as close to Naxi folk song, while the Baoshan and Baidi traditions show influence from folk songs and Lamaistic chants of nearby Tibetan communities (1993: 70–71). Which melody is applied to which scripture in which ceremony is regulated by custom, and passed down from one generation to the next; some ceremonies employ only one chant tune, others as many as five or six.

Chants, which are sung solo, fall into three categories: those for inviting and sacrificing to spirits and ancestors, which are described as smooth-flowing and respectful in mood; those for suppressing and driving out ghosts, characterized as louder, more vigorous in rhythm and very aggressive; and, most numerous, those for narrating long legends, which tend to be of steady rhythm and often narrow melodic range (Yang Zenglie 1993: 105–112).[1]

The example on CD Track 1 falls into this last category (Sangde Nuowa 1993: 73). Recorded in 1989, this is the opening of the scripture *Lv Bber Lv Raq*, chanted by He Yucai (a.k.a. He Shicheng, born 1909), a *dongba* from Zhulin Village, Dadong Township (northeast Lijiang, just south of Mingyin on Figure 3.2). There is some disagreement about the exact meaning of this scripture's title. Sangde Nuowa suggests "The shepherds migrate down the mountain," although he lists several other scholars' interpretations, including "The shepherd boy and shepherd girl come down" (1995: 30). The scripture is used almost exclusively during the ceremony *Her La Leeq Keel* (sacrifice to the wind demons), performed after the suicides of young lovers.[2] The *dongba* begins by stating that both people and birds migrated down from the mountains; he then urges youngsters to emulate the long life of trees and water rather than the evanescence of leaves, flowers, and water bubbles, and to stay put even though the stars and other natural phenomena may be in motion; he describes fathers admonishing their sons that one only lives once, and mothers reminding their daughters that flowers cannot bloom twice. The melodic range spans one octave, with five principal pitches (approximately c, e♭, f, g, c¹); the rhythm is steady, though not strictly metered; and there is frequently a pronounced slow vibrato on longer notes, something considered characteristic of Naxi folk songs.

Dongba also use a variety of percussion instruments, including large and small drums, gongs, cymbals, and bells, of which several are similar to Han and Tibetan equivalents. Considered of particular importance to the *dongba* are two drums and a bell. The *dda keq* (Chinese *da pigu*) is a wooden-framed drum with two leather faces, thirty to forty centimeters in diameter and about fifteen centimeters thick. It is suspended by four ropes attached to the frame and held in the left hand, and is hit with a stick of wood or similar material held in the right hand. The *da bbe leq* (Chinese *shouyao gu*) is a smaller drum, also with a wooden frame and two leather faces. The diameter is about fifteen centimeters and the thickness five centimeters; it has a stick protruding from the bottom of the frame by which it is held in one hand. On both sides are nailed short leather strips knotted at the end. When the drum is twisted from side to side by the right hand, these strips knock against the two surfaces, causing the drum to sound. The *zai laiq* (Chinese *panling*) is a brass bell with a diameter of about fifteen centimeters. The flare is so wide that it looks almost like a flat dish; the player uses a handle or leather thong protruding from the convex side to hold the bell in his left hand, while a small piece of wood or metal is attached to the concave side with a leather thong. When the performer agitates the handle, the wooden or metal clapper strikes the body of the bell, causing it to sound (Yang Zenglie 1993: 112–114). Several photographs show *dongba* dancing while using the bell in the left hand and the small drum in the right (Ge 1992).

Two aerophones are also used by *dongba*: the conch shell *fvl sse* (Chinese *hailuo hao*), and the yak horn *bberq ko* (Chinese *maoniu jiaohao*). Except for some chants accompanied by the small drum *da bbe leq* and bell *zai laiq*, singing is unaccompanied; instruments are primarily used to accompany the danced segments of rituals. The conch shell and yak horn play single long notes, while the percussion instruments usually delineate simple rhythmic patterns, often of two, three, or four beats. Because supernatural powers are attributed to the instruments, there are strict rules as to when they may be played and which *dongba* may use them (Yang Zenglie 1993: 114–117; Ge 1992: 70).

Dongba pictographs show many different kinds of instruments, including some wind and string instruments not known to be used by *dongba*. There is speculation that a greater variety of instruments may have been used in ceremonies in the past; at the very least the presence of such pictographs attests to the wide variety of instruments encountered and played by the Naxi (Yang Dejun 1985: 438). Although the *dongba* have no musical notation, they do possess a choreographic notation (Yang, He, and He 1990, Ge 1992).

While there is still little published on *dongba* music, even less information is available on the music of the *sainii* shamans. This is probably because the activities of such shamans are deemed "feudal superstition" (*fengjian mixin*) rather than "religion" (*zongjiao*), and thus strongly disapproved of or outlawed by the Chinese government. Hence work on their music is rendered difficult even for local researchers. However, we do possess descriptions of *sainii* ceremonies from the first half of the twentieth century from Joseph Rock. Rock describes a *sainii* and the beginning of one of his rituals thus:

> The [*sainii*] usually wears an ordinary long blue cotton gown, on his head a turban of red cloth, and on his back vari-colored paper flags which are stuck in his girdle. Smaller paper flags are stuck in his turban. His attributes of office are a sword, a small flat gong, a large iron ring on which smaller iron rings are suspended—these he shakes when he dances. Around his neck he wears a long *mani*, or rosary-like necklace of white beads made of the white conch. . . . A large barrel-like drum stretched with hide on one side lies on the ground horizontally, it is beaten by an attendant during a ceremony. . . .
>
> Before a ceremony begins, which is always at night, the [*sainii*] is given a meal by the family who have called upon him to exorcise the demons who are troubling their house, or who have afflicted them with either illness or bad luck. A table is placed in the court of the house upon which is arranged a measure of wheat or rice in which incense sticks and paper flags are inserted. The table is then moved toward the entrance of the court which faces the open door leading into the village street. The [*sainii*] first calls on Dja-ma, the personal god of the [*sainii*]. . . . He stands in an improvised chapel before a painting of [the Naxi god] Sanduo . . . with gong in hand and begins to chant . . . an invitation to the local or mountain gods. (1959: 798)

Vocal Musics

The Naxi possess a wide range of folk songs, the best known of which is the melismatic, free-rhythm melody called in Naxi *Gguq qil* (lit. "song," transliterated *guqi* in Han Chinese). Folksinger He Fengxiang, born in 1942 in Shuhe (now part of Baisha Township), told me that the words sung to this are often made up on the spot, especially if touching upon love or berating somebody. *Gguq qil* may be sung solo or as a dialogue song (Han *duige*), in which two singers face each other and sing alternately, each feeding off the wordplay of the other.[3] In some cases the words and appropriate accompanying gestures are traditionally fixed. Where there are set words, older people may criticize a young singer if he or she gets them wrong. *Gguq qil* is equally suitable for expressing love or anger, for spreading political propaganda, or indeed for any other purpose. CD Track 2 is an example of *Gguq qil*: He Fengxiang sings the love song "Bbai naiq bbaq jji huil" (The Meeting of Bees and Flowers). The words describe a courtyard of a three-storied house, in which three trees grow; each tree has three flowers growing on it, making nine in all. The courtyard also hosts three bees' nests, each housing three bees, making nine in all, so that nine pairs of bees and flowers come together. The bees and flowers are metaphors for boys and girls.[4] The fairly tense vocal quality carries well; the range is less than an octave, and many long notes display the slow, wide vibrato for which Naxi folk song is famed.

In his general surveys of Naxi music, longtime Lijiang resident Kou Bangping lists several more genres of folk songs: work songs, love songs (often sung as dialogue songs with either one man and one woman, or else in groups), funeral laments, children's songs, and "spur-of-the-minute" songs. In many "spur-of-the-minute" songs, the singer uses a short melody appropriate to his or her gender and age group (Kou lists four different melodies for girls, boys, old people, and youngsters of both sexes) and improvises words inspired by feelings of the moment (Kou Bangping 1984: 16–20; 1986: 71). Joseph Rock, resident in Lijiang for most of the second quarter of the twentieth century, was greatly impressed by Naxi youths' skill in improvisatory singing: "Their ability to keep up impromptu songs is often very remarkable. . . . When a group of boys travels together over the hills and through forests, it is by no means unusual for one to start singing extempore, while another boy will answer, and thus they will keep up improvising while wandering over their lovely country" (1939: 21). There is considerable variety in singing styles for different types of songs. In May 1989, for instance, I heard a young man and woman hundreds of feet apart singing a robust, piercing dialogue song on the mountainside above Baisha. Three years later, at a funeral in Xia Shuhe not far away, I listened to the women's laments, sung very quietly amid distraught but subdued sobbing; they were barely audible more than a few feet away.[5]

Dances with Vocal Accompaniment

Naxi folk dances, prominent both before and after 1949 at festivals, are often accompanied purely by vocal music. The participants dance and sing simultaneously, usually holding hands and performing a repetitive set of simple steps while circling to the right. CD Track 3 is the celebratory song *A li li*, now the commonest such dance in the Lijiang basin area. *A li li* developed from a Naxi folk song in the Sanba region of Zhongdian County and spread within Lijiang County only just before 1949. "A li li" are vocables that begin each verse of the song. This recording was made at a lively outdoor New Year's festival in 1992, and the words are not easy to distinguish, although one can hear two of the song's main features: the anhemitonic pentatonic melody, and the call-response structure, in which a lead singer first sings several phrases, and is then answered by everyone else in approximate unison. A very different style of dance is the famous *O ssei sseil* (better known by its Han transliteration *Worere*, or as *Remeicuo*), found among Naxi communities along the banks of the Jinsha River. Traditionally sung at funerals, it is a polyphonic two-part song in which a male chorus shouts its line roughly, while the female chorus, whose part is totally different melodically, appears to imitate the baaing of sheep (Kou Bangping 1984: 24–25; 1986: 72–73).[6]

In general, Naxi dances exemplify two important features of local musical culture: first, the frequent area-specificity of any one kind of dance; and, second, the tremendous amount of interethnic influence. Kou Bangping cites *Worere* as confined largely to the Jinsha River area, and two other song-dances as exclusive to the Naxi of Sanba, Zhongdian County (Kou Bangping 1986: 72). At the same time, the Naxi have been influenced by the dances of several other local ethnic groups, including the Tibetans, Lisu, and Yi (Zhang Yunqing 1983: 52).

Dances with Instrumental Accompaniment

There are also many dance tunes for flute (*biliq* in Naxi) and mouth organ (*ngail mo* in Naxi, *hulusheng* in Chinese). Flutes are generally made of bamboo, and may either be transverse, or recorder-style fipple flutes; the latter have a block in the mouthpiece channeling the airstream down to a window cut in the side of the instrument, and six roughly equidistant finger holes. Some of them have an extra hole above the top finger hole over which a membrane is stretched, as with the Han transverse flute *dizi*. The mouth organ is sounded by inhaling and exhaling. It consists of a gourd into which are inserted five bamboo pipes, each of which sounds when the player stops the hole drilled into its side. The pipes are held in place by wax. The lower pipe ends protrude through the bottom of the gourd, and stopping the lower end produces a second possible pitch for each pipe (Figure 4.1 shows how the instrument is held). Each pipe has a free-beating reed enclosed within the gourd wind chest. Unlike the flutes, the mouth organ can play more than one note at once, and often holds one pitch as a drone while simultaneously playing a tune. An excerpt from a mouth organ dance tune played at the May Day festival in 1992 may be heard on CD Track 4.[7] In general both flutes and mouth organs are locally made, with neither absolute pitch nor relative tuning completely standardized. It is popularly said that there are seventy-two tunes for the flute, and seventy-two for the mouth organ—which simply indicates large numbers of each.[8] Researchers have found that some tunes are peculiar to one Naxi locale, while others are in common use across the whole

FIGURE 4.1. Unidentified musician playing *hulusheng* for dancing in Dayan Town at May Day celebrations, 1992.

county among different ethnic groups (interview with Yang Zenglie, 2 May 1992). Once again, both localization and interethnic influence exist here.

Both before and since 1949 Naxi dances have been fixtures at local festivals. In May 1992 I attended an afternoon's celebrations for the "Beginning of Summer" (*Li Xia Jie*) in the village under the Puji monastery, in the Lijiang basin. Four players of the Naxi fipple flute took turns to play for the dozens of dancers who crowded into a large farm courtyard (Figure 4.2). The tunes were basically anhemitonic pentatonic, with many different tune lengths, including thirty-five beats (five groups of seven, subdivided into 4+3), twenty-two beats (three groups of four, one group of two, two groups of four), sixteen (four groups of four), fifteen (three groups of five, subdivided into 3+2), and twelve (two groups of six). Example 4.1 shows the basic tune for the first of these, which may be heard on CD Track 5; it is repeated dozens of times, each with slight ornamental variations by the flautist. The tune is divided into five seven-beat segments, and the dance steps are a repeated series of seven steps which accord with the seven beats of the flute. The dance which accompanies this seven-beat tune is performed as follows: while holding hands with the people on either side of you, leaning forward slightly, and jerking your arms downward on the beat, you circle to the right with an ever-repeating pattern of seven steps:

R L R L* L R# R*

THE MUSICAL WORLD OF REPUBLICAN LIJIANG 61

FIGURE 4.2. Wang Chaoxin playing the Naxi fipple flute for dancing at the Beginning of Summer Festival at the village under Puji monastery, May 1992.

Here, R and L stand for heavy downward steps with right and left feet, respectively; the feet are kept fairly close to the ground. L* indicates that the left foot is kicked to the right, R* that the right foot is kicked to the left. R# indicates that the right foot is brought together in a stamping movement with the stationary left foot. Both steps R are performed while moving to the right; the first step L is performed while moving to the right; the second step L moves the dancer to the left. Despite the changing directions, on aggregate each set of seven steps moves the line of dancers to the right. The flute player, who is usually standing in the middle of the circling dances, also performs the basic dance steps, and may keep a dance going for ten minutes or more before he tires. He often speeds up toward the end so that the dance gets livelier and livelier and some of the dancers fall over each other. Everybody enjoys this, especially the confusion at the end. Such dances are rambunctious, and above all good fun for all involved. At these farmyard celebrations, people of all ages took enthusiastic part in the proceedings, and the dancing went on from early afternoon to early evening.[9]

Other Instrumental Music

In common with many other southwestern minorities, the Naxi are well known for their use of the Jew's harp (*gue gueq* in Naxi, *kouxian* in Chinese). Played by both sexes, two main varieties are commonly seen. The first consists of three discrete bamboo strips with a tongue cut into each strip (see Figure 4.3). These strips are pinched between the thumb and forefinger of the left hand and held parallel just in front of the mouth; the ends project to the right of the mouth and are plucked by the index and middle fingers of the right hand. The second

f   fluttertongue

x   pitch is indeterminate, but approximately the one given

(♪) note cracks; this appears to be the pitch intended

𝄱   ornament resembling a mordent

EXAMPLE 4.1. Seven-beat Naxi dance tune played on the fipple flute by Wang Chaoxin. This basic tune is repeated many times, always with variations. The transcribed example is the first appearance of the melody as heard on CD Track 5. Actual pitch is approximately one octave higher than written.

variety is a single bamboo strip with a tongue cut in and a string attached at either end; one string is wrapped tightly around the fingers, while the other is pulled to cause the tongue to vibrate. The set of Jew's harps I bought in Dayan Town in 1989 also included an instrument similar to the first, but consisting only of one bamboo strip. The three-strip instrument is tuned so that the highest pitched strip, placed on top, sounds a minor third above the middle pitched strip, which is placed on the bottom, and a minor seventh above the lowest pitched strip, which is placed in the middle. These are the fundamental notes, but subtle overtone effects are achieved through altering the shape of the mouth, which acts as the resonating chamber. The Jew's harp among the Naxi and many other ethnic groups is particularly famous for its ability to "speak." I was unable to ascertain from interviews precisely how the "speaking" is accomplished; however, this appears to be related to the instrument's ability to reproduce the different vowels,

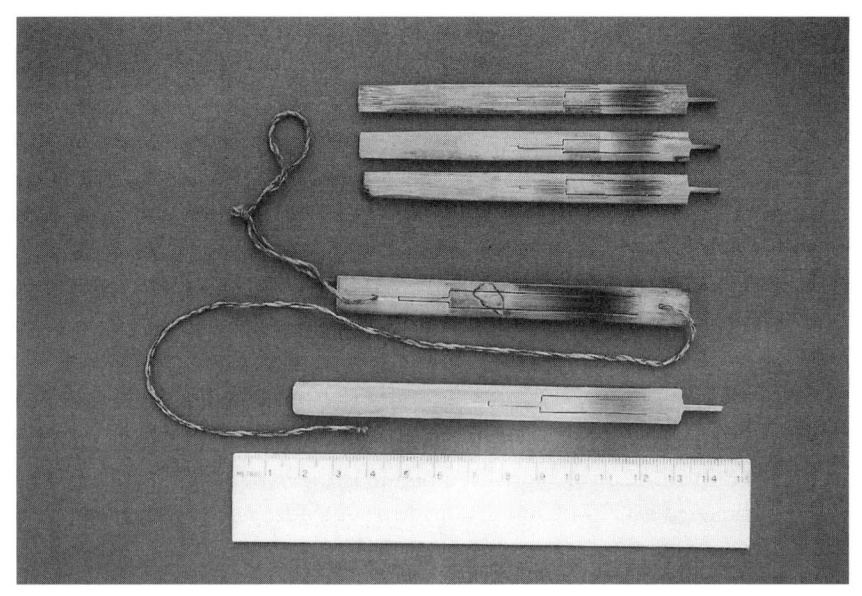

FIGURE 4.3. Three different kinds of Naxi Jew's harp purchased in Dayan Town, May 1989.

certain consonants, and possibly the tones of the Naxi language (Ying and Sun 1988: 82; Catlin 1986: 15; Rock 1939: 8).

Both before and after 1949, the Jew's harp has been particularly renowned for its role in courtship. The Russian author Goullart cites the legend of the girl Kamegamiki, the subject of a *dongba* manuscript, who used the instrument to persuade her lover to assent to a suicide pact:

> In accordance with the then prevailing etiquette, she did not broach the subject of suicide to the young man by word of mouth direct but conveyed the meaning in verse through the music of the Jew's-harp which is a national musical instrument of the Naxi and much used in love-making. Accompanying her whispered words with the harp she made a long and plaintive recital in which she used all her power and charm to persuade her lover of the hopelessness of their position, out of which the only escape was through death. He was not at all keen to follow her into the grave and raised many objections to her plan, expressing them in suitable verse, again with the help of the Jew's-harp. But she was . . . persistent . . . and finally she drove him to distraction with her promptings. (1957: 182–183)

In May 1992 I visited He Heng, an elderly woman who had moved to Dayan Town from Baoshan in northeastearn Lijiang County, and who had in earlier years been a renowned player. She spoke no Chinese, but through her daughter and daughter-in-law, who acted as interpreters, she said that one can use the Jew's harp to express any emotion, happy or sad, or to "talk love"; her daughter remembered her mother playing to herself in previous years when particularly happy or distressed.[10] CD Track 6 is Ms. He's playing of the three-strip Jew's harp. She explained the content as expressing pleasure at my visit.

Another instrument used by both the Naxi and many other ethnic groups is the leaf (see Figure 4.4). Any elliptical, smooth-surfaced leaf fresh from its tree may be used, and is discarded after playing. There are different ways to hold the leaf; Yang Houkun, a fine exponent of the instrument, used thumb and forefinger of both hands to hold it up to his upper lip. By directing the stream of air over the lower edge, he caused it to vibrate. The leaf can very effectively reproduce folk-song tunes (CD Track 7); in addition, one particular short leaf-call is recognized as a summons, often from lover to lover (Track 8).[11]

A second instrument of short-lived nature is the barley-stalk pipe (Naxi *uo uoq*, transliterated *wowo* in Chinese), made from tender shoots during the third and fourth lunar months.

> First one uses one's fingers to nip off a six to seven cm length of barley stalk. This should be a suitably tender stem from the new crop, and should have a knot at one end. The section just below the knot should be pinched between the outer edges of the two hands and rolled back and forth so that the barley stalk splits into multiple reeds about three cm long. Then, using the thumb

FIGURE 4.4. Yang Houkun playing the leaf, June 1993.

and index finger of each hand to pinch either end of the stalk, the maker exerts pressure towards the centre, causing the reeds to bulge outwards. Finally, he or she blows out the inner membrane that has been fragmented by the rubbing process, and the *wowo* is ready for a trial blow. (Yang Zenglie 1995: 71)

Half the stalk, including the end with the knot and reeds, is inserted into the mouth, with the hands cupped round the part that protrudes. Blowing into the tube causes the reeds to vibrate, so that sound is produced. While the instrument is played, the pitch is controlled by the strength and speed of the breath, the distance of the hands from the lips, and the distance of the tip of the tongue from the reeds. High pitches are produced by a fast air stream, hands close to the lips, and tongue close to the reeds. Although there are no finger holes, a skilled player can produce several notes (Yang Zenglie 1995: 71).[12]

The barley-stalk pipe seems to be particularly associated in the Naxi imagination with springtime and courtship. Mentioned in *dongba* texts, it is also cited in a couple of Han-language poems penned by Naxi literati:

> The cornfields are green, the children charming,
> The wind softly blows the willow branches.
> Willow twigs are twisted into a girl's hat,
> A barley pipe becomes a jasper flute.
> (Niu Tao, 1790–1858, in Zhao Yintang 1985: 128,
> and Yang Zenglie 1995: 68)

> A wonderful sound issues from the barley flute;
> Whoever plays it, an unreasoning passion develops.
> Wondering, looking with shyness,
> Making eyes with stealthy, sideways glances.
> (He Gengji, 1864–1951, in Zhao Yintang 1985: 236,
> and Yang Zenglie 1995: 70)

Baisha Xiyue

Probably the single most famous "indigenous" musical form of the Naxi, the funeral music known in Chinese as Baisha Xiyue (a direct translation of the Naxi term Bbesheeq Xilli) even has its own entry in the standard single-volume dictionary on Chinese music (Miao, Ji, and Guo 1985: 12). Literally "Baisha Xiyue" means "refined music from Baisha." The first serious fieldwork on the music was carried out in 1962, and resulted in two important essays by Beijing-based musicologist Mao Jizeng (1964 and 1986). He notes that before 1949 the performers were semiprofessionals who were primarily peasants but would respond to invitations to take part in funerals and sometimes ancestral sacrifices in the second and eighth lunar months (1964: 19; 1986: 114). The genre was already dying out before 1949; the 1962 field trip apparently uncovered only four performers of Baisha Xiyue: He Xidian from Changshui, Li Yulong from Lashi, Li Yunqing from Lashi, and He Chongshang from Shigu. The last of these could play only a small part of the repertoire. Consequently, information on the genre and its traditional context is somewhat patchy. All, however, agree that the music and its performers were looked down upon. It has been suggested that this was because of the music's association with funerals, which are by their nature inauspicious events. In addition, the musicians were mostly poor, and would play for anyone who could pay them, unlike the gentlemanly Dongjing associations, which would perform only for members, and generally eschewed financial profit.

The best known of the four musicians, He Xidian, wrote a brief account of Baisha Xiyue for a series on local history in Lijiang. He Xidian was born in 1906 and died in 1989 (Mu 1990: 165). He describes first his own experience:

> When I was thirteen I found time in the early mornings and evenings to study Baisha Xiyue from my uncle. This ancient music has no written scores; there is only oral transmission and osmosis, so it is hard to learn. At the end of the Qing dynasty and the beginning of the Republic it was generally known as funeral music. Whenever someone died and a funeral was organized, apart from the mourners within the household, they often invited the Baisha Xiyue ensemble to perform for the mourning of the survivors, as well as the guests' spontaneous sorrowful crying. When I had just begun to study the music, there were twelve or thirteen old people who could play it. Bereaved households often came to invite them to participate, and I used to go too to perform and get a little payment, which helped out with household expenses. I passed over thirty years in this fashion. Afterwards these old people died one after the other, and only I idled away my time. I often remember the words of my elders: from my forbears to myself, four generations of my family have studied Baisha Xiyue. (1985: 68)

Next he moves on to the problem of the origins of Baisha Xiyue. According to He's uncle, the music and musicians to perform it were first brought to Lijiang by the Mongolian Kublai Khan of the Yuan dynasty in the thirteenth century during his conquest of southern China. Kublai is said to have got on well with the Naxi ruler Mu and to have left his musicians behind as a parting gift. He Xidian says that the real name of the music is Bieshi Xieli, or "Ceremony of Thanks at Time of Parting." He attributes the alternative name Baisha Xiyue to the story that, when after some years the house of Mu was in decline and could no longer support the musicians, they split up and took their music to various villages, with some remaining at Baisha, seat of the Mu rulers (He Xidian 1985: 69–70).

He Xidian provides anecdotal evidence to support the local tradition of a Mongolian origin to this music by mentioning the 1981 visit to Lijiang of two members of the Inner Mongolian Song and Dance Troupe, who felt that the four-string plucked lute *sugudu* (used only in Lijiang County's Baisha Xiyue and Dongjing music) was Mongolian in origin (p. 71).[13] Older sources too cite a Yuan dynasty origin. The 1743 Lijiang gazetteer appears to be the earliest. The compiler observes: "The music is called Xiyue. The [bridged zither] *zheng*, [transverse flute] *di* and [four-string plucked lute] *pipa* are made the same as the Han equivalents. . . . Tradition has it that the music was left behind by men of Yuan" (*Lijiang Fu Zhilüe* 1991 [1743]: 208–209).

An early-twentieth-century commentary, however, records a different view, that the music was created by the (Naxi) people, and its name really meant "Music for the Xifan dead." The Xifan were an ethnic group now known as Pumi, large numbers of whom the Naxi ruler Mu is said to have killed in battle at Baisha (Mao Jizeng 1964: 11–12; Xuan Ke 1984a: 29; 1986a: 65). Xuan Ke adduces linguistic evidence to support his conviction that Baisha Xiyue had this latter meaning, and that it was an indigenously Naxi creation. By contrast, one of the four musicians visited in 1962, Li Yunqing, thought that the music had been brought to Lijiang by Han soldiers from Nanjing (Mao Jizeng 1964: 14). Whatever the truth of the genre's origins, it appears to have been played only in a very restricted area of Lijiang County, in the least remote communities: in some villages on the plain on which Dayan Town lies, and in a few villages near Shigu and Lashi. Baisha Xiyue seems to have been unknown among Naxi in other parts of Lijiang County, or indeed among Naxi living in other counties.

The reason for all this debate about the origins of Baisha Xiyue is its musical characteristics, atypical for the Lijiang Naxi. During the 1962 field trip, Mao Jizeng and his colleagues made recordings of some of the repertoire and also researched the instruments and traditional manner of performance. There were traditionally about nine pieces, performed in a particular order (set out in detail in Mao Jizeng 1986: 114–115). There is intense debate about the meaning of the titles and words of these pieces; this debate hinges largely on arguments about Naxi linguistics. Below I follow the translation offered by Mao Jizeng, which is based on information from He Xidian and other folk artists.[14] I list the instrumentation as given in Mao's description and transcriptions; he points out that a twelve-string bridged zither *zheng* had formerly been used, but that by 1962 no one could play it. The four-string lute *sugudu* and fipple flute were also used, although they do not appear in his transcriptions (1986: 115–146).

1. "Preface" (*Dduq* in Naxi), played on a solo transverse flute *biliq* (described as the same as the Han transverse flute *dizi*).
2. "A Letter" (*Yi Feng Shu*, a Chinese-language title), played on transverse flute, double-reed pipe *bobo*, and the bowed lutes *erhuang* and *huqin* (these instruments and the *sugudu* are described in detail later in this chapter under Dongjing music).

3. "Sansi River" (*Sail si jjiq* in Naxi), in which the same four instruments as above alternate with a solo singer.
4. "Beautiful White Clouds" (*Ai lil li jji perq* in Naxi), played by the same four instruments as above, accompanying a singer.
5. "The Princess Cries" (*Me mil ngu* in Naxi), played on a solo transverse flute.
6. "Barefoot Dance" (*Dol co* in Naxi), played on solo transverse flute, with alternating singing and dancing.
7. "Arrow Dance" (*Kail co* in Naxi), including singing and dancing; the tune is taken from part of "A Letter," but Mao does not state whether any instruments accompany this rendition.
8. "Dirge" (*Mul bvl* in Naxi), sung solo, eulogizing the deceased; this is sung as part of the third, sixth, and seventh pieces.
9. "Southern Piece" (*Nan Qu*, a Chinese-language title) for transverse flute solo. Mao does not say where this fits into the format of Baisha Xiyue.

Though Mao's transcriptions from 1962 are for an instrumental ensemble of just four people, at its largest a Baisha Xiyue ensemble included eight instrumentalists: two on the transverse flute, and one each on end-blown flute, *bobo*, *sugudu*, *zheng*, *erhuang*, and *huqin* (Mao Jizeng 1986: 114). Of these instruments, only the flutes are in common use in other forms of indigenous Naxi music. The great variety of instruments, which would be normal for Han music, is quite unusual for indigenous Naxi music; so too is their use in what appears from Mao's transcriptions to be heterophony (and in a few places polyphony, where the flute has a different melodic line from the other instruments): most Naxi instrumental music is monophonic, or monophonic with sporadic drone in the case of the mouth organ *hulusheng*. CD Track 9 is the flute solo "The Princess Cries," Track 10 a purely instrumental rendition of "Beautiful White Clouds," in which the heterophony is plainly audible.[15]

Dongjing Music

Against the Naxi soundscape within which it existed, Lijiang's Dongjing music loudly proclaimed its Han origins, confirming the evidence offered before 1949 by the quintessential Han-ness of Dongjing scriptures, deities, festivals, and costumes.

Instrumentarium

The instrumentarium alone is far more diverse than that of all other Naxi musics put together, and most of its constituent instruments are probably of Han origin.[16] Many instruments are commonly known by Han Chinese rather than Naxi names. Figure 4.5 shows a typical instrumental ensemble for this music.

The most important aerophones used in Dongjing music are a pair of bamboo transverse flutes (*dizi*, referred to colloquially in Naxi as *biliq*) with six equi-

FIGURE 4.5. Baihua Ancient Music Orchestra at a Sunday gathering, October 1991. *Left to right*: The instruments are *banhu* (two-string fiddle), *sugudu* (four-string plucked lute, half-hidden), *huqin* (two-string fiddle), *ban'gu* and *muyu* (small drum, half-hidden, and fish-shaped woodblock), *xiaocha* (small cymbals), *yunluo* and *tongling* (tuned gong set and bell), *erhuang* (two-string fiddle), *sanxian* (three-string plucked lute), *pipa* (pear-shaped four-string plucked lute), *dizi* (transverse flute), *jizi* (miniature cymbals), *dagu* (large drum).

distant finger holes and a vibrating membrane covering an extra hole located between the blowing hole and the top finger hole. These flutes are identical to Han *dizi* and are often purchased from Han makers. Their lowest pitch with all holes covered is $a\sharp^1$, and their range is over two octaves. The tongue is not used to separate notes, and many players use a heavy vibrato on long notes. This vibrato and the highly ornamented performance style may be clearly heard on CD Tracks 12 and 15. The Dongjing associations used *dizi* in identically pitched pairs, with one, described as the male (*xiong*), slimmer than the other, described as female (*ci*). A second, widespread aerophone is the double-reed *bobo*, a short cylindrical pipe made of bamboo, which traditionally had six equidistant holes. Also used in Baisha Xiyue and usually made by its player, this oboe-like instrument has a Naxi name, and is considered a local Naxi form of the *guan*, an instrument widespread among other ethnic groups in China, including the Han. The *bobo* lends a distinctive nasal tone to Lijiang's Dongjing music, which comes through clearly on CD Track 14. Pitch is controlled not only by the placement of fingers on the finger holes but also through the tightness of the embouchure, placement of lips on the reed, and strength of breath. Known traditionally for its trademark slow, wide vibrato, since the 1960s the *bobo* has also seen the introduction of extra finger holes to extend the range, and of new techniques such as fast single tonguing (Yang Zenglie 1983). The slightly modernized *bobo* used by Yang Zenglie of the Dayan Town ensemble in the 1990s has a range of just over an octave, with e♯^{1} as the lowest note. During the Qing dynasty and Republican era, two further aerophones were employed by the Dayan Town association: the end-blown flute *dongxiao*, and the double-reed pipe *guan*. While they no longer exist in Lijiang, the Han names and context imply that they were similar or identical to Han instruments of those names.

Strikingly different from the majority of indigenous Naxi musics is the presence of large numbers of chordophones. Most numerous among them are the bowed lutes (generically called *huqin*). These all have long necks made of bamboo; wooden or bamboo bodies, most with snakeskin or calfskin stretched over the front, on which a bridge rests; and a bow made of bamboo and horsehair passing between the two strings, which are tuned a fifth apart. They include the high-pitched *erhuang* (a local Han-derived name for the Han *jinghu*, with strings tuned to g♯^{1} and d♯^{2}), *banhu* (a♯^{1} and e♯^{2}), and *nanhu* (a♯^{1} and e♯^{2} or c♯^{2} and g♯^{2}); the mid-pitched *huqin* (a♯ and e♯^{1}); and the low-pitched *dihu* (colloquially known as *datongtong*, with strings tuned to A♯ and e♯). In the late twentieth century, factory-made Han *erhu* and *zhonghu* are also commonly found. Most of the bowed lutes are identical to Han instruments, and some seem to be imported from outside Lijiang; all have Han names. However, the mid- and low-pitched instruments, which lack the restraining loop (*qianjin*)[17] attached below the tuning pegs on Han bowed lutes, are always locally made, and are considered to be distinctive Lijiang variants. Typically the bowed lutes are played with fairly short, jerky bow strokes. Most players keep their left hand in first position, and they stop the strings with the inside pads of their fingers rather than with the fingertips. The bow is held underhand in the right hand.

There are also three plucked lutes used in Lijiang's Dongjing music. The three-string *sanxian* is identical to the small or southern Han *sanxian*, with a long, unfretted wooden neck and almost square body with rounded corners, covered on both sides with snakeskin. It is often played with a plectrum, and the strings are tuned in fourths (d♯, g♯, c♯^{1}).[18] The four-string *pipa* is tuned with its intervals identically spaced to the Han *pipa* (A♯, d♯, e♯, a♯), but it has a much broader, pear-shaped body. The back of the *pipa* is usually made of walnut wood, the front of Chinese catalpa. There are four frets on the neck and varying numbers on the top of the body, but usually only the top five on the body (and none on the neck) are used. The strings are stopped principally by the index and ring fingers of the left hand, and they are plucked mainly by the thumb, index, and middle fingers of the right hand. Most of the plucking motions are outward (away from the player). The four-string *sugudu* (also known as *hubo*), considered unique to the Naxi, has a long, fretless wooden neck, snakeskin (or sometimes goat- or rabbitskin) covering the front of its small, bulbous body, and strings tuned in fourths (E♯, A♯, d♯, g♯) passing over a small bridge placed about halfway up the snakeskin. The *sugudu* is usually made of walnut. The term *sugudu* is clearly not of Han derivation.[19] Most players use the left hand index finger alone to stop the strings, moving it agilely up and down the long neck and often creating small glissandi. The strings are plucked solely by the thumb and index finger of the right hand. The instrument's distinctive dotted rhythm may be seen in Example 4.2 and heard on Track 22. The dotted rhythm (shown in Example 4.2 as a dotted thirty-second followed by a sixty-fourth, then a sixteenth) is produced by first plucking inward with the index finger, then outward with the index finger, then outward with the thumb. Most other notes are played with an outward motion of the thumb. The *pipa* and *sugudu* are considered distinctively local instruments and are always made locally, although the *sanxian* used in the 1990s are usually imported from Han areas. In the Qing dynasty three Han zithers—the seven-string bridgeless *qin* and two bridged zithers, *zheng* and *se*—were also employed by the Dayan Town Dongjing association. Most of these chordophones traditionally had silk strings, although now nylon or metal is sometimes substituted. Among indigenous Naxi musics, only Baisha Xiyue seems to have used any of these string instruments. Four of Lijiang's most unusual and distinctive instruments (*bobo, pipa, huqin,* and *sugudu*) are shown together in Figure 4.6.

Two membranophones are commonly found in Lijiang's Dongjing music. The *ban'gu* is a small, flat drum about six centimeters tall and twenty-four centimeters wide, which rests on a stand. The wooden body is thick, with a hole only about two centimeters wide at the top surface of the drum, which is covered with skin held in place by studs round the bottom edge of the instrument. Consequently only the center portion of the skin acts as a vibrating membrane, so the pitch of the drum is relatively high. It is struck by a thin wooden beater. Together with the clappers (*tishou*) and the wooden fish (*muyu*) described below, it gives the beat that controls the speed of the music. The large drum (*dagu*) is an enormous drum with skin stretched over both faces, although only one is struck. It is placed on a stand, and the player sits facing one of the faces. The diameter of the faces of the drum currently used by the Dayan Town ensemble is about seventy-seven centimeters. One face is struck with two sticks, each of which has a padded head. In pre-1949 ritual performance it was used mainly for the opening drumroll that announced the start of the day's ceremonies (CD Track 11), or at climactic points in the ritual, such as in the instrumental piece "Wind on the River" (*Yi Jiang Feng*), which accompanied the sending off of the god (*songshen*) at the end of each festival (CD Track 12).

The collection of idiophones traditionally used in Dongjing music is extremely large. It includes the wooden clappers (*tishou*) and woodblock shaped like a fish (*muyu*, literally, "wooden fish"). These instruments are used in conjunction with the small drum *ban'gu* to keep the beat. The clappers consist of two slabs of wood

EXAMPLE 4.2. Opening of the Dongjing piece *Shanpo Yang* (Sheep on the Hill), as played by members of the Dayan Town Ancient Music Association. This score is not a transcription of a single performance; instead, I used my two microphones to make analytical recordings of the musicians listed below at several different performance events, and then put the transcriptions of each line together to form a composite score. In any one performance, the number of participants may vary between one and over twenty; the twelve lines given here represent an ensemble of a little under average size. The players and dates of recording are:

1. *dizi* (transverse flute)   Yang Houkun, 9 November 1991
2. *dizi* (transverse flute)   Wang Chaoxin, 16 November 1991
3. *bobo* (double-reed pipe)   Yang Zenglie, 18 October 1991
4. *erhuang* (two-string bowed lute)   He Linghan, 18 October 1991

—continued

5. *erhu* (two-string bowed lute)　　　　　　Zhang Longhan, 9 November 1991
6. *huqin* (two-string bowed lute)　　　　　Niu Weijiong, 19 November 1991
7. *dihu* (two-string bowed lute)　　　　　　Zhao Yingxian, 6 November 1991
8. *sanxian* (three-string plucked lute)　　　Wang Mingsheng, 21 November 1991
9. *pipa* (four-string plucked lute)　　　　　Niu Weijiong, 6 November 1991
10. *sugudu* (four-string plucked lute)　　　Li Cheng'gan, 14 May 1992
11. *yunluo* (cloud gong) and *tongling* (bell)　He Yi'an, 16 November 1991
12. *tishou* (clappers) and *ban'gu* (small drum)　Wang Dejiu, 16 November 1991

In line 11, the upward stems represent the cloud gong, the downward stems the bell. In line 12, the upward stems represent the clappers, the downward stems the drum. A performance of the piece "Sheep on the Hill" may be heard on CD Track 13. Actual pitch is approximately a semitone higher than written.

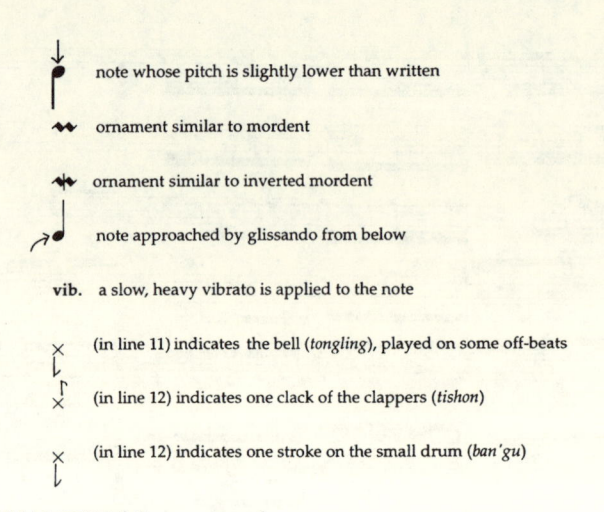

↓
♩   note whose pitch is slightly lower than written

∽   ornament similar to mordent

⊶   ornament similar to inverted mordent

↗♩   note approached by glissando from below

vib.   a slow, heavy vibrato is applied to the note

×♩   (in line 11) indicates the bell (*tongling*), played on some off-beats

×♩   (in line 12) indicates one clack of the clappers (*tishon*)

×♩   (in line 12) indicates one stroke on the small drum (*ban'gu*)

EXAMPLE 4.2. *continued*

attached together by a cord, held in the left hand and struck against each other to create a clacking sound. The wooden fish is struck by a wooden stick and has a resonant sound. The clappers are familiar from many Han traditional musics, and the wooden fish from Han Buddhist and Taoist music. Particularly prominent too is the cloud gong *yunluo*, a wooden frame on which are suspended ten small tuned gongs, struck with a single slim bamboo stick. Cloud gongs are clearly visible in the center of Figures 4.5 and 4.7, and are constructed in Lijiang so that

FIGURE 4.6. Musicians of Baihua Ancient Music Orchestra demonstrating four distinctive Lijiang instruments, August 1998. *Left to right*: He Zhiren playing *bobo* (double-reed pipe), Yi Guo'en playing *pipa* (four-string plucked lute), He Guowei playing *huqin* (two-string fiddle), He Jun playing *sugudu* (four-string plucked lute).

there are three rows of gongs on top of each other, with the tenth gong in the center on top. Always made locally, they are tuned as follows: bottom row (facing the player), right to left, $g\#^1$, $a\#^1$, $c\#^2$; middle row, left to right, $d\#^2$, $e\#^2$, $f\#^2$; highest row, right to left, $g\#^2$, $a\#^2$, $b\#^2$; top gong, $c\#^3$. Slight variations in the exact pitch of individual gongs do occur from one instrument to the next. In Lijiang the player holds the thin bamboo beater in one hand and a bell (*tongling*) in the other. Musical Example 4.2 shows how the player combines the two instruments. The *yunluo* is a fixture of Dongjing music throughout Yunnan, and indeed of much other Han ritual music. Also used are two pairs of cymbals with small and large central bosses (respectively, *nao* and *bo*); a small gong (*nao lizi* or *habagou*) struck by a flat wooden beater; a pair of small cymbals (*xiaocha*); a large gong (*daluo*); a pair of extremely resonant miniature cymbals (*jizi* or *boling*); and a small, handheld clappered bell made of copper alloy (*tongling*). The miniature cymbals and the bell are said by some musicians to come, respectively, from Tibet and Nepal; the other instruments are in common use among Dongjing associations elsewhere in Yunnan, and in other parts of China, although sometimes under different names. Several idiophones used before 1949 have been lost, including what were probably a bowl-shaped metal chime (*qing*) and a small bell suspended in a frame (*zhong*). Many of the percussion instruments can be seen in Figure 4.5; Figure 4.7 shows four of the larger idiophones in performance.

FIGURE 4.7. Dayan Ancient Music Association at a tourist concert in Dayan Town, May 1992. *Left to right*: The three standing percussionists are Yang Zenglie, playing *nao* cymbals; Zhang Longhan, playing *bo* cymbals; and Li Chenggan, playing *daluo* gong. Note also the tuned gong set *yunluo* on the table at the rear, the diagram of the eight trigrams draped over the table, and the formal long gowns and jackets of the performers.

It is not merely the instruments' construction, however, that displays Han Chinese origins: the scale they use and the way their sounds are combined also contribute to a strong sense of Han cultural presence. The scale is heptatonic, although the fourth and seventh degrees tend to be used rarely, either for ornamentation or for special effect. As in Shanghai's ensemble genre Jiangnan Sizhu, the scale is quite close to the Western diatonic major scale, although the fourth degree is somewhat sharper, and the seventh somewhat flatter (Witzleben 1995: 37). Where the first degree of the Jiangnan Sizhu scale is D, however, that of Lijiang's Dongjing music is usually close to C♯, with the *yunluo* and *dizi* being the main fixed-pitch instruments.

As for musical structure, when the melodic instruments play together, they do so in heterophony: while the basic melody is the same for all instruments, each performer interprets that melody slightly differently, depending on the quirks of his instrument and his own preferences. This characteristic may be seen in Example 4.2, a transcription of the opening of the instrumental piece *Shanpo Yang* (Sheep on the Hill) (CD Track 13). Thus the cloud gong (*yunluo*, line 11 of the transcription) is a rather cumbersome instrument, with only ten pitches available, and chimes out the simplest version of each melody; the flutes (top two lines) have large ranges and are extremely agile, allowing highly ornamented, melismatic versions of the tune to be played; the double-reed pipe *bobo* (third line) has a range of only about an octave, but can easily rearticulate repetitions of the same pitch; the four-string plucked lutes *pipa* (line 9) and *sugudu* (line 10) easily produce octave leaps; and the bowed lutes (lines 4, 5, 6, and 7) are played mainly in first position, with the left hand moving little up the neck—which allows considerable mobility, but within a narrow pitch range. CD Track 22 makes very audible the huge differences between bowed lute and *sugudu* treatments of this piece. Furthermore, within the characteristics imposed by an instrument's technical advantages and limitations, individual players often take very different approaches; in the early 1990s, one fine player of the three-string plucked lute *sanxian*, He Wenxuan, introduced elaborate glissandi all over the place, while another, He Hongzhang, largely avoided them. Moreover, while all players always follow the general melodic contours outlined most clearly by the cloud gong, each may vary his ornaments and sub-beat level formulae from performance to performance, so that no two renditions are ever quite the same (see Example 4.6). This kind of instrument-driven and individual variability within the confines of a single melodic structure is well described for Han musics of southeast China by Thrasher (1993) and Witzleben (1995). The texture created by heterophony is extraordinarily rich, so that the novice listener may doubt that everyone is playing what is basically the same tune. Lijiang's heterophonic texture is very similar to that created by Dongjing ensembles in other counties of Yunnan, and when I played recordings of the Lijiang music to friends from Hong Kong and Beijing, they immediately noted its similarity to Han instrumental genres from southeast China, especially Jiangnan Sizhu from the Shanghai region.[20] By contrast, indigenous Naxi instrumental genres other than Baisha Xiyue seldom feature several melodic instruments playing together.

The use of non-melodic percussion instruments is also characteristically Han. In Example 4.2, the clappers (*tishou*) and small drum (*ban'gu*) are used by a single player to delineate the duple beat which characterizes much Dongjing music; sometimes the wooden fish and small drum may be combined instead, especially in accompanied songs (*dadiao*). In certain pieces two pairs of large cymbals, *nao* and *bo*, play interlocking rhythms in percussion interludes, as do the small gong and small cymbals (*habagou* and *xiaocha*). This may be heard on Track 11, where two verses of the accompanied song *Bagua* (Eight Trigrams) are separated by an interlocking pattern *Bagua Wei* (Bagua Coda) played by two musicians on the *habagou* and *xiaocha*; at the end of the second verse, the two musicians switch instruments to play a similar pattern (*Bagua Wei* followed by the ending pattern *Da Xia* [Beating through to the End]) on the larger, louder *nao* and *bo* to give a sense of climactic finality as the piece concludes. In both instances, other percussion instruments keep the basic beat and the large drum underlines the interlocking patterns. Track 16, *Shoujing Jie* (Closing Ode), consists of four lines of sung verse separated by interlocking patterns played on the *nao* and *bo*. Figure 4.7 shows the *nao* and *bo* players facing each other and concentrating on an interactive interlocking pattern. Such uses of percussion are familiar not just from other Dongjing ensembles of Yunnan, but also from other parts of China (cf. Witzleben 1995: 56, and Stephen Jones 1995: 244–245).

Musical Types

Lijiang's Dongjing associations, like those elsewhere in Yunnan, typically took three or more days to perform an entire scripture. Starting from the first character of the first volume of the text, the members would sing, chant, and read their way through the entire multivolume scripture until they reached the last character of the last volume. The manner in which each passage of text was to be rendered, and the type of music used for it, were pre-detemined, so that performances of the same text differed little from one festival to the next. The ritual music of Lijiang's Dongjing associations may be divided into several distinct types, similar to Dongjing repertoires elsewhere in Yunnan. These are summarized here.[21]

1. *Dadiao* (accompanied songs): pieces in which the instrumental ensemble accompanies heterophonically the singing of passages of the scripture. The pieces have a fixed absolute pitch and the singers follow the pitch set by the instruments. Some have mainly regular verses: *Jixiang* (Good Fortune) and *Yuanshi* (Primordial) have five characters in each line; *Bagua* (Eight Trigrams) (which comes in a long version, *Quan Bagua* [Complete Eight

Trigrams], and a shorter version, *Bagua Tou* [Eight Trigrams Beginning (Section)]) has seven; *Qinghe* (Clear River) has seven, with a longer last line; and *Shi Gongyang* (Ten Offerings) has one section of five and one of seven. These five are generally considered tuneful and easy to learn, and some were applied to more than one section of scripture. More difficult are those with irregular lines, each specific to one section of scripture: *Wusheng Shenghao* (Five Appellations of the God), *Zhouzhang* (Spells), and three pieces with obscure titles, *Shi Hua*, *Shi Tong*, and *Hua Tong*. The singing voice is fairly open and relaxed, and the tunes are extremely melismatic: one syllable may endure for several beats, and follow a twisting melodic contour. In Dongjing ritual *dadiao* were usually applied to the most lyrical stanzas of the scripture. CD Track 11 is the *dadiao Bagua* (Eight Trigrams).[22]

2. *Xiaodiao* (instrumental pieces): twelve purely instrumental pieces played heterophonically by the ensemble to accompany actions such as the lighting of incense and offering of gifts to the gods. See Table 4.1 for the ten *xiaodiao* associated with the ceremony of Ten Offerings; the eleventh is *Shanpo Yang* (Sheep on the Hill), played during the lighting of incense, and the twelfth is *Yi Jiang Feng* (Wind on the River), used to send off the god at the end of the ceremony. Tracks 12, 13, 14, and 15 are all *xiaodiao*.

3. In a few sections of scripture, including the opening and closing odes for each day of the ritual, the lead singer sets the pitch and the other singers and a single flute follow him. Apart from the flute only untuned percussion accompanies these sections (a couple of gongs of the cloud gong *yunluo* are also struck, but for percussive rather than pitched effect). The singing style is similar to that of the accompanied songs. Track 16 is *Shoujing Jie* (Closing Ode) (a performance without the flute). This piece is counted by Lijiang musicians among the *dadiao*, despite its special characteristics.

4. *Daji yue* (percussion music): certain percussion patterns that routinely punctuate accompanied songs and articulate passages of chanting. Percussion patterns are frequently used to mark off one section from the next, and to close sections with a loud flourish. The percussion interludes for *Bagua* (Eight Trigrams, Track 11) and *Shoujing Jie* (Closing Ode, Track 16) are described above; note also the spectacular drumroll (*Qigu Santong*) that began each ceremony (start of Track 11). The major named percussion patterns are *Bagua Wei* (Eight Trigrams Coda), *Qian Wu Hou Wu* (Five Before, Five After), *Shiqi Shi* (Seventeen Generations), *Long Bai Wei* (Dragon Waving Its Tail), and *Da Xia* (Beating through to the End).

5. *Song* (chanting): the chanting of passages of scripture performed by all participants to simple melodic patterns of relatively narrow pitch range. Chanting of this nature was frequently used for incantations, the listing of gods' names and other passages where a large quantity of text had to be recited. Because the style was mostly syllabic and did not artificially extend the

TABLE 4.1. Order of offerings and associated instrumental pieces for the ceremony *Shi Gongyang* (Ten Offerings) from the *Liqing* (Formal Invocation) volume of the *Dadong Xianjing* (Transcendent Scripture), as carried out by the Dayan Town Dongjing association before 1949. Alternative tune titles were obtained during fieldwork, and from He Minda 1978 and Yang Zenglie 1990.

Offering	Instrumental piece
1. *Hua gongyang* (flowers)	*Wannian Hua* (Eternal Flowers) a.k.a. *Wannian Huan* (Eternal Joy)
2. *Guo gongyang* (fruit)	*Dai Wu* (meaning unclear) a.k.a. *Dai Weng* (Waiting for the Old Man) a.k.a. *Dan Wu* (Dawn Noon)
3. *Xiang gongyang* (incense)	*Lang Tao Sha* (Waves Washing the Sand)
4. *Shi gongyang* (rice)	*Man Wu Yan* (meaning unclear) a.k.a. *Man Wu Yang* (Slowly Dancing Sheep) a.k.a. *Man Wu Yang* (Wildly Dancing Sheep) a.k.a. *Guihua Xiang* (Cassia Flower Fragrance)
5. *Cha gongyang* (tea)	*Dao Chun Lai* (Spring Has Come)
6. *Yi gongyang* (garments)	*Dao Xia Lai* (Summer Has Come)
7. *Shui gongyang* (water)	*Shui Long Yin* (Water Dragon Cry) a.k.a. *Shui Lou Yin* (Water Tower Murmur)
8. *Fu gongyang* (talismans)	*Dao Qiu Lai* (Autumn Has Come)
9. *Jinjiu fadeng shuang gongyang* (alcohol and ritual lamp)	*Dao Dong Lai* (Winter Has Come)
10. *Cai gongyang* (cash)	*Liu Yao Jin* (Waving Willow Gold) a.k.a. *Liu Yao Jing* (Waving Willow Scenery)

phrase lengths of the text, unlike the extremely melismatic accompanied songs, it was possible to get through more text much faster than by singing. The constant instrumental accompaniment was the wooden fish (*muyu*), struck with a thick wooden stick by the lead singer on each syllable. Example 4.3 is a transcription of two incantations performed in this style (heard on CD Track 17). For some sections extra untuned percussion was also used.

6. *Du biaowen* (reading a memorial): similar in style to *song*, but minus the *muyu*. A single reader read a memorial to whichever god the assembly wished to address. Track 18 is part of a memorial read to the god Wenchang for his birthday.

7. Heightened speech: verbal performance type exaggerating the contours of speech intonation. When performing *jiang (xuan)* (lit. "explanation [of mysteries]"), one speaker used a heightened speech style, mostly to read com-

EXAMPLE 4.3. Two incantations chanted (*song*) by He Yi'an, accompanying himself on the *muyu* (woodblock shaped like a fish). This excerpt may be heard on CD Track 17, and the Chinese-language text and English-language explication may be

mentaries that punctuated the main scriptural text. The rhythm was free and closer than the other verbal performance types to ordinary speech rhythm. Track 19 is the opening of a passage explicating the offering of flowers to the gods. The announcement of sections was made in a similarly heightened speech style by a single speaker.

Despite the demise of Lijiang's Dongjing associations, the first four of these musical types are vibrantly alive today in the secular musical tradition that has survived. The last three were still remembered by a few elderly musicians in the early 1990s, although they were no longer heard except upon request. Ritual use of a whole gamut of musical types is widespread among revived Dongjing associations elsewhere in Yunnan.

To illustrate the mixing of musical types within the ordered sequence dictated by a text, I set out here the order of performance for the *Liqing* (Formal Invocation) volume of Lijiang's *Dadong Xianjing* (Transcendent Scripture of the Great Grotto) (see appendix A). The volume begins with several items chanted (*song*) with *muyu* (wooden fish) accompaniment, and in some cases other untuned percussion too. This initial material consists of two prefaces, then the liturgy of opening the altar (*kaitan keyi*), purification incantations, opening invocation addressed to the spirit realm (*yangqi song*),[23] formal invocation addressed to

vib.	a marked vibrato is applied to the note
(vib.)	a slight vibrato is applied to the note
(♪)	approximate pitch
	the note is approached from above by a glissando
	the note descends to an indefinite pitch via a glissando
	the note ascends to an indefinite pitch via a glissando
	the pitch is slightly higher than written
'	breath mark

---

found in Appendix C, No. 3. The first incantation begins at marker "A," the second at marker "B." The brief section before marker A is three repetitions of the name of a Heavenly Worthy. Actual pitch is approximately a semitone lower than written.

deceased kin (*liqing song*), pledge of faith (*baogao*), confession (*chanhui*), vow (*fayuan*), closing pledge of faith (*dagao*), and evocation of gods by name. This is followed by five stanzas extolling the *Transcendent Scripture*, sung to the accompanied song *Quan Bagua* (Complete Eight Trigrams); the five appellations of Wenchang, sung to the accompanied song *Wusheng Shenghao* (Five Appellations of the God); and the ceremony of the Ten Offerings, which was musically quite complex. First, incense was lit to the accompaniment of the instrumental piece *Shanpo Yang* (Sheep on the Hill); then each offering was explained by a piece of scripture using heightened speech style; this was followed by a prescribed instrumental piece different for each offering; and each instrumental piece was followed by a stanza sung every time to the same accompanied song *Shi Gongyang* (Ten Offerings). The percussion pattern *Qian Wu Hou Wu* (Five Before, Five After) concluded each rendition of the accompanied song *Shi Gongyang*. Table 4.1 sets out the order of offerings and associated instrumental pieces.

A similarly detailed prescription of performance mode existed for each of the other six volumes of the *Transcendent Scripture*, as well as for the other scriptures used.

In addition to those used in Dongjing association rituals, a few instrumental pieces played solely in non-sacred contexts were also current before 1949. Termed "miscellaneous pieces" (*zaqu*) by local scholars, these included *Xiao Bai Mei* (Little White Plum Blossom), played exclusively at funerals, and *Bubu Jiao* (Dainty Steps), played for pleasure at leisurely secular musical gatherings. These two are still widespread in Lijiang, while a few others have always been less well known (Yang Zenglie 1990: 132). In addition, the main melodic instruments each have a brief piece that is played during tuning to check intonation (CD Track 20).

Tune Titles and Notation

In addition to the instrumentarium used and the soundscape produced, the names of the melodies played for the accompanied songs and instrumental pieces proclaim their Han Chinese affinity. Most of Lijiang's tune titles are common to the repertoires of many Dongjing associations all over Yunnan. The names of the accompanied songs are mostly taken directly from the text or context of the scriptural passages they were played for, so that it is no surprise to find the same names in other locations using similar scriptures, even where the melodies differ. For example, *Jixiang* (Good Fortune) and *Wusheng Shenghao* (Five Appellations of the God) are also found in Heqing and Shiping counties and in Dali, although there is no obvious melodic overlap. Instrumental pieces, too, have names that are common among other Dongjing associations. For instance, *Yi Jiang Feng* (Wind on the River) is a title also found in Jianshui, Mile, Luxi, Lufeng, and Weishan counties, and in Baoshan and Chuxiong cities; and *Shanpo Yang* (Sheep on the Hill) exists in Heijing Town, Mengzi County, and Kunming,

Baoshan, and Qujing cities as well as in Lijiang. Furthermore, many of these tune titles are widespread in eastern China. The operatic form Kunju, found mainly in eastern China, includes tunes called *Dao Chun Lai* (Spring Has Come), *Dao Xia Lai* (Summer Has Come), *Dao Qiu Lai* (Autumn Has Come), *Dao Dong Lai* (Winter Has Come) and *Shanpo Yang* (Sheep on the Hill), all of which are titles also found in Lijiang's Dongjing music. *Bubu Jiao* (Dainty Steps) is a tune title found in many repertoires, including Cantonese instrumental ensembles; and *Wannian Hua/Wannian Huan* (Eternal Flowers/Joy) also appears with the latter name in the Taoist music of Wudang Mountain in Hubei Province and in many other repertories throughout China.[24]

Just having the same name does not, of course, guarantee that the melodies so named are identical. Much work remains to be done to ascertain the degrees of relationship among similarly named tunes in different Dongjing associations and different parts of China. However, preliminary research suggests that there is frequently a close degree of correlation. The versions of "Sheep on the Hill" from Lijiang, Mengzi, and Qujing start almost identically and have some middle passages in common, although they do diverge from one another at several points. The Lijiang version and the Kunju version correspond closely for about 60 percent of their length (Qujing Xian Gudian Yinyue Yanjiuhui, n.d.: 1; Zhongyang Yinyue Xueyuan Minzu Yinyue Yanjiusuo 1956: 63). As Example 4.4 makes clear, "Eternal Flowers/Joy" shows a particularly striking resemblance between the Lijiang and Wudang Mountain versions (Rees 1994: 412–414; Shi Xinmin 1987: 169). Melodically, therefore, at least a few of the Lijiang County Dongjing repertoire melodies are recognizably members of tune families spread all over Han China.

In terms of notation, too, Lijiang's Dongjing music fits firmly into the Han Chinese tradition. Since the Song dynasty, many Han melodic genres have used a notation called *gongchepu*. This is similar to Western solfège (*do-re-mi*), in that syllables indicate scale degrees. In the Chinese tradition, these syllables are represented on paper by simple ideographs, which are customarily written in columns and read from top to bottom, right to left. The form of *gongchepu* notation found in Lijiang is fairly standard. Table 4.2 shows the *gongchepu* symbols most commonly used in Lijiang, together with their transliterations and the equivalent scale degrees in Western solfège. The main exception to "standard" *gongchepu* is that the extra two strokes to the side of the lower octave *shang* usually indicate upper octave *shang* elsewhere in China, and the occasional presence of the same element to the side of *si* is unusual. Main beats in Lijiang's scores are usually designated by a dash to the right of the appropriate ideograph;[25] however, there is little indication in the score of how the beat is subdivided. At the most, where three pitches are indicated within one beat, they may be spaced so that there is a gap between the first and second ideographs, while the second and third are closer together, implying a rhythm of an eighth note followed by two

EXAMPLE 4.4. Versions of *Wannian Huan* (Everlasting Joy) from Lijiang and Wudang Mountain. In Lijiang this piece is also known as *Wannian Hua* (Everlasting Flowers). The upper line is the first two-thirds of the Lijiang melody transnotated from cipher notation in a recent score in the possession of He Minda of Baihua; the lower line is a transnotation of the complete Wudang Mountain melody as printed in cipher notation in Shi 1987: 169. Measure lines and note values are as in the originals. Where the Lijiang melody has extra passages not paralleled in the Wudang Mountain melody, the lower line is left blank. In two places, both marked with an "A," two quarter-note beats in the lower line lose half their length to maintain the parallelism with the Lijiang version. A complete performance of Lijiang's "Everlast-

THE MUSICAL WORLD OF REPUBLICAN LIJIANG 85

TABLE 4.2. *Gongchepu* pitch symbols commonly used in Lijiang, with their Western solfège equivalents. Note that the upper and main octave first degrees (shang/do) are the reverse of what is usually found in China.

Pitch symbol	Solfège equivalent
四 or 亻四	si (la in the bottom octave)
仩	shang (do)
尺	che (re)
工	gong (mi)
凡	fan (fa)
六	liu (sol)
五	wu (la)
上	shang (do in the upper octave)
ヽ	ditto mark (repeat the previous pitch)

sixteenths.[26] Some scores also have a syncopation sign resembling ß tipped to the left, indicating that the main beat falls in the middle of a held note. Figure 4.8 is a page of a score from Lashi Township, Lijiang, showing the piece *Shanpo Yang* (Sheep on the Hill). As usual with *gongchepu*, this should be read right to left, and up to down. Note the dashes to the side of the columns giving the main beats, the syncopation sign in columns 3 and 4, the "ditto" (repeated note) sign after the ninth character in column 3, and the sporadic use of the spacing technique where three ideographs cluster within a single main beat. (The circles are unusual among Lijiang scores, representing phrase ends but having no rhythmic function.) Example 4.5 is a transnotation of the Lashi score into staff notation. For the sake of convenience I have chosen the note C to represent the *gongchepu* symbol *shang* (*do*), although in Lijiang *shang* is usually closer to C♯. Because rhythmic subdivisions are not given (beyond the occasional spacing of three ideographs as described above), I have for the most part adopted a procedure of representing two notes to a beat as eighth notes, three as an eighth note followed by two sixteenths, four as four sixteenths, and five as one sixteenth followed by two thirty-seconds and two sixteenths. The small, circular phrase-break marks in the original are rendered by apostrophe-shaped marks above the staff in the transcrip-

---

ing Joy/Flowers" may be heard on CD track 15. Note that the skeletal melody given in this score represents only part of the full piece. The Lijiang score gives pitches a semitone higher than written, the Wudang score pitches a whole tone higher than written. I transposed the former down a semitone and the latter down a whole tone to facilitate comparison.

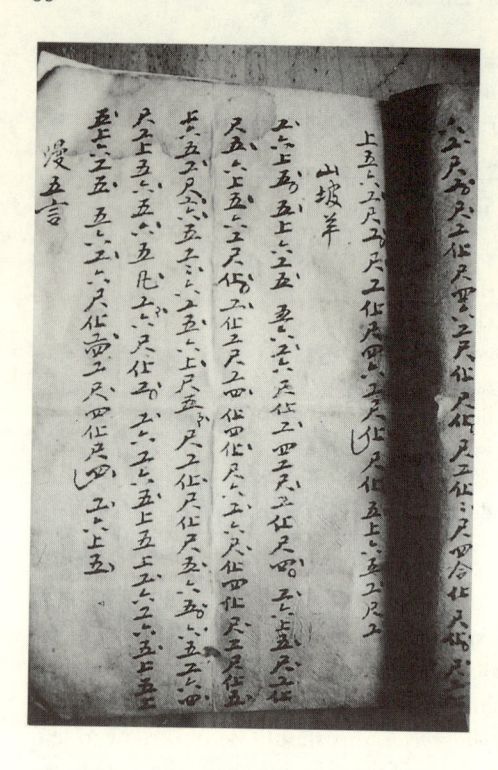

FIGURE 4.8. *Gongchepu* score from Lashi Township, showing the piece "Sheep on the Hill."

tion. The tick in the original before the last four ideographs indicates the end of the piece; I mark this by a square bracket. (The last four characters remind the reader to make a repeat.) I have chosen the quarter note to stand for the main beat designated by a dash in the *gongchepu* score; this allows easier comparison with Example 4.2. It is important to note that this is only one of several possible realizations of this score.

Historically, *gongchepu* functioned as an oral notation vital to the transmission process: during the Republican era, the commonest way for a boy to learn the repertoire was by first singing the melodies to the *gongchepu* syllables, rather as students at French conservatoires are expected to sing pieces to *do-re-mi*. Only when the Naxi boy had memorized the repertoire according to *gongchepu* was he allowed to begin playing the pieces on instruments. He Hongzheng and He Zhong, two skilled musicians who learned the Dongjing repertoire as boys in the 1940s, described the learning process:

> We'd light a stick of incense—there were no clocks in those days—and study while it burned, stopping when it was burned up. Several of us learned together—the teacher would sing a line of *gongchepu*, we had to sing it back, and so on. We had to learn orally because there was no light at night when we were learning—or at least not enough to read a score by. When each person had learned the pieces, he had to copy out his own score. (Interview, 19 December 1991)

,   represents a phrase-break indicated by a circle in the *gongchepu* score

⎯⎯⎯⎯＼   represents the end of the piece, indicated by a large tick in the *gongchepu* score

A   represents the point to which the final four-note pick-up returns to make the repeat

EXAMPLE 4.5. Transnotation into staff notation of the *gongchepu* score *Shanpo Yang* (Sheep on the Hill) from Lashi (see Figure 4.8). See Table 4.2. Note that the first degree of the scale, *shang*, is rendered as C. This aids comparison with examples 4.2 and 4.6. An ensemble performance of this piece may be heard on CD Track 13.

The process, therefore, was first to learn the *gongchepu* by rote, using it as an oral notation, and then to write it down for potential future reference. In the 1990s, many of the musicians can sing the tunes to the *gongchepu* they first learned more than half a century ago (CD Track 21). My informants then described the next stage of the learning process: "When we'd learnt the *gongchepu*, then we'd learn the bowed lutes, then gradually add the other instruments—*pipa*, et cetera." This description is very close to that given for the teaching of a ritual instrumental repertoire in a village in Hebei Province (Ben Wu 1988). Variability was built into this learning system: different scores differ slightly in the pitches represented by the solfège, especially at the sub-beat level; different people sing it slightly differently; and the same person may vary his singing and instrumental performance each time. Thus children were exposed to multiple minor variants of each piece. Example 4.6 shows the opening of "Sheep on the Hill" in five different renditions by Zhang Longhan (b.1923). The upper two are *erhu* (two-string bowed lute) performances; the next two are his singings of the *gongchepu*; and the bottom line is a *gongchepu* score he wrote out, minus any rhythmic indications, ca. 1980. Mr. Zhang was well aware that he did things slightly differently every time even when playing the same instrument. Note that he sings *shang* to represent both the first and the seventh degrees of the scale: it is rare in Lijiang for the seventh degree to be indicated with a separate symbol or syllable.

In common with many other parts of China, percussion patterns were also learned by rote according to a system of onomatopoeic mnemonics, before being realized on the instruments themselves (Ben Wu 1988: 7, Stephen Jones 1995: 260–263, Yang Yinliu 1980). Table 4.3 gives the major mnemonic syllables for Lijiang. CD Track 23 is a recitation of the syllables for the relatively short and simple percussion pattern that separates the sung lines of the opening and closing odes (*Kaijing Jie*, *Shoujing Jie*). Example 4.7 transcribes this recitation. The actual realization of this pattern may be heard on Track 16. As with the melodic skeleton, the pattern is somewhat flexible in performance. In addition, other percussion are present to keep the beat, making the texture more complex than the mnemonic implies.

Secular Music Groups

The formally constituted Dongjing associations were not the only groups in the Republican era to use Dongjing music. In and around Dayan Town, and in other parts of the Lijiang basin and Jinsha River area, secular music groups played portions of the same repertoire, mostly for informal entertainment similar to that enjoyed by the amateur Jiangnan Sizhu enthusiasts in Shanghai of the same period (Witzleben 1987). Unlike the Dongjing associations, these groups were open to any local man interested in music, and were often extremely informal. According to one elderly informant who had played in such a group in the 1940s,

THE MUSICAL WORLD OF REPUBLICAN LIJIANG

~~ ornament resembling mordent
~~ ornament resembling inverted mordent
, breath mark

EXAMPLE 4.6. Multiple interpretations of the opening to *Shanpo Yang* (Sheep on the Hill) by Zhang Longhan. The bottom line is his *gongchepu* score written in about 1980 without any rhythmic indicators. The other four lines are my transcriptions of his playing and singing: (1) *erhu* performance, recorded 14 May 1992 (CD Track 22); (2) *erhu* performance, recorded 9 November 1991; (3) singing of the *gongchepu*, recorded 17 June 1993 (CD Track 21); (4) singing of the *gongchepu*, recorded 11 May 1992. Actual pitches of Zhang's four performances vary, but are all transposed to allow comparison with each other and with examples 4.2 and 4.5. Note that he sings the syllable *shang* to represent both the first and seventh degrees of the scale.

friends would get together on an ad hoc basis to play for fun, and would teach each other new pieces. Some of the secular groups would occasionally play at funerals, thus making this kind of ritual a subsidiary arena for their music. A prominent Naxi scholar who now works in Kunming told me that during his childhood in the 1940s Dongjing music was very widespread in villages near Dayan Town. Every funeral in his village included it, and it was common to hear people singing the tunes for private amusement. Even Naxi children who otherwise spoke no Chinese could sing them accurately to *gongchepu*.

TABLE 4.3. Percussion mnemonic syllables used in Lijiang. The actual characters written to represent the sounds vary from score to score; I give those used by Yang Zenglie.

Character	Percussion syllable
火 or 合	huo (*nao* cymbals are struck together)
叉	cha (*bo* cymbals are struck together)
端 or 光	duan or guang (large gong is struck, usually with *bo* cymbals)
崩	beng (wooden fish sounds alone)
一	yi (empty beat when no instrument sounds)

When *habagou* (small stuck gong) and *xiaocha* (small cymbals) are used in place of *nao* and *bo* cymbals, the mnemonic characters are

冬	dong (*habagou*)
吉	ji (*xiaocha*)

At least one of the secular groups active in the county town in the 1940s was more tightly organized. Named the "Good Friends Music Association" (*Yiyou Yinyuehui*), it was led by an instrument maker called Li Sixian. Monthly meetings rotated round members' houses, at which everyone ate well and played music for fun; they also met on a few holidays such as Spring Festival, and played for funerals. There was a training class for prospective members, who were strictly

EXAMPLE 4.7. Recitation by He Yi'an of the percussion mnemonic syllables to the percussion interludes of *Shoujing Jie* (Closing Ode). See Table 4.3. This recitation may be heard on CD Track 23. Its instrumental realization may be heard on CD Track 16. Since the syllable *yi* stands for a rest, it is represented here by a rest. He accompanies his recitation on the *muyu* (wooden fish), but that line is omitted here.

disciplined. However, such a high degree of organization seems to have been the exception rather than the rule among the secular groups.

The secular music groups had a much more limited musical repertoire than the Dongjing associations. Since they did not perform sacred rituals or use any scriptures, they had no need for the chanting, memorial reading, or heightened speech. Most of the groups lacked the full complement of percussion instruments and left out much of the percussion music. What was left were the instrumental pieces (*xiaodiao*) and some of the accompanied songs (*dadiao*). However, the accompanied songs were played minus their words, and only those with regular verse patterns were included in the repertoires of these secular groups. This seems to be because these were less text bound, more tuneful, and easier to remember than those with more irregular patterns. The maximum potential number of pieces available to these groups, therefore, was the approximately sixteen instrumental pieces (including the non-ritual miscellaneous pieces *zaqu*), and five of the accompanied songs, minus the words. Not all of these pieces, however, would necessarily be used by each group: one elderly musician who had participated in an informal group from approximately 1930 on recollected that he and his friends had played only about seven of the instrumental pieces and three of the accompanied songs on a regular basis. In Dayan Town before 1949, members of secular groups actually outnumbered Dongjing association members, demonstrating just how far into the ordinary Naxi townsfolk this Han music had penetrated.[27] Outside Dayan Town too, many villages had by the 1940s acquired the secular Dongjing music tradition.[28]

Other Han-derived Musics

Opera

One of the most pervasive cultural phenomena of Han Chinese society for several hundred years has been the dramatic form *xiju*, generally translated "opera." A mixture of elements including singing, speaking, instrumental music, acrobatics, and elaborate costumes and makeup, Chinese opera may fulfill a ritual function or be purely secular entertainment. Like many other national minorities, the Naxi have not traditionally developed their own Naxi-language opera; urban Naxi have enthusiastically borrowed Han Chinese forms, however.

Of the various forms of opera found in Yunnan, one of the best known and most widespread is that known as Dianju (Yunnan opera). The singers are accompanied by the high-pitch bowed lute *dianhu* (similar to the *jinghu* of Peking Opera and the *erhuang* of Lijiang's Dongjing music), and often by other strings, flute *dizi*, and shawm *suona*; the percussion includes clappers, drums, cymbals, and gongs. Dianju was widespread in western Yunnan by the mid-nineteenth century. Following the suppression of the destructive Moslem rebellion, temples were rebuilt with provision for operatic stages, while temple fairs, which were the main arenas for performance, continued uninterrupted for several decades thereafter, allowing Dianju to flourish. At least a couple of opera stages were constructed at local temples in Lijiang County in the Daoguang reign of the Qing dynasty (1821–1850), although there is no record of what kind of performances took place at this time. Many such stages appear to have been built in the county during the temple reconstruction of the early Guangxu era (1875–1908). There is some documentary and oral evidence to suggest that operatic performances of various sorts were common in the late nineteenth century in Lijiang County, with troupes often invited in from outside. During the Republican era amateur Dianju groups proliferated in Dayan Town and could also be found in Jinshan, Lashi, and Shigu; they would listen to and get coaching from the professional touring troupes that visited for major religious and secular festivals. Figure 4.9 shows a contemporary amateur group; CD Track 24 is a Dianju excerpt performed by them. As in other counties in western Yunnan, opera performances of both Dianju and Sichuanese Chuanju flourished along the well-traveled commercial roads. Dianju was sufficiently popular in western Yunnan that, after 1949, the new government established state Dianju companies in some western Yunnan regions, including Lijiang Prefecture in 1961 (Yang and Gu 1986: 151, 156; Wang Zhiqiang 1989: 89–92; interview with Xi Hongyi and Wang Zhengwu, 27 July 1998).

Peking Opera too reached Lijiang. Around 1911, some recordings were brought to Lijiang, and a few Naxi intellectuals who had learned it while sojourning in Kunming or other large cities would gather from time to time to sing together.

FIGURE 4.9. Xi'an Street Dianju Club, July 1998. *Left to right*: Li Bin playing *dianhu* (two-string fiddle), Li Linshu playing *sanxian* (three-string plucked lute), Sha Yuchun playing *erhu* (two-string fiddle), Wang Zhengwu playing *xiaocha* (cymbals), Tang Shulin (male singer), Zhou Kewu playing *luo* (gong) and *bo* (cymbals), Zhao Guimei (female singer), Xi Hongyi playing *xiaogu* (drum) and *tishou* (clappers), Li Zhenpeng playing *ergu* (drum), Yang Guosheng playing *xiaoluo* (gong).

It was also performed at some festivals, such as the ten-day Dragon Fair held in the Dayan Town park in 1915. During the Second World War, there were anti-Japanese operatic activities among the Naxi (Track 1996: 32; Wang Zhiqiang 1989: 93–96).

Ritual Musics

In addition to Dongjing music and opera, much liturgical and paraliturgical music heard in the Lijiang basin before 1949 was Han derived. The Confucian sacrifice and Chinese Buddhist monks' and Taoist priests' activities were all Han Chinese in origin, and each came equipped with its own music. The music for the Confucian sacrifice was mandated by the government, which sponsored the event, and was intended to be uniform across China. The 1743 gazetteer, like many other such county histories, actually sets out in *gongchepu* (solfège) notation the exact melodies mandated at that time by the central government for each section of the ritual (*Lijiang Fu Zhilüe* 1991 [1743]: 152–153). The music for the sacrifice was very different from any other Han music, being extremely slow and stately and allowing for no individual ornamentation.[29] Though its style was syllabic (one long note per syllable), completely unlike the more melismatic, flowing Dongjing music, it was nevertheless Dongjing association members who were invited to perform it before 1949. One of them commented to me that he didn't particularly like the Confucian music, and it meant little to him compared with his beloved Dongjing music.

The Chinese-style Buddhist monks (*heshang*) carried out services such as funerals using a variety of music. According to former monk He Shiwei of Baihua, for sending off the spirits, one or other of a few Dongjing melodies was used. The instruments played were flute (*dizi*) and two two-string bowed lutes, *erhuang* and *huqin*, all familiar from the local Dongjing instrumentarium. The Buddhist scriptures, all written in Han Chinese, were either sung to one of a number of suitable tunes selected by the senior monk present (*zhangtang*) or chanted with accompaniment of the wooden fish *muyu* (song), as in other parts of China. Taoist priests also used music specific to their rituals, although it appears that none of the few surviving priests are able or willing to describe the music in detail.[30]

Paraliturgical music of non-local derivation was also commonly heard in Lijiang, at least in Dayan Town, before 1949. Professional duos, often of blind people, provided processional music for local funerals and weddings. They usually played Chinese shawm (*suona*, also known locally as *laba*), long trumpet (*dahao*), and percussion, but sometimes used other instruments too. A wedding ceremony in a moderately wealthy household from the 1920s is described thus:

> To collect the bride, four sedans were used: one for the groom, one for the bride, one for the go-between, and one for the best woman. The wedding procession travelled to [the bride's] house with the sound and excitement of Chi-

nese trumpets [i.e., *suona*], drums beating and fire crackers.... The wedding procession returned to [the groom's] house [with the same accompaniment]. (Track 1996: 133)

In addition, the musicians played flute (*dizi*), bowed lute, and gong during the wedding banquet to announce the arrival of each new dish of food (p. 135). They had low social status, and thus when playing for weddings could not sit and eat with the guests. Blind professional musicians also took part in the Confucian sacrifice, although because of their low status they stood outside the sacrificial area. They played flutes (*dizi*) and percussion when the chief ritual officiant arrived, and announced each new section of the proceedings by playing shawm (*suona*) and percussion. These blind musicians were usually Han or Bai, often from neighboring Heqing County; their profession disappeared after 1949, when elaborate rituals were discouraged.[31]

Other Musics in Lijiang County

Even before 1949, indigenous Naxi and imported Han Chinese musics were far from the sum total of the musical experiences available to the Lijiang Naxi. Living as they did interspersed with many other ethnic groups, especially the Bai, Lisu, Pumi, Yi, and Tibetans, the Naxi had ample opportunity to hear musics of these groups. Instances of interethnic musical borrowing by *dongba* and Naxi folk musicians have already been noted here. In addition, the monks of the five Tibetan Buddhist monasteries near Dayan Town used Tibetan Buddhist chant and instrumental music in carrying out their ceremonies; this music was very different from that of their Han Buddhist counterparts.

Some musical influence also came before 1949 from Christian missionaries: with a few hundred converts in Dayan Town and elsewhere, foreign missionaries introduced Western hymns, translated into the local languages. Today, among the surviving Christian community near Shigu, the mainly Lisu believers still sing these hymns in European-style harmony.[32]

The Demographics of Participation

In quite another context, that of 1960s France, Bourdieu observes that "nothing more clearly affirms one's 'class,' nothing more infallibly classifies, than tastes in music" (1984: 18). His main thesis, that an overall aesthetic outlook tied to an individual's social milieu generates specific tastes in music, art, and entertainment, can be equally well applied to other cultures. Before 1949, the likelihood of an individual Lijiang resident participating in one or more of the forms of music described above, or indeed of his or her refusal or inability to participate, was determined by a number of social and demographic factors, many interrelated: (1) professional or amateur status (of musician and music); (2) social standing; (3) ethnicity, and rural or urban environment; (4) religious affiliation; (5) age and gender.

Professional or Amateur Status

As a general rule, before 1949 the professional performance of music was *ipso facto* an indicator of low social status. For example, the Baisha Xiyue musicians, who received fees for their participation in funerals, were generally looked down upon, while the professional musicians who played processional and incidental music at weddings, funerals and the Confucian sacrifice were also considered of low status and kept at arm's length throughout the proceedings.[33] Several informants emphasized that most Dongjing associations prided themselves on never making any money out of their music and ritual, unlike religious specialists or professional musicians, and that they would not have been seen dead playing a Baisha Xiyue tune. Equally, a performer of Baisha Xiyue would be unacceptable to a Dongjing association. This is not to say that before 1949 a music's amateur status guaranteed it respectability and an uncritical following just because it was amateur: all the other factors listed above had a role to play in deciding who could participate in which kind of amateur music-making. Professional status, however, immediately conferred adverse social perceptions on the musicians and rendered the music unsuitable to non-professionals.

Social Standing

Traditionally, social standing was a major determining factor in what music one was likely to play. As noted in Chapter 3, Dongjing associations in many parts of Lijiang County and indeed Yunnan Province would admit only men of good Confucian education, moral character, and social standing. Consequently, in such areas only men with these qualifications had access to the complete musical and ritual repertoire. By achieving inclusion into this elite group, the participants also demonstrated their eligibility to take part in other highbrow musical activities, for example at the Confucian sacrifice, while simultaneously ruling themselves out of many other kinds of music-making. Baisha Xiyue and ritually used Dongjing music, for instance, were incompatible: practitioners of each were worlds removed from each other socially, and thus musically too. As late as 1992 one elderly former member of the Dayan Town Dongjing association disliked mixing Dianju or Naxi folk music with Dongjing music, even in its present secular context: he felt strongly that Dongjing music was superior, and he himself had never had anything to do with these less refined forms of music.

Even in some of the secular music groups in Dayan Town before 1949, Dongjing music seems to have been held in high regard vis-à-vis other musical forms. He Linghan, a former member of the *Yiyou Yinyuehui* (Good Friends Music Association), recollected that his teacher would fine him and the other young recruits if he caught them playing Dianju, because Dongjing music was refined and Dianju was not (interview, 16 December 1991). In more ad hoc groups, however, players were free to indulge in both forms of music if they so pleased. Consequently, not only the social standing of music-makers, but also the status they ascribed to different kinds of music helped define what music they could play and in what setting they could play it.

Ethnicity, and Rural or Urban Environment

While considerable interethnic musical influence can be proved for the Republican era, it is also true that many folk musics, especially language-dependent folk songs, were peculiar to individual ethnic groups. Even in 1990s Lijiang, I encountered mountain-dwelling Yi teenagers who came to Dayan Town on a festival day but would not participate in the Naxi dances going on raucously in the main square because, they said, Yi didn't know Naxi dances, just as Naxi couldn't dance Yi dances. (In fact, many Yi dances are quite similar in style to Naxi dances, and the Naxi dance steps are very easy to pick up, as I found out. Possibly the youths felt socially stigmatized and awkward in Dayan Town.) At the other end of the musical spectrum, according to local musicians, Dongjing associations in most parts of Lijiang were exclusively made up of Naxi before 1949.

The urban/rural divide was also a vital factor in deciding an individual's musical fate. Before 1949, certain kinds of music were simply not accessible to people living in rural areas, especially those far removed from main roads. Imported Han Chinese musics percolated only as far as communities on the major trade routes in Lijiang County. Dongjing music and Dianju were widespread, but almost exclusively in urban trading centers and surrounding areas, and along the commercial routes: the farther from these areas, the less the communication with Han Chinese parts of Yunnan Province, and the less the exposure to Han culture of any form. Conversely, Naxi residents of Dayan Town had far less exposure to indigenous Naxi musics than did their rural relatives. One elderly Dayan Town resident explained that in his youth, in the 1930s and 1940s, "we couldn't play the Jew's harp or sing folk songs; some people could, but more in the mountainous areas." Another mentioned that although people would pile into the marketplace to dance on festival days, the participants were generally farmers from nearby villages, while the Dayan Town residents generally did not take part.[34]

Religious Affiliation

Each of the religions active within Lijiang County before 1949 had its own musical repertoire. The *dongba*, operating exclusively in the Naxi language, had a repertoire of chant tunes and percussion-accompanied ritual dances peculiar to their ceremonies, as apparently did the *sainii* shamans. The Karmapa monks carried out their duties purely in the Tibetan language, using Tibetan Buddhist music similar to that in Tibetan monasteries elsewhere; the *heshang* (Chinese-style Buddhist monks) employed the Han Chinese language for their rituals, and used Chinese Buddhist music; while the Taoist priests used different music that was identifiably Taoist. The Christians sang Naxi-language hymns in European-style harmony. In other words, each set of religious professionals (and, where appropriate, devotees too) had music specific to their religion. This situation illustrates neatly a proposition made by Nketia in a West African context: that it is common for communication with a deity imported from another ethnic group to be conducted with the music and often in the language of its original group (Nketia 1970: 3; 1988: 58). While mutual influence among religious musics seems to have occurred gradually and in a piecemeal way, people I interviewed were always clear as to the necessary distinctions among the different kinds of music.

Status as a religious professional or devout believer of one or more of these religions did not necessarily restrict one's participation in musical activities available in one's area: a novice Chinese Buddhist monk might learn Dongjing repertoire in his free time, partly for use in Buddhist rituals; a *dongba* might sing work songs while tilling his fields; and a high-status Taoist priest could participate fully in a Dongjing association. One urban resident, however, mentioned that in the 1940s his father, a Christian convert, discouraged his incipient interest in Dongjing music, since it was used for non-Christian rituals.

Age and Gender

Traditionally certain folk songs were considered appropriate for young women, some for young men, and some for older people. Musical forms used primarily in courting would obviously be employed mainly by young unmarried people.

Before 1949 some musics were accessible to would-be performers regardless of gender. Many folk songs could be sung by either sex; the dances on festival days were open to both sexes, and expertise on the Jew's harp was natural for both boys and girls. However, in many cases an individual's gender in large measure dictated which musics were accessible and which were out of bounds. Some folk songs were exclusively male or female, and there were many musics from which women were excluded. All of the religious professions described above were restricted to men, although of course Christian women could take part in the hymn singing, and the lay Buddhists of the female *Mama hui* learned to chant scriptures. In secular musics, women did not generally play musical instruments other than the Jew's harp and perhaps the barley pipe, although they might sing Dianju. Dongjing music, in both its sacred and secular forms, was exclusively the preserve of men. When pressed for a reason for this exclusivity, the only answer elderly Dongjing musicians could come up with was that in the old society women had a low position, and that with their greater equality nowadays, there was no longer any impediment to their participation. Clearly both age and gender, especially the latter, were strong predictors of the musical activities of Lijiang's pre-1949 citizens.

Music as a Barometer of Republican-era Lijiang Society

Music can offer evidence of social and ethnic interaction and differentiation in extremely direct ways. As Daniel Neuman postulates, when music represents history, "music is the medium—the crucible in which time and its memories are collected, reconstituted, and preserved—and history, its message" (1991: 269). At the most obvious level, people sing about their history in epic poems and ballads: "oral genres are a people's autobiographical ethnography" (Coplan 1991: 47, citing Franz Boas). More subtly, musical style and contexts of performance, rather than simple lexical content, tell a story of identity definition and intergroup relations. In Ghana, divine pantheons and religious cults are defined and set off from one another by musical characteristics as well as beliefs and ritual; and cults imported from one group to another often retain their original language and music (Nketia 1970). The Suyá of Brazil learn and ritually perform the songs of other ethnic groups with whom they have interacted; not only does this provide clues to their history, but also "every Suyá musical performance makes history . . . in the sense that it reproduces the pattern of history: the incorporation into the life of the collectivity of the otherness of the others, and the reproduction of human beings and society through the incorporation of new melodies and texts" (Seeger 1991: 33). For the outsider, there is a "world suggested by music sounds, performances, and contexts" (Rice 1994: 6).

A musical map of Republican Lijiang is at once a map of ethnic contact, ethnic differentiation, and of social distinctions. Lexical content certainly included historiographical implications; for example, the *dongba* chants included myths of interethnic contact and migration, and the Dongjing scriptures incorporated express declarations of mainstream Chinese literatus values and allegiances. More extensively implicative, however, were musical style and performative context: who performed what, and where, and why—and how did it come to sound, look, and feel exactly as it did? Each Lijiang resident was situated at a nexus of overlapping distinctions and continua, such that the meaning he or she attached to performative forms was underlaid with highly localized referential experience. Lijiang's Dongjing music sticks out like a sore thumb within the early twentieth-century soundscape of the county, and is thus a particularly valuable tool for understanding the interactions of the local and wider worlds referenced by its aural, visual, and kinesic symbols.

5

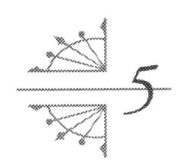

Dongjing Music and Local Interaction in Republican Lijiang

Communications in mountainous areas of early-twentieth-century Yunnan were poor, and journeys were arduous. Individual Dongjing association members from several different counties have told me of fortuitous encounters with local Dongjing groups while on business trips to other areas, and there were one or two instances of intercounty transmission of the Dongjing tradition during the Republican era;[1] but these were the exception rather than the rule. Certainly Lijiang's Dongjing music appears to have been a repertoire of almost entirely local renown and significance, and to have had little impact outside restricted areas of its home county—mainly the Lijiang basin and the banks of the Jinsha River.

Nevertheless, Lijiang's Dongjing repertoire was an active factor in the creation of local social identities, and its organization and use were important in the definition of intracounty social structures and relationships. To put it in Nketia's terms, there is evidence here of the impact of music on consciousness of identity, and of "how hierarchical structures . . . may be defined by the forms of organization and use of music" (1990: 88).

Given the status claims made implicitly and explicitly by former members of many of Lijiang's Dongjing associations, the tradition was clearly a forum for social communication. The form in which this communication was given expression was the performance of religious rituals designed to be sumptuous, solemn, and exclusive. Their social impact arose directly from their performative affect, and from the socially conditioned responses of members and nonmembers alike. Tambiah suggests that ritual action is performative in three senses: "in the Austinian sense of performative wherein saying something is also doing something as a conventional act; in the quite different sense of a staged performance that uses multiple media by which the participants experience the event intensively; and in the third sense of indexical values . . . being attached to and inferred by actors during the performance" (1981: 119). In addition, he suggests that ritual is a "disciplined rehearsal of 'right attitudes'" (p. 126), and that "social communication, of which ritual is a special kind, portrays many features that have little to do with the transmission of new information and everything to do with interpersonal orchestration and with social integration and continuity" (pp. 132–133). In the Republican era, Lijiang's Dongjing music was part of a ritual package that helped reinforce a hierarchical status quo and build solidarity among individuals and social entities. Aural, visual and kinesic elements of the ritual combined to produce an "integrated . . . experience that stimulate[d] particular modes of response and interaction" (Nketia 1988: 53), and that defined a set of relationships internal and external to the Dongjing associations.

Relationship Networks of the Dongjing Associations

Each Dongjing association in Lijiang was embedded in a network of relationships:

1. Between that Dongjing association and the nonmembers in the surrounding community
2. Between that Dongjing association and the county government
3. Between that Dongjing association and other Dongjing associations
4. Within a single Dongjing association, among its members
5. Between a Dongjing association and its gods.

Ritual performance was the major feature delineating and expressing each of these relationships.

Dongjing Associations and Nonmembers

The nature of the ritual and music carried out by the well-educated members of Lijiang's Dongjing associations reinforced their proficiency in Han cultural forms, and thus their differentiation from ordinary Naxi society around them. Visual and kinesic aspects of ritual performance drove home the Han affiliation of the form: as in other parts of Yunnan, the participants wore formal literatus gowns and jackets (*shanzi magua*) rather than local or lower-class dress; they also learned to move with stately decorum, and to practice an elaborately choreographed set of kowtows and bows to their Han gods and to one another. In addition, the singing, chanting, recitation, and ensemble performance in the rituals were audibly Han in character—both linguistically and musically. As explored at length in Chapter 4, most of the musical instruments were identical or similar to Han equivalents elsewhere, and little used in indigenous Naxi music; and many were expensive compared with homemade Naxi peasant instruments.

It is true, of course, that some of the instrumental repertoire was also played by the general population for private secular entertainment; however, the secular groups frequently lacked the more expensive instruments and most of the battery of percussion used by the Dongjing associations. Consequently, the ability to perform the entire repertoire with the complete complement of instruments, sung texts, and ritual distinguished the Dongjing association members. They thereby affirmed their corporate identity and superior sinicized status through their skill in the language, music, and expensive musical instruments of the dominant Han culture, many of which were inaccessible to the average local Naxi. Corporate status was reinforced by their communal ownership of instruments and ritual paraphernalia: individuals were not permitted to borrow these for private use. In addition, the sheer cost of providing the ritual paraphernalia and food for a multiday gathering could not fail to impress the less affluent nonmembers.

Dongjing Associations and the County Government

Twice a year for most of the Republican era, the Lijiang County government organized the state-sponsored Confucian sacrifice, and the Dayan Town Dongjing association was always summoned to provide the music for it. The members went to the Confucian temple and played the slow, stately odes mandated by the government. The musical separation between this music and that used in Dongjing ritual was clear: the Dongjing repertoire allowed substantial musical freedom, while the Confucian odes allowed little or none. The Confucian odes were sung syllabically (one long note per syllable), with little or no improvisation possible on the part of the instruments, whereas the Dongjing melodies were highly melismatic, in quicker tempo, and allowed considerable room for individual variation in performance. One of the former members, mentioning how tedious he found the Confucian music, at the same time acknowledged that the invitation to participate was certainly an honor: it was an acknowledgment of the high cultural and social status of the Dongjing association members, further buttressing their privileged position in the wider community.

Relationships among Different Dongjing Associations

The relationship between different Dongjing associations was frequently reflected in terms of musical style. Although musical repertoire was practically uniform, former association members commented to me on stylistic differences obvious to local ears. Those associations connected through a "mother-son" (*muzi*) relationship (i.e., where the longer established group had taught the newer group) tended to have fewer musical discrepancies than unrelated associations. This legacy endures among today's secular music groups: local researcher Yang Zenglie mentioned to me in 1991 that percussion patterns are almost identical between the ensembles of Dayan Town and Jinshan, while at Baihua Village, where musicians are mostly former members of Baima Dongjing association, they are quite different. The Jinshan Dongjing association was taught by He Yi'an from Dayan Town in the 1940s, while the Baima association learned from Lasha in the 1920s.

Some differences among associations as to the correct order of instrumental pieces to be played during the Ten Offerings, and as to the number of instrumental pieces known, as well as minor stylistic differences, also gave regional flavor to the various groups. This obviously was another factor, possibly involuntary, that contributed to corporate identity.[2] In addition, close relationships were maintained between associations linked through the "mother-son" tie: the groups at Gezi and Jinshan, for example, frequently exchanged visits at festival times with the association in Dayan Town, from which their teachers had been drawn.

Intraassociation Status

Relationships within a single Dongjing association were clearly defined musically, reflected visually, and emphasized by spatial planning. While the titular head (*huizhang*) might be merely a prominent local official with no relevant expertise, the two senior musico-ritual specialists, chosen by general acclaim, were the chief ritual officiant (*shanzhang*) and second ritual officiant (*fu shanzhang*). They had a high social status within their own Dongjing association based on age, respectability and, most important, degree of ritual and musical competence. Indeed, they often possessed impressive reputations among other associations too. It was these two men who held control over aural aspects of the ritual proceedings. The chief officiant was responsible for the wooden fish (*muyu*) and the small drum and clappers (*ban'gu* and *tishou*), percussion instruments that set and controlled the speed of both music and chanted sections. The second officiant played the cloud gong (*yunluo*), which gave the most basic version of the songs and instrumental pieces and acted as the visual cue for those who forgot parts of the melody.[3] Thus musical authority was vested in the men who held the highest ritual positions recognized in the association. During ritual performance, the titular head, chief ritual officiant, second officiant, and one other senior member were the only people who sat facing the statue of the god in the temple—everybody else was sideways on (see diagram in appendix B).

Dongjing Associations and Their Gods

The relationship with the two main gods espoused by the Lijiang associations, Wenchang and Guandi, both quintessentially Han Chinese deities, was maintained entirely in Han Chinese forms of communication. Not only was the language of the scriptures Chinese, but all the aural modes of performance addressed to the gods were in Han Chinese style. This reinforces the fact that the relationship between these two gods and their Naxi worshipers was the same as for Han Chinese associations elsewhere in Yunnan: Wenchang and Guandi were associated with the sinicized side of a respectable Naxi gentleman's life.

Ritual performance also underlined the relative importance of gods and men. Tambiah points out that in most societies, the longer the rite staged and "the grander the scale of the ritual's outlay and adornment, the more important . . . the ceremony is deemed to be" (1981: 150). The four annual festivals in honor of Wenchang and Guandi were each spread over at least three days and were held in the relatively spacious Wenchang or Guandi temples in Lijiang, which allowed for the full display of spectacular ritual accessories. For almost all the three days of the ritual, the ritual was communal and deity centered, with requests for blessings being made communally in general terms as dictated by the scripture in use. When individuals presented private requests for the god's consideration, the ceremony was relatively short, lasting only about forty-five minutes. The Dongjing association's contribution to a deceased member's funeral was also of only a few hours' duration, and took place in the relatively cramped quarters of a private house, clearly marking it as inferior to the god-centered rituals for the festivals of Wenchang and Guandi.

Furthermore, the gods' statues were visually and spatially differentiated from the worshipers: standing elevated on a table, they held positions of spatial superiority, backs to the wall, facing the main door of the temple. Then again, the scriptural text was in large measure addressed to or concerned with them, so that they were also the linguistic focus of the ritual. The aural elements were designed to contribute suitably to what Tambiah terms the "staged performance" by helping create the desired atmosphere of reverence. That atmosphere clearly impressed He Yi'an, taken to his first Dongjing association meeting as a seven-year-old in 1915. Warned by his father to respect Wenchang and Guandi by not looking directly at their statues, he remembered more than seventy years later that "when I entered the temple, I felt that I had entered another world. Members showed respect to the gods and to one another. Everyone spoke softly. I sensed that the temple was a holy place" (Track 1996: 29).

Ritual Performance and Social Distinctions

Returning to Tambiah's "performative approach" to ritual, it is valuable to correlate the performativity of Dongjing ritual with the social distinctions it implicitly delineated. There can be no doubt that here was a riot of "multiple media by which the participants experience[d] the event intensively": visual, aural and kinesic aspects combined to differentiate members from nonmembers, senior from junior members, and gods from men—and did so very effectively, to judge from the reactions of a seven-year-old boy. Similarly, indexical values inferred from the scale of different ceremonies, and from the attire, physical positioning, and movements of different participants, helped delineate the implied hierarchies. Dongjing association ceremonies were above all designed as displays of "right attitudes" and as means of interpersonal orchestration and social integration. They were indeed "staged performances" in which language was almost entirely formalized (and not necessarily understood in a propositional sense), and in which the performative affect was intended to reinforce the cosmological validity of the social status quo—for members and nonmembers alike.

From the musicologist's point of view, what is particularly striking is the way in which musical phenomena were instrumental in delineating intergroup identity and linking related "mother-son" associations, in defining the ritual and social status of different members of the same group, and in setting off the state-sponsored Confucian rituals from the private Dongjing ceremonies. Furthermore, the two most outstanding characteristics of the Dongjing tradition were its Han-ness as opposed to the Naxi background in which it existed, and the socially elevated literatus values it embodied; and both of these were advertised aurally by the linguistic and musical performance media adopted. Music plainly played a major role in drawing group boundaries and creating a consciousness of group cohesiveness; equally, both the form and the organization of the music involved helped define the hierarchical structures of the world in which the Dongjing associations existed and to which their rituals referred.

For an active Dongjing association member in Republican Lijiang, his membership could have a noticeable impact on his life, and might improve his social and business connections. For He Yi'an, the major part of his social life before 1949 revolved around Dongjing association meetings in Dayan Town and his activities with his friends from the group; the same had been true for his father, who died in 1929 (Track 1996). Besides maximizing the opportunity to make connections with other well-to-do men of good status and connections, membership and skill in ritual performance constituted a more general statement of cultural and social distinction. Peter Goullart, the Russian resident in Lijiang in the 1940s, attended many Dongjing association meetings in Dayan Town, and commented that "a well-to-do Naxi in the city could only be accepted as a real gentleman if he knew this ancient music or was a fully fledged Chinese scholar" (1957: 213).

Transmission

Scholars of Dongjing association history often describe a timeless status quo of privileged literati meeting for sumptuous rituals, in an ethnographic present located somewhere in the first half of the twentieth century. Yet the obvious question arises, how did an association get started? More specifically, who were the agents and what were the motivations in getting a new association off the ground? Were privilege and education sine qua nons of membership in newer groups as they were in older ones? What kind of social interactions led to and resulted from the transmission of the Dongjing tradition? How do people remember the instances of transmission that occurred?

Given the destruction and confiscation of so many documents in Lijiang since 1949, it is not surprising that the history of interassociation transmission exists entirely in oral tradition. Despite the notorious changeability of human memory and fluidity of oral tradition, it has the inestimable advantage of relying on sources "from the inside" (Vansina 1985: 197); moreover, for case studies from the early twentieth century, we are for the most part still looking at the "historical gossip" and "personal traditions" that can flesh out and counteract the blander fusions characteristic of written accounts (Vansina 1985: 17). The idiosyncracies manifest in Lijiang's tales of Dongjing association transmission add a spectrum of shades of gray to the black and white generalizations of scholarly overviews.

I rely for my data on a large number of interviews conducted with members of several of the Dongjing associations involved, and on Yang Zenglie's substantial collection of interview data (1990–1991). It was usually possible to cross-check one person's recollections with those of other knowledgeable parties, and thus build up a reasonably reliable picture of the routes the tradition traveled, despite minor discrepancies in some stories.

Early Instances of Transmission from Dayan Town, Baisha, and Lasha

By the end of the Qing dynasty (1911), there were at least five Dongjing associations in Lijiang County. These were located in Dayan Town and in the more rural areas of Baisha, Shuhe, Lasha, and Gezi. Just as the origins of Lijiang's Dongjing tradition are lost in the mists of time, so are tradition bearers uncertain which out of Dayan Town, Baisha and Shuhe was the senior group. However, oral documentation shows clearly that association members in Gezi learned the tradition from Dayan Town, and those of Lasha from Baisha, both fairly late in the Qing dynasty. These two cases are particularly interesting because they demonstrate the mechanics by which formal transmission of the entire musical and ritual repertoire from an established Dongjing association to a new one was effected.[4]

Information on transmission from Dayan Town to Gezi is especially detailed. According to He Yi'an, sometime during the Qing dynasty, possibly around the Tongzhi reign (1862–1875), the social and financial elite of the relatively wealthy area of Gezi requested that the ritual leader of Dayan Town Dongjing association teach them the musical and ritual repertoire so that they could establish an association. The cost of the altar trappings and lavish three-day ceremonies was so large that only a wealthy area could support such a group. The relationship between the two associations was maintained even into the Republican era: during He's youth, when the Dayan Town association held its twice-yearly ceremonies in honor of the god Wenchang, the members would send a letter to the Gezi group inviting them to participate. Gezi would then send four people to attend the Dayan Town meetings, both to learn from the older association and, as He Yi'an put it, "to recognize the relationship." This was a typical "mother-son" (*muzi*) relationship, a term that enshrined the generational superiority of the donor group.

The second case of Qing dynasty transmission documented in the oral tradition is that of the Lasha association receiving the musico-ritual package from the Baisha association. Fewer details are available on this instance of transmission, even though it probably occurred sometime after the first one described. Mu Zhu, a former member of the Lasha association, recalls his forebears saying that the Dongjing tradition was taught to Lasha by a Mr. Mu from Baisha, probably in the last years of the Qing dynasty. This story was independently confirmed by He Huihan, formerly of the Baisha association, who also offered "Mr. Mu's" full name as Mu Wenyu. As with Gezi, the Lasha members were usually better-off men who had received some years of a classical Chinese education.

Interassociation transmission continued during the Republican era, along much the same lines. When the residents of the rural township of Baima (the area around Baihua Village on the map in figure 3.2) wished to establish a Dongjing association in 1923, a prominent Naxi official from Baima asked Jiang Yuchuan, a leading Dayan Town association member, to teach them. When a death in the family prevented Jiang's fulfilling this request, the people at Baima turned to He Ruoqi of Lasha for help and did indeed succeed in setting up their own association.

Certain features recur in the better documented instances of interassociation transmission. It appears it was frequently a community decision, presumably by the more well-educated people, to establish a Dongjing association, after which a formal request for teaching would be made to an established association. The not inconsiderable pedagogical burden would then fall mainly on one individual's shoulders—someone recognized inside and outside his own group as particularly good at the performative aspects of the Dongjing association tradition. Despite the tremendous input of time and effort required, it was considered an honor to be asked to help establish a new group in this way. Surviving association members have maintained knowledge of the individual teachers and of the relationship between donor and receiving groups.

Throughout the Republican era the Dongjing association tradition continued to spread within Lijiang. The Hainan area and Meiquan Village in Lashi Township acquired it, probably in the early Republican era; oral reports suggest that Gao Jianming of Lasha taught in Hainan and He Ji'an of Baisha taught in Meiquan. Zhao Yuxian from Lashi was instrumental in starting an association in Shigu in about 1944. Li Baozhang, formerly of the Shuhe association, remembers his schoolteacher father taking Dongjing association scriptures and musical instruments with him during his career moves, and teaching the music and ritual in both Lashi and Weixi County, to the west of Lijiang. Laoben Village in Daju, northeast Lijiang, seems to have set up an association at some point during this period, with instruction from the Baisha association to their south.

A Curious Case: The Huangjing Association

An unusual case of transmission took place in Dayan Town in the 1930s, which points up nicely issues of social status implied at that time by possession of the Dongjing association tradition. As far back as anyone can remember, in addition to its regular Dongjing association, Dayan Town had another ritual organization known as the *huangjing ban* or *huangjing hui* (Huangjing association).[5] This organization drew its membership from the ordinary townsfolk and, until about 1930, met on the first and fifteenth of each lunar month to perform a scripture in honor of the Jade Emperor (*Gaoshang Yuhuang Benhang Jijing* [Collected Scripture on Deeds of the High Jade Emperor]). The term *huangjing* is an acronym formed from the syllables *huang* and *jing*. The method of performance was simpler than that of the Dongjing associations: the scripture was chanted (*song*), accompanied only by unpitched percussion and sometimes a flute or bowed string instrument. The social standing of the Huangjing association was much lower than that of Dayan Town's Dongjing association, so when some Huangjing association members decided they wanted to learn the Dongjing musical repertoire and start performing the major Dongjing association scriptures, they had a problem. As Wang Dejiu, one of the chief protagonists, told me, "We were young and didn't see why we couldn't do what they [Dayan Town Dongjing association] did. But the Dongjing association was haughty."

Knowing they would get no willing help from that quarter in their quest, some of the younger men opted initially for an indirect approach: they would go to the temple whenever the elite group was holding a festival and listen intently, picking up and memorizing as much of the music and ritual as they could. Wang concentrated on the percussion music, another young man, Yang Derun, on flute and stringed instruments. This was insufficient, however, to master the intricacies of the performance; so, since one of their number had worked in Shuhe and made personal connections there, they asked the more approachable Dongjing association of that area for assistance, and four elderly members of that group agreed to teach them what they needed to know. Wang estimates that it was around 1931 that the Huangjing association was first able to perform the major Dongjing association scripture, the *Dadong Xianjing* (Transcendent Scripture of the Great Grotto of Wenchang), in its entirety. The scripture itself they were given by Zeng Guocai, a Naxi official who was governor of Changning County in western Yunnan. Their performance practice was the same for this scripture as that of the Dongjing associations; but, as He Yi'an of the Dayan Town Dongjing association pointed out, their playing and singing had an obvious "Shuhe character." Like the Dongjing associations, they also used the *Guansheng Dijun Jueshi Zhenjing* (Guandi Enlightenment Scripture) to honor Guandi; this they copied by hand.

This case study of transmission neatly illustrates two of the major factors at play where the Dongjing repertoire is concerned: the importance in Dayan Town of social status as a prerequisite for access to this semisecret knowledge, as a result of which the Huangjing association had to take such a circuitous route to master a musical and ritual repertoire that existed on its doorstep; and the reliance on personal initiative and interpersonal relations in acquiring the requisite knowledge.

Two Late Case Studies: Jinshan and Shigu

As mentioned in chapter 4, secular music groups that played some of the melodic pieces from the Dongjing repertoire were extremely common throughout the Lijiang basin and other low-lying rural areas in the early twentieth century. Occasionally it happened that men who started off using Dongjing music merely for secular entertainment later converted their secular musical activities into a full-fledged Dongjing association. At least two examples of this exist in oral history, involving communities in Jinshan (formerly known as Yinglie Li), a rural township about three kilometers southeast of Dayan Town, and Shigu, a town fifty kilometers west at the first bend of the Jinsha River.[6]

By the mid-1930s, residents of Jinshan had acquired some of the instrumental pieces and accompanied songs, without any words attached, and could play them for fun. They then decided to learn the words to the *Ershisi Xiao Jing* (Classic of the Twenty-Four Exemplars of Filial Piety), the funeral text used by Dongjing associations, so that they, too, could perform it at important funerals. Members of several relatively wealthy Jinshan families requested the Dayan Town Dongjing association to recommend a teacher. The task fell to He Yi'an, a leading member of the Dayan Town group. Despite the fact that most of the players were poor farmers, and one illiterate, He was impressed by their capacity to learn, and proposed that as they already knew most of the musical pieces, instead of stopping at this one text, they should establish a full Dongjing association. They replied that they did not dare cherish such aspirations; but after he offered to teach them for free, the village leaders held a conference and assented enthusiastically. Some sense of the enormous burden on the teacher, and the respect shown by his pupils, can be gleaned from He's explanation to his biographer of the pedagogical arrangements:

> I taught them the music and the Wenchang sutras over a ten-year period. On the sixth day of Spring Festival [1937], some villagers came to my house with an offering of rice, sugar cane, and tea; they bowed before me. Later that day,

they carried my bedding to Jinshan. I lived in the village for one month; during the day the young men worked and I taught them in the evenings. I spent another month after the Torch Festival in June, or July. After several years, I went a third time during the month of December. (Track 1996: 53)

One of He Yi'an's original Jinshan pupils, Yang Jian (born 1917), described to me the technical details of their instruction. As the young men already knew the instrumental pieces (*xiaodiao*) and the tunes of most of the accompanied songs (*dadiao*), He first taught them how to fit the scriptural words to the latter pieces; after that they learned the complex percussion patterns. He also had to teach them chanting, heightened speech, and how to read memorials. In addition, he provided a complete set of ritual paraphernalia courtesy of the Dayan Town association, which had a spare set; in return, since the Dayan Town association would not accept payment for these costly presents, the Jinshan association bought a small plot of land and gave it to them. To thank He Yi'an for his efforts, the new Jinshan association did something usually reserved only for deceased mortals: in a very culturally Han gesture, they set up a spirit tablet (*paiwei*) to He on the altar. This was not the only means by which the new group recognized their relationship to the Dayan Town association and its personnel: the first time Jinshan was able to hold a meeting, in 1947, Dayan Town members were invited as honored guests and put up in the village overnight if they so desired. Thereafter, people from the Jinshan association would join those from Gezi in attending the Dayan Town association's twice-yearly Wenchang ceremonies; and even in 1991 Yang Jian emphasized that the relationship between the two groups was on a *muzi* (mother-son) basis.

In Shigu, too, men who had first played a few Dongjing pieces for secular amusement eventually added the Dongjing protocols in order to establish a full-fledged Dongjing association. One of the prime movers in this enterprise was Zhao Yuxian, an energetic and articulate man aged about eighty in 1992. Zhao was born and brought up in Lashi, which had two Dongjing associations, one of which he joined. He sought to improve his instrumental skills by visiting relatives in Dayan Town who were Huangjing association members. At about the age of twenty-seven, he moved to Shigu, and there in about 1944 he helped establish an association. As with Jinshan, some items of the musical repertoire had already arrived locally and were played without scriptural words or ritual overtones by amateur musicians. Here, however, the procedure of instruction and establishment of the association was quite informal: Zhao announced formation of the group and invited prospective members to sign up. Social and educational standing were unimportant: anyone with enthusiasm to learn was welcome. The new group acquired its ritual percussion instruments from the Zhang family of Taoist priests in Dayan Town, and its scriptures from Niujie (Niugai in Yunnan Mandarin dialect), a stop on the main road down to Dali (hence the differences between the Shigu scriptures and those elsewhere in Lijiang, described in appendix A). Shigu's Dongjing association operated for a few years until about 1949. Once again, through the initiative of one or two individuals, the repertoire in the Shigu area changed from being purely secular to one used by a genuine ritual Dongjing association.

Two Anomalies: Judian and Ludian

Judian and Ludian, two northwestern townships of Lijiang County rather remote from Dayan Town, also had Dongjing associations, but their music differed significantly from that in the rest of Lijiang County. Lijiang researcher Yang Zenglie told me of his surprise when, in the early 1990s, he went to Judian on business and encountered the local Dongjing music group marching along playing at a funeral. Hearing the opening of a popular Dongjing piece, "Ten Offerings" (*Shi gongyang*), Yang, himself a fine musician and linchpin member of the Dayan Town Dongjing ensemble, was able to join in. Fairly soon, however, he was dismayed to find that the melody took an unexpected turn, so that he could not continue. The piece, while obviously similar in places to "Ten Offerings" as played in other parts of Lijiang, had significant differences. Yang speculates that the music in Judian may have been influenced by that in Heqing County to the southeast, because many Heqing residents traveled on business to Judian and nearby Weixi and Zhongdian counties.

As for Ludian, the extracounty origins of its Dongjing association are well documented in the oral tradition:

> Ludian Township, lying in the west of Lijiang County and bordering on Weixi County, is a partly mountainous region. According to the Dongjing folk musician Wang Liang, born in 1910, during the Qing dynasty Ludian did not have a Dongjing association. In 1927 Yang Xizhen, a businessman from Muma in Dali, went to Judian on business. Because his father was ritual head of a Dongjing association, he himself was familiar with the *Transcendent Scripture of the Great Grotto of Wenchang* and its music. When the people of Ludian got to hear about this, they invited Yang Xizhen from Judian to Ludian. Wang Liang and some other men asked him to teach them, and by oral transmission he taught them the protocol of performing the scripture and the Dongjing music. At the end of six months, when they thanked their teacher, Yang Xizhen made them a present of one set of the scripture. In the same year they performed the scripture for the first time in the Guandi temple built during the Qing dynasty. (Yang Zenglie 1991: 37)

The Ludian group, some or all of whose members were Han rather than Naxi, observed three major festivals: Spring Festival on the first day of the first month; Wenchang's birthday on the third of the second month; and the Confucian sacrifice on the twenty-fifth of the eighth month (Yang Zenglie 1991: 42, 38).

Factors Affecting the Spread of Dongjing Associations

At the local level, several factors seem to have been of prime importance in influencing the history and spread of the Dongjing tradition in Lijiang. First, given the complexity of the Chinese-language scriptures, there had to be in each new association at least a quorum of members with a Chinese-language education. This quorum could exist only in the relatively sinicized areas of the county: generally the urban centers and nearby villages, and settlements along the trade routes where contact with the ouside world was frequent. Second, because of the high financial cost of establishing and maintaining an association and its festivals, only relatively prosperous parts of the county could usually support such organizations. Third, some sort of connection with an established association usually had to exist for personnel from the senior organization to be willing to make the enormous time commitment necessary to transmit the tradition. Fourth was the individual factor: men who made the decision to initiate or exploit social and economic relationships to achieve the establishment of a new association, and even to defy local attitudes when these impeded their goals.

Furthermore, the way that surviving Dongjing association members remember their histories is indicative of the way the transmission of the tradition depended on and contributed to social interaction in early pre-Communist Lijiang. Above all, the men I interviewed remembered the transmission patterns in terms of the individuals involved. Even in the early 1990s, my informants, usually by then in their eighties, recalled in detail the names and often convoluted circumstances involved in the teaching of the tradition, and felt a degree of closeness to "related" groups. To this day, the personal loyalties and affections generated by the events of many decades ago endure. He Yi'an remained on close terms with the founding members of the Jinshan group even into the 1990s; and by 1996, when the leaders of the Dayan Town music ensemble needed some experienced musicians to bolster their numbers for public concerts, it was to Jinshan that they went to invite He Yi'an's former pupils to participate.

I was fortunate in the timing of my interviews in Lijiang, in that many of the protagonists in the transmission case studies described above were still alive and remembered the events as part of their life histories. The tales had not yet receded into a more homogenized, secondhand retelling: I could watch the faces of my elderly friends as they told me about their parts in stories enacted so long ago. It was hard to ignore the impish delight with which Wang Dejiu, then quite deaf and in poor health, recalled the ingenuity with which he and his friends from the Huangjing association had circumvented the uncooperative Dayan Town Dongjing association to learn the Dongjing repertoire; or the obvious respect and affection with which Yang Jian of Jinshan spoke of his former teacher He Yi'an; or the self-deprecation with which Zhao Yuxian of Shigu described the prosaic manner in which he went about setting up his association and acquiring its instruments and scriptures. Below the bland surface narrative of the spread of the Dongjing tradition, and the generalizations about its social character, is a vibrant history of the actions, relationships, travels, and initiatives of individuals and small groups. Spreading the Dongjing associations generally involved the exploitation of existing relationships as a village sought to acquire a prestigious piece of cultural capital; it also entailed the creation and reinforcement of new personal ties and obligations as individuals spent huge amounts of time and effort teaching and learning the repertoire. Moreover, certain events in the spread of the tradition provide cultural confirmation of the degree of personal mobility even in an era of inconvenient travel. Shigu, for instance, was able to establish its association thanks to the personal migration of a leading founding member; Weixi County acquired a taste of Lijiang's Dongjing tradition as a result of the changing school appointments of Li Baozhang's teacher father; and Ludian obtained its Dongjing tradition because of the commercial peregrinations of a Dali businessman. The commonplace and the coincidental both have a place in this history, pieces of which are inextricably woven into the biographies of many local men, and resonate down the decades to the present day.

Regional Variation among Lijiang's Dongjing Associations

Just as an overview of musical life in pre-Communist Lijiang uncovered a startling array of regional diversity, so do the shades of gray revealed through the oral histories of Lijiang's Dongjing tradition alert us to the variability of individual associations. Certainly the recollections of many former association members from Dayan Town, Baisha, and Lasha bear out the scholarly generalization and common perception throughout Yunnan that Dongjing associations were exclusive clubs limited to the well-to-do literati of an area; at the same time, the evidence from Lijiang suggests that very new associations, and those in relatively poor areas, were much less exclusive.[7] The Jinshan and Shigu groups, both established in the 1940s, took any man willing to spend the time to learn the music and ritual. Jinshan even had an illiterate recruit, who learned the scriptures by rote.[8]

Similarly, the organization of associations differed from area to area, with the group in Dayan Town having the most elaborate and rigidly demarcated system of officers: (1) titular head (*huizhang*), (2) chief ritual officiant (*shanzhang*), (3) second ritual officiant (*fu shanzhang*), (4) manager (*zhishi*), (5) disciplinarian (*jiucha*), and (6) financial manager (*guanshi*) (Yang Zenglie 1990: 119).

The association head was generally someone who had held high government office even if he himself could not perform the scriptures. For instance, He Gengji (1864–1951), author of the preface to the 1938 list of members titled *Yongbao Ping'an* (Eternal Assurance of Well-Being), was association head for part of the Republican era; he had achieved the rare distinction of passing the highest civil service degree examination (*jinshi*) in 1892, and had had a distinguished career as a military official and head of Lezhi County in Sichuan Province (Yang Zenglie 1990: 117; 1991: 45). The association members stood to increase their social prestige by inviting a prominent man to be titular head, while the person so honored was able to demonstrate his own interests in refined cultural activities.

The chief ritual officiant and second ritual officiant were men chosen by their fellow members for their moral uprightness and, most important, for their intimate knowledge of the scriptures, ritual protocol, and music. They organized the ceremonies, called members together, and directed the music. The manager prepared everything for the ceremonies and supervised the ritual program; the disciplinarian watched for infringements of the rules of behavior during ceremonies and meted out penalties; the financial manager looked after property, rent, and other financial matters and organized food for meetings (Yang Zenglie 1990: 119–120).

Other Dongjing associations in Lijiang made do with fewer officers. The Lasha association had a titular association head, chief and second ritual officiants, and a manager who organized food for meetings (*huishou*). The chief ritual officiant combined the roles of chief officiant and disciplinarian. At Baisha, apart from the association head, there seems to have been no rigorous division of offices. The association Zhao Yuxian joined in Lashi had an association head and a chief ritual officiant, but the one he founded in Shigu had neither: "there was no time—we only started in 1944." In Jinshan, another late starter, the offices of association head and chief ritual officiant were vested in the same person. Overall, the more recent and more rural associations seem to have had less rigidly demarcated offices.

Funding, too, varied considerably within Lijiang County; as one might expect, the older and wealthier associations had more resources and a better established funding structure than their poorer and more rural counterparts, whose arrangements were frequently somewhat ad hoc. Some of the associations owned arable land that was rented out, with the income used to cover their expenses for festivals. Expenses for private ceremonies, such as funerals or rites for new houses, were underwritten by the member requesting them (Yang Zenglie 1990: 120–121).

Like so many associations in county seats all over Yunnan, the Dayan Town association owned both arable land, said to have been donated by the government, and two shops, the rent from which paid part of the costs incurred in putting on the annual public ceremonies (Yang Zenglie 1990: 121). Thanks to their government and business connections, members of this group were also able to think up quite inventive ways to improve their corporate income. The cholera epidemic of 1943, for instance, proved rather a boon for He Yi'an and his fellows:

> I was quite active in public affairs at this time and suggested to some friends that we visit the governor of Lijiang with a plan to build coffins. The governor agreed with our plan and sponsored it by providing seven thousand silver

dollars of public money. These funds had been donated by a rich Naxi and six coffin-makers, members of the Dongjing Society. These members organized thirty carpenters to help them make coffins. Simple coffins were provided free to the poor and higher quality coffins were sold to the wealthy at a substantial profit. The profit from these sales was used to buy salt; members of the Dongjing Society volunteered to sell the salt; the profits were used for sponsoring our gatherings. (Track 1996: 58)

Other Dongjing associations had shakier financial bases. The Baima association, if putting on a major public ceremony, would invite nonmembers to contribute money. By this means people who could not afford to invite the group to their homes could nevertheless make a meritorious contribution. The Shuhe group would sometimes perform funerals for nonmembers and collect goodwill money for doing so (this would have been anathema to the Dayan Town members). By contrast, members of the Jinshan association mostly had to come up with expenses out of their own pockets for each ceremony, although they had of course benefited from free teaching and a present of ritual paraphernalia from the Dayan Town group. The Huangjing association in Dayan Town similarly relied on individual members' contributions.

New recruits were also a source of income. When a new member was admitted to the Dayan Town association, he had to light a lamp, present a plate of rice, a box of brown sugar and a string of cash, and donate whatever item the association was short of; after that, his name was written into the official name list, and he became a formal member. At Baisha, the new recruit was expected to donate $3 and two boxes of brown sugar (Yang Zenglie 1990: 120). At Lasha, the fee for the ordinary members was $3, although richer people might be expected to pay more.

The degree of formality, wealth, social status, and hierarchical organization inherent in Lijiang's Dongjing association culture thus seems to have varied considerably within the county: the wealthy urban area, often taken as a paradigm for the Dongjing association phenomenon as a whole, was only one extreme on a continuum that stretched all the way to the relatively egalitarian approach and undifferentiated organization of the Shigu group.

Secular Groups and Social Interaction

Egalitarianism appears to have characterized the other main context for Dongjing music in Republican Lijiang, namely the secular music groups. Many such groups had no formal organization as such—several friends would simply gather and play through some of the instrumental repertoire on whatever instruments they had to hand, for their own private amusement. They tended to learn pieces from one another, all on a rather ad hoc basis. The "Good Friends Music Association" (*Yiyou*

Yinyuehui) in Dayan Town was organized enough to have regular monthly meetings and a training class for new recruits; but from the comments of former members, it seems to have had no particular claim to social exclusivity or intra-group hierarchy, being more a local leisure activity for male friends. This is not to say that these groups had no importance in social interaction—they certainly served to cement male friendships based on mutual musical interests, to provide opportunities for men to socialize within the structured setting of a communal format, and to allow for mutual respect on the grounds of musical skill. Furthermore, the very nature of the performance style, in which each player had to listen carefully to all his fellow members to blend into the subtly varying heterophony, ensured close interaction among musicians. Indeed, during my own fieldwork in Lijiang, I often heard quiet criticism of players who played too loudly, or out of tune, and thus failed to fold their own playing into the delicate texture created by the interplay of different instruments' and players' ornaments and variations.

Nevertheless, unlike most of the Dongjing associations, such secular groups lacked formalized ritual performance (other than the odd funeral) and aspirations to social status. At the most, they had a sense that their music was especially refined (*wenya*) compared with other local musics such as Dianju (Yunnan opera) or Naxi folk music.[9]

An important theme throughout this chapter has been the shades of gray lying behind the easy black-and-white judgments apparent in written accounts of Dongjing culture. Little appears as stark as the distinction between Lijiang's Dongjing associations and the secular groups that used parts of the repertoire for private entertainment and funeral observances; but even here it becomes evident from the oral histories that the boundaries were porous. As described above, Jinshan and Shigu "upgraded" from purely secular performance to full-blown Dongjing associations in the 1940s. A little earlier, three members of the Huangjing association, which had expended so much time and trouble to learn the entire Dongjing ritual and musical protocol, took the lead in spreading the custom of secular instrumental performance by teaching it to rural communities in Wuzhu, on the Zhongdian County side of the Jinsha River, in Xiangyun Village, just south of Dayan Town, and in Fuhui Village, a kilometer northwest of Dayan Town.[10] Two farmers from Fuhui Village, He Hongzhang (born 1930) and He Zhong (born 1931), recounted how Huangjing association member Yang Derun, renowned in Dayan Town as a superb musician, taught most of the instrumental pieces (*xiaodiao*) and accompanied songs (*dadiao*, minus the words) to a group of villagers including He Hongzhang's father. Yang's connection with Fuhui Village was through his father-in-law, who lived there. Apparently there was never any intention to perform Dongjing association ritual; but villagers got together to play for private entertainment on the first and fifteenth of each month, at occasions such as the Mid-Autumn Festival, and at funerals. He Hongzhang and

He Zhong estimated that their village's tradition of performance had begun in the early 1930s, and continued into the 1950s. Yang Derun was clearly comfortable moving between the worlds of Dongjing association-style ritual and secular music group performance.

Furthermore, it was quite possible for one family to participate simultaneously in a Dongjing association and a secular music group. This point is underlined by the experience of two generations of the Zhang family of Taoist priests resident in Dayan Town. The father of the family, who died in about 1933, was Lijiang's most prominent Taoist priest. He was sufficiently socially acceptable to have become a member of the Dayan Town Dongjing association, and two of his seven sons, the first and the last, followed suit. It was common for the sons of Dongjing association members to learn the music from their fathers, and at least three of Zhang's sons became competent musicians. However, the fifth son, Zhang Kuiguang, cited the family's poor finances to explain why he, universally recognized as a very skillful performer, did not join the association; instead, he used his music for entertainment purposes, playing with a well-organized secular group. Within the same family, therefore, the father played the repertoire at the Dongjing association, while his sons used it both ways depending on their personal circumstances. They were also responsible for teaching the instrumental pieces to the young Buddhist monk (*heshang*) He Shiwei, who later performed them in Buddhist rituals.[11]

There was, thus, frequent musical and social interaction between those who used Dongjing music primarily in the ritual context of the Dongjing associations, and those who played its instrumental ensemble numbers in secular groups. As with so much traditional Chinese music, different groups of users shared musical material and saw no conflict between its use in ritual and nonritual contexts.[12]

Summary

Dongjing music was an important part of social interaction in pre-Communist Lijiang for Dongjing association members and secular groups alike. Dongjing ritual included music as one of many components in a performative whole staged to affirm the validity of a sociopolitical hierarchy based as much on transethnic cultural valorization as on economic success. This performative whole articulated association identities and interassociation relationships, distinctions within and among associations, and distinctions between association members and nonmembers (cf. Nketia 1990: 88). By contrast, music itself was the overt focus of the much less self-conscious secular groups, which affirmed shared interests and friendly relations among local men in a far more informal fashion. It is important to remember, however, that local exigencies caused substantial regional variations in performance, organization and outlook among all the associations and groups discussed above; indeed, the resulting musical differences help "re-creat[e] the patterns of their history" (Anthony Seeger 1991: 33). Rather than being a static or monolithic entity, the Dongjing tradition was a wonderfully variegated and active medium in the creation, maintenance, and affirmation of social networks among its bearers.

6

The Wider World Comes to Lijiang

The Musical Impact

For most of its existence, Lijiang's Dongjing music had little observable impact outside its own county: for all its high profile within its home territory, it seldom traveled farther afield. Although a German university professor made a wax cylinder recording in 1935, and He Yi'an of the Dayan Town Dongjing association recorded a few pieces as flute solos while on a business trip to Kunming in 1947, these appear to have been isolated events that left no lasting impression on the wider world (Track 1996: 49, 64). The same is true of other musical genres: while there was certainly interethnic and intercounty diffusion of songs, dances, and religious musics, they seem to have retained a purely local importance. Though mentioned briefly in county gazetteers and other local literature, in the pre-Communist era none of these musics achieved even regional renown, let alone national fame.

Despite the overwhelmingly localized nature of Lijiang's many musics in the first half of the twentieth century, it is important to note that they did not exist in some unchanging and timeless state of isolation. Lijiang might have existed on the periphery of the Chinese state, but it was certainly not divorced from the events that have shaken southwest China, and indeed the whole nation, since the late nineteenth century. Music and dance often respond rapidly to changes in their environment; frequently, too, they preserve evidence over a long period. These are major reasons for the arguments put forward by Seeger (1940), Nketia (1964), Wachsmann (1971), Pratt (1976), Shelemay (1980), and others in favor of music as historical evidence. Provincial and national events had already had a documented impact on Dongjing music by the early years of the Republic, and they have done so increasingly with respect to all of Lijiang's musics ever since. For the sinologist, examination of the recent historical development of Lijiang's soundscape is a valuable case study of the effect on a remote county of major regional and national events.

From the Moslem Uprising to the Civil War

For this period, spanning nearly a hundred years between 1856 and 1949, documentation is richest for the Dongjing tradition, with a little information on other musical forms. In common with many other parts of Yunnan, Lijiang was badly affected by the Moslem uprising of 1856–1873, and its Dongjing associations suffered, as did their counterparts in other counties.[1] He Gengji's 1938 preface to the Dayan Town association's name list *Yongbao Ping'an* (Eternal Assurance of Well-Being) records the destruction of his Dongjing association and the loss of its ritual paraphernalia at this time, and its revival once peace was restored.

The next problem faced by this association was of national rather than regional provenance, and resulted directly from the establishment of the Republic of China in 1912. A generally anti-religious trend on the part of the government has been noted for much of the Republican era (Duara 1991); although this does not appear to have affected Lijiang much generally, in 1912 a number of local people took advantage of the new policy to smash statues in Lijiang's temples, including some of Wenchang. They also complained to the county head that the Dongjing association in Dayan Town was a feudal element that should stop its "superstitious" (*mixin*) ceremonies. The county head was himself a member of a Kunming Dongjing association, and was thus sympathetic to the Dayan Town group; he negotiated a compromise by which the association adopted the official name *Lijiang Yinyuehui* (Lijiang Music Association), but was soon allowed to resume its ritual activities.[2] This was the first time, according to my informants, that a government expressed disapproval of the association and disrupted its activities. In this instance a face-saving compromise was negotiated; but the situation underscored the vulnerablity of the Dongjing tradition to the whims of political leaders. Of equal interest is the fact that music became the front for the compromise: apparently the least politically sensitive component of the Dongjing tradition, it could be allowed to continue even if the ritual and all other facets were suspect. This was, in fact, a preview of the Communist government policy after 1949: since then, the only aspect of the Dongjing tradition that has survived in Lijiang County is the music, which flourishes in its secular incarnation.

The anti-Japanese war (1937–1945) was also marked musically in Lijiang. In March 1938, the local government organized a day of religious ceremonies in the Black Dragon Park just to the north of Dayan Town. Monks from both the Tibetan and Chinese Buddhist traditions conducted rituals praying for China's success, and the Dayan Town Dongjing association played music and recited the scripture *Wenchang Qilu Baosi Dengke* (The Wenchang Rite of Lighting a Lamp for Entreating Prosperity and Preserving Descendants) to the same end (Track

1996: 54). Anti-Japanese opera activities, both Yunnanese Dianju and Peking Opera, also flourished during the war years, at least in part under the impetus from local Naxi intellectuals who had returned from studies elsewhere in China (Wang Zhiqiang 1989: 96).

The civil war (1945–1949) too was reflected in local music making. Following the widespread Chinese tradition of fitting new words to pre-existent tunes, in 1945, the famous Naxi artist Zhou Lin,[3] a member of the Huangjing association, composed a set of patriotic words to the Dongjing association piece "Spring Has Come" (*Dao Chun Lai*). Zhou Lin's lyrics, which he taught to schoolchildren, elegized the end of the anti-Japanese war and urged peace on the warring factions in China:

> Spring comes to the desolate borderland,
> The waters of the Jinsha River sparkle with emerald sheen,
> And the Jade Dragon [Mountain][4] shines as it reflects the morning sun.
> The poplar and willow are green, the flowers are fragrant,
> And people are jubilant as they rowdily celebrate the victory.
> More difficulties make a nation prosper;
> You should remember this period of grief and joy!
> Recalling our bitter experience, no one should forget.
> Thinking of the past, the eight-year anti-Japanese war was hard,
> We have exchanged the fresh blood of tens of millions of people
> For the splendid lights of the Lantern Festival!
> The bones of the dead, not yet cold, lie on the bank of the Wuding river;
> Helping the old and young, drifting from place to place,
> Compatriots with no homes to return to long for their native place.
> Restraining immoderate revelry, prepare to display the utmost fortitude.
> How should we divide into parties and factions to strive for selfish gains and power?
> Let us seek to come together, to train [the youth]
> Engage in vigorous construction, struggle for self-strengthening.
> Each year the spring returns to the earth, and the national flag flutters forever.
>
> (Xuan 1980)

The call for parties and factions to unite reflected the uneasy alliance of Nationalist and Communist parties during the Second World War, which disintegrated soon after Japan's defeat and led to the four-year civil war won ultimately by the Communists in 1949. The choice of this piece for these words proves how widespread the Dongjing tunes were among the general populace before 1949: there would have been no point in using this melody if it were not already familiar to the children. It was ideal as a vehicle for the fiercely nationalistic sentiment felt by certain Naxi intellectuals, which they hoped to inculcate into local young people. This poem is a useful pointer to the mood of the more cosmopolitan-minded urban intellectuals of the mid 1940s.

A further musical hint that Lijiang was beginning in the early twentieth century to feel the increasing involvement of China in international interactions is given by attempts to add very foreign instruments to Dongjing music during this era: Zhou Fan of the Dayan Town Dongjing association and Zhou Lin of the Huangjing association tried to introduce not only the *yangqin* (Chinese hammered dulcimer), otherwise unknown in local musics, but also the Western violin and harmonium (Yang Zenglie 1991: 34–35). None of these instruments, however, gained a foothold in the tradition. The Christian hymn singing introduced at this time by missionaries was another international introduction of limited influence.

Liberation

The "liberation" of Dayan Town took place on 1 July 1949, and was celebrated that day by a Dianju (Yunnan opera) performance (Wang Zhiqiang 1989: 96). Ultimately, liberation had a more profound impact on local musical life than any previous national event. While its long-term ramifications unfolded only in the following years, some potent harbingers of future developments startled local observers right away. Decades later, He Yi'an recollected,

> A member of the Dongjing Society who had been involved in revolutionary activities became a government official. Secretly, he warned the members of the Dongjing Society not to hold their [next] gathering. "The new government controls everything!" he told us. "They believe that the activities of the Dongjing Society have something to do with feudal superstition. They are forbidden. You must obey them."
>
> With this stern warning . . . all subsequent Dongjing Society activities were canceled. . . . No Confucian gathering was held in September. (Track 1996: 66–67)

Ritual Dongjing activities thus ceased in Dayan Town immediately at the advent of the Communist government. It appears that the same happened soon after in other parts of Lijiang County. The Dayan Town association also handed over ten boxes of corporately owned musical instruments, scriptures, and other belongings to the government. Some were dispersed to state work-units, including professional performance troupes, the Lijiang County Library, and the Lijiang Prefecture Archive; others have since disappeared.

The Dayan Town Dongjing association was not the only one whose membership included secret revolutionaries: the Lasha group, for instance, had several such members, who would hold covert meetings during breaks from playing.[5] It was ironic that the Dongjing association ceremonies had provided a cover for meetings of the underground Party members who would ultimately contribute to the demise of the ritual Dongjing tradition in Lijiang County.

Liberation was also marked musically by the ubiquitous public performance of "politically correct" songs and dances. Russian resident Peter Goullart took a rather jaundiced view of events:

> Life in Lijiang had changed almost beyond recognition. There were daily parades of boys and girls everywhere with the eternal singing of the tune of "John Brown's Body" and hymns of praise for Mao Zedong. Old Naxi dances were prohibited and replaced by the new Communist dances which were neither attractive nor becoming. Many people donned the blue uniforms. Hired labor was abolished and all the village people had to work collectively. After their work, though tired and sleepy, they had to listen to interminable indoctrination talks at daily meetings and afterwards to dance the compulsory Communist dances. (Goullart 1957: 253)

From the 1950s through the Cultural Revolution

Theory

Mao Zedong had long been convinced of the value of literature and the arts to the Communist cause. In his "Talks at the Yan'an Conference on Literature and Art," given in 1942, he emphasized:

> There are a number of different fronts in our struggle for the national liberation of China, civil and military, or, we might say, there is a cultural as well as an armed front. Victory over the enemy depends primarily on armies with guns in their hands, but this kind of army alone is not enough. We still need a cultural army, since this kind of army is indispensable in achieving unity among ourselves and winning victory over the enemy. (McDougall 1980: 57)

He goes on in the talks to tell his audience just why literature and art are so important, revealing his awareness of the power of such media to manipulate images, transform people's opinions, and urge them to action:

> Revolutionary fiction, drama, film and so on can create all sorts of characters on the basis of real life and help the masses push history forward. For example, some people suffer from hunger and oppression while others exploit and oppress them: this state of affairs exists everywhere and no one gets upset about it; but literature and art organize and concentrate this kind of everyday occurrence, making it typical and creating a work of literature and art which can awaken and arouse the popular masses, urging them on to unity and struggle and to take part in transforming their own environment. (p. 70)

The audience to be addressed, says Mao, consists of the workers, peasants, and soldiers of the broad masses, from whom cultural workers must learn as well as studying the scientific approach of Marxism-Leninism. Curiously, given the Communist emphasis on the worth of the proletariat, he is rather dismissive of their cultural attainments: they are "illiterate, ignorant, and uncultured as a result of prolonged feudal and bourgeois rule" (p. 71). Thus cultural workers should aim both to reach a wide audience and, also, in the long run, to "raise standards." For, he argues, "if the people providing the material for wider audiences aren't on a higher level than their audience, then what is the point of trying to reach them at all?" (p. 71).

In practice, in musical terms, this "raising of standards" has usually meant the introduction of Europeanized techniques of performance and instrument manufacture to Chinese traditional musics. As mentioned in chapter 2, simple Western functional harmony frequently supplements or replaces delicate traditional heterophony; violin-influenced techniques are applied to Chinese bowed strings; professional folk "orchestras," often of several dozen players, are created to replace the traditional small folk ensembles; folk instruments are "improved" by being retuned to equal temperament and standardized through factory manufacture; families of instruments in everything from soprano to bass are constructed from traditional originals in line with the Western orchestral model, in order to add to the pitch range available and render harmonic treatment easier; and pieces are composed, or recomposed, in Western-influenced formats (Han 1979). It is frequently stated with approval that such changes make Chinese music more "scientific" (*kexue*). Mao Zedong himself told members of China's National Association of Muscians that, although it was important to maintain distinctive national characteristics and style, "in music you may apply appropriate foreign principles and use foreign musical instruments.... The general principles of Western music must be integrated with Chinese conditions.... If we can digest foreign music and absorb its strong points, this will be beneficial to us" (1979 [1956]: 9, 10, 14). What is at first glance a strange appropriation of Western influence by the Chinese Communist cultural hierarchy becomes more explicable in the light of two important factors. First, many cultural workers were intellectuals who had been influenced by trends such as the New Culture Movement, which blamed China's backwardness in the nineteenth century on the stagnant nature of traditional Chinese culture and tried to improve or replace it by the modern culture of the West. Second, until the 1960s, Chinese Communism was heavily indebted to the Soviet Union, and the Soviet model of ideologically correct musical development was to urge folk and non-European musics toward Western art music–inspired professional models.[6]

In a move very important for the cultural life of the whole country after 1949, Mao used the Yan'an talks in part to define the roles of "professional experts" and "comrades who carry out the work of reaching wide audiences":

> Our professionals should serve not only cadres but more importantly the masses as well. Gorky was active in editing factory histories, guiding village correspondents, and guiding young people in their teens, while Lu Xun also spent a great deal of time on general correspondence with students. Our professional writers should give their attention to the masses' wall newspapers and to reportage literature in the army and the villages. Our professional playwrights should give their attention to little theater groups in the army and villages. Our professional musicians should give their attention to songs sung by the masses. Our professional artists should give their attention to mass art. All of these comrades should develop close relationships with comrades who are doing the work of reaching wider audiences on the lowest level among the masses, helping and guiding them at the same time as learning from them and drawing sustenance from them, replenishing, enriching, and nourishing themselves so that their profession does not become an ivory tower isolated from the masses and from reality, devoid of meaning and vitality. (p. 73)

Mao's Yan'an talks have been honored as guiding principles of socialist art and literature since the founding of the People's Republic, and are still taken seriously; I attended the concert given by local professional and amateur musicians in Dayan Town in May 1992 to celebrate the fiftieth anniversary of their promulgation. Some idea of the particular ways in which central cultural policy was applied to the ethnic minorities may be gleaned from a speech delivered by Vice Premier Lu Dingyi at the 1964 national festival of amateur minority performances (*Quanguo shaoshu minzu qunzhong yeyu yishu guanmo yanchu*). He emphasizes the necessity of revolutionary content, and also certain needs particular to the minorities: for uniformity of content, diversity of form, and for mutual cultural influence:

> The revolutionary cultural art of the national minorities must pay attention to using ethnic forms, for thus it can be more easily accepted by the people of the national minorities. The cultural art of each nationality must be revolutionary in content and must be beneficial to socialism. On this question there must be, can only be, unanimity. But on the question of national form, flavor and characteristics, each nationality is different, and on this question there does not need to be uniformity.[7] Of course, in the socialist motherland, there should be mutual cultural exchange among all nationalities.

Lu finishes by urging unity (*tuanjie*) on the peoples and professional and sparetime cultural cadres of all China's nationalities, of course under the leadership of the Party and Chairman Mao (Lu Dingyi 1964: 5).

The effect of Mao's cultural thought and policy on performance arts and literature, and their use to further his ideological goals, have been studied at length for individual genres.[8] But using Lijiang as a case study makes it possible to look at a geographic area, rather than a single genre, as a microcosm of the new national policies. Lijiang is of further interest because the issues played out are not just those of class struggle and the progression to socialism common to the whole of China; they include also the element of interaction between Communist center and minority periphery, peculiar to China's border regions but vital to national unity and territorial integrity.

Lijiang County soon acquired the bureaucratic trappings of cultural policy common all over China. In particular, in 1953 the Lijiang County Cultural Office (*wenhua guan*) was established as the center for developing the culture of the local people, and of directing their spare-time activities. Over the years it has been responsible for collecting and editing folk literature and arts, organizing folksingers and other performers, developing extensive propaganda exercises, and putting on exhibitions connected with agricultural successes, hygiene education, calligraphy and painting and the like (Lijiang Naxizu Zizhixian Gaikuang Bianxiezu 1986: 134).[9] As elsewhere in China, a variety of professional performance troupes and cultural specialists also appeared on the scene during the 1950s and early 1960s, blending centrally mandated cultural policy with local artistic raw material. Professional musical activities mushroomed, and amateur activities were controlled, investigated, and utilized by the state as never before.

At the same time, the new county government used technology to bring news and propaganda from the rest of China into Lijiang. Lijiang County acquired its first radio receiving station in 1950, followed in 1956 by a broadcasting station that reached the Lijiang basin region. More stations followed, which for many years relayed the news, programs, and propaganda items put out by the central and provincial radio networks. The first television transmitter was set up in 1976, with limited reception over the Lijiang basin and Lashi areas. Film, too, spread as a medium from the outer world: starting with only one film projector and a single two-person projection team in the 1950s, by 1966 there were four such teams employing ten people; by the early 1970s most communes had their own units (Lijiang Naxizu Zizhixian Gaikuang Bianxiezu 1986: 148–149, 135). All these new media gradually brought news and messages from the rest of China into Lijiang, especially into the Lijiang basin area, helping draw the county more into the national picture. This latter trend is evident in much of the musical activity described below.

Dongjing Music

In accordance with the policies of encouraging and directing folk arts, the new government allowed much nonreligious traditional music making to continue, and indeed continued the custom of the Nationalist authorities of summoning local amateur musicians to play for government-sponsored events—even though these were of a somewhat different slant from the annual Confucian sacrifice and the 1933 Chrysanthemum Festival. In Dayan Town, according to He Yi'an's eyewitness account:

> In March [1950], the new government organized some musicians to form a Music Society which was divided into four groups; each group had seven or eight members. The first group were members of the Dongjing Society with myself as their leader. The second group were members of the Huangjing Society. The third group were [ordinary] citizens and the fourth group young students. Most members of the first three groups could play instruments. But the young students knew only new songs praising the new government.
>
> Each week, there were two activities: on Wednesdays, group one was in charge of finding a place and arranging the program; they played music or were taught new songs by the students. On Saturday, group two was responsible for the arrangements. We played at Spring Festival, Lijiang Martyrs' Day, the anniversary of the founding of new China (October 1st), at meetings of government officials, and when a high official of the central government died.
>
> During the Korean War, in August, the Music Society performed for five days at the . . . Cattle Fair, to encourage people to contribute money to support the army. Those who contributed could write their names on a large piece of white cloth; the cloth was later displayed as a banner. (Track 1996: 69)

Between 1950 and 1966, aficionados continued to play Lijiang's Dongjing music, albeit as a purely secular repertoire, rather in the manner of the pre-1949 secular music groups. Thus the pieces that continued to be performed after 1949 were the instrumental pieces (*xiaodiao*) and some of the accompanied songs (*dadiao*), the latter of course minus their sacred texts. During this period in Baihua Village, former members of the Baima Dongjing association would sometimes meet in small groups at private houses to play together for secular amusement. Some of the pre-1949 secular music groups both in urban and in rural areas also continued playing for private pleasure as before. In the 1950s several musicians formed a Dongjing music group in Dayan Town, headed by former Huangjing association member Yang Derun (Zhao Jingxiu 1995: 36); however, in Dayan Town the necessity of going to work on a fixed schedule at state work-units precluded daytime activities. Furthermore, every time there was a left-wing political movement the musical gatherings both in the town and in villages would cease for a few months for fear of criticism. An elderly musician from a village to the north of Dayan Town remembered an incident which occurred several years after 1949: as he went to pick up a flute at a meeting, a local leader begged him, "Please don't play any old tunes."[10]

Nevertheless, there was enough of the music going on in Dayan Town in the 1950s for Yang Houkun, then a teenager and by the 1980s a prominent local flautist, to learn it at that time from Li Chengzhen, a former member of the Huangjing association. Dongjing music heard floating through the night air in

Shigu in the early 1960s also enchanted a young military recruit from Kunming who, years later, returned to Lijiang to research its Dongjing culture (Lei Hong'an 1989–1990). It was during this period too that a group of Dongjing musicians first performed outside Lijiang: in 1954, the provincial Mass Arts Office (*qunyi guan*) summoned four well-known players to perform in Kunming, where the vice governor of Yunnan, Zhang Chong, is said to have expressed regret that so few of them made the trip (Zhao Jingxiu 1995: 35). Overall, despite a few hiatuses, Dongjing music in its secular manifestation seems to have been alive and reasonably well in Lijiang at this time, although most of my informants felt that activities did become increasingly infrequent until total cessation at the outbreak of the Cultural Revolution, when the music was demonized as part of the old society. Some of its practitioners were labeled "ox ghosts and snake spirits" (*niugui sheshen*); leading musician Yang Derun was attacked by leftist extremists, and many instruments were smashed (Zhao Jingxiu 1995: 36). Some instruments were successfully hidden by their owners and survived to be played again as the chaos ended.

Baisha Xiyue

Possibly because of its association with impoverished peasant performers, Baisha Xiyue, already on its last folk legs by 1949, "achieved the high regard of the Party and the People's Government" (Mao Jizeng 1964: 19). Like Dongjing music, Baisha Xiyue seems to have made its first trip outside Lijiang during this period. In 1956 the county government organized an amateur music group to study the repertoire from one of the four surviving exponents, He Xidian; the next year this group took part in the "Yunnan Province Amateur Song, Dance and Opera Festival" (*Yunnan sheng yeyu gewu xiqu huiyan dahui*), held in Kunming, where it was awarded a first prize (Mao Jizeng 1964: 19). From 1956 on, music workers from many different regions arrived in Lijiang to study and arrange the music. Mao concludes the historical overview of his 1964 report by reporting with satisfaction that "this year, some arts performance troupes (such as the Lijiang Song and Dance Troupe) are preparing to put it on stage, so that it may reach still more of the masses in a new guise" (p. 20).

Folk Song

As in other parts of China, folk song, with its linguistic potential, became a potent means of propaganda in Lijiang. One Naxi folk singer commented to me that the famous melody *Gguq qil* was just as suitable for singing propaganda words as for traditional content; and in an anthology of Naxi folk songs collected in 1956, thirty-one of the eighty-three songs are "new songs" (*xin'ge*) with revolutionary content (Liu Chao 1959). A 1958 article from *Renmin Yinyue* (People's

Music) describes the "old people's song group" (*qilao gehui*) of the Lijiang Naxi. After 1949, some old people used "old people's songs" (*laoren'ge*) to express their bitterness at the old society, which proved very useful: the local Party and agricultural leaders organized the elderly singers into an "old people's song group" with about three hundred members, mostly poor peasants and farm laborers over the age of fifty. From about 1952 on, for every political "movement" (*yundong*), these singers were used to spread propaganda in favor of whichever policy was being enacted (Lü Dou 1958: 30). Lijiang even produced its own local version of "Blind Abing," the folk music hero from Wuxi City (Stock 1996): the Baisha Xiyue exponent He Xidian composed many folk songs with revolutionary content in the years after 1949, made several recordings, and traveled twice to Beijing. Some of his recordings were used in a film, *Meili de Baiyun* (Beautiful White Clouds), and the music he promoted was even heard at a youth meeting in Moscow—an international first for Naxi music (Mu Yaojun 1990).

Like other ethnic groups, the Naxi were drawn into the increasingly numerous regional and national arts festivals promoted by the government. A report from the 1964 national festival of amateur minority performances (*Quanguo shaoshu minzu qunzhong yeyu yishu guanmo yanchu*) both sums up the spirit of the whole event and pinpoints a Naxi contribution:

> With sincere, deep feeling many songs expressed the incomparable love of each nationality for the Party and for Chairman Mao. The commonest theme was the eulogizing of the great Party and the great leader Chairman Mao; from firsthand experience, the laboring people of each nationality understand the source of their happy lives.
>
> "Our happiness depends entirely on the Communist Party,
> Our happiness depends entirely on Chairman Mao,
> Dance the most beautiful, the newest, the newest, the most beautiful 'A li li,'
> Sing the most beautiful, the best, the best, the most beautiful 'Nawei' song,
> To present to the dear Party,
> To present to Chairman Mao."
>
> These lines from the Naxi sang out the feelings of the people of each nationality.
>
> (Sun Shen 1964: 6)

Naxi participation in this event is mentioned as one of the highlights of local cultural history in a Lijiang County overview published in 1986 (Lijiang Naxizu Zizhixian Gaikuang Bianxiezu 1986: 135).[11]

Obviously, contemporary sources on Naxi folk song tended to emphasize the revolutionary content of the songs. How far this reflected actual grass-roots practice at the time is of course debatable; Yang Mu (1994) has pointed out the frequent discrepancy between printed accounts and actual folk song practice since 1949.

Opera and Stage Performances

After 1949, amateur Dianju and Peking Opera activities continued in Dayan Town, with the pieces performed including both traditional and revolutionary content. In 1951 the county Communist Party Committee approved the formation of a twenty-five-member Naxi Theater Troupe (*Naxi Jutuan*), (a.k.a. Naxi Art Troupe [*Naxi Wen'gongdui*]), led by Naxi artist Zhou Lin. In its one year of existence (May 1951 to April 1952), it spread revolutionary and anti-American propaganda to Lijiang villagers through an eclectic mix of performance styles, including Yangge (the northern Chinese song, dance and variety act genre borrowed for Communist propaganda in Yan'an [Holm 1991]), Dianju (Yunnan opera), choral singing, and spoken plays (Lü Zhandian 1993). Provincial and city-level troupes began to bring professional Dianju, Huadeng, Peking, and other styles of opera to Lijiang; and in 1956 Lijiang Prefecture established a professional prefectural art troupe (*wen'gongdui*), later known as the prefectural song and dance troupe (*gewutuan*). At a prefectural performance in early 1958, the Naxi "*dongba* dance" (*dongba wu*) was put on stage, shorn of its ritual context, as a dance performance, starting a tradition which has continued to the present day (Wang Zhiqiang 1989: 96–97). Lijiang County established its own "nationality art troupe" (*minzu wenyi gongzuodui*) in the early 1960s, whose members composed and performed many different dances, songs, and operatic pieces. They went into the villages to perform and to give coaching for village spare-time propaganda troupes; they also did a lot of work in collecting and editing Naxi folk songs and dances, many of which they later presented in polished versions on stage, including at the 1964 festival in Beijing (Lijiang Naxizu Zizhixian Gaikuang Bianxiezu 1986: 135).

A professional Dianju troupe was established in Lijiang Prefecture in 1961; this group averaged 171 performances a year in its first five years. Like their counterparts in Dongjing music, Baisha Xiyue and folksinging, Lijiang's Dianju performers were invited to the big city. In their case, the occasion was the Yunnan Province Revolutionary Modern Opera Festival (*Yunnan sheng geming xiandai xi guanmo yanchu dahui*) held in Kunming in October 1964; their performance of three operas they had composed, reflecting village life, attracted praise from the *Yunnan Daily* (*Yunnan Ribao*).

During the Cultural Revolution, many of the operas and performers were branded "ox ghosts and snake spirits" (*niugui sheshen*), and the troupe members were scattered, either sent back home or to cadre schools. However, soon some of them were recombined into a "Mao Zedong Thought Art Propaganda Troupe" (*Mao Zedong Sixiang Wenyi Xuanchuan Dui*), performing nationally known revolutionary theater standards such as the ballet "The White-Haired Girl" (*Baimao Nü*), the Peking Opera "The Red Lantern" (*Hongdeng Ji*), and a Dianju version of "Taking Tiger Mountain by Strategy" (*Zhiqu Weihu Shan*). The Lijiang Prefecture Dianju Troupe was not reinstated until 1979 (Wang Zhiqiang 1989: 97–99).

The Advent of the Scholars

A final national development which was to have a lasting impact on Lijiang's music was the institutionalization of ethnological and folklore research by the Communist government. The tremendous push to collect systematic ethnological data in the 1950s was accompanied by an equal desire to document the "folk literature" and "folk arts" of the People's Republic; both these phenomena have been touched upon in chapter 2. Local cultural workers in Lijiang collected folk songs in the 1950s and 1960s (He Zhiwu 1995: 2–3), and outside researchers visited Lijiang several times between 1949 and 1966. The resulting publications provide some of the most valuable non-oral material still extant on the county's historical musical life.

In 1956, Liu Chao was a member of a team sent by the Literature Research Institute of the Chinese Academy of Sciences to investigate folk song in Dali and Lijiang. Liu and one other colleague were assigned to the Lijiang portion of the research; they spent about one and a half months in Lijiang, visiting several dozen Naxi singers. Liu felt keenly the limitations of their work, noting that owing to the shortness of time they were unable to visit many parts of the county, including the north, considered the repository of the more ancient layer of Naxi culture. In addition, he was forced to rely on oral translation for the content of the songs, and did some creative editing (*jiagong*) with the final product, while attempting to preserve the original flavor (Liu Chao 1959: 1–2). More than a third of Liu's songs are "new songs" (*xin'ge*). Whatever the shortcomings of his work, Liu did at least spread awareness of the Naxi and their songs, since his anthology was published in Beijing in 1959. Short reports on Naxi music also appeared during the 1950s in the nationally distributed journal *Renmin Yinyue* (People's Music) (Zhao Jishun 1951; Lü Dou 1958).

A more profound impact resulted from a major research project undertaken in 1962. In March that year, Mao Jizeng, a scholar from the Central Conservatory of Music in Beijing, joined a group of ten men who spent more than five weeks investigating Baisha Xiyue. Mao's companions included the famous Naxi artist Zhou Lin, then assistant county head; four more Naxi who worked in culture and propaganda in Lijiang County; two composers attached to the Lijiang Prefecture Song and Dance Troupe (one Yi and one Hui); and three members of Yunnan Province Song and Dance Troupe (two Han and one Yi). Their work resulted in a detailed description of the music and surviving musicians, and in full scores of the constituent pieces. The report and scores are now available in two different formats: an internally circulated booklet bearing the imprimatur of the Chinese Music Research Institute (Mao Jizeng 1964), and a published version in the second volume of reports on Naxi social history (Mao Jizeng 1986). Two equally important results of this productive month were the recording of most of the pieces from the Baisha Xiyue repertoire, and the time spent by the members of the prefectural and provincial song and dance troupes in studying the performance techniques and style of the music. The addition of Baisha Xiyue to the professional troupes' repertoire set a proud precedent that has continued to this day of the preservation of this genre through staged performance.

At around this time, Dongjing music too was recorded by visitors from outside. A reel-to-reel tape of some Baisha Xiyue and Dongjing pieces existed in 1992 in the keeping of the Lijiang Naxi Autonomous County Song and Dance Troupe (*Lijiang Naxizu Zizhixian Minzu Gewutuan*); this was said to have been made during Mao Jizeng's visit, and was much admired for the clarity of the playing. In 1963, the Central Broadcasting Station sent people to Lijiang to record more than twenty pieces of the Dongjing repertoire, which were later aired on the central radio in Beijing (Zhao Jingxiu 1995: 36). Apart from isolated instances in 1935 and 1947, these were the first major recording projects undertaken on Lijiang's music. The copies kept in Lijiang continue to inform the playing of musicians today, and to excite aesthetic admiration.[12]

Another field trip was undertaken in September 1962 by members of several provincial-level cultural organs; they spent two months investigating Dongjing music in Lijiang, Xiaguan, Dali, and Kunming. Their report, finished in December 1962, was finally published in a provincial journal in 1983 (Zhou and Huang 1983), and certainly helped raise regional awareness of Dongjing music of several areas.

Regional and National Impact

Between 1949 and 1966, national events shaped Lijiang and its music as never before. For the first time in many years, the central government was in firm control of this part of Yunnan Province; and this was a government that followed the Soviet model of active investigation, direction, and political utilization of folk arts.

Many features stressed by Mao in his "Yan'an Talks" are evident in this period of Lijiang's musical history. Verbal performance arts in particular were clearly adapted and used for propaganda purposes; specialists from Beijing, Kunming, the local cultural office, and performing troupes went to the villages to document and learn from the traditions of the masses; and their dual task of giving professional direction to the people's spare-time musical activities and polishing local forms for stage performance realized Mao's dictum of the necessity to "raise standards." At the same time, the minority-centered issues enunciated by Lu

Dingyi in his speech at the 1964 festival of minority amateur performance were played out here. Songs that spread the central government's policy messages and expressed support for a unified China were encouraged, staged, published, and used during political movements; and Naxi art forms were given new respect—and indeed a regional and national stage—as cultural festivals proliferated.

A particularly profound effect was that on the status of professional and amateur music making. Before 1949 there were very few professional musicians living in Lijiang, and the few that did work there—such as the blind *suona* players who were engaged for weddings—were generally despised. Professional opera troupes certainly came through Lijiang, but none were based there. Suddenly, however, as in the rest of China, work as a professional musician or cultural cadre became desirable and highly sought after, since assignment to a state-sponsored work unit brought with it prestigious civil servant status, with the concomitant financial and social benefits and privileges.[13] Furthermore, it became evident that the government valued professional expertise highly, employing its specialist personnel to investigate and "raise standards" of grass-roots music making—which was thus simultaneously granted official respect as the artistic expression of the masses, and devalued as unpolished raw material to be spruced up for stage performance.

The advent of the scholars and of recording technology was also a theme common to many other areas of China.[14] For the first time in Lijiang, there were attempts at systematic documentation of the local musical culture, partially for academic purposes, but more often for practical objectives—the production of locally flavored propaganda, or the polishing and presentation of local material on the county, provincial, or, occasionally, national stage. Indeed, the emphasis on stage performance of often previously unstaged genres was a major new departure, and one presumably inspired in the main by the Soviet cultural model. For one folk genre at least, Baisha Xiyue, scholarly interest and professional staged performance almost certainly saved it from complete demise—even if the phoenix that rose from the ashes looked and sounded somewhat different from what it had been before. For the first time, cultural salvage had hit Lijiang.

A final area in which Lijiang shared in the general trends of the time was that of the decline of religious musics. The Dongjing tradition, of course, became entirely secularized soon after 1949, with both the ritual and the text-based performance forms disappearing from the scene. Likewise, the discouragement and diminution of Tibetan Buddhist, Chinese Buddhist, Taoist, *dongba* and *sainii* ceremonies entailed a reduction in the musics associated with them—although "*dongba* dance" at least was salvaged and sanitized for secular stage performance as a typical Naxi artistic form, just as *dongba* texts were eventually extracted from their ritual context and studied for their informational and cultural value (Chao 1996).

In general, the musical history of Lijiang during this period seems to have been fairly typical for the country as a whole: parallels in Han and other minority areas for the developments described here may be found throughout China. It may be valuable at this point to look at the effect of these national policies and trends on the one musical genre for which there is most evidence available, namely the Dongjing repertoire. The impact of political campaigns on Dongjing music during this period is clear: it became a totally nonritual, secular phenomenon, and much of the material culture associated with it was destroyed. Even for aficionados whose class background was "good," shifting ideological winds from time to time prevented even private playing of Dongjing music, and silenced it almost completely during the Cultural Revolution. However, the tradition of the music being played at government behest for public festivals was sporadically maintained, and the expansion under the new government in state-funded cultural research brought unexpected benefits, in the shape of the first ever serious scholarly interest in the tradition. It was a bonus for the musicians that recordings were made in the early 1960s, which are now preserved with great pride and held to be of tremendous historical and aesthetic value. The new trends ushered in by the change of government, therefore, caused the demise of the ritual branch of the Dongjing tradition and the temporary silencing of even its secular incarnation; but they nevertheless laid the groundwork for more positive developments in the years following the Cultural Revolution.

There is no doubt that national events and policies had an audible impact on Lijiang County's soundscape at this time; what is also significant is that, for the first time, Lijiang's sounds began to be heard in nonlocal settings. Thanks to the new government's enthusiasm for provincial and national festivals and cultural exchanges, Dongjing music, Baisha Xiyue, Naxi folk song, and Lijiang's own version of Dianju were performed between 1950 and 1966 in Kunming and Beijing. Recordings by Mao Jizeng and the Central Radio Station brought the sound of Dongjing music and Baisha Xiyue to the Beijing-based scholarly community, and to a wider general audience; and writings on Naxi musics began to appear in nationally distributed publications. Lijiang's music was in no way common currency in the rest of Yunnan or China by the Cultural Revolution, but the Naxi musical presence and character had been firmly established in the minds of the national musicological community, and had at least touched a wider audience through festivals and radio.

From the Death of Mao to the 1990s

Relatively little documentation is available on the effects of the Cultural Revolution on cultural life in Lijiang, but most residents agree that many forms of traditional music making went into temporary abeyance, while the nationally famous revolutionary model operas were disseminated in the county just as in the rest of the country. The late 1970s are generally depicted as a time of revival: the Lijiang Prefecture Dianju Troupe, for instance, was re-formed in 1979, and the prefectural and county song and dance troupes resumed normal activities at about this time. Amateur Dianju and Dongjing groups too re-emerged in the more relaxed atmosphere of the post-Mao era, and the modest revival of *dongba* ceremonies in remote areas allows their music to be heard again. Strictures against courtship music, such as love songs and the Jew's harp, also lessened after the Cultural Revolution, and many traditional Naxi dances flourish today both in the Lijiang basin and in remote mountainous areas. Nevertheless, some traditional Naxi musics such as the Jew's harp, folksinging, and the barley pipe are much less prevalent than they were before 1949, especially in the wealthier, low-lying areas. In the 1980s and early 1990s Dongjing music, which had been ubiquitous in the Lijiang basin, was also much attenuated; by 1991 it was played only by about ten scattered groups. People attributed this decline in traditional musics to two factors: the generational gap in transmission caused by the many political movements, especially the Cultural Revolution; and the fascination of youth in the 1980s and 1990s with television and pop music.

Indeed, what is remarkable about this most recent era is the speed at which outside cultural influences are reaching and being assimilated by the people of Lijiang. If it was political movements and central socialist cultural planning that exerted the greatest outside influence on Lijiang's music in the first thirty years of the People's Republic, it has been the open-door policy and technological advancement that have taken over as the imported cultural catalyst since then.[15]

The Media

The media explosion presaged by the introduction of radio, film, and television to Lijiang County in the first thirty years of the People's Republic has expanded its impact to an extraordinary degree since the late 1970s. By 1983 Dayan Town had two prefectural-level cinemas, with eleven more scattered throughout the county, and even the mountain-area townships had film projection teams (Lijiang Naxizu Zizhixian Gaikuang Bianxiezu 1986: 135). During my stays in Lijiang, the cinemas in Dayan Town brought popular nationally distributed films to the local public, allowing them to participate in national culture as frequently as they chose. Even more important was television: by 1988, 73 percent of the total population of the county had access to television, which provides county, provincial, and national programs (Tang and Jin 1988: 13). The programming not only encourages Chinese language acquisition among its viewers, it also serves up a steady diet of popular culture and commercial advertisements, bringing the economic reforms and the ubiquitous mainland, Taiwanese and Hong Kong popular music into people's homes.

Arguably as important as television is cassette culture. By the early 1990s when I lived in Dayan Town for several months, several shops in town did a brisk trade in music cassettes. Some of these were of Chinese opera, both local Yunnan forms such as Dianju and Huadeng, and nonlocal forms such as Peking Opera and Yueju from the Shanghai/Shaoxing area. A few were of Chinese instrumental genres, and a very small proportion of Western classical music. By far the most numerous were cassettes of Chinese-language popular songs from the mainland, Taiwan and Hong Kong: these sold like hotcakes among the urban youth. Chinese-made boom boxes also loomed in several electrical appliance shops, and were commonly bought as wedding presents (quite often complete with karaoke functions, fairy lights, and revolving plastic flowers). Domestically manufactured blank cassettes of poor quality were also sporadically available. In the villages I visited in the Lijiang basin, many rural homes had cassette players. Charles McKhann visited a number of very remote Naxi villages in 1996, including one located three days' walk from the nearest road, and reported seeing boom boxes everywhere. Cassette culture, it appears, is ubiquitous, and is in Lijiang to stay.[16]

Popular Music and Other Western-influenced Music

For the first-time visitor to Dayan Town in the 1990s, Han-language pop music may appear to be the dominant feature of the musical landscape. Since the beginning of China's "open door" policy in the late 1970s, many forms of Western-style popular culture have been enthusiastically embraced by young people throughout the country. Western-influenced Chinese-language pop songs by Taiwanese, Hong Kong, and mainland artists have proved particularly popular, both in discos, complete with flashing strobe lights and amplification systems, and on commercial cassettes. For a while in the early 1980s, the Taiwanese female pop star Deng Lijun was all the rage among urban youth; it was said that two Dengs ruled China, Deng Xiaoping by day, and Deng Lijun by night (Hooper 1985: 150–151). Since then many mainland stars have arisen, and several foreign stars have performed in China.[17]

In the run-up to the hundredth anniversary of Chairman Mao's birth (26 December 1993), one of the most popular commercial releases throughout China was the cassette set *Hong Taiyang* (Red Sun), which consists of jazzed-up "new rhythm" (*xin jiezou*) arrangements of revolutionary songs praising Mao and the Communist Party, all dating from the Cultural Revolution or the years immediately preceding it. The accompanying instruments are mainly Western, including drumset, studio strings, electric piano, and trumpets, although a few Chinese instrumental sounds are used for special effect. The harmony is conventional and rather saccharine, and the singing style is mostly typical of mainstream Chinese-style pop ballads: a fairly open, relaxed voice quality with a heavy vibrato used selectively for emotional effect. During the first half of 1992, these songs were phenomenally popular, even being piped over the loudspeakers in long-distance buses all over Yunnan Province. I remember vividly an excruciating eleven-hour journey during which the three cassettes were recycled without pause. One of the songs, *Beijing You Ge Jin Taiyang* (There is a Golden Sun in Beijing), was used in 1992 in a folk rock arrangement for a performance in Dayan Town honoring the fiftieth anniversary of Chairman Mao's "Talks at the Yan'an Conference on Literature and Art."

Lijiang County has received a considerable amount of Chinese pop song culture in the last few years. In the early 1990s, in addition to the ready availability of commercial pop cassettes in local shops, the No. 2 Guesthouse in Dayan Town held a live disco every night, which attracted a full house of young locals. Music was provided by an amplified band which featured female vocal, saxophone, trumpet, electric piano and drumset, and performed arrangements of Han Chinese pop songs. Another favorite pastime during 1992 in the county town was karaoke: facilities were provided in the youth activity center next to the No. 2 Guesthouse, where several nights a week young people, mostly men, belted out their renditions of the same songs. By 1996, pop cassettes had reached even remote mountainous Naxi villages. The enthusiasm of many young Naxi for this music was frequently cited by older people to explain the paucity of recruits for traditional music activities. In the mid-1990s, there were not as yet any Naxi-language pop songs, although by summer 1996 Tibetan-language commercial cassettes and Yi-language cassettes by the Sichuan-based group *Shanying* (Mountain Eagle) were sold alongside Han-language pop standards by street vendors in Dayan Town.

Other forms of Western and Western-influenced musics do exert some peripheral influence in Lijiang County. During my stay in Dayan Town I encountered two pianos, one privately owned and one in the youth activity center, although I saw neither being played. Dissemination of all kinds of Western music via cassettes, radio, and television does occur, even though few people take more than a passing interest and the supply is in any case limited. For instance, a Naxi friend who played in the professional Lijiang Naxi Autonomous County Song and Dance Troupe had heard Pavarotti once or twice on television, and asked me to find him some tapes of the opera singer when I went to Hong Kong in January 1992; he liked the music but could find no cassettes locally. Some schoolteachers include Western classical music along with Chinese traditional music and propaganda songs in their classes. The supply of foreign musics is constantly increasing—in summer 1998 I found an unprecedentedly eclectic display of foreign CDs and cassettes in Dayan Town's main bookstore, including Michael Bolton, Mike Oldfield, Noriko Sakai, the soundtrack to *Titanic*, L.A. Boyz, Mahler, Tchaikovsky, and Pablo Casals. Still, Chinese-language pop songs from the mainland, Taiwan, and Hong Kong are the most ubiquitous musical immigrants to Lijiang.

Song and Dance Troupes: Survival and Aesthetics

In the early 1980s, Dayan Town hosted not only the prefectural Dianju troupe, but also song and dance troupes at prefectural and county levels. The prefectural song and dance troupe, however, was abolished in 1985 to save money, although the county song and dance troupe and the prefectural Dianju troupe survived. At the end of 1992, a new organization, the Lijiang Prefecture Arts Troupe (*Lijiang Diqu Yishutuan*) was established, combining some members of the Lijiang Naxi Autonomous County Song and Dance Troupe, and almost all members of the Lijiang Prefecture Dianju Troupe. The Dianju Troupe no longer survives as an independent entity, although a somewhat reduced Lijiang Naxi Autonomous County Song and Dance Troupe continued in the late 1990s, despite the loss of many of its personnel to the new group.[18]

The mission and problems of Lijiang's professional performing troupes are typical of similar groups throughout China today. On the one hand, Lijiang Prefecture and Lijiang County require good-quality troupes to represent them at regional and occasionally national festivals; on the other, the state no longer subsidizes the arts as it used to. Several local people commented to me that the troupes lose money when they perform, and that with shrinking state subsidies they are no longer able to travel frequently to remote rural areas to entertain the peasants. Ironically, this inability to leave the urban center immediately negates one of the traditional raisons d'être of such troupes: to learn from and perform for the laboring masses. On the other hand, the prestige of maintaining a good troupe remains; and in 1996 the Lijiang Prefecture government sent about twenty young people to Kunming to train in ballet techniques for the Arts Troupe. Furthermore, the modern emphasis on seeking domestic and foreign investment has given new life to arts festivals, to which each region's professional troupes are expected to travel and advertise their locale. In western Yunnan, a regional arts festival rotates around the seven constituent prefectures every few years; in 1996 it was held in Baoshan, and Lijiang Prefecture sent its arts troupe, despite the recent destructive earthquake. Some festivals, such as the Third China Art Festival held in Kunming in 1992, are competitive, with groups from different regions vying to get their performances accepted: success brings not only kudos but also valuable visibility for an area. In addition, the new enthusiasm for enticing foreign and domestic tourists to scenic parts of Yunnan has given Lijiang's professional troupes a new outlet for their talents, as tourist concerts have proliferated since the late 1980s.[19] Lijiang's professional musicians, therefore, still serve their locale; but they do so through ever-increasing interactions with outsiders as well as through activities aimed at the local community. Economic reforms and the open-door policy rather than hardline ideological imperatives are helping determine their mission and fate.

The aesthetics of professional performance too tie Lijiang's musicians to a national cultural Weltanschauung, rather than to the local traditional musics from which they draw inspiration. Performances by the Lijiang Naxi Autonomous County Song and Dance Troupe as it existed in 1991 and early 1992 were typical of the cultural homogenization described for such groups in chapter 2. This was most immediately apparent linguistically. To render performances accessible to the widest possible range of audience members, the programs, announcements, and even most of the song words for the performances I attended were in Mandarin. Mandarin Chinese is of course both the national language and the lingua franca for minorities, who often do not understand each other's languages but have to learn Chinese in school. Use of Chinese was also necessary because the thirty-five or so troupe members included members of six ethnic groups, and some of the non-Naxi troupe members did not understand Naxi, while all the Naxi members spoke Chinese.

The troupe also employed the sort of national *musica franca* described above. In common with similar troupes all over the country, factory-issue Han Chinese and Western instruments were added to local instruments even in performance of "ethnic" items; compositions and arrangements of local folk music almost always employed simple European functional harmony foreign to all the traditional local musics; and some of the troupe members had trained at the Shanghai Conservatory of Music or the Yunnan Art Institute, and had thus introduced the polished mainstream Chinese conservatory style to Lijiang. Consequently, the troupe's style was marked by far less local color than that of the local traditional musicians from whom its arrangers borrowed (and who sometimes complained about the blandness of the resulting arrangements). The professional musicians formed part of a chain of state-supported arts troupes whose material is of eclectic provenance and whose performance aesthetic is molded at national level.

Within this aesthetic framework, the troupe strove both to eulogize the cultural assets of every group in Lijiang County, and to spread state propaganda. In a show put on for an audience of eighty Chinese tourists on 1 November 1991, for instance, there was a piece called "Spring-Summer-Autumn-Winter" (*Chun-Xia-Qiu-Dong*), which was announced as an arrangement from four similarly titled Dongjing pieces. This was played by several instruments, including some closely associated with Lijiang's Dongjing music, such as the distinctive Lijiang plucked lute *pipa*, the framed gong-set *yunluo*, and the plucked lute *sugudu*. However, the musicians additionally employed hammered dulcimer (*yangqin*) and shawm (*suona*), two Han Chinese instruments having no traditional relation to Lijiang's Dongjing music, as well as a Western cello. A singer and dancers were also introduced to what was originally purely instrumental music. The same program included a "Dance of the Lisu People," with a taped backing group of Western instruments; and the program for a concert on 21 September 1990 listed dances of the Naxi, Lisu, and Tibetan peoples. State propaganda was more prominent in a concert on 26 April 1990 for a local audience: it included newly composed songs honoring the Chinese Communist hero Lei Feng, and promoting the government birth control campaign.

The messages conveyed by this troupe were both backward- and forward-looking. In tune with longstanding policy toward minority culture, their staging of selections derived from the folk traditions of different minorities within Lijiang acknowledged the value of such grass-roots heritage; at the same time, their professionalization and stylistic homogenization of these items spoke to the desire articulated by Mao to "raise standards," which has been part of the professional cultural mandate since the 1950s. In time-honored fashion too, they were called upon to perform on the occasion of important government celebrations, and to convey propaganda messages in musical form. On the other hand, they were beginning to look outward for tourist audiences, and financial constraints prevented them from taking their shows on the road within the county as much as they would have done thirty years previously. How much influence they actually had on the aesthetic preferences of Lijiang's citizenry is hard to judge: despite their professional prestige, their performances were relatively infrequent (about once a month while I was there), audiences for concerts looked rather small, and some traditional folk musicians expressed a dislike of the lack of local flavor in their style.

Traditional Musics: A Partial Revival

In general, residents of Lijiang and Yunnanese musicologists repeat a version of the old saw: traditional Naxi songs and dances flourish in the 1990s in the mountainous townships of northwest and northeast Lijiang, while modern pop culture has taken over most successfully in the urban areas and wealthier lowland townships. Charles McKhann confirmed that during his travels in 1996 to mountainous Naxi regions, he encountered plenty of traditional Naxi music making, including work songs for agricultural activities, and singing and dancing at weddings and funerals. Dayan Town and the surrounding villages present a rather mixed picture. In the Lijiang basin area, I encountered several village teenagers who told me that they could not sing traditional folk songs, although their mothers were good singers. The same was true of performance on the Jew's harp. On the other hand, it was clear that traditional Naxi dances, especially those accompanied by flute, were flourishing and extremely popular: I often encountered them on local and national festival days, both in rural areas and in the square under the Mao statue in Dayan Town. This may be because the dance steps are easy to pick up, whereas mastery of folk song or the Jew's harp requires a longer apprenticeship which was denied to a whole generation through the political movements of the late 1950s and 1960s, and is unpalatable to teenagers accustomed to television and cassette culture.

Spare-time Dianju and Dongjing activities too have achieved a revival since the late 1970s. Dayan Town once again has a number of amateur Dianju groups which meet at members' houses to perform classics from the tradition, and by the early 1990s there were at least ten amateur Dongjing secular music groups in Lijiang County, most in Dayan Town and the surrounding valley, and the others in Lashi Township, Shigu Town, and Judian Township. At this time the sacred Dongjing tradition was completely defunct, although the secular groups often did what pre-1949 secular groups had done, playing for local funerals. The majority of their activities, however, were confined to private playing for secular enjoyment. As with many other traditional musics, the exponents tended to be middle-aged or elderly, and in 1991 musicologists and local aficionados feared that within a decade or so the music would die out entirely. (As chapter 7 shows, this has not in fact happened.)

In contrast to the apparent lack of local enthusiasm for learning local musics, the outside world has resumed its scholarly interest in folk traditions. Despite increasing problems with funding, local, provincial, and national researchers have returned to Lijiang in the 1980s and 1990s to document its musical heritage. Articles and anthologies have been published in Lijiang, Kunming, Shanghai and Beijing, and Lijiang and its Naxi inhabitants are once again firmly established in the canon of Chinese musicology. They achieve entries in the standard dictionary of Chinese music for both Baisha Xiyue and "*dongba* dance," as well as mention in the section on Dongjing music (Miao, Ji, and Guo 1985).

Furthermore, while older people frequently blame television and cassette technology for the paucity of local young recruits to traditional musics, it is these very factors that are bringing Lijiang's folk sounds to outside notice as never before. Lijiang is a beautiful area often featured on provincial and national television programs; between fall 1991 and summer 1992 Dongjing musicians were summoned from Dayan Town and Baihua Village three times to provide local music for camera crews. In addition, Chinese and foreign scholars who have arrived in the 1980s and 1990s have done so with Japanese tape recorders and video cameras in tow. Their high-quality audio and video recordings provide better documentation of folk traditions than was ever possible before, and some have been published by domestic and foreign companies.[20]

In general, therefore, the 1980s and 1990s have seen a noticeable increase in two-way interaction with the outside world. The wider world has come quite audibly to Lijiang, and Lijiang's sounds have begun to trickle out. The 1950s and 1960s introduced a regional and national dimension to the county's musical experience; the 1980s confirmed this trend, and the 1990s have broadened the arena of interaction to include an international audience. Though evidence of this can be found for several different genres, none has had such an impact, or traveled as far, as Lijiang's Dongjing music. Chapter 7 outlines the unexpected turn taken by the Dongjing revival since its shaky beginnings in the late 1970s and traces its widening trajectory of influence. Not only has this music become a major asset in Lijiang's dialogue with the wider world, its international dimension has also come full circle and fed directly back into the cultural life and outlook of the county.

7

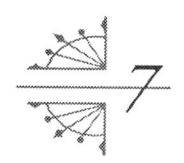

The Dongjing Music Revival

Have Music, Will Travel

Like many other forms of traditional music, Dongjing music began to experience a tentative revival at the end of the 1970s. Though this could not have occurred without the national political liberalization, the catalysts in the revival were the enthusiastic individuals who had the courage, imagination, and organizational skills to lead the way. At the same time, the tradition has experienced the same problems as its counterparts elsewhere in China—a mainly middle-aged and elderly population of aficionados, a shortage of young recruits, and financial limitations. Nevertheless, the groups still playing the music in the 1990s have solved some or all of these problems, so that there is once again a network of individual and group interaction conducted through the medium of Dongjing music in Lijiang County. Unlike before, however, this network of interaction now includes outsiders. Until the mid-1980s, Lijiang's Dongjing music retained its primarily local significance, with occasional recognition at the regional or national level; by the late 1990s, it had achieved international fame, helping focus outside attention on Lijiang County as never before. This chapter documents the means by which this transformation was achieved; it also examines the ways in which Dongjing music has once again become an active force in Lijiang society, and has indeed come to have a tangible as well as audible impact on its environment.[1]

The Beginning of the Revival

Initial Steps

The revival of Lijiang's Dongjing music began in a modest way, and one replicated throughout hundreds of other counties in China. A few individuals read the signs of political liberalization correctly, and got together again to play their music. The story of how the revival came about is still very much made up of "historical gossip" and "personal traditions" (Vansina 1985: 17): the individuals I interviewed often reminisced with pride and amusement about how they encouraged their friends to take part, and thought up ways around problems. Individual initiative was extremely important in getting the revival off the ground.

The initial revival of Dongjing music in Lijiang County is usually dated to around 1977 or 1978. He Minda (born 1945) from Baihua Village remembers playing an old tape of the music around that time; the older musicians were initially apprehensive, but eventually came together to play again. In 1979, the Huangshan Commune Ancient Music Orchestra (*Huangshan Gongshe Guyuedui*) was established, including under its aegis former members of the Dongjing associations of Lasha and Baima; it ran for two or three years, but the distance between the two sites was too great for elderly musicians to travel, so it soon split into two different ensembles, one centered on Baihua Village, with mostly Baima members, and the other on Changshui Village, with mostly Lasha members. The first orchestra head was He Xidian, the famous Baisha Xiyue musician much admired for his musical skills and poor peasant background; his reputation and good background helped lend the music social credibility.

In Dayan Town, Yang Houkun, then in his mid-thirties, helped organize a group of five or six musicians in 1977. "At first," he said, "some old comrades didn't dare come, so we did a lot of work on their thinking" (*sixiang gongzuo*). By 1983, the local government began to invite the ensemble to play again in the park on festival days. Even so, some ex-members of the Dayan Town Dongjing association were initially reluctant to join. He Yi'an, one of the most skilled surviving musicians, did not join of his own accord because he was afraid that people might criticize him as a former "landlord" for daring to play publicly. However, in 1985 he was invited to take part, and gladly did so (Track 1996: 106–107).

In Shigu, musicians began to meet again around 1980 to play, "when we heard that Dayan [Town] had done so." Musicians from Baisha and Shuhe had also begun to play again by about 1980, although there were so few left in each group that Li Baozhang of Shuhe put up a notice in Baisha announcing that the Shuhe musicians would play in Baisha and welcoming any Baisha musicians to join in. Eventually the two groups, situated very close to each other, amalgamated.

In the late 1980s and early 1990s, about ten music groups playing the Dongjing association repertoire were known to be active in different parts of Lijiang County. These included ensembles in Dayan Town, Baihua Village, Jinshan Township, Baisha Township, Changshui Village, Lashi Township, Shigu Town, and Judian Township. Not all such groups successfully maintained a revival, however: by 1991 ensembles in two villages near Dayan Town and in Longpan Township were no longer active, because too many members had died. As of 1991, only two musicians survived in Ludian (Yang Zenglie 1991: 38). Occasionally new ensembles started up: by summer 1993, a group at Xiangyun Village just south of Dayan Town had begun to get together.

One of the most pressing problems of the newly revived Dongjing music groups in the late 1970s and 1980s was the accumulation of sufficient instruments to play again. Some people had hidden their instruments during the Cultural Revolution, and could now retrieve and repair them; others knew how to make the bowed and plucked lutes, and were thus able to replace items lost; and a few instruments were bought from national and provincial factories. It was often hardest to reacquire the full complement of percussion instruments, since many of these were not routine factory issue. The Dayan Town ensemble members managed to buy their bell and some cymbals on the street and at fairs, from itinerant traders; the purchase of the set of large *nao* and *bo* cymbals was funded by a gift from Yang Dan'gui (Mrs. Rita Lou), an overseas Naxi resident in California. Since none of the revived ensembles aimed at reestablishing a ritual Dongjing association, unlike groups in other counties they did not need to replace the many lost scriptures and ritual implements. Nevertheless, the re-acquisition of instruments alone required time, money and ingenuity; and even after this problem was solved, a far bigger one remained: the paucity of recruits to keep the tradition going.

The Graying Population of Musicians in the 1980s

In 1987–1988 a survey of seven of the active groups (those in Dayan Town, Baihua Village, Jinshan Township, Baisha Township, Changshui Village, Lashi Township, and Shigu Town) was undertaken to determine the age distribution of participants. Altogether one hundred and twenty-four musicians spread among the seven groups were included in the survey. The results were as follows:

80 or over:	8 men (6.4%)
70–79:	41 men (33%)
60–69:	24 men (20%)
50–59:	19 men (15.6%)
40–49:	13 men (10.5%)
30–39:	15 men (12%)
20–29:	4 men (3.2%)
under 20:	0 men/women (0%)

(Yang Zenglie 1991: 36)

This survey clearly indicated the preponderance of elderly participants in groups playing Dongjing music: almost sixty percent were aged sixty or over in 1987–1988, and only about a quarter were under fifty years of age. This was not unexpected, given the sporadic nature of the music making between 1949 and 1966, and the total hiatus between 1966 and 1977, but it raised serious doubts about the ability of the musical tradition to endure when the pre–Cultural Revolution generation had died off. To take the Jinshan ensemble as an example, a list of active participants compiled by several of us who visited the group on 21 October 1991 revealed a thriving group of twenty-four members. However, seven were in their seventies, eleven in their mid to late sixties (64–69), and only three in their early sixties and two in their fifties (one person did not give his age). Only five were pointed out as having learned the repertoire since the revival began. In Changshui in 1992, of thirteen regular participants, two were over eighty, three under sixty, and the rest between sixty and eighty. The situation in the Baihua group was similar: He Minda supplied me with a list of twenty-two members as of 7 November 1991, of whom fifteen were sixty-five or over. The other seven included three in their fifties, three in their forties, and one man aged thirty-nine. Altogether only eight had learned the music since 1978. By summer 1993, four of those aged seventy or over had died. In the early 1990s musicians in Jinshan and Baihua often complained to me that young people were too busy to take the time to learn the demanding repertoire, and were in any case more interested in pop music.

On the other hand, the Shigu group reported a few young recruits at that time, including one or two in their twenties and one aged eighteen. The Dayan Town ensemble was also quite successful in recruiting younger members: a memorandum to the county government from 1992 lists twenty-two members, of whom six were eighty or over, two in their seventies, six in their sixties, and three in their fifties; the other five were ages forty-six, thirty-nine, thirty-nine, twenty-nine, and twenty-six (Dayan Guyuehui 1992: 1–2). A "student member" (*xueyuan*) was in his thirties. By late 1992 two more student members had begun playing with the group on a regular basis, both teenagers (one of whom, Huang Limei, was the first female participant in the entire county). In the tradition of the Dongjing associations of old, four of the seven participants under forty years of age were the children or children-in-law of older members. The Dayan Town ensemble did actively seek out young people by organizing a summer holiday training class, first held in 1989 (Dayan Guyuehui 1992: 3–4). Although very few such students had the time and dedication to master the entire repertoire and become ensemble members, they did at least gain a greater appreciation for the music. Overall, however, by the early 1990s the prospects for long-term survival of Lijiang's Dongjing music looked somewhat bleak.

Activities of Dongjing Music Groups in the 1980s and 1990s

The range of activities undertaken by the revived music groups, though somewhat different from before 1949, nevertheless remains quite broad. Probably the commonest scenario is the informal gathering at a member's house for an afternoon's or a day's playing. Until 1996 the Baihua Village ensemble met every Sunday afternoon at the house of its leader He Guowei to play through all the instrumental pieces and most of the accompanied songs, now with some scriptural words reinstated; people started arriving at 11:30 A.M., took a break for a simple lunch of noodles at about 2:00, and departed around 4:30. After a two-year hiatus caused partly by several deaths, the group met again in 1998, and expressed the hope that the meetings would continue as before. These Sunday afternoon gatherings are a purely recreational activity. In the early 1990s the Jinshan and Dayan Town groups each met once a month, rotating round the members' houses, playing for the day and breaking for an elaborate lunch (Figure 7.1). The Changshui ensemble also met once or twice a month for informal playing. The Shigu group met irregularly to play for private entertainment, as did the Baisha ensemble.

Informal recreational playing is, however, not the only activity: with the government's relaxation of controls on funerals,[2] most groups also play for the funerals of their members or members' relatives. I attended a funeral on 17 May 1992 at the village of Xia Shuhe, about ten kilometers south of Dayan Town, to which the Baihua Village ensemble was invited. The ensemble played accompanied songs (*dadiao*), without words, and instrumental pieces (*xiaodiao*) in a random order throughout the afternoon, as guests ate lunch and relatives knelt in turn before the coffin to pay their last respects to the deceased. After the deceased's

FIGURE 7.1. Jinshan Ancient Music Orchestra at a Sunday gathering, November 1991.

sons, sitting on mats in front of the coffin, had eaten "the last meal with the deceased person," an elderly ensemble member recited a memorial screed, partly in Naxi and partly in Chinese, and led the sons in making their final offerings. After this, the coffin was carried out into the courtyard, over the kneeling relatives and up the hill toward the graveyard. As it left the house the ensemble played "Wind on the River" (*Yi Jiang Feng*), the instrumental piece used in Dongjing association ritual for sending off the god (*songshen*). One of the men accompanying the coffin as it disappeared at a rapid pace up the hill carried a large cassette recorder with him, on which one could hear a tape of Lijiang Dongjing music blasting out. Four weeks later the ensemble was invited back to provide incidental music at the *siqi* memorial gathering.

The music groups of Shigu and Judian attend funerals and march along in front of the coffin, playing their instruments as it is carried to the graveyard; apparently a fashion was started in Judian by a local resident who invited the ensemble to play at his mother's funeral, after which many more such invitations were extended. The Dayan Town, Changshui, and Baisha groups also mentioned playing at funerals. However, in all cases the music is an incidental, dispensable part of the ritual: the revived groups no longer perform the *Classic of the Twenty-Four Exemplars of Filial Piety*, providing instead background music that fills in time or accompanies actions.

As before 1949, music groups occasionally assemble to play at the birthday celebrations of an elderly person; the Dayan Town group did so for the seventieth birthday of Yang Dan'gui, an overseas Naxi who has been a generous benefactor. The Baihua Village group similarly took part in a seventieth birthday celebration. At such events, there is no set order of pieces: the music is for entertainment, and any piece, especially those with auspicious names such as "Good Fortune" (*Jixiang*) and "Eight Trigrams" (*Bagua*), may be played. On such occasions "Small White Plum Blossom" (*Xiao Bai Mei*) is most emphatically not used, because of its exclusive connotation with funerals.

A further context for the music that harks back to pre-1949 days is the performance at government request. On New Year's Day 1992, for instance, the Dayan Town group performed in the park at government invitation; it also provides entertainment for visiting dignitaries when requested by the county government. Most spectacularly, a music ensemble composed in part of Dayan Town musicians and in part of members of the Lijiang County Song and Dance Troupe was sent by the county government to participate in the "Hundred Marvels of China" exhibition (*Zhongguo baijue bolanhui*) held in Canton over the winter of 1991–1992. Lijiang was asked to send an exhibition of "artwork" of the renowned *dongba*, whose unusual pictographic writing and distinctively beautiful religious paintings are still the Lijiang Naxis' main claim to fame in the eyes of the rest of China. The performing troupe sent with this exhibition as the "Dongba Culture Performance Troupe" (*Dongba Wenhua Yishu Zhanyantuan*) played largely

Dongjing music, along with some Baisha Xiyue and one or two indigenous Naxi dances. According to the disciplinary regulations for the troupe, the stated mission was "to represent Lijiang, to represent the Naxi nationality." The implication that this music would help the *dongba* exhibition to represent the Lijiang Naxi to the outside world was a little startling, given the well-known and frequently acknowledged Han Chinese derivation of the Dongjing tradition and its music. However, as I shall demonstrate in chapter 8, there is an increasing tendency nowadays on the part of local and nonlocal cultural promoters to present this musical repertoire as part of Naxi cultural heritage, even though the nonlocal origins are acknowledged.

Some of today's contexts for the music are quite innovative; for instance, the Baihua Village group played for the wedding of their leader's son. Before 1949 it was unheard of for the music to be used at a wedding; indeed, it was strongly associated with funerals. However, one member of the Dayan Town group also mentioned this new use of the music—"to detain the guests until dinner!" Most innovative of all, however, was an initiative taken in 1988 by the Dayan Town group to explore a new audience for this old music: the recently arrived foreign tourists who were beginning to discover the beauty of Lijiang's natural scenery and unspoiled nineteenth-century architecture, and the allure of its unusual minority inhabitants.

The Tourist Concerts

Foreigners in Lijiang

Despite Lijiang's isolation, and the length and danger of the journey up from Kunming before 1949, the county did feature on the itinerary of several foreign visitors in the late Qing and Republican eras. A few foreign nationals settled there for long periods; these included several missionaries, the well-known Austrian-American botanist and *dongba* scholar Joseph Rock, and a Russian employee of the Chinese government, Peter Goullart. Several other foreigners passed through on their travels and left accounts of varying degrees of detail.[3] Rock, Goullart, and the missionaries were forced to leave shortly after Lijiang came under Communist rule in 1949, and thereafter Lijiang was closed to foreigners until the 1980s.

However, in 1978 the Third Plenary Session of the Eleventh Chinese Communist Party Central Committee set in motion the economic reconstruction that has characterized the post-Mao era, and one of the spin-offs of this momentous event has been a new emphasis on encouraging foreign tourism—even in places as remote as Lijiang. Fewer than a quarter of a million foreigners visited China in 1978; the million mark was breached in 1984, and by 1993 foreign tourist arrivals had reached four and a half million. Visits by Hong Kong and Macao Chinese (classified separately from other foreign nationals) grew even more during the same period, from one and a half million in 1978 to nearly thirty-four million in 1992. Since 1987, Taiwanese tourists too have added to the numbers, reaching the one million mark in 1992. Foreign exchange earnings from all these visitors averaged a 20 percent annual increase over this period, reaching almost US $4 billion in 1992 (Zhang Guangrui 1995: 4–5). Poorer and peripheral provinces as well as the best-known sites of eastern and central China compete to attract tourists. In the northwest, Xinjiang promotes its connection with the Silk Road, its spectacular natural landscape, and its diverse Moslem ethnic minorities; these attractions netted 134,100 international visitors in 1991, up from 5,586 in 1981 (Toops 1995: 181–184). In the southwest, tourist development in chronically poor Guizhou has focused on the spectacular karst landscape and the cultural attractions of the many minority groups that make up more than one-third of the province's population. By 1994, at least twenty officially recognized ethnic tourist villages had been established there to help cater for growing tourist numbers, among which the international arrivals had leaped from thirty-seven thousand in 1991 to seventy-six thousand in 1992, and a hundred thousand in 1993 (Oakes 1995: 209–215).

The government of Yunnan Province too has jumped on the national bandwagon in attempting to attract foreign tourists, and has done so with increasing success. Foreign exchange income generated by tourism stood at only U.S. $1.75 million in 1980, but in the 1990s rose to $16.43 million in 1990, $63.79 million in 1991, $67.51 million in 1992, and more than $220 million in 1996 (Swain 1995: 223–224; *Yunnan Nianjian* 1997: 253). Like their counterparts in Xinjiang and Guizhou, the Yunnan authorities have homed in on two particular star attractions which are romanticized to appeal to travelers: the magnificent natural scenery, and the "exotic" ethnic minorities with their curious customs and costumes, who in 1996 made up about a third of the total population of forty million. The provincial government tells us:

> When you come to the highland of Yunnan . . . you will be presented with the wonders in all their majesty: the lofty mountains covered with snow, roaring flows of rivers, precipitous gorges, boundless plains, immense stretches of primitive forests and serene highland lakes . . . while other places present you a spectacular scenery of subtropical zone. . . .
>
> When you come to the highland of Yunnan, you will be interested in a variety of traditions and customs of various nationalities. . . . They still keep their own unique cultures and traditions. There are residential buildings of different styles, costumes and ornaments with a variety of colors and fashions, traditional ways and practices of different features, festivals and rites. There are also folk music and dance and beautiful legends. (Yunnan Sheng Renmin Zhengfu Waishi Ban'gongshi, n.d.: 2)

Foreign-authored travel guides see similar attractions: "Tucked between Tibet and the exotic lands of Southeast Asia, Yunnan Province is one of the least known and most beguiling regions of China. A mountainous wonderland, it is home to 24 diverse, colorful ethnic cultures. With a name meaning 'South of the Clouds,' Yunnan boasts sparkling blue skies, red earth, and green forests" (back cover of Booz 1989).

Given the undoubted success of these twin images in selling Yunnan to the outside world, it should come as no surprise that Lijiang has become one of the top tourist destinations within the province since the county was formally declared "open" in July 1985. With the spectacular scenery of the Jade Dragon Snow Mountain (*Yulong Xueshan*), the pretty canals and traditional wooden architecture of Dayan Town, and the very visible ethnic diversity on display, Lijiang has all it takes to attract adventurous tourists who wish to see more in China than the Great Wall and the terracotta warriors. English-language tour books focus on Lijiang, along with Kunming, Dali, Xishuangbanna, and Ruili, as a destination not to miss in Yunnan (e.g., Booz 1989, Cummings et al. 1991). By the late 1980s and early 1990s the public buses from Kunming, Dali, and Dukou (in Sichuan Province) disgorged dozens of young and middle-aged foreign backpackers every day. In those days there was always an element of adventure about going to Lijiang, because the county was accessible from Kunming only by an uncomfortable twenty-hour bus ride, past magnificent mountainous scenery and hairpin bends that took the breath away. An air connection was instituted in 1995, as a result of which older and less fit visitors were more numerous by the time I went back in summer 1996. Whereas in 1985 only 435 foreigners visited Lijiang, by the end of 1996 the cumulative figure had risen to over three hundred thousand, from more than sixty countries (Kou Zhengling 1996: 18). Chinese tourists from outside Yunnan seem to have discovered Lijiang around the mid-1990s; they were relatively few in number in the early 1990s, but by summer 1998 constituted the vast majority of visitors traveling for pleasure. Several million domestic visits had been made by late 1996 (Kou Zhengling 1996: 18), and numbers have skyrocketed since Dayan Town was placed on the UNESCO World Heritage List in 1997.

Lijiang County has even acquired a small number of more long-term foreign residents. A few foreigners have taught at local colleges, and several of us have spent months at a time conducting research. Four English-language dissertations from U.S. universities appeared within four consecutive years (McKhann 1992; White 1993; Rees 1994; Chao 1995), as well as other publications based on local fieldwork (e.g., Mueggler 1991; Track 1996). The scholarly world outside China has once again had Lijiang brought to its notice, in a continuation of the tradition initiated by Joseph Rock. A more popular audience, too, has been initiated into the splendors of the county, through the television and video documentary *China: Beyond the Clouds*, filmed in the 1990s by a British filmmaker, and by popular articles (e.g., Edwards 1997).

As with many other parts of the world, one of the most noticeable features about heavily touristed parts of China is the plethora of handicraft and performing arts services that have sprung up to cater to the visitors. Among Han areas, concerts are deliberately crafted to attract international tourists in Shanghai, Xi'an, and Chaozhou (Lau 1998), and performances of the Confucian sacrifice are adapted for tourists in Qufu, Shandong (Lam 1995). Among minority areas, state-run and private handicraft production aimed at the tourist trade have been documented for Xinjiang, Guizhou, and for the Sani people in Yunnan (Toops 1993, Oakes 1995, Swain 1995). In Xinjiang, the state-run Kashgar Song and Dance Troupe directs many of its performances at visitors (Mackerras 1996: 197). Similarly, in April 1989 I encountered specially organized performances for foreign and domestic tourists by young Sani villagers at the Shilin Hotel in Yunnan's Stone Forest.

Quite sensibly, the Lijiang County government and private entrepreneurs have cashed in on the evident foreign enthusiasm for minority handicrafts and arts by exploiting the most picturesque aspects of Naxi culture. Emily Chao has argued persuasively that the Lijiang government and Naxi scholars have sanitized the *dongba* religious tradition into a text- and art-based "*dongba* culture" (*dongba wenhua*), which is validated by the state-supported Dongba Culture Research Institute in Dayan Town. Shorn of its more embarrassing ritual elements, "*dongba* culture" has been invented as the core of Naxi heritage, and is now exploited by locals and nonlocals alike in the tourist market economy. As you walk along the streets of Dayan Town, you can get a chop made with your name in *dongba* pictographs; state and private shops sell paintings based on *dongba* pictographs and religious icons; and one or two local residents operate a sporadic black market in genuine *dongba* ritual texts, alledgedly from before 1949, which they sell for large sums to anyone willing to pay. Chao vividly illustrates the extremes to which the craze for "*dongba* culture" has led:

> Dongba art now sold in Lijiang is virtually anything that incorporates Naxi pictographs. Many merchants and creators of dongba art are Han Chinese or of the neighboring Bai minority. These artists and merchants do not identify themselves as Naxi, and they promote dongba culture solely for commercial purposes. While in Lijiang, I met art students from Shanghai who—aware of the foreign interest in dongba texts—had traveled across the country to the institute to copy pictographs and mass-produce them on T-shirts to sell to foreign tourists. The dongbas at the institute complain that dongba characters that appear on new commercial products of "dongba culture" are incorrectly written and make no sense, but such errors have hardly deterred their marketability. In Kunming, Naxi artists who incorporate Naxi pictographs into their otherwise modernist paintings are marketed as part of the array of "contemporary dongba culture" (*xiandai dongba wenhua*). (1996: 228)

"*Dongba* culture" may be the most visible local product exploited in the tourist trade, but it is hardly the only one. Another part of Naxi heritage frequently used for the same purpose is the sheepskin cape worn by women in the fields, and by older women even in Dayan Town. This is a heavy piece of sheepskin, decorated across the top with brightly colored discs said to represent the heavenly bodies, which cushions the body while its owner carries a heavy basket on her back. Young female employees in the tourist hotels may often be seen wearing a lighter, synthetic-looking version of this cape, rather similar to the costume worn by female members of the county song and dance troupe in Naxi numbers. Postcards that feature Naxi women invariably show them dressed in their capes; and individual leather workers in Dayan Town do a brisk trade with foreign tourists buying souvenirs, as well as with local customers purchasing their daily apparel.

Music, too, is marketed to the visitors, as is the case in many other parts of China. During my stay in Lijiang between 1991 and 1992, both the county song and dance troupe and the Dianju Troupe tried their hand at concerts for domestic and foreign tourists. However, their attempts were entirely eclipsed by the extraordinary success of a determined set of amateur Dongjing musicians, the Dayan Ancient Music Association (*Dayan Guyuehui*).

Organization of the Tourist Concerts

By 1988, Lijiang had been open to foreign visitors for three years, and the revived Dongjing music groups had been in action for approximately ten years. Occasionally visitors and the musicians would cross paths: a tourist might come across one of the playing sessions as the music floated out from a private courtyard, or was performed on a festival day in the local park; or he or she might perhaps run into one of the musicians in the street or at his shop. Those visitors who did encounter the music gave every appearance of liking it; and it occurred to some of the musicians that concerts specifically aimed at such an audience could be quite successful. Moreover, the Dongjing music ensemble of Dayan Town had an unusual advantage over other groups, amateur or professional: one of their number had been educated by missionaries and spoke fluent English. Under the circumstances, it made perfect sense for the group to apply for the necessary permissions from the governments of Lijiang Prefecture, Lijiang County, and Dayan Town to give concerts primarily aimed at foreign visitors. In July 1988 they were given leave to go ahead. The price of admission was set with the permission of the local Price Commission at 4 *yuan*, later raised to 5 *yuan* (4 *yuan* was worth a little less than U.S. $1.00). The concerts at this time were held in a picturesque old mansion in the old part of town, which housed the Dayan Town Cultural Office (*wenhua zhan*).

In these performances, the mainly elderly musicians of the Dayan Ancient Music Association (*Dayan Guyuehui*) played several Dongjing pieces, interspersed with English-language commentary from their English-speaking leader, Xuan Ke. This formula proved extremely popular with the foreign and Hong Kong tourists who initially made up most of the audience. The first concert took place on 22 July 1988. By 30 March 1992, 339 performances had been given, or about three a fortnight on average, and the total audience had reached 8,705 people from more than thirty countries (Dayan Guyuehui 1992: 5). Such was the growth in Lijiang's popularity with backpackers, and the renown of the music, that by early 1993 attendance had climbed to 13,213 people from fifty-two countries (Li and Yin 1993: 27). By summer 1993, the ensemble was performing every other evening, each time to an audience of at least thirty; by summer 1996, the concerts were nightly and drew crowds of fifty or more; by summer 1998, these had swelled to two hundred or three hundred per night. The first time I saw substantial numbers of mainland Chinese tourists in the audience was in 1996; many of them were on holiday, or traveling on business, from the newly wealthy city of Canton. Ticket prices have risen steadily, reaching 35 *yuan*, or around U.S. $4.25, in July 1998.

Thanks at least in part to its outstanding success with tourist concerts at home, the Dayan Ancient Music Association has since the late 1980s been featured many times on local, provincial, national, and foreign television, and in dozens of Chinese-language newspaper articles. The music is mentioned in numerous tour guides, both Chinese- and foreign-authored, including books from the well-known Lonely Planet, Fodor, and Rough Guide series, and in magazine features; and since the mid-1990s it has also achieved notice in English-language newspapers such as the *Times*, the *Daily Telegraph*, and the *Financial Times* in Britain; the *Straits Times* in Singapore; the *South China Morning Post* in Hong Kong; the *China Daily* in China; and the *New York Times* and *Los Angeles Times* in the United States. By fall 1998 information on the Dayan Ancient Music Association and their music was available on the Internet.[4]

When I carried out my major fieldwork in the early 1990s, many foreign tourists told me that one of their main reasons for visiting Lijiang was to catch a concert by the elderly musicians; and the same was true when I went back to Lijiang in 1996. The admiration and liking felt by thousands of visitors for Lijiang's Dongjing music were almost palpable at the dozens of concerts I attended; and this enthusiasm was generated by the ambiance skillfully created by Xuan Ke and the other performers. Uniquely among the tourist-oriented concerts I have seen in China, the Dayan Ancient Music Association gauged its particular audience brilliantly, selecting just the right combination of tradition and showmanship to keep guests coming back.

Aesthetics and Ambiance of the Tourist Concerts

This brings me full circle to my own first encounter with Lijiang's Dongjing music, in May 1989. Both the visual and the aural impression were of a romantic timelessness, somehow disconnected from the frustrations of the environment.

The concerts were held in a picturesque, if slightly dilapidated, old mansion, situated in a winding alley in the beautiful old part of Dayan Town; the electric lighting was dim, flowers grew in the courtyard, and bats flew overhead. The musicians were mostly men in their sixties and over, of whom some of the eldest had long white beards; they arrived in groups of two or three in an unhurried fashion, and took their time chatting to friends and selecting their instruments. This initial visual impression was confirmed by the formal part of the proceedings. Xuan Ke stood up and addressed the usually entirely foreign audience in fluent English. He introduced the history of the music, emphasizing the age and unchanging continuity of the musical tradition, instruments and musicians, and traced the origins of the repertoire to "temple music" of central China, now preserved in remote Lijiang. He also emphasized the "Naxi spirit" of the music, and the Naxi ethnicity of the players, introduced individual musicians of special longevity and distinction, and announced the pieces to be played. At each concert the audience was treated to a solemn rendition of several four- to eight-minute pieces of music, all in moderate tempo, and all played without any attempt at obvious virtuosity, dynamic differentiation, or even facial expression on the part of the musicians. Delicate heterophony prevailed, with no hint of the Western chords, equal temperament, and showy virtuosity that are ubiquitous in professional song and dance troupe or orchestral performances in China.

Furthermore, Xuan Ke was a charismatic speaker who read his audience well. He skillfully enhanced the atmosphere of romantic timelessness by his emphasis on history, on the remoteness of Lijiang and its Naxi inhabitants, and on the unbroken transmission of the music from the mists of time. He also pointed up the minority ethnicity of the players, and identified specifically Naxi elements in the music—particularly the four-string plucked lute *sugudu*, the double-reed pipe *bobo*, and the slow, wide vibrato used by flutes and high-pitched bowed lutes on long notes. He advertised the music widely as "traditional Naxi music," capitalizing on the foreign interest in minority culture as well as in history.

In addition, Xuan deified the oldest member of the ensemble, the incredibly photogenic He Yi'an, referring to him constantly as "our teacher," and calling on him at the end of concerts to confer a Naxi-language benediction on the audience. He Yi'an, with his elegant white beard and mustache, his dignified bearing, and his genuinely encyclopedic knowledge of Dongjing music and tradition, rose to the occasion magnificently, looking every inch the enigmatic sage. So well did he cultivate this image, indeed, that photographs of him grace the covers of a Dutch magazine (issue 148 of *Bres*, 1991), his own autobiography (Track 1996), two commercial cassettes issued in Yunnan (both volumes of *Naxi Guyue/Nakhi Music*), and the British-issued CD *Naxi Music from Lijiang*. Just as individuals were crucial to the spread of the Dongjing music tradition in the Republican era and in its revival in the late 1970s, Xuan Ke and He Yi'an became personally vital to its successful market dissemination ten years later.

Furthermore, Xuan had the inspiration to invoke the authority of the Russian author Goullart to authenticate the romantic atmosphere he and his group sought to create. In most audiences in the late 1980s and early 1990s, some members had prepared for their trip by searching out English-language travel literature on Yunnan, and at least one or two would have included Goullart's attractively written account of 1940s Lijiang in their reading. Xuan would often ask a native English speaker in the audience (preferably one with a resonant voice who was already familiar with the book) to read aloud a couple of paragraphs from Xuan's own copy. For those unfamiliar with Chinese culture, Goullart's description of the music from fifty years previously had an immediacy that made the strange setting intelligible. It also had enough in common with the concert scene to strike a familiar chord, and displayed an eloquent nostalgia for premodern times:

> The old musicians, all formally dressed in long gowns and . . . [jackets], took their seats unhurriedly, caressing their long white beards. . . . [The music] was majestic and inspiring and proceeded in rising and falling cadences. Then, as a climax, the great gong was struck. I have never heard in China such a deep and sonorous gong: the whole house seemed to vibrate with its velvety waves. Then, rising from their chairs, the elders sang a sacred ode in a natural voice and with great reverence and feeling. . . . It was a recital of the cosmic life as it was unfolding in its grandeur, unmarred by the discordant wails and crashes of petty human existence. It was classical, and timeless. It was the music of the gods and of a place where there is serenity, eternal peace and harmony. . . . Let us hope that this treasure of music in Lijiang may be secure from the ravages of the modern age. (Goullart 1957: 216–217)

The description of formal dress in long gowns became even more relevant by the early 1990s, when the Dayan Ancient Music Association had earned enough from its concerts to purchase a set of *shanzi magua* (literatus gowns and jackets) for members to wear. These had been the costume de rigeur of the Dongjing associations before 1949, and lent an even greater historicism and dignity to the proceedings than the Mao jackets and other everyday wear had done in 1989. By 1992 there was also greater emphasis on decorating the playing area with some suggestive ritual symbols, including the Eight Trigrams and, eventually, a portrait of Wenchang (see Figure 4.7). Increasingly, therefore, the tourist concerts borrowed from the solemn ritual ambiance of the former Dongjing associations—even though the entirely secular emphasis of the revived Dongjing music ensembles was far more reminiscent of the pre-1949 secular groups (Rees 1998).

In sum, the music as played at tourist concerts in the late 1980s and early 1990s clearly eschewed nonnative instruments and performing techniques; the elderly musicians played with a dignified mien, taking no apparent heed of their audience; and the location was picturesque, offering a welcome relief from the concrete and plastic otherwise so ubiquitous in China. Foreign tourists almost universally expressed their delight at the performance, cheerfully paying the ticket fee in the intermission. They expressed a genuine enthusiasm for the music, which, like related "silk and bamboo" (*sizhu*) genres in southeast China, is relatively accessible to Western ears. More than this, however, they were greatly impressed by the dignified elderly musicians, by their clear determination to keep up a longstanding artistic tradition in the face of a modernizing world (a fact emphasized by Xuan Ke in his English-language commentary), and by the fact that no obvious musical concessions were made to the presence of foreign visitors. Words used by tourists to describe this music included "traditional," "genuine," "the real thing," and "authentic."

Why have the tourist concerts been so spectacularly successful? And how have these patently commercial performances convinced the foreign audience that they are "traditional," "genuine," "authentic," and so on? As is clear from earlier chapters, Lijiang's Dongjing music was never staged for concerts before 1988—the "traditional" context was usually a ritual one, or that of informal get-togethers where the musicians played for their own pleasure, taking little interest in how bystanders might view their activities. In practice, the music sound as well as the context has altered since 1988: constant performance by the Dayan Town group of the few most tuneful Dongjing pieces has resulted in a more polished ensemble than is evident in the villages, and, ironically, in the impoverishment of repertoire actively remembered by most of the urban players. What is implied by tourists' invocation of the term "authentic" is that the performances, and Xuan Ke's interpretation of the music, are "credible and convincing," and thus "duly authorized" as culturally valid—by Xuan's commentary, by the silent but imposing elderly musicians, and by Goullart's richly evocative account (Bruner 1994: 399–400; Rees 1998).

Why do foreigners find the tourist concerts "credible and convincing"? I suggest it is because of the constant comparisons they make with other such performances attended in China. Most foreigners I interviewed expressed weariness with the usual tourist shows promoted by Chinese hotels and tour operators. I experienced a typical such show during a visit in April 1989 to the Stone Forest in Lu'nan County, near Kunming. I was quite surprised that the young Sani performers at the Shilin Hotel substituted electric organ and some obviously Han Chinese instruments for traditional Sani ones, even though it was billed as a Sani cultural show. I later found, however, that this kind of phenomenon is widespread. One British visitor to Yunnan complained of "a sanitized 'folk' music performance in a restaurant—comely maidens and youths in too-bright minority costumes pranced and posed with all the authenticity of the cheerful Cockneys in Lionel Bart musicals, and to a background of largely pre-recorded music" (Kings 1991). This kind of complaint was common among foreigners I met in Yunnan.

Lijiang's remoteness—six hundred kilometers, twenty hours by uncomfortable long-distance bus from Kunming City—ensured that most foreign visitors to the county before the institution of air service in 1995 were relatively resilient, youngish backpackers; and backpackers in particular often conform to the stereotype of what have been termed "existential" tourists—those who tend spiritually to abandon modernity and wish to get close to native peoples and their cultures (Cohen 1988: 377). For those tourists, electric pianos, strobe lights, identical sequined bodices, and corny Western harmony presented as local folk culture are an immediate turn-off. In terms of their tourist enterprise, it was a lucky inspiration that the Dayan Ancient Music Association chose not to ignore their instinctive musical conservatism when presenting their repertoire to such tourists. Instead, right from the start, they aurally and visually underlined that conservatism, painting a picture their mainly foreign audience happened to like, and hitting on a winning formula. Their strongest ally was the hundreds of obviously fabricated so-called folk or traditional performances this audience had encountered and disliked elsewhere in China.

The problem of the collision between "existential" foreign tourists and the standard "traditional," "folk," or "ethnic" music program presented to them in China is largely one of culturally informed conceptualization and expectations. While there is no one word used in Chinese which has all the ramifications of the English word "authentic," a term much employed in the musical context is "traditional" (*chuantong*). English speakers invited to hear "traditional" Chinese music as played, for instance, by the Shanghai Chinese Orchestra or equivalent professional ensembles are often dismayed to encounter a largish orchestra of standardized, equal-tempered factory-issue Chinese instruments, frequently with Western cello and bass and sometimes keyboard added. When this same orchestra then plays a mixture of modern compositions and arrangements of older pieces with simple functional harmony, a warm tone color, and dramatic dynamics apparently borrowed from the Western romantic orchestra—and clearly alien to the sound of the grass-roots folk traditions that supposedly inspire them—many foreign listeners cannot see this as "traditional" music at all. In the words of one dismayed musicologist, it "just sounds like lightweight nineteenth-century [Western] music" (Provine 1981: 13). Yet many Chinese musicians, especially those professionally trained in national conservatories such as the Central Conservatory and the China Conservatory in Beijing, or the Shanghai Conservatory of Music, see no contradiction in calling this modern style "traditional," and indeed see it as an improvement over the unarranged folk originals. This attitude harks back to the emphasis in Mao's "Talks at the Yan'an Conference" on raising the cultural level of the people, and of taking their own crude raw materials and working them up to a higher level of art. Ironically, the aesthetic preferences of "existential" foreign tourists and those of the practitioners of many amateur traditional Chinese genres are surprisingly close: most of the latter genuinely appreciate their music the way they play it, and, like many foreign visitors, find the professionalized versions rather bland and saccharine.[5]

At least for the first few years of Lijiang's Dongjing music concerts, grass-roots and tourist aesthetic preferences came together, with happy results for both. Whether this trend will continue is hard to say: many of the older members of the Dayan Ancient Music Association are dying off; one or two younger recruits have been trained in a more conservatory-influenced style of playing; traditional methods of transmission are being supplemented or replaced by new ones;[6] and Xuan Ke himself, who wields enormous influence on the direction of the group, seems to have some liking for more professional sounds. Furthermore, the composition of the audience had changed greatly by the late 1990s: whereas in the early 1990s it was mostly made up of foreign backpackers, by summer 1998 probably 80 percent appeared to be middle-class domestic tourists, mostly from the newly wealthy east coast. Certainly more attuned to the conservatorized professional style than foreign backpackers, their aesthetic preferences may not duplicate those of the original foreign visitors.

Lijiang's Dongjing Music on the Road

If the world has beaten a path lately to the door of the Dayan Ancient Music Association, the association too has found itself on the road with increasing frequency. Often in tandem with these trips have come opportunities for commercial recordings, of which several now circulate within and outside China.

Domestic Trips

The first major call to travel was when musicians of the Dayan Ancient Music Association joined members of the county song and dance troupe at the "Hundred Marvels of China" exhibition (*Zhongguo baijue bolanhui*), held in the Canton area over the winter of 1991–1992.[7] For many of those who went, especially members of the Dayan Ancient Music Association, it was the first time they had ever left Yunnan Province; and the relative wealth and flourishing free markets of the southeast were quite an eye-opener.

In Canton, the mixed troupe also recorded a commercial cassette titled *Naxi Guyue/Na-xi Music* (WS 92101), which consists mainly of pieces from the Dongjing repertoire, plus three Baisha Xiyue standards. The style, however, is not "traditional" at all. Instead, pieces on the "A" side are arranged in a style closer to that of the modern Chinese orchestra by He Zhong, a conservatory-trained member of the county song and dance troupe; those on the "B" side are similarly arranged by Xuan Ke, the English-speaking leader of the amateur group. One or two prominent local Canton musicians are also added to the players, somewhat diluting the regional flavor that remains in the pieces. Perhaps predictably, many professional musicians liked the versions of the pieces on the tape, while some of the traditional Dongjing aficionados (and foreign tourists who heard the tape afterward) found them rather bland and flavorless. The title of the cassette—*Naxi Guyue*—makes explicit the strengthening emphasis at this time on the Naxi-ness of the Dongjing repertoire. A later recording project by the Yunnan Music Video Publishing House, the two-cassette set *Naxi Music/Na-khi Music* (H-427, H-428) adheres to a more traditional style.

Following this visit to Canton, and partly in response to its growing reputation in the provincial tourist industry, the Dayan Ancient Music Association found itself invited several times in the following couple of years to Kunming. The first such trip was in September 1992, when the group performed at the Nanjiang Hotel and five prestigious provincial educational institutions, including Yunnan University, Yunnan Normal University, and Yunnan Art Institute. The second trip was in March 1993, when they played in the Kunming Theater on the occasion of the First Kunming Trade Fair. This was quickly followed by a return visit in May the same year, to provide music for the Naxi "village" in the Haigeng Cultural Scenery Tourism Zone outside Kunming.

The biggest coup of 1993, however, was the September concert tour to Beijing. Part of the groundwork for this trip was laid by Xuan Ke when he was invited in May of that year to talk on Naxi music at the Central Conservatory of Music, the China Conservatory of Music, and the Central Nationalities Institute. Nine Beijing-based organizations combined forces to issue an invitation to the "Lijiang Dayan Naxi Ancient Music Association" to visit Beijing: the National Music Committee of the China Musicians' Association, the Central Conservatory of Music, the China Conservatory of Music, the Music Research Institute, the Central Nationalities Institute, the China National Minorities Music Study Association, the China Traditional Music Study Association, the China Record Company, and the editorial board of the journal *Renmin Yinyue* (People's Music). The tour was sponsored financially and politically by the Yunnan Province Propaganda Department, the Yunnan Ethnic Cultural Arts Exchange Company (*Yunnan Minzu Wenhua Yishu Jiaoliu Gongsi*), the propaganda departments of Lijiang Prefecture and Lijiang County, and the Dayan Town Party Committee. It included performances in Beijing at the Central Party School, the Central Conservatory of Music, the Haidian Theater, and the Holiday Inn Lidu Hotel (in conjunction with an exhibition of "*dongba* art"). In Tianjin a concert was held at the Tianjin Conservatory of Music. The audiences included high-level government leaders at the Central Party School, prominent musicologists at the conservatories, foreign ambassadors at the Lidu, and Lijiang expatriates resident in Beijing.

A group of more than thirty went on this trip, of whom twenty-six were musicians drawn largely from the Dayan Ancient Music Association, with a few accomplished members of other groups added in. Four political leaders from the provincial, prefectural, county, and town levels also went, along with a photographer, a reporter, and a doctor (apparently because of the large number of very elderly musicians). This adventure was by all accounts a huge success: it rated a highly enthusiastic review in *Renmin Yinyue* (He Changlin 1993), and raised the profile not only of Lijiang's Dongjing music, but also of the county and prefecture as a whole, at provincial, national, and international levels.

Further domestic engagements followed. The city government and Party committee of Panzhihua (a.k.a. Dukou) in southern Sichuan Province invited the Dayan Ancient Music Association to give two concerts there in September 1994; they also played in Lijiang Prefecture's Huaping County on their way home. In November that year, they performed at a conference on tourist development in northwest Yunnan, at which many provincial leaders were present. The association also began to receive financial gifts from local government and financial institutions supporting its goal of establishing an academy to encourage children to study Dongjing music. Domestic trips have continued since then; in November 1999, for example, the musicians performed at the Shanghai International Arts Festival.

International Trips

The reflexivity that has pervaded anthropological writing for some years now has also invaded ethnomusicological writing. No longer does the ethnomusicologist necessarily claim to remain a fly on the wall, standing apart from the musics s/he studies. Shelemay puts it well: "Most ethnomusicologists are well aware that they do not study a disembodied concept called 'culture' or a place called the 'field,' but rather encounter a stream of individuals to whom they are subsequently linked in new ways" (1996: 51). Shelemay, for instance, found herself involved, sometimes unexpectedly, in aspects of the transmission of Syrian and Ethiopian Jewish music. One of the themes of this book has been the interaction of individuals in the maintenance and dissemination of Lijiang's Dongjing music tradition; and in documenting the first international tour, I find myself a major actor in my own narrative.

I revisited Lijiang in summer 1993, and had tea one afternoon with Xuan Ke, leader of Dayan Ancient Music Association, and Yang Zenglie, the secretary. Xuan and Yang showed me all the documentation concerning their coming trip to Beijing, and spoke of how delighted they were to have the opportunity to raise awareness of Lijiang's music—and of Lijiang itself—in this manner. Many of their fellow musicians, too, were thrilled by the prospect of an expedition to the nation's capital, which most had never had the opportunity to visit before. Given the success of Dongjing music among the foreign tourists in Lijiang, they continued, would not an international concert tour be the next logical step? And would I perhaps be in a position to try to jump-start such an endeavor? Given that I was still a graduate student at this stage, without any relevant connections in Europe or North America, this was quite a challenge; but I promised to do what I could. Friends who had had experience of bringing Asian folk ensembles to Europe suggested Britain's Asian Music Circuit, a promoter of traditional Asian musics that had successfully sponsored a tour by a Buddhist ensemble from Tianjin earlier in 1993. The two east/southeast Asia specialists for Asian Music Circuit expressed immediate enthusiasm for the tape of the music I gave them, and worked extremely hard over the following two years to clear the bureaucratic and financial hurdles in organizing a Naxi visit.

The tour took place in October 1995, with nine members of the Dayan Ancient Music Association and their accompanying official billed as "Chinese Naxi Musicians" (Asian Music Circuit 1995). They performed to packed houses at the Purcell Room and the Chinese Embassy in London, the Royal Northern College of Music in Manchester, and the Midlands Arts Centre in Birmingham; Xuan Ke and I also shared the lecture portion of demonstration recitals at the School of Oriental and African Studies in London, the University of Hull, and Oxford University. In addition, the group recorded the CD *Naxi Music from Lijiang* for the British company Nimbus; this was released in spring 1997. The reception in England was invariably enthusiastic, with the cassettes the musicians had brought with them selling like hotcakes. One of the reasons for the degree of interest in them was the popularity in Britain of the TV documentary *Beyond the Clouds*, which had been shown not long before. Although no Dongjing music was used in this documentary, the Asian Music Circuit flier reminded the public of the connection: "Many people will be familiar with the town of Lijiang and its people through the fascinating TV documentary series *Beyond the Clouds* which gave a vivid portrayal of life in the town. Many intrepid visitors to Lijiang have ventured down the narrow streets and alleyways of the old town, their destination a small courtyard where these musicians give regular concerts" (Asian Music Circuit 1995). Thus did two totally independent British encounters with Lijiang come together and reinforce one another, to the great benefit of the touring Naxi musicians.

The British tour was noted in the London and Yunnan press: it was preceded by quite lengthy features in the *Times* and the *Daily Telegraph* (Christmas 1995, Clough 1995), and written up in the *Chuncheng Wanbao* (Spring City Evening News) in Kunming (Yang Xinhong 1995). In addition, it was the subject of an article published in a special issue of *Yulong Shan* (Jade Dragon Mountain), a cultural magazine of Lijiang Prefecture (He Jiaxiu 1996b). Photos of the tour are particularly prominent in the magazine. The association members also came equipped with their own Panasonic video camera, which they requested me to use to document some of their concerts. They asked me to include any distinguishing features of the concert hall—such as the huge organ at the Royal Northern College of Music—and to concentrate on the reactions of the British audience rather than on the performance itself. After all, they explained, footage of their performances had been shown many times inside and outside China; what they wanted was footage of the British reaction, to show on local Lijiang TV back home. It was an interesting adjustment of roles, with me now employed to document what they felt was valuable in the tour for their relatives, friends, and fellow Lijiangers.

After the success of the British tour, several other foreign trips were mooted for the Dayan Ancient Music Association. The next one to come off was an appearance at the Hong Kong Arts Festival in February 1997; it included one concert at Government House, and one at the Hong Kong City Hall Concert Hall (Xuan and Yang 1997). In May 1998, the ensemble performed at the Bergen International Festival, at the invitation of the Norwegian government. This was followed in September that year by a European tour taking in Switzerland, Italy, Germany, and France, and in April 1999 by a trip to Taiwan.

The Kudos of National and Foreign Attention

Generally speaking, in China great emphasis is placed on validation from the perceived political and/or cultural center. There is a range of national- and province-level festivals, prizes, and competitions in all artistic spheres, and people express a rightful pride in their achievement if they win one of these. International awards are also highly valued; in the 1950s and since the 1980s, for instance, the Chinese government has placed great emphasis on Chinese students' successes in international music competitions.[8]

Thus Lijiang, which before its recognition by UNESCO in 1997 must have rated close to the boondocks in the national imagination, values its national and international approbation very highly. In the 1996 special issue of the Lijiang Prefecture magazine *Yulong Shan*, many of the photographs are of Dongjing musicians visiting the tourist sites and meeting prominent politicians, diplomats, and academics in Kunming, Beijing, and England. The names and statuses of VIPs included are carefully documented. An undated promotional leaflet (Zhongguo Lijiang Dayan Naxi Guyuehui, n.d.) enumerates all kinds of interactions, major and minor, between members of the Dayan Ancient Music Association and foreign visitors, starting with a visit by a group of fourteen Dutch amateur music enthusiasts in September 1988. Congratulatory banners from organizations as august as the Central Conservatory of Music, and as fleeting as a Taiwanese tour group, adorned the walls of the concert area in summer 1996; and a prominently displayed advertisement showing the way to the newly opened *Guyue Gong* (ancient music palace) announced in English, "Traditional Na khi music concert and introduction to musical instruments/famous folk orchestra has traveled abroad/ every evening 8:00 pm" (all spelling and phrasing as in the original).

This national and international recognition clearly impresses Chinese journalists as well. The author of the *Chuncheng Wanbao* article mentioned above leads off with Xuan Ke's having given a scholarly talk at Oxford University (Yang Xinhong 1995). A five-page feature on Lijiang in the English-language *Beijing Review* devotes a whole section to "Naxi Ancient Music," stressing the British tour and the enthusiasm of an Italian medical college graduate for local Dongjing music. In a similar vein, it mentions Goullart's connection with the county, and the interest shown by UNESCO (Kou Zhengling 1996). At a more personal level, many of the musicians were obviously thrilled by the chance to travel to the provincial and national capitals, and even more by the unusual opportunity to go overseas. As I discovered later, in the 1990s a successful application for a British visa was considered a rare coup in Yunnan.

Clearly, the national and international recognition and performance opportunities that have proliferated since the early 1990s have brought great personal kudos to many of the musicians involved, and substantial cultural capital to Lijiang County and the Naxi, who gain ever greater exposure in the outside world. What is equally important is the effect that all of this has had on the place of Dongjing music in contemporary Lijiang society, since the influences on both the music and its environment are plainly very different from those of the first half of the twentieth century.

Dongjing Music and Lijiang Society in the 1980s and 1990s

In chapter 5, I discussed the place of Dongjing music and associations in Lijiang County before 1949. The conceptual framework for the chapter arose from two sources: Rice's admonition to build the individual factor into musical historiography (1987), and Nketia's emphasis on music as an active rather than passive cultural phenomenon (1990). I argued from the evidence presented that Dongjing music was part of a ritual package that defined and articulated group and class hierarchies and identities; and I shall argue similarly for Dongjing music as it exists in purely secular form in Lijiang in the late twentieth century. In the 1990s, however, the impact of Dongjing music upon its extramusical environment goes beyond confirmation, definition, and articulation of preexisting boundaries and worldviews: for the first time, it brings tangible economic advantages that would be absent if the music were not played.

The Economic Impact

Lijiang County is very dependent on domestic and foreign tourism to generate much-needed income; the local tourist department estimates that by the year 2010, tourism earnings will constitute more than half the county's annual revenue (Kou Zhengling 1996: 21). Just as the government of Yunnan Province pushes the twin tourist attractions of beautiful natural scenery and fascinating ethnic cultures, so does the *Beijing Review's* reporter tell us that "visitors are enraptured by Lijiang's unique natural scenery and culture" (Kou Zhengling 1996: 18). One of the cultural phenomena on which Kou dwells at greatest length is "Naxi Ancient Music"—in fact, Lijiang's Dongjing music as purveyed by the Dayan Ancient Music Association. I have mentioned earlier in this chapter the numerous guide books, magazine features, and newspaper articles introducing the music as one of Lijiang's star attractions; it usually goes hand-in-hand with some or all of "*dongba* culture," the famous Ming dynasty murals at Baisha,[9] Naxi female attire and supposed matriarchal survivals, picturesque buildings in Dayan Town, and the grandeur of the Jade Dragon Snow Mountain.

Lijiang's Dongjing music is clearly a very important factor in attracting tourists to the county. Many foreigners I spoke to in the early 1990s cited the music as a major reason for their decision to include Lijiang on their itinerary, and by summer 1998 most of the audience consisted of domestic tourists—suggesting that for them too it has become a focus of interest. The same year, the new luxury Guanfang Hotel and the Dongba Palace (*Dongba Gong*), a tourist entertainment center, both showcased ensembles playing Dongjing music. While the music is only one of a number of attractions that happened to congregate in the same county, it is plainly an important one.

Yet the economic impact of Dongjing music is not confined to its benefits to Lijiang's tourist trade as a whole: it also has a tangible effect on the economic well-being of individuals. During the early 1990s, each tourist concert by the Dayan Ancient Music Association guaranteed 5 *yuan* to each performer, while the remainder of the profits from ticket sales went into the group bank account, helping pay for new instruments, instrument repairs, furniture, and subsidies to any member temporarily hospitalized. The non-concert income of the association members varied: one or two at this time earned as much as 400 *yuan* a month, while others were surviving on pensions of only 30 or 40 *yuan*. Thus concert fees of up to 80 *yuan* per month constituted a sizable addition to almost everybody's income. By summer 1998 there was a four-tier pay system, with the most experienced musicians getting a little more than 600 *yuan* a month. Furthermore, while the lion's share of the tourist bonanza has gone to the musicians of Dayan Town, some others have benefited too. By summer 1996 the Dayan Ancient Music Association had lost so many of its most knowledgeable elderly members that it was paying nightly for a taxi to import three aged players from Jinshan; and the Sunday afternoon get-togethers of the Baihua Village ensemble have from time to time received busloads of foreign visitors who stay for part of their playing session. Unlike the urban musicians, however, the Baihua ensemble has gone little further than to welcome such visitors and invite them to contribute any money they see appropriate to the corporate coffers, to help pay for instrument construction and repair; they do not alter their leisurely pace or relaxed postures to take account of their audience. Nevertheless, they told me that they found the occasional windfalls quite helpful, and indeed asked me to write out English-language posters encouraging donations. Opportunities for regular employment increased in the late 1990s: the new ensemble playing in 1998 at the Guanfang Hotel and the Dongba Palace provided employment for thirty or so muscians, mostly drawn from Dayan Town and surrounding villages. For a few dozen Dongjing musicians, therefore, income generated by tourist interest has proved very useful.

Networks of Relationships of the 1980s and 1990s

To the outsider, the most visible impact of Dongjing music in Lijiang today may be the economic advantages it has brought with it to certain individuals and groups, and to the county as a whole. However, this is by no means the whole story. Just as in the first half of the twentieth century, the music plays a role in intracounty personal and communal interactions and identity formation. This is not to say, of course, that the scenario is the same as before 1949: for a start, the ritual Dongjing associations, which gave such strong expression to social status and literatus values and beliefs, are defunct. There seems to be no special social cachet attached to membership in the revived secular music groups; and the gods have long since exited the scene, except in the minds of some of the older men. Nevertheless, certain modes of social interaction continue to be defined in musical terms.

Intergroup relations continue to be important. The historical *muzi* (mother-son) relationships between such ensembles as those of Dayan Town and Jinshan Township are still remembered, and are given concrete expression by the closer musical ties between ensembles thus related. Overall, today's groups have cultivated friendly and egalitarian relations with one another, occasionally exchanging personnel, loaning instruments, and in 1991 joining in a music festival together.

Within any one group, senior knowledgeable members are still greatly respected, but performance roles are less differentiated in today's ensembles than they were in the ritual Dongjing associations of years ago: capable people take turns playing the *muyu* (wooden fish) and other controlling percussion. In the rural ensembles of the early 1990s, usually the only officers selected were the *duizhang* (head) and sometimes his deputy. Financial affairs were simple, since everybody contributed grain or money toward communal meals. The Dayan Ancient Music Association, reflecting its more complex financial affairs, designated an accountant and secretary, who by summer 1998 were joined by a nonplaying support staff of several young people. Most of today's ensembles are probably similar in internal relations to the more organized secular groups of the 1940s. Indeed, they retain one important function of both Dongjing associations and secular groups from the first half of the twentieth century: they are fora in which friends and family members with similar interests get together to make music and socialize in a group setting.

However, as was the case historically, the relationship between each music group and the county government is still crucial: government approval was essential to the revival of the music in the late 1970s, and critical to the Dayan Ancient Music Association's tourist enterprise in the late 1980s. Just as in the first half of the twentieth century, the urban musicians frequently perform at government invitation for festivals and special events, thus simultaneously garnering local respect and contributing to the community's celebrations and endeavors. Though many other aspects of the social environment have changed for Lijiang's Dongjing music, this feature is notable for its consistency.

In addition to the intracounty social networks, of course, a new kind of interaction has arisen: that between the musicians of the Dayan Ancient Music Association, and to a lesser extent those of Baihua Village, and the outside world. This is one relationship that is entirely a product of the 1980s, and indeed could not have happened before the opening of Lijiang County to foreign visitors in July 1985. Moreover, this relationship is inextricably linked to the way the government of Lijiang presents the county and its inhabitants to outsiders. Dongjing music has thus become a cultural ambassador for both Lijiang County and the Naxi, whether at home or on the road.

Changes in the Dongjing Tradition

Lijiang's Dongjing music has since 1949 sloughed off its sacred associations and emerged as an entirely secular music, albeit one that is put to a large number of uses in contemporary society. Although the numbers of musicians involved in its performance in the early 1990s probably did not greatly exceed two hundred—substantially fewer than in the 1940s—it has nevertheless achieved a widening level of renown and significance. Known only at county level before 1949, it has progressed from sporadic regional and national recognition in the first thirty-nine years of the People's Republic to national and international fame since the institution of tourist concerts in 1988. Recognition has also been assisted by the increasing dissemination of commercial recordings since 1992 (see discography). Musical traditions are constantly changing, simultaneously shedding and acquiring meanings; it is worth examining what these changes have been in the case of Lijiang's Dongjing music, given the rapidity of developments since the late 1980s.

Music Making for Pleasure and Profit

Most of the music making that went on through the medium of Lijiang's Dongjing music betwen 1949 and 1988 was for private pleasure. Since then, the musicians of the Dayan Ancient Music Association have done most of their music making for profit. They, alone of all the ensembles active on the plain around the urban area, succeeded in attracting several young recruits in the early 1990s—probably because they could offer a small income in return for the dedication needed to learn the tradition. The leap from purely recreational to mostly commercial performance was a large one; and some scholars of tourism have posited that commoditization of previously noncommoditized culture results in a loss of meaning for the culture producers (e.g., Greenwood 1977: 135).

This does not, however, seem to have been the case in Lijiang in the early 1990s. Although they played the same pieces several times a week, the Dayan Ancient Music Association members always turned up enthusiastically to their monthly private assemblies, during which they played Dongjing music all day long. Instead of the tourist concert format replacing the informal secular format, they ran the two comfortably in tandem. The "meaning," at least in terms of enthusiasm for and interest in the repertoire for its own sake rather than just for the money it could make, was clearly as strong as ever for most participants. Erik Cohen argues:

> Folk musicians, who play for money to an external audience, may be excited by the opportunity to present their art and proud to display their competence. There is no reason to assume that their music lost all meaning for them, merely because they have been paid for performing it. It would be absurd to argue that all popular music is meaningless for the artists merely because it is commercialized. . . . Just as a new cultural product can become with time widely accepted as "authentic," so it can, although changed through commoditization, acquire a new meaning for its producers. . . . [It] may become a culturally significant self-representation before an external public. (1988: 381–382)

It was obvious in the early 1990s that the Dayan Town musicians were proud of their music, and of the interest foreigners showed in it, at a time when young local enthusiasts were few and far between. It retained its aesthetic appeal for the performers while acquiring a commercial function. Whether this aesthetic pleasure will survive the strain of the nightly performances of the late 1990s, as opposed to the thrice-weekly concerts of 1992, is difficult to say. Certainly members of village groups remote from Dayan Town and the main tourist sites will continue to play largely for their own amusement, with the odd funeral thrown in, since they have little prospect of a paying audience.

The Easing of the Transmission Crisis

One of the biggest worries voiced by Dongjing musicians in the early 1990s was the paucity of young and middle-aged recruits to the tradition. The grim picture painted by the survey of 1987–1988, in which about 40 percent of the active participants were age seventy or over, and 60 percent sixty or over, had not changed greatly by the time I arrived in Lijiang three years later.

Since then, however, things have improved for some groups. When I revisited the Jinshan ensemble in June 1996, members were delighted to introduce me to several young and early-middle-aged men who had taken up the music since my previous visit. When I asked why they had decided to learn the repertoire, most of these enthusiastic recruits mentioned the fear that the music would die out, pride in it as local cultural heritage, and an aesthetic liking for it. A few younger people had also attached themselves to the Baisha ensemble, previously one of the least functional, and were attending rehearsals at which the musicians played both Dongjing pieces and—a new departure—Baisha Xiyue pieces. Given the concentration of tourist attractions in Baisha, especially the famous murals and temples, and a new center for *dongba* culture exhibits and souvenirs, they were aiming to start performances, especially of Baisha Xiyue, for visitors. When I revisited Baihua Village in August 1998, five men in their twenties and three teenagers (two of them female) were present, and the teenagers told me that one village nearby had about twenty-five youngsters learning the music. These teenagers earned some money from the music by playing in the Guanfang Hotel group.

The Dayan Ancient Music Association has had the greatest resources to recruit younger members, and indeed their membership list from early 1996 (published at the back of the January 1996 issue of *Yulong Shan* magazine) gives the names of thirteen people under thirty. They started a summer training class for interested youngsters in 1989, and with the purchase in 1996 of their own historic mansion and its renovation as a *Guyue Gong* (ancient music palace), instituted a permanent "Naxi Music Academy," which welcomed almost a hundred children to the summer school held in 1998 (Figure 7.2). They also supplied teachers for an incipient ensemble in Daju. Most of the musicians I questioned thought that the respect for Lijiang's Dongjing music shown by the outside world had made many local young people realize that the music was a piece of local and even ethnic heritage worth studying and preserving, rather than a boring relic played by old people. Many also pointed out the economic motivation that some youngsters probably felt. Certainly many people displayed greater optimism in the late 1990s about the survival of the Dongjing repertoire than they had at the beginning of the decade.

Why Is the Dongjing Repertoire Purely Secular Today?

Given the vitality of the musical repertoire in the 1980s and 1990s, why has Lijiang County failed to revive even one ritual Dongjing association? As observed in chapter 3, most counties and cities that retain Dongjing music have also revived the ritual associations in some shape or form. No completely satisfactory answers have arisen to this question. The commonest suggestion, usually from people familiar with county governments in Yunnan, is that the Lijiang County

FIGURE 7.2. Xuan Ke, leader of the Dayan Ancient Music Association, in July 1998, standing in front of the "Ancient Music Palace" established by the association in 1996.

administration is relatively conservative and is reluctant to allow too overt a religious revival. It is certainly true that whereas in places such as Weishan County and Dali religious activities are readily observable even within a kilometer or so of the government center, one never sees major activities in or around the county seat in Lijiang. Buddhist monasteries remain almost uninhabited, there are no more Taoist priests, and the closest to the county town that any of my informants has recently seen a *dongba* ceremony was in a village sixteen kilometers away.

Probably the conservatism of the county government does have something to do with the exclusively secular use of the Dongjing repertoire today; but practical problems may also be a factor. As far as I know, only one scripture remained in private hands after 1949, and all the ritual paraphernalia and most of the musical instruments belonging to the Dongjing associations disappeared. To set up a full-blown ritual association is expensive, and ironically enough, the place in Lijiang County best able to spend that sort of money, Dayan Town, is home to one of the few contemporary ensembles whose older members had belonged mostly to secular music groups before 1949. Consequently, the town group lacks expertise and probably motivation for such an undertaking. In fact, when in July 1992 the county government wanted to stage a one-time performance of the Ten Offerings (apparently to provide research material and generate publicity for

Lijiang and its cultural heritage), it took days of rehearsals to get the ceremony right because only one member of the Dayan Ancient Music Association, He Yi'an, had a clear recollection of the ritual, and he had to coach the others. That this government-sponsored performance has not to my knowledge been followed by others organized privately suggests that the motivation among the majority of players for such a revival is simply not there.

Furthermore, while most of the Dongjing aficionados whom my Chinese co-researchers and I interviewed in other parts of Yunnan indicated that their Dongjing music had been used mainly in association rituals before 1949, many ordinary Naxi already enjoyed their Dongjing music as secular entertainment in the first half of the twentieth century; thus in the 1980s the revived Lijiang secular groups already had a previously blossoming secular model on which to base their activities—one that was apparently lacking in other areas. Consequently it may have been a natural step simply to stop at secular performance, which has a long and honorable tradition in the county.

Lijiang's Dongjing music has traveled a long way literally and metaphorically since the first half of the twentieth century. It has lost some roles, gained others, opened up to women and outsiders, and found itself interpreted and reinterpreted in a bewildering variety of ways, which are discussed in the following chapter. Above all, like so much traditional Chinese culture, it has become a "cultural symbol recycled and diffused in everyday social living to create new meanings and to reinforce new . . . interests" (Siu 1990: 767).

8

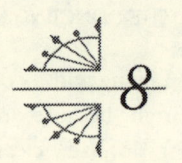

Representation and Ethnicity

Ethnographies, suggests Edward Bruner, "are guided by an implicit narrative structure, by a story we tell about the peoples we study" (1986: 139). He offers as an example the different "dominant" stories behind ethnographic writing on Native Americans in the 1930s and 1940s, when the paradigm was of a glorious past, disorganized present, and assimilated future, and in the 1970s, when it had changed to an exploited past, resistant present, and ethnically resurgent future (pp. 139–140). Many such "dominant stories" have been identified, and their effects on perception and public policy identified, in the past two decades. Said's critique of orientalism (1979) is of course an outstanding example, as is McKhann's fine explication (1995) of the Morganian paradigm as applied by Chinese ethnologists working on the Naxi and Mosuo. Nor is it only writers describing other groups who can be seen to be working within powerfully implicative frames of reference: authors writing the history of their own country or ethnic group may be equally influenced by a story they wish to tell, or a contention they wish to prove (Hobsbawm and Ranger 1983; Hanson 1989; Duara 1995).

The identification and critique of such frames of reference, or "narrative structures," have recently proliferated in musical scholarship too. Scholarship on African music has been discussed with particular vigor, although writings on many other subjects, including the Western art music tradition, have come under similar scrutiny.[1] Nor has Chinese musical scholarship escaped the deconstructionist knife. Yang Mu has argued eloquently that, as a result of China's ideological climate, "certain important facets of Chinese folk song culture have been distorted, and some misleading information has been disseminated" (1994: 318). The changing representations of the life and music of blind Abing, socialist China's folk music hero, have also been minutely analyzed (Stock 1996), and Joseph Lam (1995) has investigated the paradigms behind reconstruction in the mainland and Taiwan of the Confucian sacrifice. Such critiques can tell the reader much about the worldview of earlier writers (and not infrequently something about the author of the critique, too). They represent, in fact, what Neuman calls "reflexive music history," or "the history of music history" (1991: 269).

In this chapter, I tackle the material presented in the preceding chapters on Lijiang's music from a fresh angle, or rather a series of fresh angles: how it has been and is being represented by different agents. By invoking descriptions and opinions offered by people of diverse ethnic and cultural backgrounds, I aim to establish the frames of reference within which they perceive these musical phenomena. From this, one may gather valuable information both on the potential biases of sources of information and on the social expectations and attitudes obtaining at different times and among different people. This is important not merely because of the commentary it offers on attitude differentiation and attitudinal change over time, but also because of the impact that such attitudes have had and still do have on the development of musical traditions.

Following, I deal first with the problem of nomenclature, and then with interpretations offered by different commentators that illuminate shifting "implicit narrative structures." While I consider all aspects of Lijiang's musical life as they arise, my main focus is on the Dongjing tradition.

Names Attached to the Dongjing Tradition

The name attached to an object or tradition may be loaded with cultural resonance, and is often of extreme importance in indicating how the namers view the named item. Recent researches in Chinese politics have affirmed that in this arena the selection of words to describe certain sensitive items and issues is of major significance. The naming of cultural traditions may be equally instructive (Schoenhals 1992; Guy 1995).

Before 1949, a variety of names was attached to the Dongjing associations and secular groups. The appellations discussed here were confirmed in interviews[2] and appear in several documentary sources. Formally, the Dongjing associations were referred to as *dongjinghui* (lit. Dongjing associations); this is the term used in He Gengji's preface to the Dayan Town association name list *Yongbao Ping'an* (Eternal Assurance of Well-Being) from 1938, and in writer Zhao Yintang's vignettes of Lijiang (1984 [1948]: 154). Colloquially, nonmembers commonly termed the associations *tanjingban* (scripture discussion groups) (Zhao Jingxiu 1995: 34), or, at least in Baisha, *wenrenhui* (literati association). The secular music groups, by contrast, had names indicating their musical interests: Pineflower Orchestra (*Songhua Yuedui*), Good Friends Music Association (*Yiyou Yinyuehui*), Cultured Music Association (*Wenming Yuehui*), and so on (Yang Zenglie 1990:

120). He Linghan and Sun Ziming, former members of such groups, said that they usually referred to their activities as *iuqqil duel*; *iuqqil* is a Naxi borrowing of the Han Chinese word for musical instruments, *yueqi*, and *duel* is the Naxi verb "to play" (the phrase is confirmed in Zhao Jingxiu 1995: 34). By contrast, the Dongjing association members' activities were referred to as *tanjing* (discuss scriptures). Indigenous terms for the Dongjing associations, secular music groups, and their activities before 1949, therefore, distinguished a vital difference: the former were sacred groups that performed scriptures, the latter secular groups whose focus was instrumental music. This confirms the contextual information garnered from informants and documentary sources, and set out in chapter 3.

Since 1949, the terminology has changed somewhat. A *gongchepu* (Chinese solfège notation) score from Baisha, probably copied some time in the 1950s, is titled *Baisha guyue* (Baisha ancient music). A brief article in *Renmin Yinyue* (People's Music) on Naxi music from 1951 mentions *dongjing yinyue* (Dongjing music) (Zhao Jishun 1951: 31). The 1962 fieldwork report by Zhou Yongxian and Huang Lin (1983 [1962]) refers throughout to *dongjinghui* and *dongjing yinyue*. *Dongjing yinyue* is also the term used in passing by Mao Jizeng in his work on Baisha Xiyue (1964: 27), and in some scholarly articles of the 1980s and 1990s (e.g., Chong Xian 1989; Yang Zenglie 1990–1991; Sangde Nuowa 1994). By the 1980s and 1990s, however, especially outside the scholarly sphere, the term *guyue* (ancient/old music) had become more usual. Lijiang's Dongjing repertoire is frequently referred to as *Lijiang guyue* (Lijiang Ancient Music) (Zhang Yunqing 1983: 47, 51; Li and Wang 1984: 82–83; Naxizu Jianshi Bianxiezu 1984: 151; Kou Bangping 1984: 26 and 1986: 73; Zhang Xingrong 1990: 77–78; Sangde Nuowa 1994: 66), or as *Naxi guyue* (Naxi Ancient Music) (Xuan Ke 1980; Dayan Guyuehui 1992; Zhang Xingrong 1990: 77; Li and Yin 1993: 26–27; Yi 1993; Yang Xinhong 1995; many articles in the January 1996 special issue of *Yulong Shan* [Jade Dragon Mountain]; Xuan and Yang 1997; He Yong 1998: 23).[3]

Two commercial cassettes appeared in the early 1990s, both titled *Naxi Guyue* (ZAX-9103 and WS 92101). The former contains arranged versions of several genres of music from the Lijiang Naxi, but played by professional, mainly non-Naxi, musicians. It includes three pieces of Dongjing music. The latter consists mainly of arrangements of Dongjing music with a few Baisha Xiyue items. A third commercial tape, recorded in a deliberately more "authentic" style by members of the Dayan Town Ancient Music Association, is titled *Lijiang Dongjing Yinyue* (Dongjing Music from Lijiang), although the English-language inlay notes are headed "An Introduction to Nakhi Music." A later two-cassette set is once again titled *Naxi Guyue* (H-427, H-428).

The groups that play Lijiang's Dongjing music for secular entertainment invariably include the term *guyue* in their official names. For example, *Baihua Guyuedui* (Baihua Ancient Music Orchestra), *Baisha Guyuedui* (Baisha Ancient Music Orchestra) and *Jinshan Guyuedui* (Jinshan Ancient Music Orchestra). The

Dayan Town group is usually referred to as *Dayan Guyuehui* (Dayan Ancient Music Association), although the report they submitted to the Lijiang Prefecture authorities on the proposed trip to Beijing in 1993 was issued under the name of *Lijiang Dayan Naxi Guyuehui* (Lijiang Dayan Naxi Ancient Music Association). The same report was stamped *Zhongguo Lijiang Dayan Naxi Guyuetuan* (China Lijiang Dayan Naxi Ancient Music Troupe) (Lijiang Dayan Naxi Guyuehui 1993). A review of their trip published in *Renmin Yinyue* (People's Music) refers to the group as *Lijiang Naxi Guyuetuan* (Lijiang Naxi Ancient Music Troupe) (He Changlin 1993). In 1989 the Dayan Town ensemble and the Lijiang County Trade Union collaborated in organizing a summer course to train middle-aged and young people in Dongjing music; the class was called *Naxi Guyue Jiyi Peixunban* (Naxi Ancient Music Training Class) (Dayan Guyuehui 1992: 3–4).

Overall, therefore, there has been a significant shift in nomenclature over the last fifty years. For obvious reasons, the terms *tanjingban* (scripture discussion group) and *dongjinghui* (Dongjing association) are never heard in contemporary speech, unless specifically referring to the past. The phrase *iuqqil duel* (play instruments) was commonly used as late as the 1960s (Zhao Jingxiu 1995) and was still well known in the early 1990s. Scholarly works generally refer to Lijiang's Dongjing music as *dongjing yinyue* (Dongjing music), but increasingly the preferred term in ordinary discourse is *guyue*, prefaced in print either by "Lijiang" or by "Naxi." All the groups that still perform the music call themselves *guyuedui* or *guyuehui*. Several elderly informants commented that *guyue* is a modern term.

This enthusiasm for the word *guyue* (ancient/old music) or for *gu* (ancient/old) in other combinations is reflected in other parts of Yunnan, and indeed elsewhere in China. For example, the first officially published book on Dongjing music was titled *Dali Dongjing Guyue* (Ancient Dongjing music of Dali) (Dali Shi Xiaguan Wenhuaguan 1990). In China as a whole the instruments known traditionally as *qin* (seven-string bridgeless zither) and *zheng* (multiple-string bridged zither) are today commonly called *guqin* and *guzheng* ("ancient *qin*" and "ancient *zheng*"). With the antitraditional iconoclasm of the Cultural Revolution now well past, to be able to claim antiquity for an item or tradition is to increase its value as part of China's cultural heritage. Because the term "Dongjing" is not mentioned in the names of performing groups, the former religious associations of the music are deemphasized; the focus is instead on the musical repertoire pure and simple.

A final point of importance is the habit nowadays of prefixing "Lijiang" or "Naxi" to the word *guyue*. Presumably the increased contact with the outside world caused by the improvements in communications since the 1950s has resulted in a need to specify the geographical or ethnic origin of this repertoire. While awareness of the music was confined to Lijiang, this need did not exist; but documents and publications today are often aimed at a far wider audience, so that such specification has become a necessity. The current habit of emphasizing the geographical or ethnic origin may also be a reflection of the fact that the music has in recent years come to be a useful cultural ambassador for Lijiang Naxi Autonomous County. It thus carries out a new function inside and outside Lijiang, and one that is marked by an appropriate adjustment of nomenclature.

The vagaries of nomenclature, therefore, are a valuable guide to the contexts in which this music has existed in this century, and to the perceptions of its users, of other members of the community, and of outsiders. Before 1949, different names for the sacred and secular groups and for their activities neatly distinguished between the primarily sacred and exclusively secular contexts. Since 1949, the enthusiasm for the term *guyue* reflects not only the search for a safe secular name, but also the awareness of the value reattached in the years since the Cultural Revolution to what is historical or antique. By promoting themselves as preservers of "ancient" music, today's musicians are tapping into the social and political respectability conferred on protectors of a venerable cultural heritage. The cultural capital generated by possession of a tradition valued in this way may also translate into economic gains, since the "ancient-ness" of the music has definitely become a selling point in the tourist and media market. Moreover, the prevalence of the prefix "Naxi" (even more than "Lijiang") during the mid-1990s seems indicative of the way the music is increasingly seen—and marketed—as an integral part of a specifically Naxi heritage.

Representations from before 1949

Chinese Accounts

Documentary and literary sources from before 1949 seldom offer explicitly evaluative comments on Lijiang's music. Some musical instruments and musical activities are mentioned in *dongba* manuscripts and Han-language poems by Naxi literati, although such references are usually brief. Often, a mention of music helps evoke a desired atmosphere; for instance, a set of Han-language poems by Niu Tao (1790–1858), one of which is translated in chapter 4, conjures up a scene of rural beauty through mention both of Lijiang's natural environment and of local musical activities such as playing the *hulusheng* (mouth organ), barley-stalk pipe, and flute and singing and dancing (Zhao Yintang 1985: 127–129).

Documents written or compiled by officials working in Lijiang refer occasionally to local music. In addition to giving a brief description of Baisha Xiyue, the local official Guan Xuexuan observed in 1743 that "each of the different kinds of barbarians has its own songs and leaping song-dances" (*Lijiang Fu Zhilüe* 1991 [1743]: 208). He used the usual derogatory term of that time for non-Han peoples (*yiren*), often translated into English as "barbarian," but otherwise passed no subjective judgment on what he had seen and heard. The 1895 county gazetteer similarly mentions Baisha Xiyue, but offers no subjective comments (*Lijiang Fu Zhi* 1895: first fascicle, folio 121).

The 1934 report by Lijiang County acting head He Wenxuan on the previous year's Chrysanthemum Festival describes in glowing terms the effect of what was almost certainly Dongjing music on the audience: the music was so fine that people listened in a reverent silence. In addition, He Wenxuan anticipates a major "implicit narrative structure" which will resurface in the late 1980s and early 1990s, that of the precious ancient tradition lost in the rest of China but preserved by good fortune in remote Lijiang:

> Last year on the Double Ninth [the ninth day of the ninth lunar month], we held the first Chrysanthemum Festival. There was a massive attendance; officials and people enjoyed themselves for three days, with ten thousand people coming from far and near. We added instrumental music, which was so fine that the people didn't make a sound. The tone of the [four-string plucked lute] *hubo* [otherwise known as *sugudu*] was especially redolent of refined antiquity. This *hubo*, and indeed the ancient music which was transmitted to Lijiang when Kublai Khan of the Yuan dynasty crossed the [Jinsha] river [ca. 1253], are said by the music histories to be lost. This however does not refer to Lijiang in Yunnan, where there are still many people who can play [the *hubo*]. Consequently after the flower competition was over, we continued with a piece of refined music for the *hubo*, together with [the four-string plucked lute] *pipa* and [the endblown flute] *xiao*. The tourists were delighted, feeling increasingly as though floating to and fro [with the music]; everywhere they were orderly, reverent and silent. (quoted in Yang Zenglie 1991: 44)

None of these three early accounts are particularly informative; however, none were written by or for specialists or travel enthusiasts, being instead passing references noted by the authors while engaged on official administrative business.

Still briefer, but expressive of similar affect, is the mention of Dongjing music by well-known Naxi author Zhao Yintang. Writing in 1948 of the Dongjing and Huangjing associations, she notes that "the music is refined, the mood harmonious. The history of the two associations dates from the transition to direct Chinese rule [1723]" (1984 [1948]: 154). More deeply engaged is He Gengji's 1938 preface to the Dayan Town Dongjing association's name list *Yongbao Ping'an* (Eternal Assurance of Well-Being), translated in its entirety in chapter 3. It describes the Dongjing association ambience as follows: "the scholars were upright, the protocols were strict, the music was sonorous, and it flourished in a civilized fashion." The emphasis in both of these accounts is on the refined, morally uplifting, and socially respectable nature of the music and its setting.

A Foreign Viewpoint: Peter Goullart

The only known foreign account of Lijiang's Dongjing music from before 1949 is that by the Russian observer Goullart (1957: 213–217).[4] I have cited Goullart's description before as evidence for the high regard in which the music was held, and as a contributor to the nostalgic ambiance of the tourist concerts, but concentrate here on the "implicit narrative structure" framing his depiction. Asserting that the music was brought to Lijiang by the Chinese general Zhuge Liang in the third century A.D., Goullart stresses very much the angle of Lijiang's remoteness permitting the preservation of arts lost elsewhere in China. Indeed, he appears to espouse a romantic desire to find in Lijiang's tradition the pure roots of classical Chinese music:

> Lijiang has ever remained peaceful and isolated, and could devote itself to the perpetuation of cherished ancient arts. Indeed, it was China that had to sacrifice the purity of her music and drama to the whims of vulgar Mongol and Manchu conquerors.... The conquests did harm to Chinese civilization and culture, and music perhaps suffered most at the hands of the invaders. The present-day Chinese falsetto singing and the discordant and shallow music of Chinese theatres are no more representative of the ancient classical music of China than modern jazz is representative of classical Greek music. Some esoteric Taoist monasteries have preserved fragments of the classical music and they perform it in their ceremonies and dances, but the instruments and the score they use are far less genuine than those preserved by the Naxi....
>
> Let us hope that this treasure of music in Lijiang may be secure from the ravages of the modern age. (1957: 215, 217)

In these accounts from before 1949, therefore, we find two main "implicit narrative structures" in the description of Dongjing music. First, He Wenxuan, Zhao Yintang, He Gengji, and Peter Goullart all emphasize the serenely spiritual, morally uplifting, and socially respectable nature of the music. Second, He Wenxuan and Goullart both stress that the Naxi have preserved an ancient tradition lost in the rest of China. Interestingly, there is no mention of a specifically Naxi character to the music.

Representations from 1949 to the Cultural Revolution

Dongjing Music

It is since 1949 that descriptions of Lijiang's music have become more detailed. The 1962 fieldwork report on Yunnan's Dongjing tradition (Zhou and Huang 1983 [1962]), in addition to reporting a wealth of factual detail, also gives many value-laden judgments on the Dongjing tradition in Lijiang and the other main centers covered, Dali, Xiaguan, and Kunming. For example, "most of these who presided [over Dongjing associations] were the local "gentry" or businessmen; local officials also lent their support. As for sources of revenue, most [associations] had exploitative income from fixed capital in the form of land rent and interest from shops. . . . Dongjing associations were inseparable from feudal superstition" (1983 [1962]: 78–79). The vocabulary used, especially "exploitative" (*boxue*) and "feudal superstition" (*fengjian mixin*), places the associations firmly in the litany of social evils. On the other hand, there seems to be an attempt to salvage the purely musical aspects of the tradition: "the artists of the Dongjing associations were mostly [amateur] music enthusiasts" (p. 79). The word used for "artists," *yiren*, is politically neutral, as is the term "enthusiasts" (*aihaozhe*); in the early 1960s amateur music groups were perfectly acceptable, and indeed often organized by cultural officials. Zhou and Huang carry on to point out the musical validity of the Dongjing repertoire, and its recognition by local officials:

> Dongjing music is a favorite with the people in all areas of Yunnan, and has an extensive basis among the masses. In accordance with the Party policy of allowing the hundred flowers to blossom, in recent years Dongjing musicians, organized by cultural officials in each area, perform [the music] in their free time. . . . In addition, music organizations and music workers from Yunnan and elsewhere take Dongjing music very seriously. (p. 79)

This tendency, to praise Dongjing music for its musical value while denigrating the religious and organizational aspects of the tradition, is a pre-echo of naming strategies adopted by many revived Dongjing associations and music groups throughout Yunnan in the 1980s: the names they selected tended to emphasize their musical rather than ritual activities and histories.

Other Lijiang Musics

Musics in Lijiang other than the Dongjing tradition also began to receive evaluative mention between 1949 and the Cultural Revolution. Beijing-based folk song collector Liu Chao comments that "Naxi songs are numerous, beautiful, and full of special character" (1959: 1). Two articles appearing in *Renmin Yinyue* (People's Music) in the 1950s note that "the Naxi are very fond of song and dance" (Zhao Jishun 1951: 31), and that they are "good at singing and dancing" (Lü Dou 1958: 30). The invocation of this latter phrase, *neng'ge shanwu*, foreshadows its ubiquitous employment to characterize all national minorities in the 1980s and 1990s. Thus even in the 1950s we can see the "motif of the music-making minority" implicit in these brief musicological descriptions.

Representations since the Cultural Revolution

Music Other Than Dongjing Music: Chinese Writings

The greatest flurry of widely disseminated literature on Lijiang's music has occurred since the early 1980s, often as part of wider studies or, increasingly, travel guides.

The 1986 article by Kou Bangping, long a cultural cadre in Lijiang, is one of the fullest overviews of the musical world of the Naxi, and contains a fair number of value judgments in addition to a comprehensive factual survey of many different genres.[5] The article starts with general statistics on the Naxi. He then describes Naxi performing arts in general terms with a number of set-phrase clichés:

> The Naxi are an ethnic group whose members are industrious, brave, good at singing and dancing, and have a long cultural tradition. . . . Naxi folk music is wide-ranging in content, various in form, melodically ingenuous and rhythmically rich. It has its own characteristic artistic style and a clear regional flavor. . . . Folksongs are . . . inseparable from the lives of the masses. If you walk through Naxi villages, large or small, all about you you will hear attractive sounds of singing and see all kinds of happy song and dance activities. It reflects all the thoughts and emotions, customs and habits and moral practices of the Naxi people. (p. 71)

This description is reminiscent of Guan Xuexuan's 1743 observation that each of Lijiang's ethnic groups had its own songs and dances (*Lijiang Fu Zhilüe* 1991 [1743]: 208).

Kou Bangping is not the only 1980s commentator to describe the Naxi as "good at singing and dancing" (*nengge shanwu*): exactly the same phrase appears in an overview of Naxi history (Naxizu Jianshi Bianxiezu 1984: 147). In the same vein, "the characters for singing in the [*dongba*] pictographs are proof that the Naxi of former times loved singing and were good at it [*aige shanchang*]" (Yang Dejun 1985: 434). Descriptions by active local Naxi musicians too take this tack: the preface to a collection of Naxi folk songs from 1987 announces that "Naxi folksongs are extremely rich and varied, and have their own artistic characteristics; they are . . . a precious legacy of ethnic culture" (Zhal, Hoq, and Hoq 1987). A Chinese-authored English-language guide to Lijiang takes a similar approach:

> The Naxi are one of China's many minority nationalities with a long and brilliant history and culture, centered on Lijiang County. . . . The Naxi have a variety of colorful dances, including primitive dances, Dongba classical dances, group dance and modern dances. . . . The two-volume Naxi classical dance book written in pictographic characters, "The Dance Modes," records several hundred dancing movements of 60 dances. During a visit to Lijiang, Dai Ailian, Vice-Chairman of both the International Dancers' Association and the Chinese Dancers' Association, highly praised these traditional dances. (Tang and Jin 1988: 30, 39–40)

This emphasis on the achievements of the Naxi in the performing arts is entirely in accord with the policy toward national minority culture described in chapter 2: it celebrates the ethnic diversity of China, validates the contributions of minority groups, and shows respect for non-Han cultural heritages. All this is diametrically opposed to the often dismissive attitudes displayed by the Han majority toward minority peoples and their cultures before 1949, and displays a deliberate concern for minority pride. At the same time, all the descriptions cited fit into the "motif of the music-making minority" identified in chapter 2. The Naxi, like the other national minorities in China, are depicted as naturally gifted at singing and dancing; moreover, as the evidence shows, this characterization goes back at least as far as the 1950s.

Dongjing Music: Chinese Writings

A further theme of great interest in these publications on the music of the Lijiang Naxi is the handling of the Dongjing music repertoire. Kou Bangping explains that although "Lijiang Ancient Music" (*Lijiang guyue*) was borrowed from the Han Chinese in the Ming and Qing dynasties and has a definite flavor of the eastern Chinese Jiangnan Sizhu instrumental ensemble genre, its many years of modification in Lijiang have imbued it with "definite Naxi stylistic color" (1986: 73). Another essay points out that ethnic Naxi flavor has been added to the Han Chinese *sizhu* style, so that now "Lijiang Ancient Music" has a special identity which is an amalgam of Naxi and Han elements (Naxizu Jianshi Bianxiezu 1984: 151). Similar statements are made in a handbook on the Naxi (Li and Wang 1984: 82–83), in a Chinese-language guidebook (Li and Yin 1993: 26–27), and in a newspaper article (Liu Can 1998). This is in interesting contrast to a brief comment from a 1951 article on Naxi music: only eleven characters in the Chinese text cover Dongjing music, and it is described purely as "borrowed in from the Han in ancient times" (Zhao Jishun 1951: 31). Overall, it is the more recent writings that seem most likely to emphasize Naxi artistic input into the tradition.

A commercial cassette of Lijiang music that includes Dongjing pieces takes a similar line, although introducing in addition the theme of preservation in a remote area of a "living museum"/"living fossil" otherwise lost in the rest of China. *Naxi Guyue/Na-Xi Music* (WS 92101) contains both Dongjing and Baisha Xiyue pieces. The inlay notes, which are in Chinese only, are headed "Naxi Ancient Music: an ancient music treasure of the motherland," and explain:

> There are two parts to Naxi Ancient Music. The first is . . . Baisha Xiyue, created seven hundred years ago by the Naxi forefathers. It is . . . one of the earliest large-scale ensemble pieces in the world, and was termed by Lü Ji, former chairman of the Chinese Musicians' Association, "a living fossil of Chinese music." The second is Lijiang's ancient Dongjing music, which is an unusual form of music created by the melding of central China's Taoist music with Naxi folk music. It has a long history and has wide currency among the Naxi people. It has miraculously preserved a part of the . . . music of the Tang, Song and Yuan dynasties already lost in central China.

A similar emphasis on preservation of an ancient Chinese music in a remote place may be found in the bilingual inlay notes to the cassette *Lijiang Dongjing Yinyue* (Dongjing Music of Lijiang), which are headed "An Introduction to Nakhi Music": "With the gradual introduction of western culture into Chinese life, this musical style almost ceased to exist. Fortunately, in the remote and isolated area of southwest China known as Lijiang, the Nakhi people continued to enjoy traditional culture including Dong Jin music. Their preservation of this ancient musical style has helped to create a living museum today."

This particular set of notes introduces a new idea, of this music as medicine:[6]

Music is medicine. It can bring life or death. Both players and listeners must always be careful!

Scientific research worldwide has revealed that the only music which is healthy is religious music. This does not mean music from the gods or Buddhism but rather true religious music which can only come from an expression of the heart in combination, as Confucius points out, with the control of human rules. In this way the music will bring all participants back into harmony with nature eliminating noise and war while promoting silence and peace. In contrast, uncontrolled music can only kill. . . .

We hope the Music will be enjoyed by both research scholars and those persons who exercise for good health. The listener must place himself in a very quiet location putting his whole heart into the performance. He should clear his mind of any outside distractions and concentrate totally on the music. Only in this way can he truly believe that music is medicine.

The Dayan Ancient Music Association's 1993 trip to Beijing produced a plethora of commentaries on their music. A substantial review by musicologist He Changlin appeared in *Renmin Yinyue* (People's Music). He gives a romanticizing write-up that emphasizes the great age of the major performers. The general tenor of his article may be gleaned from the title, "Guobao maicang zai Ximalaya yunling shenchu" (A national treasure hidden in the recesses of the cloud peaks of the Himalayas).

The article first introduces Lijiang, its Dongjing music, and the elderly musicians in florid language, then goes on to summarize the background to the scriptures formerly used and to the music itself. He Changlin points out that many of the tunes are common to genres in eastern China and suggests that Lijiang's Dongjing music preserves some features of Tang dynasty music. He ends by noting in picturesque language two recent deaths among the elderly musicians, the ill health and poverty of the survivors and the lack of young recruits, and makes a final appeal to the god Wenchang, whom at one point he addresses as "Comrade Divine Lord" (*Dijun Tongzhi*), to adjust cultural policy to ensure preservation of "your, our, even more all Chinese people's and all mankind's precious cultural legacy" (p. 25). This impassioned outpouring to Wenchang is somewhat unexpected in an official publication. Other points He touches upon en route include the alleged medicinal properties of the music and its wide international renown.

Speakers at the meeting convened at the Central Conservatory of Music in honor of the Beijing concert trip emphasized some of these same themes. Renowned musicologist Yuan Bingchang opened the meeting by stressing that Lijiang's Dongjing music is a cultural treasure both of China and of mankind as a whole; other speakers touched upon its antiquity and healthful qualities, and hoped for its continuance among younger Naxi. Another famous music scholar, Shen Qia, sounded the first note of caution: he feared the damage that commercialization could do to the music through daily performance for hordes of enthusiastic foreigners. He praised the way the Japanese have treated their "intangible cultural assets," and recommended that Lijiang's Dongjing music receive the same careful handling (Yuan Bingchang et al. 1993).

Three years later, in the context of a very different kind of publication, the English-language weekly *Beijing Review*, journalist Kou Zhengling first reports enraptured foreign reactions to "Naxi Ancient Music," then summarizes what he understands to be the value of the tradition, in terms very similar to those cited above:

> In fact, Naxi music is a combination of Taoist and court music popular throughout the Tang and Song dynasties (618–1279). The latter was lost, while the former managed to miraculously survive and has been lovingly handed down to present generations.
>
> Domestic musicologists noted that Lijiang's unique geographic location hindered the development of local economy, but provided a rare shelter for ancient culture. Naxi music is actually the ancient music of China, scholars say, and its survival helps explain China's musical history. (1996: 20)

Trends in Chinese Writings on Lijiang's Music

What, then, are the "implicit narrative structures" that guide these Chinese-authored representations of Lijiang's music? Several distinct trends are obvious in the writings since 1949:

1. In writings on Naxi music in general, the Naxi are portrayed as naturally good at singing and dancing, and as incorporating the performing arts into their daily lives. This is a typical portrayal of a national minority and is repeated in many works on other minorities.
2. Naxi music in general is depicted as having its own distinctive Naxi flavor.
3. Lijiang's Dongjing music is portrayed as an import from the Han Chinese, but some writings, especially those from the 1980s and early 1990s, emphasize that it is overlaid with distinctively Naxi musical style.

4. Lijiang's Dongjing music is frequently described as a precious historical relic lost in the rest of China but preserved by good fortune in remote Lijiang. This trend of the 1980s and 1990s is anticipated by the 1934 report. Newspapers hit this theme particularly hard from the mid to late 1990s (Dayan Guyuehui, n.d. [1998]).
5. In tune with its time, the 1962 fieldwork report depicts the Dongjing associations as exploitative and bound up with feudal superstition, but concedes the artistic value of the music.
6. In the 1990s the supposed medicinal properties of Lijiang's Dongjing music are touted; this is probably related to the romantic spiritual ambiance increasingly associated with the repertoire through the carefully staged atmosphere of the tourist performances.
7. Music scholar He Changlin brings in the motif of the "endangered tradition," by emphasizing the age of the elderly musicians and the lack of young recruits.
8. Music scholar Shen Qia warns of the dangers of overcommercialization of the tradition.

Each of these trends may be correlated with extramusical developments. The fifth is a very specific symptom of its time. The first two are appropriate to the government policy toward minority culture outlined in chapter 2: the cultural inheritance of the minorities is to be salvaged and respected, and the minorities are to "be the real masters in their own house in culture." In addition, insisting on the distinctiveness of each ethnic group's culture also lends credence to the official classification system, which has an often debatable theoretical and empirical basis, but whose validity underlies the entire minority policy espoused by the Chinese government. A similar desire to stress the distinctiveness of minority artistic traditions probably informs the frequent assertion that Lijiang's Dongjing music has been indissolubly melded with local Naxi folk music, resulting in the creation of a distinctive Lijiang Dongjing style.

On the other hand, the increasingly romanticized picture of Dongjing music and its spiritual qualities painted by the tourist concerts and the many tourist guidebooks, introductory articles, and television programs no doubt underlies the portrayal of Lijiang as stalwart preserver of a valuable ancient heritage lost in the main part of China (despite the presence of other Dongjing musicians throughout Yunnan who play similar repertoires), and of the music as being spiritually and possibly physically beneficial. The medicinal aspect is also frequently mentioned by Xuan Ke in his English commentaries at tourist concerts. The atmosphere of reverence and the antique setting make the idea sufficiently plausible that I have seen several tourists claim to feel physical benefits from listening. The media often stress the exotic remoteness and beauty of Lijiang, thus bolstering its claim to be a place time forgot and consequently a possible repository of culture long since lost in central China.

Finally, many Chinese musicologists privately and sometimes publicly bemoan the loss of traditional musics, thanks in part to the Cultural Revolution and in part to the recent improvement in communications, and observe the diminution of authentic performance practices when folk genres are commercialized. The comments of He Changlin and Shen Qia are typical of such frequently expressed recent scholarly concerns.

Dongjing Music: What Foreigners Say

Descriptions in present-day foreign-authored travel guides are generally fairly brief. That in the guide published by Lonely Planet is quite typical. Speaking of the Dayan Town tourist concerts, it notes that the musicians are Naxi, that the music is "Taoist temple music lost elsewhere in China," and that one is offered "a rare chance to hear Chinese music as it must have sounded in classical China" (Cummings et al. 1991: 740). Clearly the major angle is preservation by the Naxi of ancient music from central China. Magazine articles too tend to take this line. For example, a Dutch author writes that this "traditional Chinese music" comes from the Han and Tang dynasties, and even from the time of Confucius; and that while it is lost in the rest of China, it is preserved in Lijiang by the Naxi (Paulzen 1991: 39; see also Clough 1995; Edwards 1997: 67).

English-language newspaper articles include all the above themes, and frequently touch too on the endangered nature of the tradition, its medicinal properties, and the triumph of its revival after the Cultural Revolution. Understandably, the authors cite Xuan Ke, the only English-speaking musician, as the source of their information on all these points (e.g., Christmas 1995; Clough 1995; Jack 1996; Leong 1996; Norman 1997; Farley 1999).

Many foreign tourists in Lijiang talked to me about the Dongjing music they had heard, mostly at the tourist concerts, but sometimes at Baihua Village. Apart from liking the "authenticity" of the music and being impressed by the elderly performers, many tourists had picked up from Xuan Ke's English-language commentary and from the visual evidence of the average age of the musicians that this music was in danger of dying out. One British tourist, who had heard only the Baihua group, wrote an account of his encounter with the "unique, ancient music" of the "Naxi orchestra," regretting its likely demise because of the obvious lack of young recruits. He also compared the Baihua group's amateur, unstaged musical gatherings favorably with a professionally staged, "sanitized 'folk' music performance" put on in a Kunming restaurant by students from the Yunnan Nationalities Institute (Kings 1991). This observer's account sums up well the impressions of many of the tourists I met: sorrow at the apparently likely demise of the music, liking for the "authenticity" of its presentation in contrast to specially staged minority arts shows seen elsewhere, enthusiasm for its "antiquity," and a perception of the music as identifiably "Naxi."

Comparison of Chinese- and Foreign-authored Accounts

Most foreigners are unable to read Chinese-language works and thus do not have access to the opinions of Chinese commentators, except for the very few English-language articles and the occasional oral exchange of views, usually with Xuan Ke. Equally, most Chinese do not have access to the writings of foreign authors. Given this situation, how do Chinese-authored and foreign-authored accounts compare?

Most foreign writers mention only Dongjing music, while some Chinese commentators refer to Dongjing music as part of the overall Naxi musical world. Foreign authors do, however, frequently emphasize three major themes in common with recent Chinese authors: the preservation of a historical cultural relic in a remote area; the "Naxi-ness" of the musicians or their music, or both; and as expressed in writing by He Changlin and frequently orally by the musicians themselves, the endangered nature of the tradition. Those foreign accounts based on interviews with Xuan Ke often add the idea of the music as medicine, and the triumph of the post–Cultural Revolution revival. Furthermore, the foreign accounts have a definitely romanticized tinge to them highly reminiscent of He Changlin's article and the inlay notes to the commercial cassettes cited above. The atmosphere of regret for the apparent passing of a tradition is reminiscent of the salvage ethnography so popular in the first half of this century.

It is not surprising that there are so many points in common between the representations by foreign and nonlocal Chinese authors and commentators. Both are "outsiders" to Lijiang's life and culture, and inclined to view the Naxi of Lijiang in the same way: as an exotic people living in a beautiful, remote location. In addition, many Chinese citizens as well as foreigners are concerned about the disappearance of traditional cultural forms in the modern world and like to hunt for them in out-of-the-way places.

Dongjing Music: The Tradition Bearers Speak

The 1980s and 1990s have seen a considerable number of writings by local people on the Dongjing music tradition, and not surprisingly the tone differs depending on the purpose of the document or article. Among scholarly works by those currently active in the musical tradition, the most notable are the two-part article by Yang Zenglie (1990–1991) and the briefer overview by Chong Xian (1989). The former is remarkable for its meticulous research and objective writing style. The latter is also based on detailed fieldwork and maintains a generally objective tone. Overall, in these scholarly descriptions there is little sign of the "implicit narrative structures" so evident in most of the writings discussed above.

This changes when one looks at treatments directed at a particular audience other than scholarly readers. For instance, in a 1992 report to the Dayan Town government on the Dayan Ancient Music Association's activities, the emphases are quite apparent. Concerning the "concerts of Naxi Ancient Music for foreigners," the preamble explains,

> Naxi Ancient Music (otherwise known as Lijiang Dongjing music) is a precious legacy of the outstanding traditional culture of the Chinese peoples. It is an exquisite product, a very special musical genre created by the melding of the culture of the Han and Naxi ethnic groups. The Dayan Ancient Music Association is an amateur musical performing group of the masses, a folk activity handed down for generations.
>
> [The aim of the organization is] to carry on and to disseminate this outstanding ethnic culture that is Naxi Ancient Music; to preserve this traditional musical living historic relic in a systematic and complete fashion; and to begin scholarly research [on the music]. [Our aim in doing this is] to help in the construction of socialist spiritual culture in Lijiang, and in the construction of material civilization. [We also aim to] improve the visibility of the renowned historical town [i.e., Dayan Town], and to contribute to the vigorous development of Lijiang's economy. (Dayan Guyuehui 1992: 1)

The report goes on to list in detail the sources of income for the association and their outgoings, which included assistance to impoverished members when sick, and donations to the 1991 flood disaster relief in central China and to the fund for the Third China Art Festival held in February 1992 in Kunming. Their other pro bono activities include the "Naxi Ancient Music Training Class" intended to help pass the music on to local youngsters. Regulations for members include the maintenance of good moral behavior and the responsibility on the part of the younger participants to assist the elderly musicians and do the heavy fetching and carrying.

In this report, the association clearly emphasizes the social legitimacy and utility of the music. It is a folk activity of the masses, a blend of Naxi and Han culture especially precious for its antiquity. It can promote the socialist culture and economic development of Lijiang County, and raise its profile in the outside world. Its players are people of good moral character who quite genuinely contribute to worthy causes. In short, they are a boon to Lijiang, and to Naxi cultural heritage.

A further twist in representation occurred in the context of the Dayan Ancient Music Association's trip to Beijing in September 1993 to perform at several high-profile venues. The enterprise was named "Classical music returns to the capital after four hundred years" (*Yayue huan jing sibai nian*). This is a clear reference to the oral tradition that the sixteenth-century Naxi ruler Mu Gong obtained Dongjing music from the Chinese capital and preserved it in Lijiang (Yang Zenglie 1990: 116; also reiterated many times by He Yi'an in interviews, 1991–1992). According to a document summarizing the arrangements, the purpose of the enterprise was multifold:

This event "Classical music returns to the capital" is not only an exceptional opportunity to display the ancient cultural art of the Naxi ethnic group to China and the outside world, it is also a chance to introduce and promote the local products of Lijiang Prefecture, and the natural resources available for tourism. [We can use this] opportunity to raise awareness of the renowned historical town [i.e., Dayan Town] and the beautiful scenery of the Jade Dragon [Snow Mountain] for tourists. (Lijiang Dayan Naxi Guyuehui 1993: 3)

To achieve this economic end, the document recommends that local Lijiang enterprises contact the organizers to get advertising space on the programs.

Several conceptual themes are competing here for attention. The title of the event underlines the angle of "preservation in a remote area of Chinese music otherwise lost." On the other hand, Dongjing music is at least a part of "the ancient cultural art of the Naxi ethnic group," so it has value as a Naxi symbol. Finally, the music is portrayed as an advertising opportunity for the economic development of Lijiang, a means to spread Lijiang's name in the outside world. It is also pointed out that the trip could gain recognition for Yunnan Province as a whole. The event received promises of financial and administrative support from the Yunnan Province Committee Propaganda Department, the Yunnan Ethnic Cultural Arts Exchange Company, and the governments of Lijiang Prefecture, Lijiang County, and Dayan Town (Lijiang Dayan Naxi Guyuehui 1993: 3–5). Obviously each group felt that the trip was worth backing—thus underlining just how important Lijiang's Dongjing music has become as a tool of local, ethnic, and even regional representation.

As I have indicated, local officials have an important influence on musical and cultural life. Lijiang's Dongjing musicians have been fortunate to have had the support of several officials who have worked hard to promote the music and facilitate their activities. For example, He Jiaxiu, the head of the propaganda department of the Lijiang Prefecture Party Committee, has offered consistent support and assistance. He was selected as the official to accompany nine musicians from the Dayan Ancient Music Association on their tour of England, and even took the trouble to learn some percussion parts so that he could participate in the performance. His summary of his views regarding the future of the music appears in the January 1996 special issue of the prefectural cultural magazine *Yulong Shan* (Jade Dragon Mountain), and represents a very important local viewpoint: that of an official actively engaged in the cultural scene. He reiterates many of the points mentioned by other local and non-local writers with regard to the antiquity of the tradition, the service the Naxi have performed by preserving this precious national heritage in Lijiang, and the value of the music to the tourist business; he also affirms the need to encourage performance of the music and the making of cultural products related to "Naxi Ancient Music," such as films, TV programs, cassettes, and CDs (He Jiaxiu 1996a). He plainly sees both the cultural value and the economic and advertising potential of the Dongjing tradition, rather as the Dayan Ancient Music Association does.

Local writing directed at the non-local Chinese and foreign audience for Lijiang's Dongjing music is a little different in emphasis. Here I take as an example the introductory program notes authored by association leader Xuan Ke for the Dayan Ancient Music Association's tour to Hong Kong in February 1997. Themes stressed include the antiquity of the music, its central Chinese origins, its refinement and employment by the literati, its preservation in remote, mountainous Lijiang, and the strenuous efforts to propagate an endangered tradition in the face of the encroachment of pop music and culture. "The Naxi people are committed to preserving some of the world's most precious cultural heritages," the first paragraph explains (Xuan and Yang 1997: 6). The romanticizing tone is reminiscent of Peter Goullart and He Changlin—not surprisingly, given the outsider audience at which the notes are directed.

Spoken Introduction to "Naxi Ancient Music" at the Tourist Concerts

Finally, I should like to turn to one form of oral documentation that has not so far been treated: the oral presentation that Xuan Ke, leader of the Dayan Ancient Music Association and their public spokesman, makes to all the tens of thousands of tourists who attend their concerts. In the 1980s and early 1990s, when the vast majority of tourists were foreign nationals, he usually spoke in English alone, but since domestic tourists have become the majority in the late 1990s, the presentation is now bilingual in English and Chinese. When speaking Chinese, Xuan always refers to the Dongjing repertoire as *Naxi Guyue* (Naxi Ancient Music). He invariably emphasizes that only the Naxi in their remote homeland have kept the ancient music from central China which came to Lijiang generations ago and has been handed down from father to son ever since. In addition, he stresses the difficulty of recruiting young people to learn the music, and often points out that some of the ticket money is used to help fund the "Naxi Ancient Music Training Class." A brilliant improviser, Xuan Ke is able to work in practically any material to make his point. For example, on 28 November 1991, he pointed to me playing with the ensemble, and said,

> Before she came, the Naxi children would not learn this good music . . . so after the foreign student, she comes to Lijiang and learned this only, never go to the ballroom for disco . . . so they [were surprised]. They said, "Maybe this good music, good music. Could we learn this music from your orchestra, Mr. Xuan Ke?" I said, "You are welcome, the door is opened." So now we can receive many. (taped speech)

I have never knowingly met a young Naxi who was inspired by my example to take up the music, but it nevertheless gets across Xuan Ke's point: most of the practitioners of Dongjing music are elderly, and popular music is so attractive to young local people that very few want to spend the time and trouble to learn the repertoire, so the training class is a necessity.

At the many tourist concerts I attended between 1989 and 1993, while Xuan Ke frequently reiterated that "everything here borrowing from other people" (i.e., most aspects of the Dongjing tradition were imported from outside Lijiang, from the Han), he was nevertheless keen to emphasize the Naxi contribution to the music. He introduced the double-reed pipe *bobo* as belonging specifically to the Naxi, and credited it with contributing to the "spirit of Naxi music" he felt existed in the Dongjing pieces. He frequently stated that "everyone here [is] Naxi,"[7] and his concern for the lack of young recruits was expressed in terms of "Naxi children" ignoring the music. By 1998, perhaps reflecting the fact that his tourist audience was now mostly (Han) Chinese, he gave particular emphasis to the angle of "Naxi preservation of ancient Han music" rather than to identifiably Naxi sounds.[8]

In addition, as described in chapter 7, Xuan Ke does his best to contribute to the atmosphere of rarified and timeless exoticism exuded by the picturesque setting and the solemn dress and demeanor of the musicians. He always emphasizes the ages of the oldest musicians, often adding a year or two for effect, and offers engaging anecdotes about individual instruments. This spoken presentation is vital to the commercial success of the concerts. The imperative need to locate an English-speaking substitute for Xuan Ke when he went to Canton in winter 1991–1992, as well as his own increasing national and international celebrity, have graphically demonstrated the central place of his interpretation in the presentation of the music to visitors.

Ethnicity

How important is the concept of Naxi ethnicity in the representations of Lijiang's Dongjing music now being created? Obviously it differs from one representer to the next, and from one intended audience to the next. Certainly "Naxi-ness" is an important part of the impression that tourists and much of the outside world have received during the 1990s. Even though the Han Chinese origins are stated by almost all authors, in most cases it is explained that the music has a mixture of Han and Naxi characteristics, or the Naxi ethnicity of its performers is emphasized. The recent popularity of the term *Naxi Guyue* (Naxi Ancient Music) in Chinese-language written and oral materials suggests an increasing identification of the ethnic group with the genre; this is observable in the documents and advertisements circulated within Lijiang itself, and in the Chinese-language newspaper articles the outside world sees. Furthermore, the inclusion of musicians playing largely Dongjing pieces in the 1991 trip to Canton as part of the Dongba Culture Performance Troupe inevitably helped tie this music to the ethnic identity of the Naxi, since it was thus associated with the archetypal symbol of Naxi ethnicity, the indigenous *dongba*. Similarly, the group that traveled to Beijing in 1993 was named the "China Lijiang Naxi Ancient Music Troupe," which cannot help but reinforce the impression that there is something specifically Naxi about the music played. Furthermore, both these high-profile concert trips involved the promotion of Lijiang Naxi Autonomous County; and a cultural program advertised as representing Lijiang may reasonably be assumed to have strong Naxi characteristics. While the Han Chinese origins of the Dongjing repertoire are proudly acknowledged, its Naxi affiliation is greatly stressed.

Outsiders, therefore, are likely to receive the impression that Naxi input into the Dongjing repertoire is extremely substantial; or even that Lijiang's Dongjing music is "Naxi Ancient Music" pure and simple. This is significant, since the music has recently become so important in creating an identity for and attracting tourism and investment to Lijiang Naxi Autonomous County. But how do the Naxi themselves view the music? Advertisements directed at young people to learn the music refer to the training class "for Naxi Ancient Music." This promotes a view of the music as an important part of specifically Naxi cultural heritage.[9] My Naxi friends, who usually refer to the music in casual conversation with me as *guyue* (ancient music), are aware of the Han Chinese origins of the Dongjing repertoire; but they also draw completely valid stylistic parallels between certain features of Dongjing music performance and the performance practice of other local musical genres. This applies especially to some of the instruments and to the slow, wide vibrato heard both in Lijiang's Dongjing music and in Naxi folk songs.

The frequent emphasis on Lijiang's Dongjing music as marked to a great extent by Naxi influence, and on its validity as a cultural ambassador for Lijiang Naxi Autonomous County, may be clarified by reference to the history of ethnic awareness in China, set out in detail in chapter 2. In 1940s Lijiang, Dongjing music in its ritual context was a badge of sinicized sophistication and consequent high social status. Even some of the secular groups looked upon it as a particularly refined form of music—in contrast to, for example, the local opera Dianju or folk dances. By the early 1990s, on the other hand, when the music had long since been revived in purely secular form, the local government, entrepreneurs, and some of the musicians themselves had begun to underline the Naxi affiliation of the music. As noted in chapter 7, by 1996 the Dayan Ancient Music Association had many recruits aged forty-five and under, for whom the pre-1949 resonances of the music are slight. Far from eschewing folk dances, as I was told that urban Dongjing association members did, some of these younger people routinely participate in any and all local musical activities; one in particular, a farmer and butcher, is a mainstay of the ensemble, and is also in great demand for miles around as a flute player for rural festival dances. In explaining his participation in several different kinds of music making, including Dongjing music, he said, "I like the music of my ethnic group." This suggests that he views all these musical genres as Naxi in nature.

The reasons for these developments probably have to do with changes in class and ethnic consciousness. In the 1940s, the distinction between those who played the music in the context of the Dongjing associations and those who took part in Naxi-language folksinging and peasant dancing was essentially one of class; those who aspired to political, economic, and social leadership, especially in Dayan Town, expressed their class affiliation by an overt rejection of indigenous local musical and dance forms, leaving them to the illiterate peasant masses. They expressed their higher class status by cleaving to the cultural pursuits of the dominant ethnic/cultural group of their political world, the Han Chinese, and were proud to do so. There were pragmatic advantages to be gained from this: it drew a boundary between them and the illiterate Naxi peasants and affirmed their elite status; it gained them respect from officials and other literati; and it brought them closer to educated Han Chinese, with whom they interacted on an equal footing in the Han-dominated wider world.

This was the situation, then, up to 1949. Thereafter, performance of Dongjing music was sporadically disrupted for about thirty years. By the early 1990s, when the renaissance of the music was well under way, the tradition had been reincarnated as a firmly secular art form, and one with a strong Naxi rather than class identity. There are several possible reasons for this. First, in the intervening forty years, it had become politically and often economically useful to emphasize one's identity as a national minority, even if one's descent had previously been a matter of little consequence (David Wu 1990: 3). There is no doubt that the self-identity of the Lijiang Naxi was established long before 1949 (Goullart 1957: 205–206; McKhann 1995: 48; Naxizu Jianshi Bianxiezu 1984: 1). Thus it was natural to espouse and encourage a definitively Naxi culture when it became advantageous to emphasize this preexisting identity. Second, the sharp class distinctions overtly emphasized in the 1940s have become anachronistic anathema in a socialist state that destroyed the landlord class in its first couple of years. Third, government policy positively encourages national minorities to develop and claim their own distinct and differentiated art forms. Fourth, as described in chapter 7, the recent influx of foreign and domestic tourists to Lijiang has led to a self-conscious ethnicity in the way the Naxi present themselves to outsiders.

Conscious motivation certainly plays a part in all of this; but in addition, especially for those born since 1949, the government version of ethnic identity has been inculcated through official education and media for years. On the evidence of fieldwork carried out in the mid-1990s, one scholar suggests that "state education involuntarily supports—perhaps even creates—a focus on ethnic identity." In the Naxi case, state education—and local reaction to it—has "been instrumental in the development of a stronger and forcefully expressed ethnic identity" (Hansen 1999: 84–85). This modern sense of identity impelled by internal and external forces, and the "unexamined assumptions" it brings in its wake, have become a reality (Bentley 1987: 28). In Bourdieu's terms, the government's ethnicity policies, when added to pre-existing notions of ethnic identity, have contributed to the molding of a certain *habitus* among minorities and Han Chinese alike. In Lijiang, the unconscious set of assumptions and practices which comprise this *habitus* make it quite logical for the Naxi inhabitants of Lijiang to respond to certain new stimuli by stressing their "Naxi-ness," even in spheres where the environment and outlook of fifty years ago would have made such a response unlikely. The ingraining of government policy in the consciousness of both ethnic minorities and the Han majority probably explains why Lijiang's Dongjing music has recently acquired the new name "Naxi Ancient Music," a term never traditionally used. It has attracted international admiration and generated substantial income both for the individual musicians and for Lijiang Naxi Autonomous County as a whole, at least in part because of the Naxi ethnicity of its performers; so it is logical to emphasize its Naxi qualities, even though these are presumably no more or less present than they were before 1949.

Summary: Representation of Music in Lijiang

From the foregoing examples it is obvious that the examination of representations of Lijiang's music can offer valuable information on the frames of reference of different authors at different times in history, writing for different audiences. Not only can we illuminate the frames of reference within which the writers are operating, and thus elucidate the diverse meanings the music holds for different parties, we can also gather valuable information on extramusical historical developments. Praise in the early twentieth century for the refinement and civilized nature of Dongjing music (with no hint of any specifically Naxi input) suggests a traditional Confucian, Han-oriented cultural mindset. Recent praise for the Naxi as "good at singing and dancing" and the frequent presentation in local documents of Dongjing music as a valuable part of Naxi heritage help underscore the impact of the current nationalities policy at the local level. Overt acknowledgment of the music as a cultural flagship for Lijiang capable of bringing in outside investment and trade also indicates a mindset dominant in the increasingly free-market 1990s. Perhaps most significantly, the examination of all these different representations allows us to compare and contrast the frames of reference of "internal" and "external" audiences (cf. Graburn 1976: 5–6), and the impact of the increase in the latter on the former. With the wide recognition now accorded Lijiang's Dongjing music, and the generation gap among the performers, there are several different "implicit narrative structures" all existing simultaneously. Some of these "implicit narrative structures" interact and influence the tradition itself; in the late 1980s and early 1990s, for instance, Xuan Ke actively inserted Goullart's romantic account of Dongjing associations from the 1940s into the picture he painted for his largely foreign audience. The success of this picture among outside visitors then contributed to the commercial viability of the genre, which in turn helped push its candidacy as a cultural ambassador for Lijiang. The music's success in this role has actually fed back into its own survival: almost certainly its new prestige and the chance of financial gain have been factors motivating some of the dozens of young recruits who learn the tradition in the late 1990s. Some of these phenomena are of course visible from the secondhand depiction of events which constitutes the bulk of ethnographic writing. However, an examination of the "dominant stories" underlying the interpretations of different agents, and the vocabulary with which they tell them, often sheds fresh light on the subject. In the case of Lijiang's Dongjing music, the "stories people tell" constitute a major part of the evidence for the development of the tradition. That these "stories" can co-exist and interact is demonstrated by the ease with which so many authors and commentators incorporate both the angle of the "endangered, precious remnant of lost Han Chinese music" and the importance of identifiably Naxi input into the tradition.

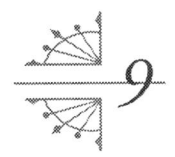

Conclusion

From Dongjing Music to Naxi Ancient Music

In the twentieth century, Lijiang's Dongjing music has been exalted ritual music, refined secular entertainment, funeral music, tool of patriotic and political propaganda, object of musicological interest, emblem of place and ethnicity, and an economic asset in the socialist market economy and the tourist trade. Over the last fifty years it has also traveled a trajectory of geographically widening recognition and significance.

Initially a music with both sacred and secular roles, it has been a totally secular phenomenon since 1949. Traditionally an amateur activity, many of whose proponents would not have been seen dead making money from it, since 1988 it has been put to both amateur and commercial uses. Before 1949 a music of purely local significance, it gradually gained sporadic recognition at provincial and national level, and since 1988 has achieved national and international acclaim through tourist performances, commercial recordings, and concert tours to Canton, Beijing, Shanghai, Hong Kong, Taiwan, and six European countries.

Interpretations of the meaning of the music, too, have changed over time. The snob value and high cultural prestige implicitly predicated on the Han Chineseness of Dongjing music in local society before 1949, especially in its ritual context, have become anachronistic, giving way to an increased emphasis on its Naxiness as it interacts with an outside world ever more interested in minority identity and culture. This new emphasis on ethnic rather than class affiliation is strongly underlined in the written and oral evidence presented in chapter 8, and may be attributed to the pervasive influence of the government's nationalities policy, the fascination of visitors with the remote and the exotic, and the music's consequent utility in commercial and tourist promotion. Thanks to these factors, allied to the improvement in communications in the late twentieth century, Lijiang's Dongjing music has become Naxi Ancient Music.

Minority Music and the Socialist State

Like the Soviet Union before it, Communist China has explicitly rejected previous governments' overt preference for cultural assimilation of its ethnic minorities. Given the government's keen interest in management and development of the arts in directions compatible with the policies of the socialist polity, this has created the preconditions for private and public performance of musics closely identified with those ethnic minorities. The importance of such preconditions was vividly demonstrated when they largely disappeared during the Cultural Revolution, taking much minority (as well as Han) culture with them for several years. For most of the history of the People's Republic, however, there has been overt encouragement of minority arts forms, even if these have often been heavily reworked and reinterpreted in the public sphere. The Naxi and other minorities can pursue many of their traditional musics (other than those too closely allied to "feudal superstition" or anti-Communist sentiments) with the overt approval of the state, which has itself seen the value of utilizing and adapting such musics for purposes of political and, more recently, economic persuasion.

Because of the enthusiasm of most socialist states for giving firm direction to folk arts and folklore scholarship, examination of the minority music scene frequently offers valuable evidence of a government's approach to ethnic diversity. Like China, the Soviet Union espoused an explicit policy of recognition of national identities and cultures rather than overt compulsory Russification, and thus generally encouraged both the training of minority performers from favored ethnic groups (Slobin 1971; Levin 1979; Muhambetova 1995) and scholarship on minority traditions (e.g., Beliaev 1975 [1962]), albeit within boundaries defined for political reasons by the state (Zemtsovsky and Kunanbaeva 1997). Like China, too, the Soviet Union promoted domestic and international performances by minority arts troupes. Nevertheless, at the professional level in both countries, there has been an obvious emphasis on the "improvement" of folk and minority musics in line with the Marxist-inspired belief in the higher level of Western art-music-style harmony, polyphony, and orchestral organization; this has resulted in a tendency toward countrywide professional homogenization. While this stands in ironic opposition to the overt goal of promoting cultural diversity, it is perhaps an unintended musical metaphor for the successful resolution of socialist national unity with ethnic diversity—a resolution explicitly assumed in the common Chinese statement that "our country is a unified multiethnic socialist country" (*woguo shi yi ge tongyi de duo minzu de shehuizhuyi guojia*).

In contrast to China's overt encouragement of minority cultural activities, which has facilitated and directed so much private and public minority music-making, other socialist governments have gone in the opposite direction, seeking to outlaw artistic symptoms of ethnic diversity. In Mongolia, a country of more than twenty distinct peoples, the Stalinist regime wished to deny ethnic differences as well as extirpate religion in order to create a "unified national socialist identity"; as a result, performance traditions that challenged those goals were eradicated or forcibly changed. For example, composite versions of oral epics collected from different Mongolian peoples were published, with no acknowledgment that certain epics were particular to specific peoples (Pegg 1995: 77–78). Despite the Soviet Union's overt encouragement of ethnic diversity within socialist guidelines, this did not extend to the folklore of certain disfavored peoples repressed under Stalin, such as the Volga Deutsch and the Crimean Tartars (Zemtsovsky and Kunanbaeva 1997: 19). In the 1980s, the Bulgarian government pursued a vigorous policy of monoethnicism against its ethnic Turks, Gypsies, and Pomaks—Moslem groups making up more than 17 percent of the total population of 8.5 million. This included discouraging or banning traditional Moslem clothing and certain types of folk music identified with these groups, such as *zurna* (shawm) playing, and *kyuchek*, a distinctive type of Gypsy music and dance (Silverman 1989: 147–148). When a popular "wedding music" influenced by Turkish, Gypsy, and non-Bulgarian groups spread widely in the 1980s, the government tried to control the phenomenon through auditions and registration; and prestigious state music festivals attempted to dictate the aesthetics of performing groups more in line with the government's vision of correct Bulgarian music (Rice 1994: 247–255).

As noted, investigating the status of minority art forms in socialist states can inform us as to the practical treatment of ethnic diversity in those countries—which may or may not entirely reflect enunciated policy. At a microlevel, looking at how individual musicians and groups act within and against the constraints and opportunities of their environment offers useful case studies of the degree of individual agency instrumental in musical change, and of the active roles music may play as its meaning is interpreted in its social setting—for example, as a validating element (revolutionary songs and model operas in China), a subversive metaphor (Bulgarian wedding music), or an expression of identity and means of economically advantageous communication with the outside world.

It is these last two factors that have come into play as Naxi musicians have taken advantage of China's political and economic liberalization to leap into the artistic marketplace. As Rice notes, economic liberalization in a socialist country "generate[s] a music system responsive to economic demands" (1994: 242); and in this case, perspicacious and talented individuals grasped the opportunity to repackage a local music in a form attractive to tourist customers increasingly interested in minority culture. Furthermore, the music's economic success has helped make it one of several important symbols of Naxi identity, itself a concept in tune with the stated policy of the Chinese government, and one with valuable benefits for Lijiang in terms of national and international visibility. A happy coincidence of individual, ethnic, governmental, and tourist interests has allowed Lijiang's Dongjing music to affect its locale in ways unthought of before the late 1980s.

Theoretical Perspectives

In chapter 1, I cited Nketia's suggestion that we move from a view of music as a passive recipient of extramusical influences to one of music as an active agent in its environment. Lijiang's Dongjing music has played an active social role in a century full of political upheavals. Use, transmission, and stylistic differences within the repertoire have helped articulate and differentiate relations based on social class, intergroup interaction, intragroup hierarchy, and egalitarian friendship. More recently the music has been a major factor in the presentation of Lijiang and the Naxi to the outside world; it has also brought money to the county and to individual musicians.

Indeed, individuals have loomed large in the study on which this book is based. To be sure, the overall political, economic, and social environment provides the necessary preconditions for the music to function; but it is individuals who are demonstrably the catalysts in making things happen. The Dongjing association tradition could not have spread around Lijiang County had individuals not had the inspiration and commitment to transmit and learn it; the post–Cultural Revolution revival was orchestrated by several courageous and energetic men who took a visible lead; and, as we have seen, the recent engagement with the outside world has relied to an enormous extent on the English-language and public relations skills of a single musician. Rice asks, "How do people historically construct, socially maintain and individually create and experience music?" (1987: 473). Chapters 5 through 8 have offered diachronic answers to all these questions; a related question which has arisen unbidden through the reliance in this book on interview data has been, "How do people remember music history?" As the fifth chapter shows, to a large degree the answer is, "individually": even decades after the fact, oral history is for its protagonists a tapestry of individual actions and small-group decisions, superimposed on a background of national events.

One of the chief values of this study, in fact, is its ability to relate national events and trends in China's recent history to daily life in a small, rather remote county nearly four thousand kilometers from the national capital. Music, as many writers dealing with Africa have suggested, can offer useful historical evidence from a distinctive perspective. I would suggest that the value of Lijiang's music to historians is twofold. In the first place, the florescence, adaptation, destruction, and revival of musical forms act as a barometer both of intracounty social and political conditions, and increasingly, of the impact of national events, policies, and decisions on the Chinese periphery. The second contribution of musical evidence is more subtle, but relates to one of the paradigms of music history enunciated by Neuman: that of "immanent music history," in which "music 'writes' or in some manner represents history: a history not so much of music itself as of its creators or consumers" (1991: 269). I suggested in chapter 4 that one can view the musical activities of Republican Lijiang as a map, with people's participation in music and dance largely defined by their ethnic group and social status, and by their position as urban or rural, male or female, old or young. The same is, of course, true for the Communist period described in chapter 6, although the auditory parameters have expanded in some directions and contracted in others since 1949. Paul Stoller (1989) has argued for a greater consideration of sensory evidence in ethnographic writing, and I suggest that Lijiang County offers proof of the validity of this approach. In many cases one can actually hear, see, and feel ethnic interaction in borrowed music and dance: one can trace shared tunes and styles across counties and ethnic groups, hear the difference between a Naxi folk dance and the Dongjing repertoire, and pick out the introduction of Western harmony and instruments into certain commercial recordings of Lijiang's music—sensory evidence of a local and national history at ineffable work.

My own introduction to the tangled tale of Naxi Ancient Music was entirely via the history "immanent" in the music I heard that spring night in 1989: I wanted to understand why the "traditional Naxi music" played by the Naxi musicians sounded so similar to Han instrumental ensemble genres I knew from the east coast. Sun Jiong, representative of the Yunnan Province China Overseas Tourism Company, was no doubt thinking largely of the immediate audiovisual affect of the famed tourist concerts when he described Lijiang's Dongjing music as "echoes of history" (1996); yet at a deeper level, much of Lijiang's recent history is indeed "written" into its music and into people's understanding of that music. What echoes back to us is stories of ethnic interactions, changing social mores and ideologies, individual travel and initiative, and an ever-increasing engagement with the world beyond the county boundaries.

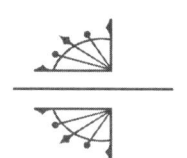

Appendix A

Dongjing Scriptures of Lijiang County

The version of the *Transcendent Scripture of the Great Grotto of Wenchang* from Lijiang County[1] is almost identical to that used in Baoshan City in west Yunnan.[2] It consists of seven fascicles, all of which were sung and recited at each Wenchang festival. In the order of performance, these fascicles are:

1. *Kaitan Yiwen* (Rite of Opening the Altar)
2. *Yuqing Wuji Zongzhen Wenchang Dadong Xianjing Liqing Quanjuan* (Complete Formal Invocation of the Transcendent Scripture of the Great Grotto of Wenchang)
3, 4, 5. *Yuqing Wuji Zongzhen Wenchang Dadong Xianjing juan shang, juan zhong, juan xia* (Transcendent Scripture of the Great Grotto of Wenchang, first fascicle, second fascicle, third fascicle)
6. *Yuqing Wuji Zongzhen Wenchang Dadong Shenzhou Quanjuan* (Complete Divine Spells of the Transcendent Scripture of the Great Grotto of Wenchang)
7. *Wenchang Qilu Baosi Dengke* (The Wenchang Rite of Lighting a Lamp for Entreating Prosperity and Preserving Descendants).

The *Rite of Opening the Altar* begins with an eight-line opening ode and continues with ten stanzas purifying the participants and regulating the conduct of the ritual. Then comes a brief "Divine Spell" (*Zhanjuan shenzhou*), followed by five texts:

a. *Taishang Hunyuan Laojun Shuo Chang Qingjing Jing* (The Scripture of Perpetual Purity and Quietude as Spoken by Laozi) (Taoist Canon, Harvard-Yenching Index [HY] 620)

b. *Taishang Dongxuan Lingbao Shengxuan Xiaozai Huming Miaojing* (The Wondrous Scripture Which Staves Off Calamity and Protects Life) (Taoist Canon, HY 19)

c. *Taishang Lingbao Tianzun Shuo Rangzai Du'e Zhenjing* (The True Scripture Which Exorcises Calamity and Overcomes Misfortune, as Spoken by the Lingbao Heavenly Worthy) (Taoist Canon, HY 357)

d. *Wushang Yuhuang Xinyin Jing* (The Jade Emperor Heart-Seal Scripture), an important theoretical work in *neidan* (inner alchemy)[3] (Taoist Canon, HY 13)

e. *Wenchang Dijun Yinzhi Wen* (The Wenchang Tract of the Quiet Way [translation by Suzuki and Carus, 1906]).

The fascicle concludes with a closing invocation (*yangqi*) and ode (*shoujing jie*).

The fifth of these texts, *The Wenchang Tract of the Quiet Way*, has been extensively researched and translated. Of late Ming origins, the present-day text was first printed in 1689; only sixteen characters have been added since then. Most editions attribute the text to Wenchang (van der Loon 1962). It expresses a mixture of Confucian and Buddhist moral maxims of filiality, good citizenship, and kindness to people and animals. Foreign commentators note the wide distribution of the text throughout China in the late nineteenth century (e.g., Suzuki and Carus 1906: 3). Its moral maxims appear to have been written deliberately in easily comprehensible Chinese so as to appeal to the common people (Eichler 1882–1883: 94).

The second of the seven fascicles in the Lijiang scripture, the *Complete Formal Invocation of the Transcendent Scripture of the Great Grotto of Wenchang*, includes purification incantations, invocations to the spirit realm and to deceased kin, and other prefatory matter (see chapter 4 for a detailed list and manner of performance). It is very similar to the second fascicle of the text HY 103 in the Taoist Canon, except that it concludes with the ceremony of Ten Offerings (*Shi Gongyang*). Many scriptures used by Yunnan Dongjing associations include a ceremony of ten offerings to the relevant deity. In Wenchang's case the order is always as follows: flowers (*hua gongyang*), fruit (*guo gongyang*), incense (*xiang gongyang*), rice (*shi gongyang*), tea (*cha gongyang*), garments (*yi gongyang*), water (*shui gongyang*), talismans (*fu gongyang*), a double offering of fermented beverages and lamp (*jinjiu fadeng shuang gongyang*), and cash (*cai gongyang*). It is unusual in Yunnan for the Ten Offerings to come in the *Complete Formal Invocation of the Transcendent Scripture of the Great Grotto of Wenchang*: with the exception of this version of the scripture, peculiar to Lijiang County and Baoshan City, the Ten Offerings always appears in the fascicle *Yuqing Wuji Zongzhen Wenchang Dadong Xianjing juan zhong* (e.g., in texts used in Yongsheng, Dali, Xiaguan, Weishan, Chuxiong, Heijing, Lufeng, Kunming, Tonghai, Jianshui, Mengzi, and Luxi).[4]

The three central fascicles of the scripture (*Yuqing Wuji Zongzhen Wenchang Dadong Xianjing juan shang, zhong, xia*) are basically identical to the version titled *Dongjing Shidu* from the *Daozang Jiyao* (Collected Essentials of the Taoist Canon). This version has only twenty-four stanzas in the main text. The language of the stanzas of the main text is obscure and is understood by very few Dongjing association members. The content concerns the practice of *xiulian*, or self-cultivation through physical and meditative exercises (Zhang Xingrong 1998: 87). He Yi'an, former association member from Dayan Town, commented that his private practice of *qigong* (often translated "Chinese yoga") enabled him to understand the text better than most, but that there were still parts that were difficult for him. Two prefaces to the first of these fascicles are dated 1728 and 1736.

The three sections (*juan shang, juan zhong, juan xia*) of the sixth of the Lijiang fascicles, *Complete Divine Spells of the Transcendent Scripture of the Great Grotto of Wenchang*, all begin with an "opening ode" (*kaijing jie*). In each case this is followed by a section of the "Great Grotto Divine Spells" (*Dadong shenzhou*). The third section (*juan xia*) ends with three sets of stanzas in which three deities extol the scripture (*Yuanhuang Da Tiandi zan Dadong Jing ershiwu shi, Zhengyuansou Zhenren zan Dadong Jing gu shi shishou, Qinghe Laoren zan Dadong Jing gu shi shisi shou*). The language of the "Divine Spells" is sufficiently obscure that none of my Lijiang informants understood the contents. The first two sections may be found in the Taoist Canon, HY 78, and most of the third in HY 386.

The seventh fascicle of the Lijiang scripture, the short *Wenchang Rite of Lighting a Lamp for Entreating Prosperity and Preserving Descendants*, calls upon and professes faith in Wenchang, his relatives, and other divine beings; toward the end the petitioner(s) insert(s) a memorial explaining the purpose of the day's ceremony. Models for these memorials are given in the *Shuwen Digao* (Memorials Manuscript) hand copied in 1905, one copy of which exists in the Lijiang County Library.

In a typical three-day ceremony honoring Wenchang, each day began with the *Rite of Opening the Altar*. The first day continued with the *Complete Formal Invocation* and the first fascicle of the *Transcendent Scripture*. The second day featured the reading of a memorial, then performance of the second and third fascicles of the *Transcendent Scripture*. The third day was devoted to the *Complete Divine Spells* before sending off the god (*songsheng*) with the aid of the *Wenchang Rite of Lighting a Lamp* (Yang Zenglie 1990: 136–138).

The Lijiang *Guandi Enlightenment Scripture* has four fascicles:

1, 2, 3. *Guansheng Dijun Jueshi Zhenjing, juan shang, zhong, xia* (Guandi Enlightenment Scripture, first fascicle, second fascicle, third fascicle)

4. *Guansheng Dijun Danfeng Chaoyang Baochan* (Guandi Precious Repentance).

The first three fascicles are used in practically the same form by the Nanya Music Society (*Nanya Yinyue She*), a Dongjing association in Dali.

The first fascicle contains three prefaces, two of which are dated, to 1776 and 1678. They are followed by the *Guansheng Dijun Baoxun* (Precious Instructions of Guandi), dated 1775. The central text of the first fascicle is the *Jueshi Jingwen* (Enlightenment Scripture). This text is mentioned by Eichler as being one of the tracts popular throughout China in the late nineteenth century (1882–1883: 147).[5] It focuses on a number of moral maxims strikingly reminiscent of *The Wenchang Tract of the Quiet Way*. The second fascicle centers on the ten offerings to Guandi, which differ slightly from those to Wenchang: flowers, fruit, incense, rice, garments, cash, tea, water, talismans, and a double offering of fermented beverages and a lamp. The core of the third fascicle is eighteen chapters that stress the maintenance of health and good fortune and avoidance of disaster through the practice of traditional (Confucian) virtues. These chapters appear almost verbatim in the text *Sanjie Fumo Guansheng Dijun Zhong Xiao Yi Zhenjing* (Guandi True Scripture of Loyalty, Filial Piety, and Righteousness), which appears in the 1971 edition of the *Collected Essentials of the Taoist Canon*, volume 23.

The fourth fascicle centers on eight sections that discuss the sins of omission resulting from neglect of the traditional virtues. These are: failure to show proper respect to heaven and earth (*bu jing tiandi*); disloyalty to rulers (*bu zhong junwang*); unfilial behavior (*bu xiao fumu*); breach of friendly relations with brothers (*bu you xiongdi*); disrespect to teachers and elders (*bu gong shizhang*); mistrust in dealings with friends (*bu xin pengyou*); failure to distinguish the proper spheres of husband and wife (*bu bie fufu*); and failure to promote harmonious relations in one's homeland (*bu he xiangli*).

Appendix B

Temple Interior for Dongjing Ceremonies in Dayan Town

The diagram in this appendix is based on a hand-drawn one by Yang Zenglie (an amplification of his original diagram [1990: 128]). Working largely from information supplied by He Yi'an, formerly of the Dayan Town Dongjing association, Yang offers an excellent description of the temple interior during Dongjing ceremonies (pp. 124–129). I summarize this description below, amplifying in places from my own interviews with He Yi'an and Zhang Longhan.

The diagram shows the general layout of the temple and the seating plan. It assumes a ceremony for Wenchang. Each of the eight tables in front of the offering table seated two men, and was adorned with one of the eight trigrams (*bagua*); the sixteen positions thus created were known as the "principal seats" (*zhengwei*) and were reserved for longstanding association members. Newer members sat closer to the walls of the temple, in no particular order. The only instruments with immutable positions were those indicated on the diagram; there were no predetermined places for any of the other instruments, although there had to be a pair of flutes (*dizi*), one on each side. Players responsible for the large cymbals (*nao* and *bo*), the large drum (*dagu*), the large gong (*daluo*), the chime (*qing*), and the bell (*zhong*) could also play other instruments, since these instruments were struck only occasionally.

The "sacred curtain" (*shenzhang*) was a backdrop suspended from the wall of the temple behind the main ritual table. It no longer exists, but was probably embroidered with celestial beings and auspicious symbols.

The small ritual table (*xiao jingzhuo*) was positioned on the main ritual table (*da shenzhuo* or *wanjuan zhuo*). On the small ritual table were placed the bronze statues of three

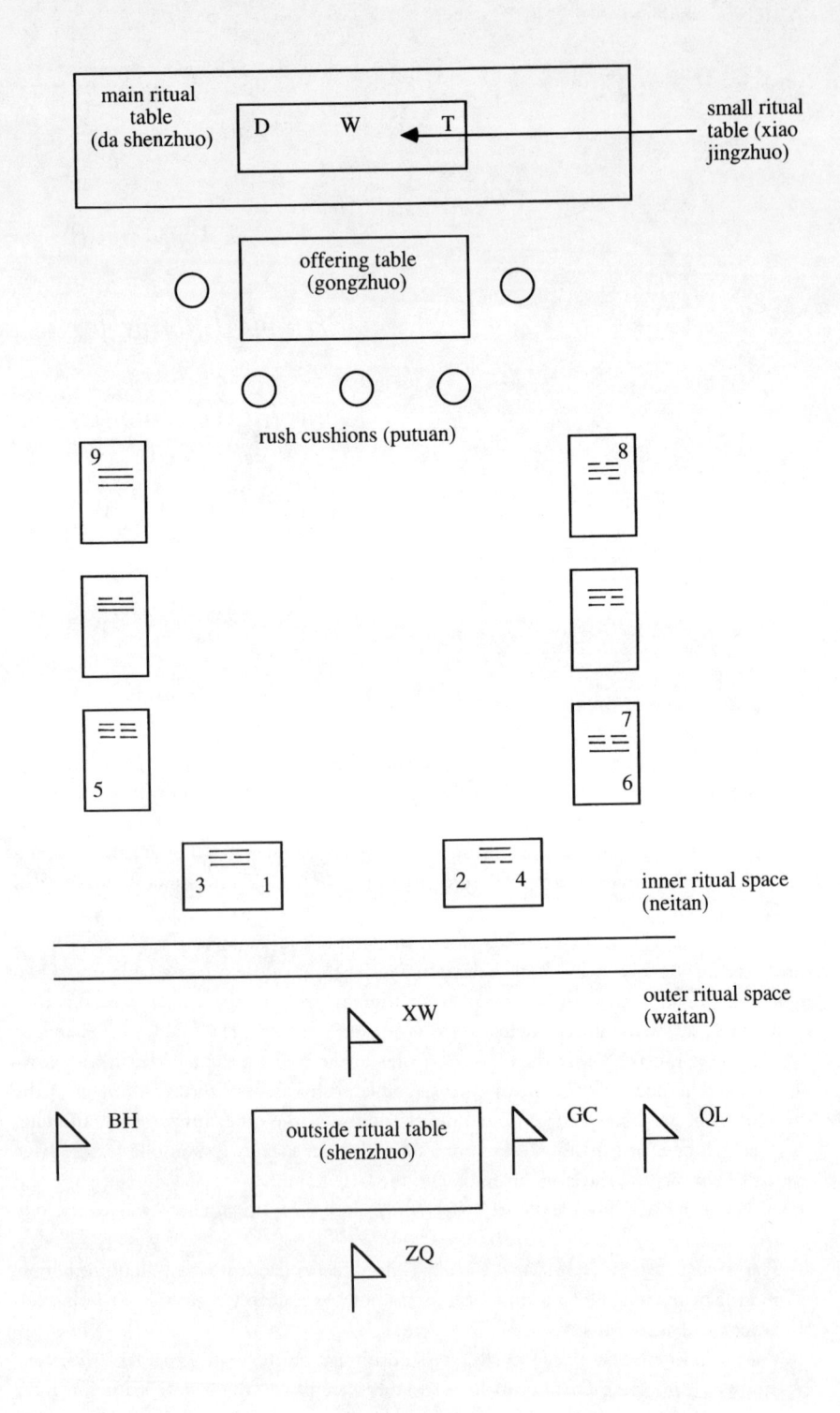

| main ritual table (da shenzhuo) | D   W   T | ← small ritual table (xiao jingzhuo) |

offering table (gongzhuo)

rush cushions (putuan)

9 ☰

8 ☷

☷

☷

5 ☷

6 ☷ 7

3 ☷ 1   2 ☷ 4

inner ritual space (neitan)

outer ritual space (waitan)

▷ XW

▷ BH   outside ritual table (shenzhuo)   ▷ GC   ▷ QL

▷ ZQ

W	statue of Wenchang
T	statue of Tianlong
D	statue of Diya
GC	pennant to the left is that of Gouchen (Angular Array)
XW	two pennants, of Xuanwu (Black Tortoise) and the seven northerly constellations
BH	two pennants, of Baihu (White Tiger) and the seven westerly constellations
QL	two pennants, of Qinglong (Blue Dragon) and the seven easterly constellations
ZQ	two pennants, of Zhuque (Vermilion Bird) and the seven southerly constellations
1	seat for *shanzhang* (chief ritual officiant), playing *muyu* (woodblock), *ban'gu* (small drum), and *tishou* (clappers)
2	seat for *fu shanzhang* (second ritual officiant), playing *yunluo* (cloud gong) and *tongling* (bell)
3	seat for *dagu* (large drum)
4	seat for *huizhang* (association head)
5	seat for *bo* (large cymbals with large bosses)
6	seat for *nao* (large cymbals with small bosses)
7	seat for *daluo* (large gong)
8	seat for *zhong* (bell)
9	seat for *qing* (chime)

gods, with Wenchang in the middle and his acolyte Tianlong to his left and acolyte Diya to his right. Tianlong held a copy of the *Dadong Xianjing* (Transcendent Scripture of the Great Grotto), while Diya held a jade *ruyi* sceptre. The Dayan Town association's statue of Wenchang had been bought from Zitong County in Sichuan, the god's place of origin, by He Gengji (1864–1951), one of the last heads of the association, during his sojourn as governor of Lezhi County in Sichuan Province. If performing a ceremony in honor of Guandi rather than Wenchang, the central statue would be that of Guandi, with his acolytes Guanping (holding a seal) and Zhoulun (holding a broadsword) to his left and right. (For associations that lacked statues, wooden deity tablets [*shengpai*] engraved with each god's name could be substituted.) Behind the gods' statues were a pair of fans with small circular mirrors nailed to the top and, beneath, depictions of dragons, phoenixes, peacocks, and white cranes. Underneath the fans were two bronze concave mirrors, each with nine small mirrors inset around their sides. To the sides of the gods' statues, possibly on the main ritual table, were six wooden deity tablets, three to the left and three to the right, each engraved with the name of another god.

On the main ritual table to either side of the small table were two pots (*qiantong*) holding bamboo slips (*jiechi*). Each of these slips specified the number of kowtows to be performed as penance for infringement of association discipline. It was the job of the disciplinarian (*jiucha*) to watch out for such infractions as tardy arrival, failing to replace the cover on a scripture when it was finished, disarrangement of clothing, smoking in the temple, disarranging the instruments, playing out of tune, being noisy in the temple, and the like; when he noticed this kind of behavior, he would present the malefactor with a slip out of the pots, and the culprit would have to take the slip, perform his penance immediately, and then return the slip to the pot. Altogether there were twenty possible infractions.

In front of the small ritual table was placed a white sandalwood *ruyi* sceptre engraved with the characters for the three stars of Orion's belt (*Fu Lu Shou*); this had been bought from Guangdong Province in southeast China. In front of the sceptre was an incense container, and in front of the incense container were five tin plates, each cast with the character for longevity (*shou*). The middle plate held a *ruyi* sceptre, the first left civil garments, the first right military garments, the second left the book *Dadong Falu* (Great Grotto Talismans), and the second right a copper alloy incense burner. Behind the small ritual table in the middle was a "spirit lamp" (*shendeng*), and (presumably on the main table) there were also small lamps representing the constellations of the Big Dipper (*Beidou Qixing*), Sagittarius (*Nandou Liuxing*), and Orion's belt (*Fu Lu Shou Sanxing*).

In front of the main ritual table was placed an offering table (*gongzhuo*), also known as "eight immortals table" (*baxian zhuo*), which was hung round with an embroidered cloth decorated with dragons and phoenixes and the characters *Guixiang Baodian* (Cassia Fragrance Precious Hall). On this were placed a silver bowl of ritually pure water, a bronze incense burner, two candlesticks burning scented oil, and cups containing tea and fermented beverages.

To either side of the offering table was placed a rush cushion (*putuan*), with three more in front of it; these were for association members whose ritual duties or role making offerings brought them to this area, to cushion their knees while kneeling or kowtowing.

The final adornments inside the temple, in the *neitan* (inner ritual space), were four rows of cloth streamers hanging down from the roof. From back to front, the first row consisted of thirteen long, rectangular streamers, each listing the name of one of Wenchang's relatives. The second consisted of ten larger such streamers, each listing the name of a heavenly worthy (*tianzun*). The third was made up of twenty-four small such streamers, each with the name of another Taoist, Buddhist, or Confucian deity. The fourth row consisted of two large cylindrical streamers, each displaying part of the text from the *Shenzhou* (Divine Spells) volume of the *Transcendent Scripture*.

Outside the main hall of the temple, in the *waitan* (outer ritual space), another ritual table (*shenzhuo*) was placed facing the offering table inside. It was hung with a vertical red drape, over which was placed a piece of yellow cloth, on which were four Chinese characters in black: *Lingbao xuantan* (Lingbao mysterious/profound altar). On the table was a large incense burner. By the side of the table was a pennant with the characters Gouchen (Angular Array), representing the center. To its north were pennants with the characters for Xuanwu (Black Tortoise), emblem of the north, and the seven northerly constellations; to its south, pennants with the characters Zhuque (Vermilion Bird), emblem of the south, and the seven southerly constellations; to its east, pennants with the characters Qinglong (Blue Dragon), emblem of the east, and the seven easterly constellations; and to its west, pennants with the characters Baihu (White Tiger), emblem of the west, and the seven westerly constellations. The pennants for Gouchen, Xuanwu, Zhuque, Qinglong, and Baihu were rectangular, while those for the four sets of constellations were triangular.

Overall this layout is quite similar to those I have observed elsewhere among currently active Dongjing associations in Yunnan, except that I have never seen the musicians' tables decorated in this fashion with the eight trigrams, or pennants of this nature in the outer ritual space. It should be noted that while most Dongjing associations show certain generic similarities in their ritual setup, each one also has its own peculiarities, even within a single county. He Minda's drawing of the layout before 1949 at Baihua, based on his father's and uncle's recollections, is similar to Yang's for Dayan Town, but the arrangement of musical instruments differs slightly.[1] Layouts for today's Dongjing associations of Jianshui County and Baoshan City may be found in Zhang Xingrong 1998: 223, 225.

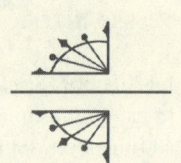

Appendix C

Chinese Texts

This appendix contains the texts to the Han-language sung tracks on the CD. It should be noted that original texts to which I had access for items 1, 2, 5, and 6 are written primarily in simplified characters, so that I have converted them into full-form characters here.[1]

1. Words to *Bagua* (Eight Trigrams), Track 11.
The text was provided by Yang Zenglie. Punctuation is as in his original.

> 元始天王降吉祥，惟願慈悲降道場。今晨合會增福壽，皈依元始大法王。

> "Primordial Heavenly King, grant us your favor; may your compassion extend to the altar. Let this morning's assembly gain fortune and longevity. We surrender unto the Primordial Great Legal King."

2. Words to *Shoujing Jie* (Closing Ode), Track 16.
The text was provided by Yang Zenglie. Punctuation is as in his original.

> 大道不遠在身中，萬法皆空性不空。神性不空元炁注，炁歸元海壽無窮。

> "The great Tao is close, it resides in one's person. The myriad teachings are vacuous, while nature is not. Spirit nature is not vacuous, the original *qi* (life-force) pours in. The *qi* returns to the original ocean and longevity is boundless."

3. Words to two chanted incantations, Track 17.
The text is the first two of the ten incantations that purify the ritual participants at the beginning of the *Kaitan Yiwen* (Rite of Opening the Altar), the first fascicle of the Lijiang County version of the *Transcendent Scripture of the Great Grotto of Wenchang* (manuscript version hand copied in 1947 and preserved by He Yi'an). The recorded selection begins with a repeated invocation of a Heavenly Worthy, then continues with the first incantation, 息慮真言 (true words on clearing the mind). The second incantation, 調氣真言 (true words on harmonizing the breath), follows without a break. I leave a line-break

before each incantation to show where it begins. To assist the reader in following the recording with this text, I use the sign ， to indicate where the performer takes breaths. The period at the end of the first line marks both a breath and the end of the initial invocation of the Heavenly Worthy. There are no punctuation marks in the original text.

開甬，衍奧天尊，開甬衍奧天尊，開甬衍奧天尊。

藐玆寸胸萬欲，交蒙，驅馳南北，顛倒西東，本無塵垢，亦非苦空，敬之敬之，主一而終，放心速收，咫尺天宮，

氣本浩然，靜乃動先，蹶者趣者，中斯餒焉，以默以緩，呼吸綿綿，客感皆寂，太和始全，屏如不息對越在天，

The recording then fades out as the first few characters of the next incantation are sung.

The first incantation concerns the quelling of thoughts, with the aim of attaining a state of mental stillness. The second aims to bring respiration under control.

4. Words to the extract from the reading of a memorial, Track 18.
The text is from the manuscript of memorial texts 疏文底稿 handwritten by Niu Baoqing. Dated 1905, it is preserved in the Lijiang County Library, and was hand copied by me in 1992. In performance the sixth line here is slightly altered by the singer. I give the singer's text rather than the exact original. Division into text lines is as in the original. There are no punctuation marks in the original.

…伏以
旭日輝春法像森羅環桂殿
祥煙結篆霓旌郁麗靄文宮
群仙供珍果以稱觴下民式效
諸真捧瓊漿而介壽邊士翹瞻澡雪宿垢中藏戰兢惟寅上賀恭惟
九天開化梓潼文昌元皇帝君更生永命天尊　陛下

The recording then fades out as the next two lines are sung:

代天宣化
助國救民
…

This is the memorial for the ceremony carried out in honor of the birthday of the god Wenchang on the third day of the second month. Wenchang is the god named in the sixth line.

5. Words to the extract of heightened speech, Track 19.
The text was hand copied in 1988 by Yang Zenglie from the text 文昌大洞仙經闡微行十供養禮玄文全卷. Dated 1922, the text is preserved in the Lijiang County Library. It contains the spoken explications of each of the Ten Offerings of the *Transcendent Scripture of the Great Grotto of Wenchang*. I include the punctuation from Yang's original. This is the opening of the explication of the first offering, that of flowers.

帝君曰。人身以血氣而成。本之二氣靈秀。一元主宰。並行不悖。榮衛交濟。自己元神。自太虛而來。寄父母胎孕而生。三元會合。名之曰人。血氣充盈。運行不礙。血

氣衰敗。元神何依。故人不可以種種情慾。戕賊生根。當知時時保護。依幻修真。養血氣以留元神。

The recording fades out as the explication continues with the characters

凝元神…

The text is put in the mouth of Wenchang, referred to here as 帝君. It explains that the body is made from blood and *qi* (life-force), and that one's primordial spirit comes from the Great Void, to be given birth by one's father and mother. Man is made by the coming together of the Three Primes. He should avoid carnal desires and nourish his blood and *qi* to retain his primordial spirit. The section that continues after the end of this excerpt finishes by explaining that the offering of flowers is dedicated to the Primordial Heavenly King 元始天王.

6. Words to the Dianju (Yunnan opera) scene, Track 24.
The text was supplied by Xi Hongyi. The scene performed is "Vying for the Umbrella" 搶雨傘, from the opera *Tiger Head Encampment* 虎頭寨. It is in *huqin* singing style 胡琴唱腔. Punctuation is as in the original.

(倒板)　(旦) 干戈起滅狼煙
(机頭)　(生) 兄妹們失落在中途路邊,
(旦) 在中途得遇君家面,
(生) 不辭千里送你回還
(旦) 我的父在朝為官宦, 提拔君家做大官,
(生) 好倒好男女同路不相伴, 又恐旁人説閑言。
(旦) 真金不怕火來煉, 樹正那怕月照偏。
(生) 娘含紅了臉 (旦) 君子登陽關
(生) 日落天將晚 (旦) 紅日照西山
(生) 庵堂寺內鐘鼓擂
(旦) 處處茅屋起火煙
(生) 到前途。 (旦) 找旅店。
(生) 咱二人 (旦) 把身安,
(生) 到晚來 (旦) 缺少一個知心人兒, 相陪伴。

(Daoban melody) (female)　In the war there is smoke everywhere.
(Jitou melody) (male)　Brother and sister have lost their way mid-journey by the side of the road.
(female)　To have the chance to run into you in the middle of my journey . . .
(male)　I would not avoid the trouble of going a thousand *li* to see you safe to your home.
(female)　My father is an official at court, and could promote you to a high official position.
(male)　That's good, but if an unmarried man and woman travel together, I fear people may gossip.
(female)　True gold does not fear the test of fire, a tree that grows straight does not fear the slanting moonlight.

(male)   You are blushing.
(female)   I trust you will behave as a gentleman.
(male)   The sun is setting, it is getting late in the day.
(female)   The red sun lights the western mountains.
(male)   Inside the temple the bell and drum sound.
(female)   From the houses all around smoke from cooking dinner is rising.
(male)   Let's press ahead.
(female)   And look for a hostel.
(male)   Let us both
(female)   Settle down.
(male)   When it gets to night
(female)   I will not have an intimate friend to keep me company.

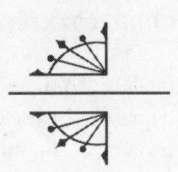

Appendix D
Glossary of Chinese Characters

This glossary is divided into eight sections: ethnic groups, place names, personal names, tune titles, musical instrument names and other musical terms, terms associated with Dongjing associations and Dongjing music groups, scriptural titles and terms, and miscellanous terms. Alphabetization is according to individual Chinese characters, so that, for instance, in the fifth section, *qilao gehui* comes before *qianjin*, since the first characters are *qi* and *qian*.

Ethnic Groups

Bai	白	Naxi	納西
Dai	傣	Pumi	普米
Han	漢	Qiang	羌
Hui	回	Sani	撒尼
Kucong	苦總	Shui	水
Lahu	拉祜	Wa	佤
Lisu	傈僳	Yi	彝
Miao	苗	Zhuang	壯
Mosuo	麼梭		

Place Names (Counties, Townships, Towns, Villages)

Baihua	白華	Changning	昌寧
Baima	白馬	Changshui	長水
Baisha	白沙	Chuxiong	楚雄
Baoshan (city in west Yunnan)	保山	Dacan	大倉
		Daju	大具
Baoshan (township in Lijiang)	寶山	Dali	大理
		Dayan Zhen	大研鎮

212

GLOSSARY OF CHINESE CHARACTERS

Dongchuan	東川	Muma	木馬
Fuhui	福慧	Ninglang	寧蒗
Gezi	格子	Niujie (Niugai)	牛街
Gejiu	個舊	Puji	普濟
Hainan	海南	Qiqu Shan	七曲山
He Jia Cun	何家村	Qiubei	丘北
Heqing	鶴慶	Qujing	曲靖
Heijing	黑井	Sanba	三壩
Huaping	華坪	Shigu	石鼓
Huili	會理	Shiping	石屏
Jianchuan	劍川	Shizong	師宗
Jianshui	建水	Shuhe	束河
Jinshan	金山	Simao	思茅
Jingdong	景東	Tengchong	騰沖
Judian	巨甸	Tonghai	通海
Kaiyuan	開遠	Weishan	巍山
Lasha	剌沙	Weixi	維西
Lashi	拉市	Wenshan	文山
Laoben	老本	Wudang Shan	武當山
Lezhi	樂至	Xiaguan	下關
Li Jia Cun	李家村	Xia Shuhe	下束河
Lijiang	麗江	Xiangyun	祥雲
Lijiang Naxizu Zizhi Xian	麗江納西族自治縣	Xin'ansuo	新安所
		Xinping	新平
Longpan	龍蟠	Yanxing	鹽興
Longquan	龍泉	Yao'an	姚安
Ludian	魯甸	Yinglie Li	英烈里
Lufeng	祿豐	Yongning	永寧
Luxi	瀘西	Yongsheng	永勝
Luoping	羅坪	Zhaotong	昭通
Meiquan	美泉	Zhongdian	中甸
Mengzi	蒙自	Zhujie	朱街
Mile	彌勒	Zhulin	竹林
Muli	木里	Zitong	梓潼

Personal Names (Deities, Yunnan Musicians, Historical Figures in Lijiang)

Names whose exact form varied or seemed uncertain are given in parentheses.

Baihu	白虎	Gouchen	勾陳
Che Xuelin	車學林	Guandi	關帝
Chen Qiuyuan	陳秋元	Guanping	關平
Diya	地啞	Guanyin	觀音
Fuyuan Kaihua Wenchang Silu Hongren Dijun	輔元開化文昌司祿宏仁帝君	He Chenglin	和呈麟
		He Chengxing	和誠興
		He Chongshang	和崇尚
Gao Jianming	高建明	He Fengxiang	和鳳翔

He Gengji	和庚吉	Li Zhenpeng	李振鵬
He Guowei	和國偉	Ma Zhiqing	馬値卿
He Hanwei	和漢偉	Mu Gong	木公
He Heng	和恆	Mu Shaoxian	木紹先
He Hongxing	和鴻興	Mu Shu	木樞
He Hongzhang	和鴻章	Mu Tai	木泰
He Hui	和惠	(Mu Wenyu)	木文育
He Huihan	和惠涵	Mu Zhu	木柱
(He Ji'an)	和集安	Niu Baoqing	牛保慶
He Jiaxiu	和家修	Niu Shiguang	牛世光
He Jianwei	和建偉	Niu Weijiong	牛維炯
He Jun	和鈞	Qinglong	青龍
He Linghan	和凌漢	Sanduo	三多
He Maogen	和茂根	Sha Yuchun	沙玉春
He Minda	和民達	Sun Ziming	孫子鳴
He Ruoqi	和若祺	Tang Shulin	唐樹林
He Ruxiang	何汝相	Tianlong	天聾
He Shangchao	和尚朝	Wang Chaoxin	王朝信
He Shicheng	和世誠	Wang Dejiu	王德久
He Shikun	和士坤	Wang Liang	王良
He Shiwei	和士偉	Wang Mingsheng	王明生
He Wenxuan (musician)	和文選	Wang Yiliang	王以良
He Wenxuan (1930s official)	何文選	Wang Zhengwu	王正武
		Wenchang	文昌
He Xidian	和錫典	Xi Hongyi	習宏一
He Yi'an	和毅庵	Xuan Ke	宣科
He Yitian	和義田	Xuanwu	玄武
He Yongfu	和永福	(Yang Bangwei)	楊邦衛
He Yucai	和育才	Yang Dan'gui	楊丹桂
He Zegan	和則甘	Yang Derun	楊德潤
He Zhiren	和執仁	Yang Guosheng	楊國聖
He Zhong (of Dayan Town)	和中	Yang Houkun	楊后昆
		Yang Jian	楊鑑
He Zhong (of Fuhui Village)	和忠	Yang Xizhen	楊錫珍
		Yang Zemin	楊澤民
Huang Erya	黃爾雅	Yang Zenglie	楊曾烈
Huang Limei	黃麗梅	Yi Guo'en	易國恩
Jiang Yuchuan	江玉川	(Zeng Guocai)	曾國才
Li Baozhang	李豹章	Zhang Kuiguang	張奎光
Li Bin	李彬	Zhang Longhan	張龍漢
Li Cheng'gan	李承干	Zhao Guimei	趙桂美
Li Chengzhen	李成珍	Zhao Yingxian	趙應先
Li Linshu	李林書	Zhao Yuxian	趙煜賢
(Li Sixian)	李四先	Zhou Fan	周樊

Zhou Kewu	周克武	Zhoulun	周侖
Zhou Lin	周霖	Zhuque	朱雀

Tune Titles

A li li	阿里里	Man Wu Yang	慢（漫）
Bagua	八卦		舞羊
Bagua Tou	八卦頭	Nanqu	南曲
Bagua Wei	八卦尾	Qian Wu Hou Wu	前五後五
Bubu Jiao (Jiao/Jiao/Jia)	步步嬌（嬌／交／加）	Qinghe Laoren	清河老人
		Quan Bagua	全八卦
		Shanpo Yang	山坡羊
Da Xia	打下	Shi Gongyang	十供養
Dai Weng	待翁	Shi Hua	十華
Dai Wu	代五	Shiqi Shi	十七世
Dan Wu	旦午	Shi Tong	十通
Dao Chun Lai	到春來	Shuilong Yin	水龍吟
Dao Dong Lai	到冬來	Shuilou Yin	水樓吟
Dao Qiu Lai	到秋來	Wannian Hua	萬年花
Dao Xia Lai	到夏來	Wannian Huan	萬年歡
Guihua Xiang	桂花香	Wusheng Shenghao	五聲聖號
Huatong	華通	Xiao Bai Mei	小白梅
Jixiang	吉祥	Yifeng Shu	一封書
Lang Tao Sha	浪淘沙	Yi Jiang Feng	一江風
Liu Yao Jin	柳搖金	Yuanshi	元始
Liu Yao Jing	柳搖景	Zhouzhang	咒章
Long Bai Wei	龍擺尾	Zouzhang	奏章
Man Wu Yan	慢五言		

Musical Instruments, Genres, Titles, and Terms

Baimao Nü	白毛女	da tongtong	大筒筒
Baisha Xiyue	白沙細樂	dihu	低胡
ban'gu	板鼓	dizi	笛子
Beijing You Ge Jin Taiyang	北京有個金太陽	dianhu	滇胡
		Dianju	滇劇
Bieshi Xieli	別時謝禮	dingxiang	叮響
bo	鈸	dongxiao	洞簫
bobo	波伯	du biaowen	讀表文
boqing	鉢磬	duige	對歌
dadiao	大調	ergu	二鼓
dagu	大鼓	erhu	二胡
dahao	大號	erhuang	二簧
daji yue	打擊樂	geming gequ	革命歌曲
daluo	大鑼	gongchepu	工尺譜
da pigu	大皮鼓	guyue	古樂

guqin	古琴	panling	盤鈴
guzheng	古箏	pipa	琵琶
guan	管	qigu santong	起鼓三通
habagou	哈巴狗	qilao gehui	耆老歌會
hailuo hao	海螺號	qianjin	千斤
Hongdeng Ji	紅燈記	qin	琴
Hong Taiyang	紅太陽	qing	磬
hubo	胡撥	sanxian	三弦
hulusheng	葫蘆笙	se	瑟
huqin	胡琴	sheng	笙
Huadeng	花燈	shouyao gu	手搖鼓
jizi	擊子	sizhu	絲竹
Jiangnan Sizhu	江南絲竹	song	誦
jiang xuan	講玄	sugudu	速古篤
jinghu	京胡	suona	嗩吶
kouxian	口弦	tishou	提手
Kunju	崑劇	tongling	銅鈴
Jingju	京劇	wen'gongtuan	文工團
Lijiang Diqu Dianjutuan	麗江地區滇劇團	xiju	戲劇
		xiao	簫
Lijiang Naxizu Zizhixian Minzu Gewutuan	麗江納西族自治縣民族歌舞團	xiaocha	小鑔
		xiaodiao	小調
		xiaogu	小鼓
Lijiang Guyue	麗江古樂	xiaoluo	小鑼
maiguan	麥管	xin jiezou	新節奏
maoniu jiaohao	氂牛角號	xuan	宣
Mao Zedong Sixiang Wenyi Xuanchuan Dui	毛澤東思想文藝宣傳隊	yangge	秧歌
		yangqin	揚琴
		yinqing	引磬
muyu	木魚	yunluo	雲鑼
Naxi Guyue	納西古樂	zheng	箏
Naxi Jutuan	納西劇團	Zhiqu Weihu Shan	智取威虎山
nao	鐃	zhonghu	中胡
nao lizi	鬧哩子		

Dongjing Associations, Festivals, and Terms; Dongjing Music Groups

anlong diantu	安龍奠土	Dandao Hui	單刀會
bagua	八卦	Dayan Guyuehui	大研古樂會
baxian zhuo	八仙桌	dongjinghui	洞經會
Baihua Guyuedui	白華古樂隊	Fu Lu Shou Sanxing	福祿壽三星
Baisha Guyuedui	白沙古樂隊	fu shanzhang	付善長
Baoshu Xue	保庶學	Ganying Hui	感應會
Beidou Qixing	北斗七星	gonghui	公會
Changshui Guyuedui	長水古樂隊	gongzhuo	供桌
da shenzhuo	大神桌	Guyue Gong	古樂宮

GLOSSARY OF CHINESE CHARACTERS

Guansheng Shengdan	關聖聖誕	ruyi	如意
guanshi	管事	Sanyuan Hui	三元會
Guixiang Baodian	桂香寶殿	Sanyuan She	三元社
Hongren Hui	宏仁會	shanzhang	善長
huangjingban	皇經班	shendeng	神燈
huangjinghui	皇經會	shenzhang	神帳
Huangshan Gongshe Guyuedui	黃山公社古樂隊	shenzhuo	神桌
		shengpai	聖牌
huishou	會手	siqi	四七
huizhang	會長	sishi	司事
jiechi	戒尺	Songhua Yuedui	松花樂隊
Jinshan Guyuedui	金山古樂隊	songshen	送神
jiucha	糾察	songsheng	送聖
Kunming Dongjing Yinyue Yanjiuhui	昆明洞經音樂研究會	songzang	送葬
		tanjing	談經
Lijiang Dayan Naxi Guyuehui	麗江大研納西古樂會	tanjingban	談經班
		waitan	外壇
Lijiang Naxi Guyuetuan	麗江納西古樂團	wanjuan zhuo	萬卷桌
		Wenchang Fu Shengdan	文昌父聖誕
Lijiang Yinyuehui	麗江音樂會	Wenchang Shengdan	文昌聖誕
Lingbao xuantan	靈寶玄壇	wenrenhui	文人會
lingqian gongyang	靈前供養	Xiaguan Dongjing Yinyuehui	下關洞經音樂會
Miaoshan Xue	妙善學		
Moshi Bu Wang	沒世不忘	xiao jingzhuo	小經桌
Naxi Guyue Jiyi Peixunban	納西古樂技藝培訓班	Yiyou Yinyuehui	益友音樂會
		yizhibu	藝旨簿
Nandou Liuxing	南斗六星	Yongbao Ping'an	永保平安
Nanya Yinyue She	南雅音樂社	zhengwei	正位
neitan	內壇	zhishi	執事
paiwei	牌位	Zhongguo Lijiang Dayan Naxi Guyuetuan	中國麗江大研納西古樂團
putuan	蒲團		
qiantong	簽筒		
qiuzi	求子	zhushou	祝壽
Qujing Xian Gudian Yinyue Yanjiuhui	曲靖縣古典音樂研究會	Zunsheng Hui	尊聖會

Scriptural Titles and Vocabulary

Anlong Diantu Jing	安龍奠土經	bu gong shizhang	不恭師長
an tudi shenzhou	安土地神咒	bu xiao fumu	不孝父母
baogao	寶告	bu xin pengyou	不信朋友
bao gongyang	寶供養	bu you xiongdi	不友兄弟
bu bie fufu	不別夫婦	bu zhong junwang	不忠君王
bu he xiangli	不和鄉里	cai gongyang	財供養
bu jing tiandi	不敬天地	cha gongyang	茶供養

chanhui	懺悔	Quan Bagua	全八卦
Dacheng Miaofa Lianhua Jing	大乘妙法蓮花經	Sanjie Fumo Guansheng Dijun Zhongxiao Zhongyi Zhenjing	三界伏魔關聖帝君忠孝忠義真經
Dadong Falu	大洞法籙	Shi Gongyang	十供養
Dadong Fulu	大洞符籙	Shi Wang Jing	十王經
Dadong Shenzhou	大洞神咒	shoujing jie	收經偈
Dadong Xianjing	大洞仙經	shoujing shang juan fayuan	收經上卷發願
Dadong Zhenjing	大洞真經	Shuwen Digao	疏文底稿
dagao	大誥	shui gongyang	水供養
Daozang Jiyao	道藏輯要	Taishang Dongxuan Lingbao Shengxuan Xiaozai Huming Miaojing	太上洞玄靈寶昇玄消災護命妙經
Dongjing Shidu	洞經示讀		
Duren Jing	度人經		
Ershisi Xiaojing	二十四孝經		
fayuan	發願		
fu gongyang	符供養		
Gaoshang Yuhuang Benhang Jijing	高上玉皇本行集經	Taishang Hunyuan Laojun Shuo Chang Qingjing Jing	太上混元老君說常清淨經
Guansheng Dijun Baoxun	關聖帝君寶訓	Taishang Lingbao Tianzun Shuo Rangzai Du'e Zhenjing	太上靈寶天尊說禳災度厄真經
Guansheng Dijun Danfeng Chaoyang Baochan	關聖帝君丹鳳朝陽寶懺		
Guansheng Dijun Jueshi Zhenjing	關聖帝君覺世真經	Taishang Wuji Zongzhen Wenchang Dadong Xianjing	太上無極總真文昌大洞仙經
guo gongyang	果供養		
hua gongyang	花供養	tianzun	天尊
jin'guang shenzhou	金光神咒	tiaoqi zhenyan	調氣真言
jinjiu fadeng gongyang	金酒法燈供養	Wenchang Dadong Xianjing	文昌大洞仙經
jinjiu fadeng shuang gongyang	金酒法燈雙供養	Wenchang Dijun Yinzhi Wen	文昌帝君陰騭文
jing kou shenzhou	淨口神咒	Wenchang Qilu Baosi Dengke	文昌祈祿保嗣燈科
jing tiandi shenzhou	淨天地神咒		
jing xin shenzhou	淨心神咒	Wushang Yuhuang Xinyin Jing	無上玉皇心印經
juan shang, juan zhong, juan xia	卷上、卷中卷下	xilü zhenyan	息慮真言
Jueshi Jingwen	覺世經文	xiulian	修煉
kaijing jie	開經偈	Xuehu Jing	血湖經
kaitan keyi	開壇科儀	yangqi	仰啟
Kaitan Yiwen	開壇儀文	yangqi song	仰啟頌
liqing	禮請	Yuanhuang Da Tiandi zan Dadong Jing ershiwu shi	元皇大天帝讚大洞經二十五詩
liqing song	禮請頌		
neidan	內丹		
Qinghe Laoren zan Dadong Jing gu shi shisi shou	清河老人讚大洞經古詩十四首	Yuqing Wuji Zongzhen Wenchang Dadong Shenzhou Quanjuan	玉清無極總真文昌大洞神咒全卷

GLOSSARY OF CHINESE CHARACTERS

Yuqing Wuji Zongzhen Wenchang Dadong Xianjing	玉清無極總真文昌大洞仙經	Zhanjuan shenzhou	展卷神咒
		Zhengyuansou Zhenren zan Dadong Jing gu shi shi shou	鄭淵藪真人讚大洞經古詩十首
Yuqing Wuji Zongzhen Wenchang Dadong Xianjing Liqing Quanjuan	玉清無極總真文昌大洞仙經禮請全卷		

Other Terms and Names

aige shanchang	愛歌善唱	qigong	氣功
aihaozhe	愛好者	Quanguo shaoshu minzu qunzhong yeyu yishu guanmo yanchu	全國少數民族群眾業餘藝術觀摩演出
Aomen Ribao	澳門日報		
Beijing Qingnian Bao	北京青年報		
Beijing Wanbao	北京晚報		
bianjiang diqu	邊疆地區	Renmin Ribao	人民日報
bianjiang minzu	邊疆民族	shanzi magua	衫子馬褂
boxue	剝削	Shang Bao	商報
chahanzhang guanmin guan	茶罕章管民官	sixiang gongzuo	思想工作
		tuguan	土官
Chuncheng Wanbao	春城晚報	tusi	土司
ci	雌	tu tongpan	土通判
Dayan Zhen Wenhuazhan	大研鎮文化站	tuanjie, fanrong, jinbu wenya	團結繁榮進步文雅
daode	道德	wenyi wei renmin fuwu, wei shehuizhuyi fuwu	文藝為人民服務，為社會主義服務
Dijun Tongzhi	帝君同志		
dongba	東巴		
Dongba Wenhua Yanjiushi	東巴文化研究室	xianjin minzu	先進民族
		Xiangsheng	相聲
Dongba Wenhua Yishu Zhanyantuan	東巴文化藝術展演團	xiong	雄
		xiucai	秀才
fengjian mixin	封建迷信	xiuzhen guniang	修真姑娘
gaitu guiliu	改土歸流	yayue huan jing sibai nian	雅樂還京四百年
gongming	功名		
Guangming Ribao	廣明日報	yiren (barbarian)	夷人
heshang	和尚	yiren (artist)	藝人
jinshi	進士	yiyi zhiyi	以夷治夷
lao yiren	老藝人	Yong Bailian	詠白蓮
Lijiang Bao	麗江報	youya you yu, jinzhang bu zu	悠雅有餘，緊張不足
Lijiang Xian Wenhuaju	麗江縣文化局		
		Yulong Xueshan	玉龍雪山
Li Xia Jie	立夏節	Yunnan Minzu Wenhua Yishu Jiaoliu Gongsi	雲南民族文化藝術交流公司
mei you weidao	沒有味道		
minzu	民族		
muzi	母子	Yunnan Minzu Xueyuan	雲南民族學院
nengge shanwu	能歌善舞		
niugui sheshen	牛鬼蛇神	Yunnan Ribao	雲南日報

Yunnan sheng yeyu gewu xiqu huiyan dahui	雲南省業餘歌舞戲曲會演大會	Zhongyang Minzu Daxue	中央民族大學
Yunnan Sheng Weiyuanhui Xuanchuan Bu zhangtang	雲南省委員會宣傳部掌堂	Zhongyang Minzu Xueyuan	中央民族學院
		Zhongyang Yinyue Xueyuan	中央音樂學院
Zhongguo baijue bolanhui	中國百絕博覽會	zizhi	自治
		zouhun	走婚
Zhongguo Changpian Gongsi	中國唱片公司		

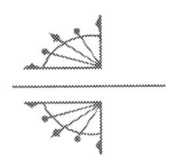

Notes

Chapter 1

1. The term *dongjing* refers to the main scripture used by these groups and is explained in Chapter 3.

2. E.g., Yung 1984 on changes to Cantonese opera; Lau 1996a and b on post-1949 developments in the solo *dizi* (transverse flute) solo repertoire; Yung 1989b on the *guqin* (seven-string zither); Holm 1991 on Yangge (a song and dance form); and Kraus 1989 on piano music. Developments in minority performing arts are discussed by Thrasher (1990) and Mackerras (1984, 1996).

3. Lijiang's Dongjing music has until recently received relatively little scholarly attention. The most detailed sources are Chong 1989, Yang Zenglie 1990–1991, Sangde Nuowa 1994, Rees 1994, and Rees 1996. There is also a delightfully impressionistic description by a Russian resident of Lijiang in the 1940s (Goullart 1957: 213–217), and a brief but informative local memoir (Zhao Jingxiu 1995).

4. E.g., Nketia 1963; Ames 1973; Witzleben 1987; Bohlman 1991a; Slobin 1992: 189–191.

5. E.g., Nketia 1964; Wachsmann 1971; Pratt 1976; Shelemay 1980; Loza 2000.

Chapter 2

1. Note, however, that sometimes the court and Chinese officials despaired of the native peoples—the Qianlong emperor in 1751 ordered the closure of charitable schools for the Miao on the basis that they were naturally unintelligent, and after learning to read, preferred "vile" books to the morally uplifting variety (Jenks 1994: 43–44).

2. For population statistics, see the 1990 census (*Zhongguo 1990 Nian Renkou Pucha Ziliao*). Many scholars have pointed out the problematic nature of the term "Han," since the regional and group identities of those subsumed under this catchall label, such as Hakka, Cantonese, and Subei people, are often as strong as "nationality" identities. Studies of these and related issues include Lamley 1981; Gladney 1991: 306–312; Honig 1992; Constable 1996; and Ebrey 1996. In this book I use the term "Han" as it is generally understood, indicating those people whose ancestors were bearers of mainstream Chinese languages and civilization, and who are now certified as such by their official Han label.

3. Schools in remote areas sometimes teach in the local ethnic language. In Phala, three hundred miles northwest of Lhasa, for instance, children at the primary school are taught

only Tibetan (Goldstein and Beall 1989: 779). A variety of policies is in effect in other minority regions (see, for example, Borchigud 1995, and Mackerras 1996: 141–145). Less remote areas usually operate exclusively in Chinese: Harrell notes that Nuosu (Yi) children in Panzhihua, Sichuan Province, are taught only Chinese at school, despite the existence of a modern standardized script for their own language—which is actually used in the schools of nearby Liangshan Yi Autonomous Prefecture (1990: 527). When I acquired a textbook written in the modern standardized Naxi script in Lijiang, I found that none of my local friends could read it, since they do not learn it in school.

4. The theory and application of these ideas are well discussed by Harrell (1995b: 22–27) and McKhann (1995), who has drawn Western readers' attention to recent critiques by Chinese scholars. Problems with the application of Stalin's classification criteria have been identified by anthropologist Huang Shuping, who argues for a greater emphasis on culture, and for research into ethnology theory that takes account of Western scholarship (1989). Tong Enzheng has delivered a comprehensive criticism of Morganian-Engelsian evolutionary theory (1989). On the history of Soviet and other influences in Chinese ethnology, see Guldin (1994).

5. See Harrell 1995a and Brown 1996 for many instances of individuals and groups manipulating, working within, and resisting state norms, categories, and expectations. For the Naxi, see Hansen 1998.

6. One of the earliest genres turned to Communist propaganda use was the music–dance–variety act form Yangge (Holm 1991), but many other popular traditional genres were also employed. Xiangsheng (humorous dialogue) was given revolutionary subject matter, folk songs were turned into revolutionary songs, and Peking and regional operas were converted into "model" operas (Link 1984; Wong 1984; Yung 1984).

7. The most outstanding example of this was "Blind Abing," a street musician who was discovered just before his death in 1950 and immortalized as the archetypal romantic folk musician in the works of musicologist Yang Yinliu and others, and even in a film and on TV (Stock 1996).

8. Du Yaxiong has drawn Western readers' attention to the fact that one important function of musical research in the People's Republic of China has been "to give service to the composers" (1992: 9). Ben Wu makes a similar point in his discussion of musical scholarship on Tibet, and he contrasts this with the research aims of most Western scholars (1998: 36–37). A rare "insider" story of how one minority folk dance was researched and then transformed choreographically and musically to suit professional performance on the national stage is offered by Chin Ming (1963).

9. The history of research on minority music from the 1940s to the early 1990s is examined by Wu Guodong (1991). Yang Fang (1995) has published an informative brief account for Yunnan Province, 1940s to 1960s.

10. During my studies at the Shanghai Conservatory of Music between 1987 and 1989, I frequently heard teachers and students of traditional Chinese instruments practicing Mozart and Bach concertos on their instruments, and developing techniques appropriate to those pieces. Western influence on Chinese traditional music began in the early twentieth century (Han 1979: 12–17), and proceeded apace after 1949 with the introduction of Soviet musical models into the conservatories and song and dance troupes. On the development of the Chinese music conservatories, see Schimmelpenninck and Kouwenhoven 1993, and Stock 1996, ch. 6.

11. Note that this has happened also to traditional Han musics. There is frequently a pronounced aesthetic divide between conservatory-trained musicians, who often find the "authentic" style of traditional amateurs dull, stagnant, and "unscientific" (*bu kexue*), and the amateurs, who complain that the professional arrangements of their music "lack flavor" (*meiyou weidao*). This issue is sympathetically explored by Witzleben (1995: 27–30). Similar adaptation of folk forms to a Western art music-inspired harmonic and pedagogic morphology was common in the formerly socialist countries of Eastern Europe and the U.S.S.R; see for example Buchanan 1991 and Rice 1994 on Bulgaria, as well as Slobin 1971, Levin 1979, Levin 1996, and Muhambetova 1995 on Uzbekistan and Kazakhstan.

12. Quotations from, respectively, Liu Chao 1959: 227; Zhongguo Yishu Yanjiuyuan Yinyue Yanjiusuo 1983: 1; "Washan" Bianjibu 1985: 1; Yang Tongshan et al. 1980: 26.

13. The lively place of singing, instrumental music and sometimes dancing in traditional Han society is described in hundreds of publications; among the most accessible in English are Tuohy 1988, Holm 1991, Stephen Jones 1995, and Schimmelpenninck 1997. In the first half of the 1990s, karaoke and disco dancing were ubiquitous in large cities and small towns alike.

14. For an in-depth study of "Miao albums," see Hostetler 1995.

Chapter 3

1. The descent and marriage systems of the Mosuo fascinate Chinese ethnologists, who have produced a plethora of books and articles on the subject. Important books include *Yongning Naxizu Shehui ji Muxizhi Diaocha* (1986), *Ninglang Yixu Zizhixian Naxizu Shehui ji Jiating Xingtai Diaocha* (1987), and *Ninglang Yizu Zizhixian Yongning Naxizu Shehui ji qi Muxizhi Diaocha* (1988). There is also an English-language dissertation on the subject (Shih 1993).

2. These include several county histories, the earliest dating from the eighteenth century (listed in Li Xiaoyuan 1988: 317–318); two genealogical chronicles of the Mu family, hereditary Naxi rulers of Lijiang; memorial stones of the Mu family; six eulogistic biographies of famous Mu rulers; and a printed copy from 1646 of the letters of recognition granted to Mu chiefs by successive Ming emperors. Most of these sources are treated in great detail by Rock (1947). One of the genealogical chronicles, with illustrations and an introduction dated 1545, is published in a French translation by Chavannes (1912).

3. On Lijiang's economic development, see Lijiang Naxizu Zizhixian Gaikuang Bianxiezu 1986; Yunnan Sheng Cehuiju 1980; Mueggler 1991; and Goullart 1957.

4. I follow McKhann in using Naxi Pinyin to transliterate *sainii* and *paq*, but retain regular Hanyu Pinyin for *dongba* instead of using Naxi Pinyin *dobbaq*, since *dongba* is the more familiar form. A detailed description of the *sainii* may be found in Rock 1959.

5. The most influential works include Guo and Yang 1985 and 1991, which also offer extensive bibliographies of mainly Chinese-language books, articles, and translations; the many translations of ritual texts by scholars of the Dongba Culture Research Institute and other Yunnan institutions; dictionaries of Naxi pictographs, especially Li Lin-ts'an 1953 and Fang and He 1981; several works by Li Lin-ts'an; many works by Joseph Rock (see Chock, Bryan, and Marks 1963 for bibliography); Jackson 1979; and McKhann 1992. A partial summary of the recent state of research is given in Jackson 1989. Goullart (1957, chs. 11 and 12), gives graphic descriptions of *dongba* ceremonies he witnessed in the 1940s;

Chao (1995, ch. 4, and 1996) offers a fascinating insight into contemporary exploitation of the *dongba* phenomenon in modern ethnic image building.

6. The uncomfortable relationship between the government of the People's Republic of China and its peoples' religious practices has been examined in many publications. For the tremendous chronological and regional variations, and the local negotiations that characterize the post–Cultural Revolution resurgence, see MacInnes 1972; Madsen 1989; Munro 1989; Siu 1989; Saso 1990; Gladney 1991; Luo 1991; and Dean 1993.

7. The Chinese spoken in Lijiang is a subdialect of Yunnanese Mandarin, a distinctive form of the standard northern language (Gui 1990).

8. Naxi men also participated in the imperial civil service examinations until their abolition in 1905, and the successful candidates often became officials in other counties.

9. Information is derived from personal visits, unless otherwise stated. The exceptions are Tengchong, Heqing, and Shiping counties, for which information was supplied by Zhang Xingrong, who made personal visits; Nanjian County (Liu Wenzhi 1993); and Kaiyuan County, for which information was supplied by Sun Xibing of the Kaiyuan County Cultural Office (*Kaiyuan Xian Wenhuaguan*). More detailed English-language discussion of Yunnan's Dongjing associations may be found in Rees 1994, ch. 3; the major provincewide Chinese-language study is Zhang Xingrong 1998.

10. Revivals of some kind have occurred in Jingdong County and Gejiu City, although it is unclear if they include ritual activities as well as music (Zhang Xingrong 1998: 465, *Gejiu Shi Wenhua Zhi* 1988: 125). There has been no revival in some other places, including Zhaotong City and Xinping County (personal communication, Zhang Xingrong, October 1993), Luoping County (personal communication, Lei Hong'an, February 1992), Mile, Fengqing, and Changning counties (personal observation), and Huaping, Qiubei, and Simao counties (Yuan Yuancong 1993: 104; Yin 1991: 4; Ouyang 1991: 2).

11. Many associations did traditionally have plentiful written records of their membership and, in some cases, of their history, too, but relatively few survive in the 1990s. Informants usually pointed to one or more of the following events as responsible for destruction of their documents: the violent Yunnan Moslem rebellion of 1856–1873; the immediate aftermath of the Communist victory in 1949, following which many associations saw their belongings confiscated; and the Cultural Revolution of 1966–1976, during which many documents in private hands and libraries were burned.

12. The term *dongjinghui* is found in gazetteers from the counties of Qiubei (1921, first fascicle), Yiliang (1921, second fascicle, folio 34), Luquan (*Yunnan Sheng Luquan Xianzhi* n.d. [1925]: 168), and Shunning (now Fengqing) (1948, quoted in Zhang Xingrong 1998: 465). Descriptive mentions of what appear to be Dongjing associations occur in several other gazetteers, including those from Zhennan Prefecture (*Yunnan Sheng Zhennan Zhou Zhilüe* n.d. [1892]: 144), the counties of Chuxiong (*Yunnan Sheng Chuxiong Xianzhi* 1967 [1910]: 31), Dali (1914, sixth fascicle, folio 6), Jingdong (*Yunnan Sheng Jingdong Xianzhi Gao* n.d. [1923]: 192), Zhaotong (*Yunnan Sheng Zhaotong Xianzhi Gao* 1967 [1936]: 428), and Yao'an (1988 [1949]: 792–793).

13. When I visited Dali and Xiaguan with Zhang Xingrong of the Yunnan Art Institute, we inquired after all these historical documents mentioned in Dali Shi Xiaguan Wenhuaguan 1990, and were told that they had been burned during the Cultural Revo-

lution. However, handwritten copies of two of them, made about 1960 by Xiaguan expert Li Chun, still exist in his keeping, and he kindly allowed us to inspect them. Outline histories of several major associations, past and present, are given in Dali Shi Xiaguan Wenhuaguan 1990: 606–610.

14. Interviews with members of Yongsheng Dongjing association, 18 March 1992; with Tian Shihua of Luxi, 15 February 1992; and with Peng Youshan of Kunming, 29 March 1992.

15. Interviews with Dongjing association members in Jianshui, 28 January 1992, and in Heijing, 14 March 1992; for Xinping see "Xinping dongjing yinyue shiwen" 1988: 1.

16. Interviews with Ma Zhiqing of Xiaguan, 27 October 1991; and He Ruxiang of He Jia Cun, 23 March 1992.

17. Interviews with Che Xuelin of Chuxiong, 17 June 1992; Zhao Congkuan of Weishan, 8 March 1992; Ma Zhiqing of Xiaguan, 16 March 1992; Wang Yiliang of Jianshui, 27 January 1992; Yang Jian of Jinshan, Lijiang, 20 November 1991.

18. Despite the upheavals in China this century, Wenchang is once again worshiped in Zitong County, his place of origin, and is still credited with moralizing planchette texts in Taiwan (Kleeman 1988: 108; Jordan and Overmyer 1986).

19. On the *Dadong Zhenjing*, see Robinet 1983 and 1993; on the formation of the Taoist Canon and its different editions and indices, see Boltz 1987 and 1993. Yunnan variants of the *Dadong Xianjing* are discussed in Rees 1994: 89–93. On the contents of the Lijiang version, see appendix A.

20. For an exhaustive list of Dongjing festivals throughout Yunnan, see Zhang Xingrong 1998: 35–39. Zhang also describes all the main scriptures used (pp. 150–198).

21. Interview with He Ruxiang of He Jia Cun, 14 March 1992; and several interviews with He Yi'an of Dayan Town.

22. A loyalty to and nostalgia for one's hometown is a well-known feature of Chinese culture. In the reform era since the late 1970s, it is common for Chinese people who left their hometown in or before 1949 to make return trips and renew old friendships and business partnerships. Frequently they also support artistic or ritual activities characteristic of the locale. Overseas Chaozhouese, for example, have demonstrated enthusiasm for and given donations to music groups performing traditional genres from their home region in southeast China (Dujunco 1994: 146–150; Lau 1998: 123–129). At least two Dongjing music organizations in Yunnan have benefited in like fashion from local emigrés.

23. Formal classes have been organized by groups in Xiaguan, Mengzi County Town, and Lijiang's Dayan Town; female recruits have been welcomed in Weishan, Luxi, and Mengzi county towns, and in Dayan Town and Baihua Village in Lijiang; children of older members figure prominently in Chuxiong City and Dayan Town, and entrepreneurs in Dali and Chuxiong.

24. These different modes of performance may be heard on several commercial recordings of Dongjing music, among which the most accessible outside China are *Dongjing Music in Yunnan, China* (Nanjian County, 1995), *Naxi Music from Lijiang* (1997), and *Dongjing Music* (field recordings from five other counties, 1998).

25. A similar observation on the differences between Confucian state ritual and Taoist ceremonies is made by Picard (1991: 54).

26. Both membership lists are preserved in the Lijiang Prefecture Archive, which kindly permitted me access to the 1938 list (the preface to this is reproduced by Yang Zenglie [1991: 44–45]). Zhou and Huang (1983 [1962]: 91–93) report that in 1962 the Lijiang County Library held several nineteenth-century Dongjing scriptures, the earliest of which dated from 1818. I did not see these in 1992 and 1993. Yang Zenglie reports that a historical account of the Dayan Town association written in the early nineteenth century was destroyed during the Moslem Rebellion of the mid-nineteenth century, and a similar document from the late nineteenth century was lost in 1949 (1990: 116–117).

27. Information on the festivals of Lijiang's Dongjing associations is based on interviews with He Yi'an of Dayan Town, 23 October 1991, 18, 19, and 27 November 1991, and 30 December 1991; Li Baozhang of Shuhe, 1 June 1992; He Huihan of Baisha, 3 June 1992; Yang Jian of Jinshan, 20 November 1991; as well as on the work of Yang Zenglie (1990–1991).

28. This scripture appears not to have survived in Lijiang after 1949.

29. Interviews with He Yi'an of Dayan Town; with He Huihan of Baisha, 11 November 1991; with He Minda of Baihua, 7 November 1991; with Mu Zhu of Baihua, formerly of Lasha, 6 November 1991; and with Zhao Yixian of Shigu, 2 June 1992. The general picture was confirmed exhaustively by casual comments from elderly people, former association members and nonmembers alike, and in Yang Zenglie 1990: 119.

Chapter 4

1. Sangde Nuowa considers chants used at funerals a separate, fourth category (1993: 71).

2. I am grateful to Xuan Ke for arranging the recording session on 9 May 1989 and to Ge Agan for explaining the content in detail (interview, 22 August 1998). For a vivid account of the frequent love suicides in 1940s Lijiang, and of this *dongba* ceremony, see Goullart 1957, ch. 12. For a scholarly explanation, see Rock 1939. Excerpts of *dongba* music and dance may be found on the videos *Local Customs and Music* and *The Instrument Kingdom in Yunnan, China*.

3. Dialogue songs are sung in several different parts of China, usually with one male and one female partner. They are found among both national minorities and the Han. Kunming's Cuihu Park was famous in the late 1980s and early 1990s for the singers who gathered there on Sunday afternoons (Rees 1990: 30–31; Thrasher 1990: 6).

4. Translation by Xuan Ke (during recording session, 20 May 1992), further interpretation by He Zhong (interview, 1 August 1998).

5. Two recent compilations of Naxi folk songs include more than a hundred, in Naxi with Chinese translations (Kou, Wang, and He 1995, with musical notation; and He Zhiwu 1995, without musical notation).

6. *A li li* and *Worere* are both included in the *JVC Video Anthology of World Music and Dance*, East Asia Tape 4. The singing for *Worere* may also be heard on the CD *Baishibai*. For a transcription of *Worere* and a set of articles on the dance, see Xuan 1984b, 1986b, 1990, and 1991.

7. The gourd mouth organ (*hulusheng* in Chinese) is widespread among Yunnan's minorities. Its construction is described by Yuan and Mao (1986: 123–126) and Thrasher (1990: 43). A major anthology (Zhang Xingrong 1990) includes transcriptions of pieces

from the Kucong, Lahu, Lisu, Naxi, Pumi, Wa, and Yi. Sometimes, as in Figure 4.1, a second gourd is attached to the top of the lowest-pitched pipe.

8. Several instrument-accompanied Naxi dances are shown on the *JVC Video Anthology of World Music and Dance*, East Asia Tape 4, and on the videos *The Instrument Kingdom in Yunnan, China*, Vol. 2, and *Local Customs and Music*, Vol. 2. Two dances played on the fipple-flute (and a beautiful rendition of the *Gguq qil* folk song melody) may be found on the CD *Naxi Music from Lijiang*.

9. Stevan Harrell notes the presence of similar dances all over the Tibeto-Burman area. In the Liangshan Yi Autonomous Prefecture in Sichuan Province, dance tunes have even been standardized to a tape and are taught in the schools, while in the villages the tape suffices when there is no flautist, or when the flautist is taking a break (personal communication).

10. The Naxi Jew's harp is featured on the *JVC Video Anthology of World Music and Dance*, East Asia Tape 4, and the videos *The Instrument Kingdom in Yunnan, China*, Vol. 2, and *Local Customs and Music*, Vol. 2. Jew's harp tunes for the Naxi, Bai, Lisu, Nu, and Yi minorities may be found in Zhang Xingrong 1990. On its use in courtship among the Liangshan and Chuxiong Yi, see Thrasher 1990: 24, 40; for the Sani, see Rees 1990: 33–34.

11. Zhang Xingrong's anthology includes tunes for the leaf from the Miao, Shui, Yi, and Zhuang (1990). I saw the leaf being played by the Sani in Lu'nan County in April 1989. On Chinese historical sources for the leaf, see Thrasher (1990: 55–56), who also gives a detailed description of the playing technique and context among the Yi (pp. 57–59). The leaf is mentioned in a foreign account of Chuan Miao music from before 1949, which notes that it is used for "love-making" and "in times of trouble to summon members of the clan" (Agnew 1939: 15).

12. The Wa of Ximeng County, Yunnan Province, have a similar instrument (Yuan and Mao 1986: 154); I am grateful to Laurence Picken for pointing this out.

13. For discussion of a possible Mongolian connection, see also Mao Jizeng 1964: 9, and 1986: 110; Mo'er Jihu 1991; and Zhao Kuanren 1989.

14. Note, however, that some scholars, notably Xuan Ke, dispute this interpretation (1984a, 1986a).

15. This recording is by Baisha Ancient Music Orchestra, a group of Dongjing musicians coached by He Maogen, the flautist in Track 9, who learned the music from He Xidian. Therefore the performance is somewhat overlaid by Dongjing flavor.

16. Because nomenclature is not completely standardized, some Dongjing instruments have several different names and/or written forms. For the sake of consistency, in the glossary I follow the precedents set in the first major publication on Lijiang's Dongjing music (Yang Zenglie 1990–1991), which supplements here the information I gathered myself during fieldwork. Supplementary information was also gleaned from Yuan and Mao 1986, Sangde Nuowa 1994: 74, and from Ge Agan (interview, 22 August 1998). I list the instruments according to the standard Sachs-Hornbostel classification system of aerophones, chordophones, membranophones, and idiophones (Hornbostel and Sachs 1961 [1914]). In giving pitches, I adhere to the convention that C is the note two octaves below middle C, c the note one octave below, c^1 middle C itself, c^2 upper C, and so on. Because *shang* (the equivalent of *do* in Chinese solfège) is usually equivalent to approximately C# in Lijiang's Dongjing music, I give instrument pitches assuming a *shang* of C#.

17. On the importance and history of the restraining loop, see Stock 1991: 23–24.

18. I did see one player in Dayan Town using the large Han *sanxian* instead, but everyone else uses the small form.

19. Several scholars and musicians have noted the similarity in appearance to the Mongolian instrument *huobusi* (He Xidian 1985: 71; Zhao Kuanren 1989; Yuan and Mao 1986: 243); indeed, this similarity is often cited to support the idea of a Mongolian origin to Baisha Xiyue, in which the instrument is also used. Although within Yunnan the *sugudu* is commonly considered unique to Lijiang's Dongjing music and Baisha Xiyue, I saw an instrument of very similar appearance used by Han Dongjing association musicians in Xin'ansuo, Mengzi County, in summer 1993.

20. Southeastern instrumental genres including Jiangnan Sizhu may be heard on the CD *Sizhu Silk Bamboo: Chamber Music of South China*.

21. Information on technical musical features of Lijiang's Dongjing repertoire as played by former Dongjing associations is derived primarily from numerous personal interviews with He Yi'an, a former member of the Dayan Town Dongjing association; from Yang Zenglie 1990–1991; and from personal discussions with He Minda and Yang Zenglie. Yang Zenglie sets out the entire application of musical types to the *Transcendent Scripture of the Great Grotto* (1990: 136–138).

22. More *dadiao* may be found on the CD *Naxi Music from Lijiang*.

23. Although my discussions with He Yi'an appeared to indicate that *yangqi song* was chanted in the same manner as the other initial material in this volume, Yang Zenglie and He Minda point to a special melody for at least some *yangqi song* sections (personal communication).

24. Information on tune titles is based on Dali Shi Xiaguan Wenhuaguan 1990, Zhang Xingrong 1998, and on several regional anthologies: *Kunming Dongjing Yinyue* (1983), Chong Xian 1986, Tang Xin 1988, *Lufeng Xian Heijing Dongjing Yinyue* (1991), Shiping Xian Dongjing Yinyue Xiehui 1992, Qujing Xian Gudian Yinyue Yanjiuhui, n.d., Yang Guanghong, n.d.

25. I was able to photograph four booklets of Lijiang's Dongjing pieces handwritten in *gongchepu* notation. That owned by the Baihua Ancient Music Orchestra (Baihua Guyuedui) is dated 1924. None of the other three—which are from Dayan Town, Baisha, and Hainan Village in Lashi Township—bear a date, although their owners suggested possible dates around the middle of the twentieth century. I am grateful to He Guowei, Li Chenggan, He Huihan, and He Minda for permitting me access to these scores. Zhang Longhan generously gave me a score he had written in both *gongchepu* and cipher notation around 1980. Most of these scores represent main beats with a single dash to the right of the pitch symbols, but contain no further indication of metrical organization. However, the Baihua score treats *dadiao* (accompanied songs) differently: it indicates the initial unmetered long notes with triangles, and for the rest of each *dadiao* notates a meter of four main beats, representing the first beat of each cycle with a circle, and the other three beats with single dashes. Zhang Longhan's score has no rhythmic indicators at all, although he leaves spaces between phrases. Yang Zenglie emphasizes the high degree of individual variation found among Lijiang's scores (1991: 30–32).

26. In some Chinese musical genres, *gongchepu* scores use more complex rhythmic signs to show whether a piece has a pattern of two, four, or eight main beats (Yang Yinliu 1962: 13–21). Comprehensive explanations and discussions of *gongchepu* may be found

in Yang Yinliu 1962 and Xue Zongming 1983: 230–402. English-language descriptions include Pian 1967: 96–98 for Song dynasty sources; Yung 1989a: 14–18 for Cantonese opera; Stephen Jones 1995 for Beijing's Zhihua Temple and northern and southern instrumental groups; and Ben Wu 1988 for a village in Hebei Province.

27. Interviews with Zhao Yingxian of Dayan Town, 30 November 1991; Ge Agan of Kunming, 19 September 1991; Niu Weijiong, 4 December 1991; He Linghan, 16 December 1991; Sun Ziming, 20 December 1991 (all of Dayan Town).

28. Interviews with Yang Jian of Jinshan Township, 20 November 1991; He Hongzhang and He Zhong of Fuhui Village, near Dayan Town, 19 December 1991; Zhao Yuxian of Shigu, 2 June 1992.

29. While the exact music for the Confucian sacrifice has been revised many times, its solemn, dignified feel may be sensed from the CD *Taiwan, Republic of China: The Confucius Temple Ceremony.*

30. Interview with former Buddhist monk He Shiwei of Baihua, 31 May 1992, and personal communication from Yang Zenglie on Taoist music.

31. Interviews with He Yi'an, 18 November 1991; Xuan Ke, 21 November 1991; and Sun Ziming, 20 December 1992 (all of Dayan Town).

32. Interview with He Shiwei of Baihua, 31 May 1992; also personal communications from Xuan Ke. On Christian music among the Yunnan minorities, see Yang Minkang 1990.

33. The low status of professional musicians, especially blind ones, was common throughout China, as in many other countries, before 1949.

34. Interviews with Zhao Yingxian, 30 November 1991; and Xuan Ke, 21 November 1991 (both of Dayan Town).

Chapter 5

1. Cases documented in oral tradition include transmission from Heijing Town (then county seat of Yanxing County, now in Lufeng County) to Huili in Sichuan Province (Liu Yue 1991: n.p.); and from Dali to Ludian Township, Lijiang County (Yang Zenglie 1991: 37).

2. For similar minor differences in repertoire arrangement and performance in other group-defined musical settings, see Slobin 1992: 189.

3. This was because everybody could see the player hitting the ten tuned gongs. Therefore someone with an imperfect memory could watch which gong the *fu shanzhang* was hitting and thus himself play the correct note. This sometimes happens with today's secular music groups too, and was a technique recommended to me when I was learning the music!

4. Information is derived from interviews with He Yi'an of Dayan Town, 29 April 1992; Mu Zhu, formerly of Lasha, 6 November 1991 and 3 May 1992; He Huihan of Baisha, 11 November 1991 and 3 June 1992; He Hongxing of Changshui, 30 May 1992; Li Baozhang, formerly of Shuhe, 1 June 1992; Yang Zenglie, 3 August 1998; also from Yang Zenglie 1990: 118, 1991: 40–41.

5. This association is mentioned by Zhao Yintang in her vignettes of Lijiang (1984 [1948]: 154). Information on the Huangjing association and its acquisition of the Dongjing tradition was obtained from interviews with Wang Dejiu, formerly of the Huangjing association (21 November 1991 and 26 May 1992); He Yi'an of the Dayan Town Dongjing association (4 May 1992); and from Yang Zenglie 1990: 120.

6. Information on the Jinshan and Shigu cases is derived from interviews with Yang Jian of Jinshan, 20 November 1991; He Yi'an of Dayan Town, 30 December 1991 and 29 April 1992; Zhao Yuxian of Shigu, 2 June 1992; and from He Yi'an's autobiography (Track 1996).

7. Information in this section is derived from a series of interviews with He Yi'an of Dayan Town, and from interviews with Mu Zhu, formerly of Lasha, 6 November 1991; He Huihan of Baisha, 11 November 1991; Zhao Yuxian of Shigu, 2 June 1992; Yang Jian of Jinshan, 20 November 1991; He Minda of Baihua, 7 November 1991; Li Baozhang, formerly of Shuhe, 1 June 1992; and Wang Dejiu, formerly of the Huangjing association, 21 November 1991; also from Yang Zenglie 1990–1991 and Track 1996.

8. Charles McKhann points out (personal communication) that the apparent relaxation in educational qualifications in the newer groups may also be a symptom of the general decline of the traditional literatus system, dealt a deathblow by the abolition of the imperial civil service examinations in 1905.

9. Interviews with Zhao Yingxian, 30 November 1991; Niu Weijiong, 4 December 1991; He Linghan, 16 December 1991; and Sun Ziming, 20 December 1991 (all of Dayan Town); also the brief article by Zhao Jingxiu (1995).

10. Interviews with He Hongzhang and He Zhong of Fuhui Village, 19 December 1991; and with Wang Dejiu, formerly of the Huangjing association, 26 May 1992.

11. Personal communications from Zhang Kuiguang and Zhang Longhan; interview with He Shiwei, 31 May 1992.

12. Compare Chen Dacan 1989: 166; Jones 1995; Tsao 1989: 112–126. Ethnomusicological research from around the world suggests that while such sharing and borrowing of repertoire between ritual and non-ritual, or sacred and secular, contexts is quite common in many cultures (e.g., al Faruqi 1983: 25, and Nketia 1987: 174), in some cases local custom results in the conception of a rigid division between the two (e.g., Ellingson 1987: 163, and Shelemay 1982: 52).

Chapter 6

1. For example, the associations in Chuxiong (interview with Che Xuelin, 9 March 1992) and Dali (Dali Shi Xiaguan Wenhuaguan 1990: 607).

2. Yang Zenglie kindly brought this episode to my notice (interview, 13 November 1991); He Yi'an of the Dayan Town association later confirmed the facts. It is also described by Track (1996: 141).

3. Zhou Lin (1902–1977) was a nationally recognized artist born in Shigu, Lijiang County. He had a varied career as soldier, schoolteacher, and, after 1949, cultural official. He was well known for his skills in music and other facets of culture as well as in the visual arts. For some years prior to 1949 he taught Chinese at the high school level in Lijiang (Zhou Shanfu 1990). Setting new words to old tunes was not unknown in Lijiang's Dongjing tradition: in 1944 the Dongjing association member Zhou Fan set the poem "White Lotus" (*Yong Bailian*) to the instrumental piece "Water Dragon Cry" (*Shui Long Yin*) (Yang Zenglie 1991: 35).

4. The Jade Dragon Snow Mountain (*Yulong Xueshan*) is Lijiang's major landmark, towering over Dayan Town.

5. Interview with He Yitian of Changshui, formerly of Lasha, 30 May 1992.

6. The Soviet model of musical development has been well explained in English by Muhambetova: "According to the Marxist point of view, the basis (i.e., means of production and production relations) should correspond to the superstructure (i.e., culture, art, science, and ideology). In musicology, a theory was worked out, according to which each stage of social economic development corresponded very strictly to a particular level of musical culture, which in turn is represented by certain genres, forms and means of musical language and by types of professionalism. The history of musical culture was regarded as encompassing the evolution from monody . . . to polyphony, with its forms and genres. European polyphony, which, according to this conception, had replaced medieval monodic thinking in Europe, was the aim of all cultures. The creation of polyphonic genres provided the necessary correspondence of superstructures and basis in the cultures of the oriental peoples [of the Soviet Union] who had been proclaimed as members of socialist nations" (1995: 73). Mark Slobin offers a more concrete exposition of the consequences: "Soviet writers concluded [that] it [would] be necessary for the Uzbeks to bring their music 'up to the level of world culture,' a phrase which seemed to me to indicate that it should sound as much like Tchaikovsky as possible" (1971: 7). Note a similar trend in Bulgarian theorizing (Silverman 1989: 149).

7. Compare Lenin's slogan about "nationalities" and art: art should be "nationalist in form, socialist in content" (quoted in Levin 1979: 155).

8. See, for example, Hegel (1984) on fiction and drama; Holm (1991) on Yangge; Kraus (1989) on the piano; Lau (1996a and b) on *dizi* (transverse flute) music; Link (1984) on Xiangsheng; Schimmelpenninck and Kouwenhoven (1993) on the Shanghai Conservatory of Music; Shih Hwa-Fu (1959) and Hung (1993) on storytelling; Wong (1984) on revolutionary songs; Yang Mu (1994) on the selective representation of China's folk song culture; Yung (1984) on Cantonese opera; and Yung (1989b) on the seven-string zither *guqin*.

9. Another important cultural organ, Lijiang County Library, was established in 1957 (Lijiang Naxizu Zizhixian Gaikuang Bianxiezu 1986: 134). This library houses many surviving Dongjing association scriptures from Dayan Town.

10. Information on this period is derived from many interviews and observations from musicians active at this time; also from Zhao Jingxiu's article (1995).

11. An anthology of songs performed at this festival was published (Yinyue Chubanshe Bianjibu 1965); it includes two Naxi numbers (pp. 145–147).

12. The catalogue of recordings held by the Music Research Institute in Beijing includes many Naxi folk songs, Baisha Xiyue, and Lijiang Dongjing recordings collected in 1962. Some items from all these categories are dated 1961, and listed as having been dubbed by the Institute, implying the existence of some original recordings from before that date. There are also a few folk song recordings listed from the 1950s, and several recordings and dubbings from after the Cultural Revolution (Li Jiuling 1994: 196–198; 317–318). One local musician commented that some visitors in the 1960s had urged the Dongjing musicians to play faster, criticizing them for being too refined and insufficiently lively (*youya you yu, jinzhang bu zu*).

13. On the propensity of the new government for absorbing writers and artists into the state's cultural apparatus, see McDougall 1984.

14. Scholarly research and recording of Chinese music had begun well before 1949, but received an unprecedented impetus from the formation of a national network of cultural institutions under the Ministry of Culture (Jones 1995: 52–54; Wong 1991). Among national minorities, the Naxi were one group out of many whose music was researched and recorded as never before in the 1950s and early 1960s. The catalogue of sound recordings held by the Music Research Institute in Beijing includes recordings from this period for many other groups (Li Jiuling 1994), and the China Record Company even put out commercial records of the music of some minorities ("Gramophone Discs: National Minority Music," 1964). Among the most famous research and salvage missions of this period was the project on the Twelve Mukam of the Uighur minority of Xinjiang Province (Wan 1963).

15. Unless otherwise stated, information for this section is derived from personal observation and interviews in urban and lowland rural areas, and from personal communications from Charles McKhann and Yang Zenglie on remote mountainous regions.

16. Note the parallel with "cassette culture" in India (Manuel 1993).

17. For a recent English-language overview of the development of popular music in the mainland, see Bernoviz 1997. On Chinese popular culture in general, see Zha 1995.

18. The history and changing names of Lijiang's professional performance troupes are quite complex. The prefectural "art troupe" (*wenyi gongzuodui*, or *wen'gongdui* for short), established in 1956, was renamed the prefectural "song and dance troupe" (*gewutuan*) in the 1960s. The county "nationality art troupe" (*minzu wenyi gongzuo dui*), established in the early 1960s, was the precursor of what was known by the 1980s as the county "nationality song and dance troupe" (*minzu gewutuan*). The "Lijiang Prefecture Art Troupe" (*Lijiang Diqu Yishutuan*) formed in 1992 from the merger of the prefectural Dianju troupe and part of the county nationality song and dance troupe was renamed in the late 1990s "Lijiang Prefecture Nationality Song and Dance Troupe" (*Lijiang Diqu Minzu Gewutuan*). I am grateful to He Zhong for providing information on this subject in the early and mid 1990s, and to Yang Zenglie for elucidation of the entire history in a recent letter (6 January 2000).

19. Mackerras notes a definite trend toward professional minority troupes directing their performances at visitors from outside their region. By October 1994 the Kashgar Song and Dance Troupe in Xinjiang (northwest China) was contracting out 70 percent of its annual performances to organizations such as tourist hotels (1996: 197).

20. For example, on the CD *Baishibai: Songs of the Minority Nationalities of Yunnan*; in the *JVC Video Anthology of World Music*; and in the domestically produced video sets *Local Customs and Music—Ethnic Music in Yunnan* and *The Instrument Kingdom in Yunnan, China*.

Chapter 7

1. Apart from printed sources cited, information on the mechanics of the revival was obtained through personal observation, and through interviews with Ge Agan of Kunming, 20 September 1991; He Minda of Baihua, 7 November 1991; Xuan Ke of Dayan Town, 31 October and 5 November 1991; He Linghan of Dayan Town, 16 December 1991; Yang Zenglie of Dayan Town, who has also carried out fieldwork in Shigu and Judian, 27 April 1992; He Yitian of Changshui, 30 May 1992; He Hongxing of Changshui and He Minda of Baihua, 30 May 1992; Yang Houkun of Dayan Town, 24 May 1992; Li

Baozhang of Shuhe, 1 June 1992; and Zhao Yuxian of Shigu, 2 June 1992. Other post–Cultural Revolution musical revivals are well described by Jones (1995, ch. 4) and Dujunco (1994, ch. 6).

2. From 1949 on the new government discouraged elaborate funerals. Since the late 1970s some funerals, especially outside the urban area of Dayan Town, are once again being celebrated with some ritual content and incidental or processional music.

3. In addition to Rock's own voluminous works, inventoried in a bibliography (Chock, Bryan, and Marks 1963), a selection of his photographs has been published (Aris 1992). There is also a biography (Sutton 1974), and a retrospective on his work in *National Geographic*, to which he contributed several articles (Edwards 1997). Goullart published a popular account of his years in Dayan Town (1957). An earlier visitor to write substantially was Bacot (1913). Lijiang is also mentioned more briefly by several other travelers, including Courtellement (1904), Johnston (1908), Andrews and Andrews (1918), and Reitlinger (1939).

4. The scrapbook kept by the Dayan Ancient Music Association (Dayan Guyuehui, n.d. [1998]) includes newspaper articles since the late 1980s from all levels of the domestic Chinese-language press, including many mentions in the local *Lijiang Bao* (Lijiang News) and provincial *Chuncheng Wanbao* (Spring City Evening News) and *Yunnan Ribao* (Yunnan Daily). Newspapers from other parts of China mentioning the music include the *Beijing Wanbao* (Beijing Evening News), *Beijing Qingnian Bao* (Beijing Youth Daily), *Guangming Ribao* (Guangming Daily), and the best-known national paper, *Renmin Ribao* (People's Daily). Chinese-language newspapers from Macao (*Aomen Ribao* [Macao Daily News]) and Manila (*Shang Bao* [Commercial News]) have also picked up New China News Agency reports on the music. Chinese-authored guidebooks include Tang and Jin (1988: 38–39), Li and Yin (1993: 26–27), and He Yong (1998: 23–25). Foreign-authored guides include Booz (1989: 136–137); Cummings et al. (1991: 740), and later editions of the Lonely Planet China guide; Knowles 1995 and later editions of Fodor's China guide; Atiyah, Leffman, and Lewis (1997); and Mayhew and Huhti (1998: 375–376). Magazine features include Paulzen 1991, Kou Zhengling 1996, and Edwards 1997. For the three British newspapers, see Christmas 1995, Clough 1995, and Jack 1996; for the *Straits Times*, see Leong 1996; for the *South China Morning Post*, see Norman 1997; for the *China Daily*, see Mao Jingbo 1998; for the two United States newspapers, see Hessler 1997 and Farley 1999. The Norwegian press reported the 1998 tour to Norway. The Internet site accessible in 1998 was www.sinohost.com/yunnan_travel/lijiang/lijiang_music.html.

5. The clash between the Chinese conservatory establishment and non-Chinese musicologists over the validity of the term "traditional," and the aesthetic desirability of injecting Western functional harmony, equal temperament, instrumental forms and techniques into Chinese music, is best set out in a spirited exchange conducted at the Second Oriental Music Festival held in Durham, England, in August 1979 (Fang 1981, Provine 1981, Thrasher 1981). The aesthetic gulf between professional and amateur performers of a traditional Chinese music is well illustrated by the case of Shanghai's instrumental genre Jiangnan Sizhu (Witzleben 1987). The traditional amateurs find the professional, harmonized arrangements by conservatory musicians lacking in feeling and flavor, despite their technical sophistication. At the same time, "most conservatory students find [the] new arrangements far more attractive than the 'unimproved' music played by amateur groups. Many performers and scholars in professional circles feel that the amateur *sizhu*

musicians are hopelessly conservative, unable to appreciate anything new, and unwilling to see their music develop" (Witzleben 1987: 246). To hear "authentic" and "arranged" minority folk music side by side, listen to the CD *A Happy Miao Family*; this includes both "authentic" folk songs and song and dance troupe compositions.

6. Many young musicians in the Dayan Town group learned not by the traditional rote repetition of *gongchepu* (solfège) versions of the pieces as described in chapter 4, but by a mixture of reading detailed scores in cipher notation, listening to their elders, and hearing recordings. In Jinshan and villages around Baihua, *gongchepu* is still used. It is unclear as yet how changing methods of transmission will affect the music in the future (Rees, n.d.).

7. Information on the domestic trips is derived from several sources, including personal communications from several musicians on the Canton trip in 1991–1992; documents including the formal invitation to the Dayan Ancient Music Association to visit Beijing (Zhongguo Yinyuejia Xiehui et al. 1993), the association's memorandum on the trip (Lijiang Dayan Naxi Guyuehui 1993), and an undated publicity leaflet (Zhongguo Lijiang Dayan Naxi Guyuehui, n.d.); and interviews with Xuan Ke and Yang Zenglie during the association's visit to England in October 1995.

8. Note the Chinese reaction to pianist Fou Ts'ong's third prize in the 1955 Chopin Competition: "Fou Ts'ong immediately became a Chinese national hero. . . . Fou was the first Asian musician to be honored in an important international competition by Westerners for playing European music. . . . From this point, Fou Ts'ong's career was a matter of interest to the Party's chief leaders" (Kraus 1989: 81). In 1987 I attended an exhibition marking the sixtieth anniversary of the Shanghai Conservatory of Music, at which every domestic and international prize ever won by a teacher or student at the conservatory was proudly listed.

9. These murals are discussed in several sources, including Lijiang Xian Wenhuaguan 1986.

Chapter 8

1. On Africa, see Nketia 1986a and 1986b, and Agawu 1992 and 1995; for other musics, see Bohlman 1991b, Racy 1991, Shiloah 1991, Treitler 1991, Potter 1996.

2. I discussed nomenclature in detail during several interviews and informal meetings with He Yi'an of the Dayan Town Dongjing association; He Huihan of the Baisha association; He Linghan and Sun Ziming, who had played before 1949 in secular groups in Dayan Town; and Kunming-based Naxi scholar Ge Agan.

3. A Chinese-authored English language travel guide uses the term "Ancient Tune of Lijiang," clearly a direct translation of *Lijiang guyue* (Tang and Jin 1988: 38). Occasionally the term "Lijiang Ancient Music" or "Naxi Ancient Music" is also intended to include Baisha Xiyue or other types of traditional Naxi music.

4. In chapter 4 I cite a few brief mentions by Peter Goullart and Joseph Rock of Naxi musics other than the Dongjing tradition; but because they are mostly factual rather than evaluative, I do not repeat them here.

5. Kou Bangping, a member of the Hui (Moslem) minority, was a music worker in Lijiang for many years from 1956 on, although he had moved to Dali before I went there.

6. The first time I heard anyone mention this idea was when a Chinese professor from Canton, a *qigong* (Chinese yoga) enthusiast, attended a tourist concert in Dayan Town in 1992, and commented that the music seemed to him to have healthful qualities. This

theme was taken up immediately by Xuan Ke, the English-speaking leader of the group, and I have seen it reappear in print several times since.

7. Actually a few ensemble members are Han Chinese.

8. By summer 1998, Xuan Ke had also added a couple of new items to the program: a flute solo from Baisha Xiyue, and solo folk songs sung by a young Naxi woman. This injected a strongly Naxi flavor into part of the program, as well as adding more musical variety for his ever-bigger audiences.

9. In a casual conversation in June 1996, a young Han Chinese who ran a café in Lijiang told me that, had she been Naxi, she would have been interested in joining the training class. I pointed out that Naxi language skills were not necessary to learn the music, but she still seemed to feel that it was Naxi music that a Han could not play. There are in fact several Han who do participate. Nevertheless, her comment shows how much Lijiang's Dongjing music is now considered a specifically Naxi heritage.

Appendix A

1. Descriptions of the scriptures are based on a 1947 hand-copied *Transcendent Scripture of the Great Grotto of Wenchang* preserved by He Yi'an of Dayan Town; and on two copies of a 1903 woodblock *Guandi Enlightenment Scripture* preserved in Lijiang County Library. More detailed discussion of Lijiang's texts may be found in Rees 1994: 151–164.

2. It differs greatly, however, from versions used in counties and cities closer to Lijiang, including Yongsheng, Dali, and Xiaguan.

3. "Inner alchemy" is discussed in English by Robinet (1989), who defines it as "a method of finding illumination by returning to the fundamental order of the cosmos" (p. 299).

4. I encountered one exception in Lijiang County to the rule that the Ten Offerings appear in the *Complete Formal Invocation* volume. The Dongjing association in Shigu, which began its activities about 1944, obtained its scriptures not from another part of Lijiang County, but from Niujie (Niugai in local Yunnan Han dialect), a stop on the road to Dali (interview with Zhao Yuxian, 2 June 1992). Clearly the version of the *Transcendent Scripture of the Great Grotto of Wenchang* available in Niujie was one of the majority in Yunnan in which the Ten Offerings come in the second fascicle of the *Transcendent Scripture*.

5. Part of the text which appears in the Lijiang and Dali scriptures has been translated into German and English (Doolittle 1872: 373–376).

Appendix B

1. Sangde Nuowa's diagram of the temple layout for a Dongjing ceremony is also very similar, although the placement of the trigrams differs (1994: 78).

Appendix C

1. I am indebted to Judith Boltz for clarifying the content and meaning of the scriptural texts included here (first through fifth excerpts), and to Bell Yung for advice on translating the Dianju (Yunnan opera) scene (sixth excerpt).

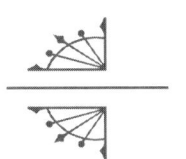

Bibliography

For Chinese-language items, Chinese characters are given for authors' names, article and book titles, and journal titles.

Abbreviations
LJWSZL—*Lijiang Wenshi Ziliao* 麗江文史資料 (Lijiang cultural and historical records)
MZYSYJ—*Minzu Yishu Yanjiu* 民族藝術研究 (Research into ethnic arts)
MZYY—*Minzu Yinyue* 民族音樂 (National music)
RMYY—*Renmin Yinyue* 人民音樂 (People's music)
YLS—*Yulong Shan* 玉龍山 (Jade Dragon Mountain)
YNMZCBS—Yunnan Minzu Chubanshe (Yunnan Nationalities Publishing Company)
YNRMCBS—Yunnan Renmin Chubanshe (Yunnan People's Publishing Company)
ZJXYJ—*Zongjiaoxue Yanjiu* 宗教學研究 (Religious studies research)

Agawu, Kofi. 1992. "Representing African Music." *Critical Inquiry* 18.2: 245–266.
———. 1995. "The Invention of 'African Rhythm'." *Journal of the American Musicological Society* 48.3: 380–395.
Agnew, R. Gordon. 1939. "The Music of the Ch'uan Miao." *Journal of the West China Border Research Society* 11: 9–22.
Ames, David Wason. 1973. "A Sociocultural View of Hausa Musical Activity." In *The Traditional Artist in African Society*, edited by Warren L. d'Azevedo, 128–161. Bloomington: Indiana University Press.
Andrews, Roy Chapman, and Yvette Borup Andrews. 1918. *Camps and Trails in China*. New York: D. Appleton.
Aris, Michael. 1992. *Lamas, Princes, and Brigands: Joseph Rock's Photographs of the Tibetan Borderlands of China*. New York: China House Gallery/China Institute in America.
Asian Music Circuit (British concert promoters). 1995. Flier for British concert tour of Dayan Ancient Music Association.
Atiyah, Jeremy, David Leffman, and Simon Lewis. 1997. *China: The Rough Guide*. London: Rough Guides.
Backus, Charles. 1981. *The Nan-chao Kingdom and T'ang China's Southwestern Frontier*. Cambridge: Cambridge University Press.
Bacot, J. 1913. *Les Mo-so*. Leiden: E. J. Brill.

Beliaev, Viktor M. 1975. *Central Asian Music: Essays in the History of the Music of the Peoples of the U.S.S.R.* Translated by Mark Slobin and Greta Slobin. Middletown, CT: Wesleyan University Press. First published in Russian, 1962.

Bentley, G. Carter. 1987. "Ethnicity and Practice." *Comparative Studies in Society and History* 29.1: 24–55.

Bernoviz (Baranovitch), Nimrod. 1997. "China's New Voices: Politics, Ethnicity, and Gender in Popular Music Culture on the Mainland, 1978–1997." Ph.D. dissertation, University of Pittsburgh.

Bohlman, Philip V. 1991a. "Of *Yekkes* and Chamber Music in Israel: Ethnomusicological Meaning in Western Music History." In *Ethnomusicology and Modern Music History*, edited by Stephen Blum, Philip V. Bohlman, and Daniel M. Neuman, 254–267. Urbana: University of Illinois Press.

———. 1991b. "Representation and Cultural Critique in the History of Ethnomusicology." In *Comparative Musicology and Anthropology of Music*, edited by Bruno Nettl and Philip V. Bohlman, 131–151. Chicago: University of Chicago Press.

Boltz, Judith Magee. 1987. *A Survey of Taoist Literature, Tenth to Seventeenth Centuries.* Berkeley: Institute of East Asian Studies, University of California.

———. 1993. "Notes on Modern Editions of the Taoist Canon." *Bulletin of the School of Oriental and African Studies* 56.1: 87–95.

Booz, Patrick R. 1989. *An Illustrated Guide to Yunnan.* Hong Kong: Guidebook Company. First published in 1987.

Borchigud, Wurlig. 1995. "The Impact of Urban Ethnic Education on Modern Mongolian Ethnicity, 1949–1966." In *Cultural Encounters on China's Ethnic Frontiers*, edited by Stevan Harrell, 278–300. Seattle: University of Washington Press.

Bourdieu, Pierre. 1977. *Outline of a Theory of Practice.* Translated by Richard Nice. Cambridge: Cambridge University Press. First published in French, 1972.

———. 1984. *Distinction: A Social Critique of the Judgement of Taste.* Translated by Richard Nice. Cambridge: Harvard University Press. First published in French, 1979.

Brown, Melissa J., ed. 1996. *Negotiating Ethnicities in China and Taiwan.* Berkeley: Institute of East Asian Studies, University of California.

Bruner, Edward. 1986. "Ethnography as Narrative." In *The Anthropology of Experience*, edited by Victor W. Turner and Edward M. Bruner, 139–158. Urbana: University of Illinois Press.

———. 1994. "Abraham Lincoln as Authentic Reproduction: A Critique of Postmodernism." *American Anthropologist* 96.2: 397–415.

Buchanan, Donna A. 1991. "The Bulgarian Folk Orchestra: Cultural Performance, Symbol, and the Construction of National Identity in Socialist Bulgaria." Ph.D. dissertation, University of Texas at Austin.

Catlin, Amy. 1986. "The Hmong and Their Music . . . A Critique of Pure Speech." In *Hmong Art: Tradition and Change*, edited by Joanne Cubbs and Ruth DeYoung Kohler, 11–18. Sheboygan, WI: John Michael Kohler Arts Center.

Chao, Emily Kay. 1995. "Depictions of Difference: History, Gender, Ritual and State Discourse among the Naxi of Southwest China." Ph.D. dissertation, University of Michigan.

———. 1996. "Hegemony, Agency, and Re-presenting the Past: The Invention of Dongba Culture." In *Negotiating Ethnicities in China and Taiwan*, edited by Melissa J. Brown, 208–239. Berkeley: Institute of East Asian Studies, University of California.

Chavannes, Edouard. 1912. "Documents historiques et géographiques relatifs à Li-kiang." *T'oung Pao* (2nd series), 13: 565–653.

Chen Dacan 陳大燦. 1989. "Tongyi daoqu zai ge di liuchuan zhong de bianhua" 同一道曲在各地流傳中的變化 (Regional variations of a Taoist tune). In *Studies of Taoist Rituals and Music of Today*, edited by Pen-yeh Tsao and Daniel P. L. Law, 166–180. Hong Kong: Society of Ethnomusicological Research in Hong Kong.

Ch'en, Fu-yen. 1975. "Confucian Ceremonial Music in Taiwan with Comparative References to Its Sources." Ph.D. dissertation, Wesleyan University.

Cheung, Siu-woo. 1996. "Representation and Negotiation of Ge Identities in Southeast Guizhou." In *Negotiating Ethnicities in China and Taiwan*, edited by Melissa J. Brown, 240–273. Berkeley: Institute of East Asian Studies, University of California.

Chin Ming. "How the Peacock Dance Reached the Stage." *China Reconstructs* 12.3: 10–11.

Chock, Alvin K., E. H. Bryan, Jr., and Loy Marks. 1963. "Bibliography of J. F. Rock." *Taxon* 13.3: 98–102. (First published in *Hawaiian Botanical Society Newsletter*, January 1963.)

Chong Xian 崇先, comp. 1986. "Yunnan Heqing Dongjing Yinyue" 雲南鶴慶洞經音樂 (Dongjing music of Heqing, Yunnan). Mimeographed score.

———. 1989. "Lijiang dongjing yinyue chutan" 麗江洞經音樂初探 (Preliminary investigation of Dongjing music of Lijiang). *MZYSYJ* 7: 32–39, 31.

Christmas, Linda. 1995. "Have Gongs, Will Finally Travel." *Times* (London), 5 October (photocopy).

Clark, Paul. 1987. "Ethnic Minorities in Chinese Films: Cinema and the Exotic." *East-West Film Journal* 1.2: 15–31.

Clough, Juliet. 1995. "A Thousand Years of Music and Tao." *Daily Telegraph* (London), 7 October: A3.

Cohen, Erik. 1988. "Authenticity and Commoditization in Tourism." *Annals of Tourism Research* 15: 371–386.

Constable, Nicole, ed. 1996. *Guest People: Hakka Identity in China and Abroad*. Seattle: University of Washington Press.

Coplan, David B. 1991. "Ethnomusicology and the Meaning of Tradition." In *Ethnomusicology and Modern Music History*, edited by Stephen Blum, Philip V. Bohlman, and Daniel M. Neuman, 35–48. Urbana: University of Illinois Press.

Courtellement, Gervais. 1904. *Voyage au Yunnan*. Paris: Plon-Nourrit.

Cummings, Joe, and Robert Storey. 1991. *China—A Travel Survival Kit*. 3rd ed. Melbourne, Australia: Lonely Planet.

Dali Shi Xiaguan Wenhuaguan 大理市下關文化館, ed. 1990. *Dali Dongjing Guyue* 大理洞經古樂 (Ancient Dongjing music of Dali). Kunming: YNRMCBS.

Dali Xianzhi Gao 大理縣志稿 (Draft gazetteer of Dali County [Yunnan Province]). 1916.

Dayan Guyuehui 大研古樂會. 1992. "Baogao" 報告 (Report). Manuscript, kept by Dayan Ancient Music Association.

Dayan Guyuehui 大研古樂會. n.d. (1998). Scrapbook of newspaper cuttings from Chinese and foreign press.

Deal, David. 1976. "Policy towards Ethnic Minorities in Southwest China, 1927–1965." *Journal of Asian Affairs* 1.1: 31–38.

Dean, Kenneth. 1993. *Taoist Ritual and Popular Cults of South-East China*. Princeton, NJ: Princeton University Press.

Diamond, Norma. 1988. "The Miao and Poison: Interactions on China's Southwestern Frontier." *Ethnology* 27.1: 1–25.

———. 1995. "Defining the Miao: Ming, Qing, and Contemporary Views." In *Cultural Encounters on China's Ethnic Frontiers*, edited by Stevan Harrell, 92–116. Seattle: University of Washington Press.

Doležalová, A. 1983. "Nationalism and Literature of National Minorities of the People's Republic of China." In *Proceedings of the Fourth International Conference on the Theoretical Problems of Asian and African Literatures*, edited by M. Gálik, 83–90. Bratislava: Literary Institute of the Slovak Academy of Sciences.

Doolittle, Justus. 1872. *A Vocabulary and Handbook of the Chinese Language*, vol. 2. Foochow: Rozario, Marcal.

Dreyer, June Teufel. 1976. *China's Forty Millions: Minority Nationalities and National Integration in the People's Republic of China*. Harvard East Asian Series No. 87. Cambridge: Harvard University Press.

Du Yaxiong 杜亞雄. 1992. "Recent Issues in Music Research in the People's Republic of China." *Association for Chinese Music Research Newsletter* 5.1: 9–12.

———. 1993. *Zhongguo Ge Shaoshu Minzu Minjian Yinyue Gaishu* 中國各少數民族民間音樂概述 (An outline of the folk music of the national minorities of China). Beijing: Renmin Yinyue Chubanshe.

———. 1994. "Caifeng he caifengzhe de pinde" 采風和采風者的品德 (Fieldwork and fieldworkers' ethics). *Zhongguo Yinyue* 中國音樂 (Chinese music) 56: 17–19.

Duara, Prasenjit. 1988a. *Culture, Power, and the State: Rural North China, 1900–1942*. Stanford: Stanford University Press.

———. 1988b. "Superscribing Symbols: The Myth of Guandi, Chinese God of War." *Journal of Asian Studies* 47.4: 778–795.

———. 1991. "Knowledge and Power in the Discourse of Modernity: The Campaigns against Popular Religion in Early Twentieth-Century China." *Journal of Asian Studies* 50.1: 67–83.

———. 1995. *Rescuing History from the Nation: Questioning Narratives of Modern China*. Chicago: University of Chicago Press.

Dujunco, Mercedes. 1994. "Tugging at the Native's Heartstrings: Nostalgia and the Post-Mao 'Revival' of the *Xian Shi Yue* String Ensemble Music of Chaozhou, South China." Ph.D. dissertation, University of Washington.

Ebrey, Patricia. 1996. "Surnames and Han Chinese Identity." In *Negotiating Ethnicities in China and Taiwan*, edited by Melissa J. Brown, 19–36. Berkeley: Institute of East Asian Studies, University of California.

Edwards, Mike. 1997. "Our Man in China." *National Geographic* 191.1: 62–81.

Eichler, R. 1882–1883. "The K'uen Shi Wan; Or, the Practical Theology of the Chinese." *China Review* 11: 93–101, 146–161.

Ellingson, Ter. 1987. "Music and Religion." In *The Encyclopedia of Religion*, edited by Mircea Eliade, vol. 10, 163–172. London: Collier Macmillan Publishers.

Fang Guoyu 方國瑜 and He Zhiwu 和志武. 1981. *Naxi Xiangxing Wenzi Pu* 納西象形文字譜 (Dictionary of Naxi pictographs). Kunming: YNRMCBS.

Fang Kun 方堃. 1981. "A Discussion on Chinese National Musical Traditions." Translated by Keith Pratt. *Asian Music* 12.2: 3–11. Originally published as "Guanyu Zhongguo minzu yinyue chuantong de yici taolun—Zhongyang Yinyue Xueyuan Minyuetuan zai Yingguo Dulun dongfang yinyue jie" 關於中國民族音樂傳統的一次討論—中央音樂學院民樂團在英國杜倫東方音樂節 (A discussion on Chinese national musical traditions—the Central Conscrvatory Chinese Music Ensemble at the Oriental Music Festival in Durham, England) in *RMYY* 178 (1980): 38–40.

Farley, Maggie. 1999. "Himalayas Are Alive with Music of China." *Los Angeles Times*, 19 January: A1, A8.

Faruqi, Lois Ibsen al. 1983. "What Makes 'Religious Music' Religious?" In *Sacred Sound: Music in Religious Thought and Practice*, edited by Joyce Irwin, 21–34. Chico, CA: Scholars Press.

Fei Hsiao Tung (a.k.a. Fei Xiaotong). 1981. *Toward a People's Anthropology*. Beijing: New World Press.

Fitzgerald, C. P. 1941. *The Tower of Five Glories*. London: Cresset Press.

Fu Maoji. 1985. "Language Policies toward National Minorities in China." Translated by Sharon J. Mann. *Anthropological Linguistics* 27.2: 214–221.

Ge Agan 戈阿幹. 1992. *Dongba Shenxi yu Dongba Wupu* 東巴神系與東巴舞譜 (The Dongba pantheon and Dongba dance notation). Kunming: YNRMCBS.

Gejiu Shi Wenhuaju 個舊市文化局, ed. 1988. *Gejiu Shi Wenhua Zhi* 個舊市文化志 (Cultural records of Gejiu City). No other publication details.

Gladney, Dru C. 1991. *Muslim Chinese: Ethnic Nationalism in the People's Republic*. Harvard East Asian Monographs No. 149. Cambridge: Council on East Asian Studies, Harvard University.

———. 1994. "Representing Nationality in China: Refiguring Majority/Minority Identities." *Journal of Asian Studies* 53.1: 92–123.

Goldstein, Melvyn, and Cynthia Beall. 1989. "The Remote World of Tibet's Nomads." *National Geographic Magazine* 175.6: 752–781.

Gong Yin 龔蔭, ed. 1985. *Ming Qing Yunnan Tusi Tongzuan* 明清雲南土司通纂 (Compilation on the native officials of Yunnan in the Ming and Qing dynasties). Kunming: YNMZCBS.

Goullart, Peter. 1957. *Forgotten Kingdom*. London: Readers' Union/John Murray.

Graburn, Nelson H. H., ed. 1976. *Ethnic and Tourist Arts: Cultural Expressions from the Fourth World*. Berkeley: University of California Press.

"Gramophone Discs: National Minority Music." 1964. *Peking Review* 7.3: 35.

Greenwood, Davydd J. 1977. "Culture by the Pound: An Anthropological Perspective on Tourism as Cultural Commoditization." In *Hosts and Guests: The Anthropology of Tourism*, edited by Valene L. Smith, 129–138. Philadelphia: University of Pennsylvania Press.

Gui, Ming Chao. 1990. "Yunnanese and Kunming Chinese: A Study of the Language Communities, the Phonological Systems, and the Phonological Developments." Ph.D. dissertation, University of Texas, Arlington.

Guldin, Gregory Eliyu. 1994. *The Saga of Anthropology in China: From Malinowski to Moscow to Mao*. Armonk, NY: M. E. Sharpe.

Guo Dalie 郭大烈 and Yang Shiguang 楊世光, eds. 1985. *Dongba Wenhua Lunji* 東巴文化論集 (Collected essays on Dongba culture). Kunming: YNRMCBS.

———, eds. 1991. *Dongba Wenhua Lun* 東巴文化論 (Research on Dongba culture). Kunming: YNRMCBS.

Guo Songyi 郭松義. 1990. "Lun Ming Qing shiqi de Guanyu chongbai" 論明清時期的關羽崇拜 (The cult of Guan Yu in Ming and Qing times). *Zhongguo Shi Yanjiu* 中國史研究 (Research in Chinese history) 47: 127–139.

Guy, Nancy A. 1995. "Peking Opera as 'National Opera' in Taiwan: What's in a Name?" *Asian Theatre Journal* 12.1: 85–103.

Han, Kuo-Huang. 1979. "The Modern Chinese Orchestra." *Asian Music* 11.1: 1–40.

Hansen, Mette Halskov. 1998. "Fostering 'Love of Learning': Naxi Responses to Ethnic Images in Chinese State Education." In *Reconstructing Twentieth-Century China: State Control, Civil Society, and National Identity*, edited by Kjeld Erik Brødsgaard and David Strand, 280–309. Oxford: Clarendon Press.

———. 1999. *Lessons in Being Chinese: Minority Education and Ethnic Identity in Southwest China*. Seattle: University of Washington Press.

Hanson, Allan. 1989. "The Making of the Maori: Culture Invention and Logic." *American Anthropologist* 92: 890–902.

Harrell, Stevan. 1990. "Ethnicity, Local Interests, and the State: Yi Communities in Southwest China." *Comparative Studies in Society and History* 32.3: 515–548.

———, ed. 1995a. *Cultural Encounters on China's Ethnic Frontiers*. Seattle: University of Washington Press.

———. 1995b. "Introduction: Civilizing Projects and the Reaction to Them." In *Cultural Encounters on China's Ethnic Frontiers*, edited by Stevan Harrell, 3–36. Seattle: University of Washington Press.

———. 1995c. "Jeeping against Maoism." *Positions* 3.3: 728–758.

———. 1996. "The Nationalities Question and the Prmi Prblem." In *Negotiating Ethnicities in China and Taiwan*, edited by Melissa J. Brown, 274–296. Berkeley: Institute of East Asian Studies, University of California.

He Changlin 何昌林. 1993. "Guobao maicang Ximalaya yunling shenchu—wei Lijiang Naxi Guyuetuan jin Jing yanchu zuo" 國寶埋藏喜馬拉雅雲嶺深處—為麗江納西古樂團晉京演出作 (A national treasure hidden in the recesses of the cloud peaks of the Himalayas—for the performance in Beijing of the Lijiang Naxi Ancient Music Troupe). *RMYY* 338: 20–25.

He Gengji 和庚吉. 1938. "Yongbao Ping'an Xu" 永保平安序 (Preface to "Eternal Assurance of Well-Being"). Manuscript, kept in Lijiang Prefectural Archive.

He Jiaxiu 和家修. 1996a. "Naxi guyue de jin yi bu baohu he kaifa" 納西古樂的進一步保護和開發 (Further protection and development of Naxi Ancient Music). *YLS* 74: 43–45.

———. 1996b. "Naxi guyue zhenhan Ying Lun" 納西古樂震撼英倫 (Naxi Ancient Music hits London, England). *YLS* 74: 101–113, 99.

He Minda 和民達, comp. 1978. "Lijiang Dongjing Yinyue" 麗江洞經音樂 (Lijiang's Dongjing music). Mimeographed score.

He Xidian 和錫典. 1985. "Bieshi Xieli—Baisha Xiyue" 別時謝禮—白沙細樂 (Baisha Xiyue). *LJWSZL* 1: 68–71.

He Yong 和勇. 1998. *Lijiang Lüyou Zhinan* 麗江旅游指南 (Guide to tourism in Lijiang). Kunming: YNRMCBS.

He Zhiwu 和志武. 1995. *Naxizu Min'ge Yizhu* 納西族民歌譯注 (Naxi folk songs, translated and annotated). Kunming: YNRMCBS.

Hegel, Robert E. 1984. "Making the Past Serve the Present in Fiction and Drama: From the Yan'an Forum to the Cultural Revolution." In *Popular Chinese Literature and Performing Arts in the People's Republic of China, 1949–1979*, edited by Bonnie S. McDougall, 197–223. Berkeley: University of California Press.

Hessler, Pete. 1997. "Into the Past at China's Edge." *New York Times*, Travel Section, 11 May: 8–9, 32.

Hobsbawm, Eric, and Terence Ranger, eds. 1983. *The Invention of Tradition*. Cambridge: Cambridge University Press.

Hoh Chih-Hsiang, tr. 1946. *The Constitution of the Republic of China*, bilingual Chinese-English edition. Shanghai: Shangwu Yinshuguan.

Holm, David. 1991. *Art and Ideology in Revolutionary China*. Oxford: Clarendon Press.

Honig, Emily. 1992. *Creating Chinese Ethnicity: Subei People in Shanghai, 1850–1980*. New Haven, CT: Yale University Press.

Hooper, Beverley. 1985. *Youth in China*. Ringwood, Victoria: Penguin Books Australia.

Hornbostel, Erich M. von, and Curt Sachs. 1961. "Classification of Musical Instruments." Translated by Anthony Baines and Klaus P. Wachsmann. *Galpin Society Journal* 14: 3–29. First published as "Systematik der Musikinstrumente: Ein Versuch" in *Zeitschrift für Ethnologie* 46.4–5 (1914): 553–590.

Hostetler, Laura. 1995. "Chinese Ethnography in the Eighteenth Century: Miao Albums of Guizhou Province." Ph.D. dissertation, University of Pennsylvania.

Hsieh, Jiann. 1986. "China's Nationalities Policy: Its Development and Problems." *Anthropos* 81: 1–20.

Hsu, Francis L. K. 1943. *Magic and Science in Western Yunnan: The Problem of Introducing Scientific Medicine in a Rustic Community*. New York: International Secretariat, Institute of Pacific Relations.

———. 1952. *Religion, Science and Human Crises: A Study of China in Transition and Its Implications for the West*. London: Routledge & Kegan Paul.

Hu Jiaqiang 胡家強, comp. 1991. "Lufeng Xian Heijing Dongjing Yinyue" 祿豐縣黑井洞經音樂 (Dongjing music of Heijing, Lufeng County). Mimeographed score.

Huang Fu 黃富. 1990. "Xinping daojiao yinyue, fojiao yinyue ji qi yitong" 新平道教音樂、佛教音樂及其異同 (Taoist and Buddhist music of Xinping and their differences and similarities). *MZYSYJ* 18: 31–37.

Huang Lin 黃林. 1990. "Yunnan dongjing yinyue de shisuxing he suiyixing ji qi fazhan quxiang chutan" 雲南洞經音樂的世俗性和隨意性及其發展趨向初探 (Preliminary investigation of the secularization and development of Dongjing music in Yunnan). Mimeograph.

Huang Shuping 黃淑娉. 1989. "Minzu shibie ji qi lilun yiyi" 民族識別及其理論意義 (Ethnic identification and its theoretical significance). *Zhongguo Shehui Kexue* 中國社會科學 (China social science) 1989.1: 107–116.

Huang Zhen 黃鎮. 1982. "Fanrong shaoshu minzu wenyi chuangzuo, tigao ge minzu renmin wenhua shuiping" 繁榮少數民族文藝創作，提高各民族人民文化水平 (Promote cultural creativity among the national minorities, raise the cultural level of each nationality). In *Zhongguo Wenyi Nianjian 1981* 中國文藝年鑑 1981 (China literature and art yearbook 1981), edited by Su Yiping 蘇一平 and Bai Ying 白鷹, 708–709. Beijing: Wenyi Yishu Chubanshe.

Hung, Chang-tai. 1993. "Reeducating a Blind Storyteller: Han Qixiang and the Chinese Communist Storytelling Campaign." *Modern China* 19.4: 395–426.

Jack, Andrew. 1996. "Dr. Ho's Magic Formula Eases the Pain." *Financial Times* (London), 23/24 March: 13.

Jackson, Anthony. 1979. *Na-khi Religion*. The Hague: Mouton.

———. 1989. "Naxi Studies: Past, Present and Future." In *Ethnicity and Ethnic Groups in China*, edited by Chien Chao and Nicholas Tapp, 133–147. New Asia Academic Bulletin No. 8. Hong Kong: New Asia College, Chinese University of Hong Kong.

Jenks, Robert D. 1994. *Insurgency and Social Disorder in Guizhou: The "Miao" Rebellion, 1854–1873*. Honolulu: University of Hawaii Press.

Jin Anjiang 金安江 and Luo Shidan 羅世丹. 1991. *Shaoshu Minzu Diqu Xingzheng Guanli* 少數民族地區行政管理 (The administration of national minority areas). Guiyang: Guizhou Minzu Chubanshe.

Jing Dexin 荊德新, ed. 1986. *Yunnan Huimin Qiyi Shiliao* 雲南回民起義史料 (Historical materials on the Moslem uprising in Yunnan). Kunming: YNMZCBS.

Johnston, R. F. 1908. *From Peking to Mandalay*. London: John Murray.

Jones, Stephen. 1995. *Folk Music of China: Living Instrumental Traditions*. Oxford: Clarendon Press.

Jones, Stephen, Chen Kexiu, Jing Weigang, and Liu Shi. 1992. "Funeral Music in Shanxi." *Chime* 5: 4–29.

Jordan, David K., and Daniel Overmyer. 1986. *The Flying Phoenix: Aspects of Chinese Sectarianism in Taiwan*. Princeton, NJ: Princeton University Press.

Kings, Michael. 1991. "The Last Naxi Musicians?" Unpublished manuscript.

Kleeman, Terry Frederick. 1988. "Wenchang and the Viper: The Creation of a Chinese National God." Ph.D. dissertation, University of California, Berkeley.

Knowles, Christopher. 1995. *Fodor's Exploring China*. New York: Fodor's Travel Publications.

Kou Bangping 寇邦平. 1984. "Naxizu yinyue gaishu" 納西族音樂概述 (Overview of Naxi music). *MZYY* 4: 16–28.

———. 1986. "Naxizu de minjian yinyue" 納西族的民間音樂 (Folk music of the Naxi). *Zhongguo Yinyue* 中國音樂 (Chinese music) 22: 71–73, 18.

———, Wang Qiongbi 王瓊璧, and He Minda 和民達, eds. 1995. *Naxizu Minjian Gequ Jicheng* 納西族民間歌曲集成 (Anthology of Naxi folk songs). Kunming: YNMZCBS.

Kou Zhengling. 1992. "Kunming Builds Ethnic Culture Tourist Zone." *Beijing Review* 35.14: 36.

———. 1996. "Lijiang: An Ancient City Embraces the Modern World." *Beijing Review* 39.52: 17–21.

Kraus, Richard Curt. 1989. *Pianos and Politics in China: Middle Class Ambitions and the Struggle over Western Music*. New York: Oxford University Press.

"Kunming Dongjing Yinyue" 昆明洞經音樂 (Dongjing music of Kunming). 1983. 2 vols. Mimeographed score.

Lam, Joseph S. C. 1995. "The Yin and Yang of Chinese Music Historiography: The Case of Confucian Ceremonial Music." *Yearbook for Traditional Music* 27: 34–51.

Lamley, Harry J. 1981. "Subethnic Rivalry in the Ch'ing Period." In *The Anthropology of Taiwanese Society*, edited by Emily Martin Ahern and Hill Gates, 282–318. Stanford: Stanford University Press.

Lau, Frederick. 1996a. "Forever Red: The Invention of Solo *Dizi* Music in Post-1949 China." *British Journal of Ethnomusicology* 5: 113–131.

———. 1996b. "Individuality and Political Discourse in Solo *Dizi* Compositions." *Asian Music* 27.2: 133–152.

———. 1998. "'Packaging Identity through Sound': Tourist Performances in Contemporary China." *Journal of Musicological Research* 17.2: 113–134.

Lee, James. 1982. "The Legacy of Immigration in Southwest China, 1250–1850." *Annales de démographie historique* 1982: 279–304.

Lei Hong'an 雷宏安. 1987. "Yunnan dongjinghui chutan" 雲南洞經會初探 (Preliminary investigation into the Dongjing associations of Yunnan). *ZJXYJ* 11: 85–91.

———. 1989–1990. "Lijiang dongjinghui diaocha" 麗江洞經會調查 (Investigation into the Dongjing associations of Lijiang). *ZJXYJ* 15: 47–54; 16: 28–34.

———. 1990. "Qujing diqu dongjinghui kaocha" 曲靖地區洞經會考察 (Investigation of the Dongjing associations of Qujing Prefecture). *Qujing Shizhi Tongxun* 曲靖史志通訊 (Qujing history newsletter) 15: 14–21.

———. n.d. "Dongjinghui" 洞經會 (Dongjing associations). In "Qujing Diqu Minzu Zhi" 曲靖地區民族志 (Ethnic record of Qujing Prefecture), vol. 2, 270–287. Mimeograph.

Lei Hong'an and Peng Youshan 彭幼山. 1986. "Yunnan dongjing yinyue chutan" 雲南洞經音樂初探 (Preliminary investigation into Dongjing music of Yunnan). *ZJXYJ* 8: 43–50.

Leong, Weng Kam. 1996. "20-Year Struggle to Restore the Sounds of Naxi Tribesmen." *Straits Times* (Singapore), 22 May (photocopy).

Levin, Theodore C. 1979. "Music in Modern Uzbekistan: The Convergence of Marxist Aesthetics and Central Asian Tradition." *Asian Music* 12.1: 149–158.

———. 1996. *The Hundred Thousand Fools of God: Musical Travels in Central Asia (and Queens, New York)*. Bloomington: Indiana University Press.

Lew, Alan A., and Lawrence Yu, eds. 1995. *Tourism in China: Geographical, Political and Economic Perspectives*. Boulder, CO: Westview Press.

Li Fugen. 1995. "A Living Encyclopedia of Chinese Ethnic Groups." *China Today*, North American Edition 44.1: 10–12.

Li Jinchun 李近春. 1986. "Lijiang Naxizu de wenhua xisu he zongjiao xinyang" 麗江納西族的文化習俗和宗教信仰 (The cultural customs and religious beliefs of the Naxi of Lijiang). In *Naxizu Shehui Lishi Diaocha* 納西族社會歷史調查 (Investigation of Naxi social history), vol. 2, 28–66. Kunming: YNMZCBS.

Li Jinchun and Wang Chengquan 王承權. 1984. *Naxizu* 納西族 (The Naxi). Beijing: Minzu Chubanshe.

Li Jiuling 李久玲, ed. 1994. *Zhongguo Yishu Yanjiuyuan Yinyue Yanjiusuo Suo Zang*

Zhongguo Yinyue Yinxiang Mulu 中國藝術研究院音樂研究所所藏中國音樂音響目錄 (Catalogue of sound recordings of Chinese music preserved in the Music Research Institute of the Chinese Academy of Arts). Ji'nan: Shandong Youyi Chubanshe.

Li Li 李理, and Yin Haitao 殷海濤. 1993. *Lijiang Daoyou* 麗江導游 (Guide to Lijiang). Dehong: Dehong Minzu Chubanshe.

Li Lin-ts'an 李霖燦. 1953. *Moxie Xiangxing Wenzi Zidian* 麼些象形文字字典 (A Dictionary of Mo-so Hieroglyphics). N.p.: Shuowenshe.

Li Xiaoyuan 李小緣, ed. 1988. *Yunnan Shumu* 雲南書目 (Yunnan bibliography). Kunming: YNRMCBS.

Liang Yu 梁宇. 1986. "Yunnan minzu zaju diqu de yinyue gongrong" 雲南民族雜居地區的音樂共融 (Musical blending in multiethnic areas of Yunnan). *MZYY* 13: 21–29.

Lijiang Dayan Naxi Guyuehui 麗江大研納西古樂會. 1993. "Guanyu 'Yayue huan jing' huodong de anpai yijian" 關於 '雅樂還京' 活動的安排意見 (Opinions on the arrangements for the trip "Refined music returns to the capital"). Mimeograph.

Lijiang Fu Zhi 麗江府志 (Lijiang gazetteer). 1895. 8 volumes.

Lijiang Fu Zhilüe 麗江府志略 (Lijiang gazetteer). 1991. Reprinted by Lijiang Xian Xianzhi Weihui Ban'gongshi from 1743 original.

Lijiang Naxizu Zizhixian Gaikuang Bianxiezu 麗江納西族自治縣概況編寫組, ed. 1986. *Lijiang Naxizu Zizhixian Gaikuang* 麗江納西族自治縣概況 (Overview of Lijiang Naxi Autonomous County). Kunming: YNMZCBS.

Lijiang Xian Wenhuaguan 麗江縣文化館. 1986. "Lijiang bihua jianjie" 麗江壁畫簡介 (Introduction to Lijiang's murals). In *Naxizu Shehui Lishi Diaocha* 納西族社會歷史調查 (Investigation of Naxi social history) vol. 2, 67. Kunming: YNMZCBS. (First compiled in 1961.)

Link, Perry. 1984. "The Genie and the Lamp: Revolutionary Xiangsheng." In *Popular Chinese Literature and Performing Arts in the People's Republic of China, 1949–1979*, edited by Bonnie S. McDougall, 83–111. Berkeley: University of California Press.

Liu Can 劉燦. 1998. "Naxi Guyue jianjie" 納西古樂簡介 (Brief introduction to Naxi Ancient Music). *Yinyue Shenghuo Bao* 音樂生活報 (Musical life), 5 February: A2.

Liu Chao 劉超. 1959. *Naxizu de Ge* 納西族的歌 (Songs of the Naxi). Beijing: Renmin Wenxue Chubanshe.

Liu Chi Ping, Yip Chuen Leung, Tang Jun, Cheung Yuet Sim, Yiu Lai, and Wong Mei. N.d. *Shenzhen "Splendid China" Miniature Scenic Spot*. Translated by Au Lai Wa and Ko Yik Hing. Hong Kong: China Travel Advertising Hong Kong Limited.

Liu Jiesheng 劉杰生. 1991. "Shiping de dongjinghui" 石屏的洞經會 (Shiping's Dongjing associations). *Shiping Xian Wenshi Ziliao* 石屏縣文史資料 (Shiping County cultural and historical records) 4: 170–172.

Liu Shao-Chi (Liu Shaoqi). 1954. *Report on the Draft Constitution of the People's Republic of China*. Peking: Foreign Languages Press.

Liu Tieshan 劉鐵山. 1953. Letter to the editor under the heading "Shaoshu minzu gequ chuangzuo de fengge wenti he yuyan wenti" 少數民族歌曲創作的風格問題和語言問題 (The problems of style and language in composition of national minority songs). *RMYY* 16: 63.

Liu Wenzhi 劉文治. 1993. "Nanjian Dongjing yinyue" 南澗洞經音樂 (Dongjing music of Nanjian). *Nanjian Wenshi Ziliao* 南澗文史資料 (Nanjian cultural and historical records) 1: 136–138.

Liu Yue 劉悦. 1991. Preface to "Lufeng Xian Heijing Dongjing Yinyue" 祿豐縣黑井洞經音樂 (Dongjing music of Heijing, Lufeng County), compiled by Hu Jiaqiang 胡家强. Mimeograph.

Loon, Piet van der. 1962. Summary of Sakai Tadao 酒井忠夫, "Inshitsubun no seiritsu ni tsuite" 陰騭文の成立について (The history of the *Yinzhi Wen*) (*Toyo Shukyo* 東方宗教 [Eastern religions] 12: 1–13). In *Revue bibliographique de sinologie* 3 (1957): 343. Paris: Mouton.

Loza, Steven. 2000. "The African Role in Latin American *Mestizaje*." Paper presented at the Department of Ethnomusicology, University of California, Los Angeles, 3 March.

Lu Dingyi 陸定一. 1964. "Hui laodong you hui congshi wenyi huodong de ren shi zui hao de wenyi gongzuozhe" 會勞動又會從事文藝活動的人是最好的文藝工作者 (The best cultural workers are those who can undertake labor as well as cultural activities). *RMYY* 140: 2–5.

Lü Dou 綠豆. 1958. "Naxizu de 'qilao gehui'" 納西族的'耆老歌會' ("Old people's song groups" of the Naxi). *RMYY* 69: 30.

Lü Zhandian 呂占典. 1993. "Huiyi Naxi Jutuan" 回憶納西劇團 (Remembering the Naxi Theater Troupe). *LJWSZL* 12: 95–98.

Luo Zhufeng, ed. 1991. *Religion under Socialism in China*. Translated by Donald E. MacInnes and Zheng Xi'an. Armonk, NY: M. E. Sharpe.

Ma Yao 馬曜, ed. 1991. *Yunnan Jianshi* 雲南簡史 (Brief history of Yunnan). 2nd ed. Kunming: YNRMCBS. 1st edition published 1983.

MacInnes, Donald E. 1972. *Religious Policy and Practice in Communist China*. New York: Macmillan.

Mackerras, Colin. 1984. "Folksongs and Dances of China's Minority Nationalities: Policy, Tradition, and Professionalization." *Modern China* 10.2: 187–226.

———. 1996. *China's Minority Cultures: Identities and Integration since 1912*. New York: St. Martin's Press.

McDougall, Bonnie S. 1980. *Mao Zedong's "Talks at the Yan'an Conference on Literature and Art": A Translation of the 1943 Text with Commentary*. Michigan Monographs in Chinese Studies No. 39. Ann Arbor: Center for Chinese Studies, University of Michigan.

———. 1984. "Writers and Performers, Their Works, and Their Audiences in the First Three Decades." In *Popular Chinese Literature and Performing Arts in the People's Republic of China, 1949–1979*, edited by Bonnie S. McDougall, 269–304. Berkeley: University of California Press.

McKhann, Charles Fremont. 1992. "Fleshing out the Bones: Kinship and Cosmology in Naqxi Religion." Ph.D. dissertation, University of Chicago.

———. 1995. "The Naxi and the Nationalities Question." In *Cultural Encounters on China's Ethnic Frontiers*, edited by Stevan Harrell, 39–62. Seattle: University of Washington Press.

———. 1997. "The Left-Handed Kowtow: Naxi Mythic Versions of Naxi-Han-Tibetan-Mongol Relations." Paper presented at the Association for Asian Studies annual meeting, Chicago.

———. 1999. "Tears of Chairman Mao: Some Preliminary Observations on Tourism Development in Lijiang." Paper presented at the International Conference on Anthropology, Chinese Society and Tourism, held in Kunming, Yunnan, 18 September–3 October, and revised for the Lijiang International Dongba Culture and Arts Festival, held in Lijiang, Yunnan, 15–20 October.

Madsen, Richard. 1989. "The Catholic Church in China: Cultural Contradictions, Institutional Survival, and Religious Renewal." In *Unofficial China: Popular Culture and Thought in the People's Republic*, edited by Perry Link, Richard Madsen, and Paul Pickowicz, 103–120. Boulder, CO: Westview Press.

Manuel, Peter. 1993. *Cassette Culture: Popular Music and Technology in North India*. Chicago: University of Chicago Press.

Mao Jingbo. 1998. "Naxi Elders Preserve Their Music Traditions." *China Daily*, 27 January (photocopy).

Mao Jizeng 毛繼增. 1964. "Baisha Xiyue" 白沙細樂 (Baisha Xiyue). Mimeograph, Zhongguo Yinyue Yanjiusuo.

———. 1986. "Guanyu 'Beishi Xili' de diaocha baogao" 關於'北石細哩'的調查報告 (Report on an investigation into Baisha Xiyue). In *Naxizu Shehui Lishi Diaocha* 納西族社會歷史調查 (Investigation of Naxi social history), vol. 2, 109–150. Kunming: YNMZCBS.

Mao Zedong. 1979. "A Talk to Music Workers (August 24, 1956)." *Beijing Review* 22.37: 9–15.

Mayers, Wm. Frederick. 1869–1870. "On Wen-Ch'ang, the God of Literature, His History and Worship." *Journal of the North-China Branch of the Royal Asiatic Society* (New Series), 6: 31–44.

Mayhew, Bradley, and Thomas Huhti. 1998. *Southwest China*. Hawthorn, Victoria, Australia: Lonely Planet Publications.

Miao Tianrui 繆天瑞, Ji Liankang 吉聯抗, and Guo Naian 郭乃安, eds. 1985. *Zhongguo Yinyue Cidian* 中國音樂辭典 (Dictionary of Chinese music). Beijing: Renmin Yinyue Chubanshe.

Mo'er Jihu 莫爾吉胡. 1991. "Bieshi Xili kaozheng" 別時細哩考證 (Research on Baisha Xiyue). *Yinyue Yishu* 音樂藝術 (Musical art) 47: 1–5.

Moseley, George, translator and commentator. 1966. *The Party and the National Question in China*, by Zhang Zhiyi. Cambridge: M.I.T. Press.

Mu Yaojun 木耀鈞. 1990. "He Xidian shilüe" 和錫典事略 (A brief biography of He Xidian). *LJWSZL* 9: 164–165.

Mueggler, Erik. 1991. "Money, the Mountain, and State Power in a Naxi Village." *Modern China* 17.2: 188–226.

Muhambetova, Asiya Ibadullaevna. 1995. "The Traditional Musical Culture of Kazakhs in the Social Context of the 20th Century." *World of Music* 37.3: 66–83.

Munro, Robin, editor and translator. 1989. "Syncretic Sects and Secret Societies: Revival in the 1980s." Special issue of *Chinese Sociology and Anthropology* 21.4.

Naxizu Jianshi Bianxiezu 納西族簡史編寫組. 1984. *Naxizu Jianshi* 納西族簡史 (A brief history of the Naxi). Kunming: YNRMCBS.

Neuman, Daniel M. 1991. "Epilogue: Paradigms and Stories." In *Ethnomusicology and Modern Music History*, edited by Stephen Blum, Philip V. Bohlman, and Daniel M. Neuman, 268–277. Urbana: University of Illinois Press.

Ninglang Yizu Zizhixian Naxizu Shehui ji Jiating Xingtai Diaocha 寧蒗彝族自治縣納

西族社會及家庭形態調查 (Investigation into the society and household organization of the Naxi of Ninglang Yi Autonomous County). 1987. Kunming: YNRMCBS.

Ninglang Yizu Zizhixian Yongning Naxizu Shehui ji qi Muxizhi Diaocha 寧蒗彝族自治縣永寧納西族社會及其母系制調查 (Investigation of the society and matriarchal system of the Yongning Naxi of Ninglang Yi Autonomous County). 1988. Kunming: YNRMCBS.

Nketia, J. H. Kwabena. 1963. *Drumming in Akan Communities of Ghana*. Edinburgh: Thomas Nelson and Sons.

———. 1964. "Historical Evidence in Ga Religious Music." In *The Historian in Tropical Africa*, edited by J. Vansina, R. Mauny, and L. V. Thomas, 265–283. London: Oxford University Press.

———. 1970. "African Gods and Music." Typescript.

———. 1986a. "African Music and Western Praxis: A Review of Western Perspectives on African Musicology." *Canadian Journal of African Studies* 20.1: 36–56.

———. 1986b. "Perspectives on African Musicology." In *Africa and the West: The Legacies of Empire*, edited by Isaac James Mowoe and Richard Bjornson, 215–253. Contributions in Afro-American and African Studies No. 92. New York: Greenwood Press.

———. 1987. "Music and Religion in Sub-Saharan Africa." In *The Encyclopedia of Religion*, edited by Mircea Eliade, vol. 10, 172–176. London: Collier Macmillan.

———. 1988. "The Intensity Factor in African Music." *Journal of Folklore Research* 25.1–2: 53–86.

———. 1989. "Musical Interaction in Ritual Events." *Concilium—Revue internationale de théologie* 1989.2: 114–124.

———. 1990. "Contextual Strategies of Inquiry and Systematization." *Ethnomusicology* 34.1: 75–97.

Norman, Kirsty. 1997. "Echoes of a Living Tradition." *South China Morning Post*, 9 February: 4.

Oakes, Timothy S. 1995. "Tourism in Guizhou: The Legacy of Internal Colonialism." In *Tourism in China: Geographic, Political, and Economic Perspectives*, edited by Alan A. Lew and Lawrence Yu, 203–222. Boulder, CO: Westview Press.

Ouyang Zheng 歐陽正. 1991. "Simao dongjing yinyue jianshu" 思茅洞經音樂簡述 (A brief description of Dongjing music of Simao). In "Yunnan Sheng Shoujie Zongjiao Yinyue Xueshu Yantaohui Lunwen Huibian" 雲南省首屆宗教音樂學術研討會論文彙編 (Papers from the First Conference on Religious Music Research in Yunnan Province). Mimeograph.

Pan Wei-Tung. 1945. *The Chinese Constitution: A Study of Forty Years of Constitution-making in China*. Washington, D.C.: n.p.

Paulzen, Herbert. 1991. "De man die niet kan liegen" (The man who cannot lie). *Bres* 148: 38–48.

Pegg, Carole. 1995. "Ritual, Religion and Magic in West Mongolian (Oirad) Heroic Epic Performance." *British Journal of Ethnomusicology* 4: 77–99.

Pian, Rulan Chao. 1967. *Song Dynasty Musical Sources and Their Interpretation*. Cambridge: Harvard University Press.

Picard, François. 1991. *La musique chinoise*. Paris: Minerve.

Potter, Pamela. 1996. "Musicology under Hitler: New Sources in Context." *Journal of the American Musicological Society* 49.1: 70–113.

Pratt, K. L. 1976. "Music as a Factor in Sung-Koryo Diplomatic Relations." *T'oung Pao* 62.4–5: 199–218.

Provine, Robert C. 1981. "Reactions" [to "A Discussion on Chinese National Musical Traditions" by Fang Kun]. *Asian Music* 12.2: 11–14.

Qiubei Xianzhi 邱北縣志 (Gazetteer of Qiubei County [Yunnan Province]). 1921.

Qujing Xian Gudian Yinyue Yanjiuhui 曲靖縣古典音樂研究會. n.d. (before 1992). "Gudian Dongjing Qupu" 古典洞經曲譜 (Classical Dongjing music). Mimeographed score.

Racy, Ali Jihad. 1991. "Historical Worldviews of Early Ethnomusicologists: An East-West Encounter in Cairo, 1932." In *Ethnomusicology and Modern Music History*, edited by Stephen Blum, Philip V. Bohlman, and Daniel M. Neuman, 68–91. Urbana: University of Illinois Press.

Ramsey, S. Robert. 1987. *The Languages of China*. Princeton, NJ: Princeton University Press.

Rees, Helen. 1990. "Report on Fieldwork—Music in Northern Yunnan." *Chime* 1: 30–35.

———. 1994. "A Musical Chameleon: A Chinese Repertoire in Naxi Territory." Ph.D. dissertation, University of Pittsburgh.

———. 1995. "Domestic Orientalism: The 'Motif of the Music-making Minority'." Paper presented at the annual conference of the Society for Ethnomusicology, Los Angeles.

———. 1996. "Musical Assertion of Status among the Naxi of Lijiang County, Yunnan." In *Harmony and Counterpoint: Ritual Music in Chinese Context*, edited by Bell Yung, Evelyn S. Rawski, and Rubie S. Watson, 76–104. Stanford, CA: Stanford University Press.

———. 1998. "'Authenticity' and the Foreign Audience for Traditional Music in Southwest China." *Journal of Musicological Research* 17.2: 135–161.

———. n.d. "What Is the Point of the Score? Notation, Performance, and Transmission in a Chinese Music Ensemble." Unpublished manuscript.

Reitlinger, Gerald. 1939. *South of the Clouds: A Winter Ride through Yün-nan*. London: Faber and Faber.

Rice, Timothy. 1987. "Toward the Remodeling of Ethnomusicology." *Ethnomusicology* 31.3: 469–488.

———. 1994. *May It Fill Your Soul: Experiencing Bulgarian Music*. Chicago: University of Chicago Press.

Robinet, Isabelle. 1983. "Le Ta-tung chen-ching: Son authenticité et sa place dans les textes du Shang-ch'ing ching." *Mélanges chinois et buddhiques* 21: 394–433.

———. 1989. "Original Contributions of *Neidan* to Taoism and Chinese Thought." In *Taoist Meditation and Longevity Techniques*, edited by Livia Kohn, 297–330. Michigan Monographs in Chinese Studies No. 61. Ann Arbor: Center for Chinese Studies, University of Michigan.

———. 1993. *Taoist Meditation: The Mao-Shan Tradition of Great Purity*. Translated by Julian F. Pas and Norman J. Girardot. Albany: State University of New York Press. Originally published in French as *Méditation taoiste* (Paris: Dervy Livres, 1979).

Rock, Joseph F. 1925. "Land of the Yellow Lama: National Geographic Society Explorer

Visits the Strange Kingdom of Muli, beyond the Likiang Snow Range of Yunnan Province, China." *National Geographic Magazine* 47.4: 447–491.

———. 1939. "The Romance of ²K'a-²Mä-¹Gyu-³Mi-²Gkyi: A Na-khi Tribal Love Story Translated from Na-khi Pictographic Manuscripts." *Bulletin de l'École Française d'Extrême-Orient* 39.1: 1–155.

———. 1947. *The Ancient Na-khi Kingdom of Southwest China.* 2 vols. Harvard-Yenching Institute Monograph Series Nos. 8 and 9. Cambridge: Harvard-Yenching Institute.

———. 1959. "Contributions to the Shamanism of the Tibetan-Chinese Borderland." *Anthropos* 54: 796–818.

———. 1963. *The Life and Culture of the Na-Khi Tribe of the China-Tibet Borderland.* Wiesbaden: Franz Steiner.

Rowe, William T. 1994. "Education and Empire in Southwest China: Ch'en Hung-mou in Yunnan, 1733–38." In *Education and Society in Late Imperial China, 1600–1900*, edited by Benjamin A. Elman and Alexander Woodside, 417–457. Berkeley: University of California Press.

Said, Edward. 1979. *Orientalism.* New York: Vintage Books.

Sakai Tadao 酒井忠夫. 1960. *Chugoku Zensho no Kenkyu* 中國善書の研究 (Research on Chinese morality tracts). Tokyo: Kobundo.

Samson, Valerie. 1991. "Music as Protest Strategy: The Example of Tiananmen Square, 1989." *Pacific Review of Ethnomusicology* 6: 35–64.

Sangde Nuowa 桑德諾瓦. 1993. "Naxizu dongba changqiang de xuanlü fengge ji fenlei" 納西族東巴唱腔的旋律風格及分類 (Melodic style and categories of Naxi Dongba chant melodies). *Zhongyang Yinyue Xueyuan Xuebao* 中央音樂學院學報 (Journal of the Central Conservatory of Music) 52: 70–74.

———. 1994. "Naxi wenhua zhong de gudai yinyue yicun" 納西文化中的古代音樂遺存 (The remains of ancient music in Naxi culture). *Yishu Xue* 藝術學 (Study of the arts) 11: 27–112.

———. 1995. "Dongba yishi yinyue de ruogan diaocha yu yanjiu" 東巴儀式音樂旳若干調查與研究 (Investigation and research into Dongba ceremonial music). *Zhongguo Yinyuexue* 中國音樂學 (Musicology in China) 41: 29–43.

Saso, Michael. 1990. *Blue Dragon White Tiger: Taoist Rites of Passage.* Washington, D.C.: Taoist Center.

Schein, Louisa. 1997. "Gender and Internal Orientalism in China." *Modern China* 23.1: 69–98.

Schimmelpenninck, Antoinet. 1997. *Chinese Folk Songs and Folk Singers: Shan'ge Traditions in Southern Jiangsu.* Leiden: Chime Foundation.

Schimmelpenninck, Antoinet, and Frank Kouwenhoven. 1993. "The Shanghai Conservatory of Music—History and Foreign Students' Experiences." *Chime* 6: 56–91.

Schoenhals, Michael, ed. 1992. *Doing Things with Words in Chinese Politics: Five Studies.* Berkeley: Institute of East Asian Studies, University of California.

Seeger, Anthony. 1991. "When Music Makes History." In *Ethnomusicology and Modern Music History*, edited by Stephen Blum, Philip V. Bohlman, and Daniel M. Neuman, 23–34. Urbana: University of Illinois Press.

Seeger, Charles. 1940. "Folk Music as a Source of Social History." In *The Cultural Approach to History*, edited by Carolyn F. Ware, 316–323. New York: Columbia University Press.

Shelemay, Kay Kaufman. 1980. "'Historical Ethnomusicology': Reconstructing Falasha Liturgical History." *Ethnomusicology* 24.2: 233–258.

———. 1982. "Zema: A Concept of Sacred Music in Ethiopia." *World of Music* 24.3: 52–67.

———. 1996. "The Ethnomusicologist and the Transmission of Tradition." *Journal of Musicology* 14.1: 35–51.

Shi Xiao 式嘯. 1985. "Pumizu minjian yinyue jianjie" 普米族民間音樂簡介 (Overview of Pumi folk music). *MZYY* 6: 48–53.

Shi Xinmin 史新民, ed. 1987. *Zhongguo Wudang Shan Daojiao Yinyue* 中國武當山道教音樂 (Taoist music of Wudang Mountain, China). Beijing: Zhongguo Wenlian Chuban Gongsi.

Shih, Chuan-kang. 1993. "The Moso: Sexual Union, Household Organization, Ethnicity and Gender in a Matrilineal Duolocal Society in Southwest China." Ph.D. dissertation, Stanford University.

Shih Hwa-Fu. 1959. "Old Bards Sing New Ballads." *China Reconstructs* 8.2: 14–16.

Shiloah, Amnon. 1991. "An Eighteenth-Century Critic of Taste and Good Taste." In *Ethnomusicology and Modern Music History*, edited by Stephen Blum, Philip V. Bohlman, and Daniel M. Neuman, 181–189. Urbana: University of Illinois Press.

Shiping Xian Dongjing Yinyue Xiehui 石屏縣洞經音樂協會. 1992. "Shiping Xian Dadong Xianjing Yinyue Qupai ji Jingwen Changqiang" 石屏縣大洞仙經音樂曲牌及經文唱腔 (Instrumental and vocal melodies of the Transcendent Scripture in Shiping County). Mimeographed score.

Siguret, J., trans. 1937. *Territoires et populations des confins du Yunnan*. Peiping: Editions Henri Vetch. Reprinted in 1971 by Ch'eng Wen Publishing, Taipei.

Silverman, Carol. 1983. "The Politics of Folklore in Bulgaria." *Anthropological Quarterly* 56.2: 55–61.

———. 1989. "Reconstructing Folklore: Media and Cultural Policy in Eastern Europe." *Communication* 11.2: 141–160.

Siu, Helen F. 1989. "Recycling Rituals: Politics and Popular Culture in Contemporary Rural China." In *Unofficial China: Popular Culture and Thought in the People's Republic*, edited by Perry Link, Richard Madsen and Paul Pickowicz, 121–137. Boulder, CO: Westview Press.

———. 1990. "Recycling Tradition: Culture, History, and Political Economy in the Chrysanthemum Festivals of South China." *Comparative Studies in Society and History* 32.4: 765–794.

Slobin, Mark. 1971. "Conversations in Tashkent." *Asian Music* 2.2: 7–13.

———. 1992. "Europe/Peasant Music—Cultures of Eastern Europe." In *Worlds of Music: An Introduction to the Music of the World's Peoples*, edited by Jeff Todd Titon, 167–208. 2nd ed. New York: Schirmer.

Smith, Kent Clarke. 1970. "Ch'ing Policy and the Development of Southwest China: Aspects of Ortai's Governor-Generalship, 1726–1731." Ph.D. dissertation, Yale University.

Stalin, Joseph. 1934. *Marxism and the National and Colonial Question*. Marxist Library No. 38. New York: International Publishers.

Stock, Jonathan. 1991. "A Phoenix Crying at Sunset—Origins and Social Context of the Erhu." *Chime* 3: 20–31.

———. 1996. *Musical Creativity in Twentieth-Century China: Abing, His Music, and Its Changing Meanings*. Rochester, NY: University of Rochester Press.

Stoller, Paul. 1989. *The Taste of Ethnographic Things: The Senses in Anthropology*. Philadelphia: University of Pennsylvania Press.

Sun Jiong 孫炯. 1996. "Lishi de huiyin" 歷史的回音 (Echoes of history). *YLS* 74: 98–99. First published in a publicity leaflet (Zhongguo Lijiang Dayan Naxi Guyuehui, n.d.).

Sun Shen 孫慎. 1964. "Huanhu quanguo shaoshu minzu qunzhong yeyu yishu guanmo yanchu de juda chengjiu!" 歡呼全國少數民族群眾業餘藝術觀摩演出的巨大成就! (Acclaim the splendid results of the national festival of minority nationality mass amateur arts performance!). *RMYY* 140: 6–8.

Sutton, S. B. 1974. *In China's Border Provinces: The Turbulent Career of Joseph Rock, Botanist-Explorer*. New York: Hastings House.

Suzuki, Teitaro, and Paul Carus, trans. 1906. *Yin Chih Wen: The Tract of the Quiet Way with Extracts from the Chinese Commentary*. Chicago: Open Court Publishing.

Swain, Margaret Byrne. 1995. "A Comparison of State and Private Artisan Production for Tourism in Yunnan." In *Tourism in China: Geographic, Political, and Economic Perspectives*, edited by Alan A. Lew and Lawrence Yu, 223–233. Boulder, CO: Westview Press.

Tambiah, Stanley. 1981. "A Performative Approach to Ritual." *Proceedings of the British Academy* 65: 113–169.

Tang Xin 唐鑫. 1988. "Yunnan Weishan Dongjing Guyue Quxuan" 雲南巍山洞經古樂曲選 (Anthology of Dongjing pieces from Weishan, Yunnan). Mimeograph.

Tang Zhilu and Jin Zhuotong. 1988. *Lijiang*. Beijing: New World Press.

"Third China Art Festival Opens." 1992. *Beijing Review* 35.9: 9.

Thrasher, Alan. 1981. "Reactions" [to "A Discussion on Chinese National Musical Traditions" by Fang Kun]. *Asian Music* 12.2: 14–16.

———. 1990. *La-Li-Luo Dance-Songs of the Chuxiong Yi, Yunnan Province, China*. Danbury, CT: World Music Press.

———. 1993. "Bianzou—Performance Variation Techniques in Jiangnan Sizhu." *Chime* 6: 4–21.

Tong Enzheng. 1989. "Morgan's Model and the Study of Ancient Chinese Society." *Social Sciences in China* 10.2: 182–205.

Toops, Stanley. 1993. "Xinjiang's Handicraft Industry." *Annals of Tourism Research* 20.1: 88–106.

———. 1995. "Tourism in Xinjiang: Practice and Place." In *Tourism in China: Geographic, Political, and Economic Perspectives*, edited by Alan A. Lew and Lawrence Yu, 179–202. Boulder, CO: Westview Press.

Track, Norman. 1996. *Song of a Water Dragon*. Jamaica Plain, MA: YMAA.

Treitler, Leo. 1991. "The Politics of Reception: Tailoring the Present as Fulfilment of a Desired Past." *Journal of the Royal Musical Association* 16.1: 280–298.

Tsao, Pen-yeh. 1989. *Taoist Ritual Music of the Yu-Lan Pen-Hui (Feeding the Hungry Ghost Festival) in a Hong Kong Taoist Temple*. Hong Kong: Hai Feng Publishing.

Tuohy, Sue. 1988. "Imagining the Chinese Tradition: The Case of Hua'er Songs, Festivals and Scholarship." Ph.D. dissertation, University of Indiana, Bloomington.

Vansina, Jan. 1985. *Oral Tradition as History*. Madison: University of Wisconsin Press.

Wachsmann, Klaus P., ed. 1971. *Essays on Music and History in Africa*. Evanston, IL: Northwestern University Press.

Wan Tung-Shu. 1963. "The Twelve Mukam of Sinkiang Saved and Revived." *China Reconstructs* 12.2: 38–41.

Wang Lianfang 王連芳. 1986. *Yunnan Minzu Wenti Lilun Yanjiu yu Shijian* 雲南民族問題理論研究與實踐 (Theoretical research and practice in the nationalities question of Yunnan). Kunming: YNMZCBS.

Wang Zhihong 王志泓. 1991. "Ming, Qing Naxizu shufa jianshi" 明清納西族書法簡史 (Naxi calligraphy during the Ming and Qing dynasties). *LJWSZL* 10: 48–54.

Wang Zhiqiang 王志強. 1989. "Lijiang xiju gaishu" 麗江戲劇概述 (Overview of theater in Lijiang). *LJWSZL* 7: 84–89.

"Washan" Bianjibu '佤山' 編輯部, ed. 1985. *Ximeng Wazu Min'ge* 西盟佤族民歌 (Folk songs of the Wa of Ximeng). Kunming: YNRMCBS.

White, Sydney Davant. 1993. "Medical Discourses, Naxi Identities, and the State: Transformations in Socialist China." Ph.D. dissertation, University of California, Berkeley.

Witzleben, J. Lawrence. 1987. "*Jiangnan Sizhu* Clubs in Shanghai: Context, Concept and Identity." *Ethnomusicology* 31.2: 240–260.

———. 1995. *"Silk and Bamboo" Music in Shanghai: The Jiangnan Sizhu Instrumental Ensemble Tradition*. Kent, OH: Kent State University Press.

Wong, Isabel. 1984. "Geming Gequ: Songs for the Education of the Masses." In *Popular Chinese Literature and Performing Arts in the People's Republic of China, 1949–1979*, edited by Bonnie S. McDougall, 112–143. Berkeley: University of California Press.

———. 1991. "From Reaction to Synthesis: Chinese Musicology in the Twentieth Century." In *Comparative Musicology and Anthropology of Music*, edited by Bruno Nettl and Philip Bohlman, 37–55. Chicago: University of Chicago Press.

Wu, Ben. 1988. "How Music Is Transmitted in a Typical Chinese Folk Group." *International Council for Traditional Music, UK Chapter Bulletin* 21: 5–12.

———. 1998. "Music Scholarship, West and East: Tibetan Music as a Case Study." *Asian Music* 29.2: 31–56.

Wu, David Y. H. 1990. "Chinese Minority Policy and the Meaning of Minority Culture: The Example of Bai in Yunnan, China." *Human Organization* 49.1: 1–13.

Wu Guodong 伍國棟. 1991. "Cong huangwu zou xiang fanmao: shaoshu minzu yinyue yanjiu sishi nian" 從荒蕪走向繁茂—少數民族音樂研究四十年 (From wasteland to florescence: forty years of research on minority nationality music). *Zhongguo Yinyuexue* 中國音樂學 (Musicology in China) 24: 4–12.

Wu Mingxian 吳明銑. 1981. "Dongjing yinyue qianyan" 洞經音樂前言 (Dongjing music: preface). Photocopy of manuscript.

Wu Xueyuan 吳學源. 1990. "Yunnan 'Dongjing' yinyue gaishuo" 雲南'洞經'音樂概說 (A survey of "Dongjing" music in Yunnan). In *Zhongguo Yinyue Guoji Yantaohui Lunwen Ji* 中國音樂國際研討會論文集 (Papers from the International Conference on Chinese Music [held in Hong Kong in 1988]), edited by Qiao Jianzhong 喬建中 and Cao Benye (Pen-yeh Tsao) 曹本冶, 205–230. Ji'nan: Shandong Jiaoyu Chubanshe.

"Xinping dongjing yinyue shiwen" 新平洞經音樂釋文 (Dongjing music of Xinping). 1988. In "Xinping Xian Minjian Qiyuequ Jicheng" 新平縣民間器樂曲集成 (Anthology of folk instrumental music in Xinping County), 1–17, 100–102. Mimeograph.

Xiong Xiyuan 熊錫元. 1986. "Dui Sidalin minzu dingyi de yidian kanfa" 對斯大林民族

定義的一點看法 (My understanding of Stalin's definition of Nation). *Minzu Yanjiu* 民族研究 (Ethnicity research) 42: 17–18.

Xuan Ke 宣科. 1980. Score of "Dao Chun Lai" 到春來 (Spring Has Come) with words by Zhou Lin 周霖. Mimeograph.

———. 1984a. "Baisha Xiyue xiaoyi" 白沙細樂小議 (My view on Baisha Xiyue). *MZYY* 4: 29.

———. 1984b. Transcription of *Remeicuo* 熱美蹉. Unpublished manuscript.

———. 1986a. "Baisha Xiyue tanyuan" 白沙細樂探源 (Investigation of the origins of Baisha Xiyue). *LJWSZL* 3: 65–74. A slightly revised version was published in *Minzu Yinyue Lunji* 民族音樂論集 (Papers on ethnic music), edited by Yang Fang 楊放, 269–279. Kunming: YNRMCBS, 1991.

———. 1986b. "Naxizu duosheng min'ge 'Remeicuo' de yuanshi zhuangtai" 納西族多聲民歌'熱美蹉'的原始狀態 (The original state of the polyphonic Naxi folk song Remeicuo). *LJWSZL* 3: 32–61.

———. 1990. "Remeicuo de laili" 熱美蹉的來歷 (Origin of Remeicuo). *Yizhou* 藝舟 (Ship of art) 3: 68–73.

———. 1991. "Dui *Remeicuo de laili jing* de taolun" 對《熱美蹉的來歷經》的討論 (A Study of the Dongba manuscript "The Origin of the Sseiq Mei Dance"). In *Dongba Wenhua Lun* 東巴文化論 (Research on Dongba culture), edited by Guo Dalie 郭大烈 and Yang Shiguang 楊世光, 593–599. Kunming: YNRMCBS.

———. n.d. "Lijiang Jidujiao Xiaoshi" 麗江基督教小史 (Brief history of Christianity in Lijiang). Unpublished manuscript.

Xuan Ke and Yang Zenglie 楊曾烈. 1997. Program notes for Hong Kong concerts of Dayan Naxi Ancient Music Association.

Xue Zongming 薛宗明. 1983. *Zhongguo Yinyueshi Yuepu Pian* 中國音樂史樂譜篇 (Chinese music history, notation volume). 2nd ed. Taipei: Taiwan Shangwu Yinshuguan.

Yang Dejun 楊德鋆. 1983. "Naxi gudai yinyue gaitan" 納西古代音樂概談 (Overview of Naxi ancient music). *MZYY* 1: 34–38.

———. 1985. "Dongba yinyue shulüe" 東巴音樂述略 (Overview of Dongba music). In *Dongba Wenhua Lunji* 東巴文化論集 (Collected essays on Dongba culture), edited by Guo Dalie 郭大烈 and Yang Shiguang 楊世光, 434–444. Kunming: YNRMCBS.

———, He Fayuan 和發源, and He Yuncai 和雲彩. 1990. *Naxizu Gudai Wudao he Wupu* 納西族古代舞蹈和舞譜 (Ancient Naxi dances and dance notation). Beijing: Wenhua Yishu Chubanshe.

Yang Fang 楊放. 1995. "Yunnan wushi nian minzu minjian yinyue gongzuo lüeying" 雲南五十年民族民間音樂工作掠影 (Glimpses at fifty-year work on folk and ethnic music in Yunnan) (first part). *Yunnan Yishu Xueyuan Xuebao* 雲南藝術學院學報 (Journal of Yunnan Art Institute) 10: 8–10.

Yang Guanghong 楊光宏, comp. n.d. (before 1992). "Mile Dongjing Yinyue" 彌勒洞經音樂 (Dongjing music of Mile). Mimeographed score.

Yang Ming 楊明 and Gu Feng 顧峰, eds. 1986. *Dianju Shi* 滇劇史 (History of Dianju). Beijing: Zhongguo Xiju Chubanshe.

Yang Minkang 楊民康. 1990. "Yunnan shaoshu minzu jidujiao yinyue wenhua chutan" 雲南少數民族基督教音樂文化初探 (Preliminary investigation of the Protestant musical culture among Yunnan's minority nationalities). *Zhongguo Yinyuexue* 中國音樂學 (Musicology in China) 21: 82–88.

Yang Mu. 1994. "Academic Ignorance or Political Taboo? Some Issues in China's Study of Its Folk Song Culture." *Ethnomusicology* 38.2: 303–320.

Yang Qichang 楊啟昌. 1991. "Lüetan Naxizu diqu de lamajiao" 略談納西族地區的喇嘛教 (Brief discussion of Lamaism in Naxi areas). *LJWSZL* 10: 6–27.

Yang Tongshan 楊通山, Meng Guangchao 蒙光朝, Guo Wei 過偉, and Zheng Guangsong 鄭光松, eds. 1980. *Dongzu Min'ge Xuan* 侗族民歌選 (Anthology of Dong folk songs). Shanghai: Shanghai Wenyi Chubanshe.

Yang Xinhong 楊新紅. 1995. "Hun zai qingyin liu yun jian" 魂在清音流韻間 (The spirit lies in the clear sounds and flowing melody). *Chuncheng Wanbao* 春城晚報 (Spring City evening news), 17 December: 8.

Yang Yinliu 楊蔭瀏. 1962. *Gongchepu Qianshuo* 工尺譜淺説 (Brief discussion of solfège). Beijing: Yinyue Chubanshe.

———. 1980. *Shifan Luogu* 十番鑼鼓 (Shifan luogu [music]). Beijing: Renmin Yinyue Chubanshe.

———. 1981. *Zhongguo Gudai Yinyue Shi Gao* 中國古代音樂史稿 (Outline history of ancient Chinese music). Beijing: Renmin Yinyue Chubanshe.

Yang Zenglie 楊曾烈. 1983. "Naxizu minjian yueqi 'bobo' ji qi gaige" 納西族民間樂器'波撥'及其改革 (The Naxi folk instrument "bobo" and its reform). *Yueqi* 樂器 (Musical instruments) 51: 20–21.

———. 1990–1991. "Lijiang dongjing yinyue diaocha" 麗江洞經音樂調查 (Investigation of the Dongjing music of Lijiang). *LJWSZL* 9: 114–138; 10: 30–47.

———. 1993. "Dongba yinyue" 東巴音樂 (Dongba music). *LJWSZL* 12: 104–118.

———. 1995. "'A Barley Pipe Becomes a Jasper Flute': The Naxi Folk Instrument Wowo." Translated by Helen Rees. *Chime* 8: 67–75. An expanded version of "Naxizu yiguan duohuang yueqi 'wowo' qianshi" 納西族一管多簧樂器'窩破'淺識 (The "wowo": a Naxi instrument with one pipe and multiple reeds). In *Minzu Yinyue Lunji* 民族音樂論集 (Collected papers on ethnic music), edited by Yang Fang 楊放 and Wu Xueyuan 吳學源, 256–264. Kunming: YNMZCBS, 1991.

Yao'an Xianzhi 姚安縣志 (Gazetteer of Yao'an County [Yunnan Province]). 1949. Reprinted by YNRMCBS, Kunming, 1988.

Yi Gong 一弓. 1993. "Gulao yinyue de huisheng" 古老音樂的回聲 (Echoes of ancient music). *Lijiang Bao* (Lijiang news), 30 November: 3.

Yiliang Xianzhi 宜良縣志 (Gazetteer of Yiliang County [Yunnan Province]). 1921.

Yin Mingguang 尹明光. 1991. "Qiubei 'dongjing yinyue' chutan" 邱北'洞經音樂'初探 (Preliminary investigation of "Dongjing music" in Qiubei). In "Yunnan Sheng Shouji Zongjiao Yinyue Xueshu Yantaohui Lunwen Huibian" 雲南省首屆宗教音樂學術研討會論文彙編 (Papers from the First Conference on Religious Music Research in Yunnan Province). Mimeograph.

Ying Youqin 應有勤 and Sun Keren 孫克仁. 1988. "Kouxian de zonghe kaocha" 口弦的綜合考察 (Comprehensive investigation into the Jew's harp). *Zhongguo Yinyuexue* 中國音樂學 (Musicology in China) 11: 77–89.

Yinyue Chubanshe Bianjibu 音樂出版社編輯部, ed. 1965. *Quanguo Shaoshu Minzu Yeyu Yishu Guanmo Yanchu Gequxuan* 全國少數民族群眾業餘藝術觀摩演出歌曲選

(Anthology of songs from the national festival of minority nationality mass amateur arts performance). Beijing: Yinyue Chubanshe.

Yongning Naxizu Shehui ji Muxizhi Diaocha 永寧納西族社會及母系制調查 (Investigation of the society and matriarchal system of the Yongning Naxi). 1986. Kunming: YNRMCBS.

Yuan Bingchang 袁炳昌, He Changlin 何昌林, Qin Pengzhang 秦鵬章, Zhao Feng 趙渢, Tian Liantao 田聯滔, Shen Qia 沈洽, Xue Liang 薛良, Xiu Hailin 修海林, and Feng Guangyu 馮光鈺. 1993. Speeches given at the Central Conservatory of Music conference in conjunction with the concert tour to Beijing and Tianjin by the Dayan Ancient Music Association. Texts given in *Lijiang Bao* 麗江報 (Lijiang news), 30 November: 2–3.

Yuan Bingchang 袁炳昌 and Mao Jizeng 毛繼增, eds. 1986. *Zhongguo Shaoshu Minzu Yueqi Zhi* 中國少數民族樂器志 (Musical instruments of the ethnic minorities of China). Beijing: Xin Shijie Chubanshe.

Yuan Yuancong 袁遠琮. 1993. "Huaping dongjing yinyue shiqing lüeshu" 華坪洞經音樂史情略述 (Outline of the history of Dongjing music in Huaping). *Huaping Xian Wenshi Ziliao* 華坪縣文史資料 (Huaping County cultural and historical records) 2: 95–105.

Yung, Bell. 1984. "Model Opera as Model: From Shajiabang to Sagabong." In *Popular Chinese Literature and Performing Arts in the People's Republic of China, 1949–1979*, edited by Bonnie S. McDougall, 144–164. Berkeley: University of California Press.

———. 1989a. *Cantonese Opera: Performance as Creative Process*. Cambridge: Cambridge University Press.

———. 1989b. "La musique du guqin: du cabinet du lettré à la scène de concert." *Cahiers de musiques traditionelles* 2: 51–62.

Yunnan Cidian 雲南辭典 (Yunnan dictionary). 1993. Kunming: YNRMCBS.

Yunnan Nianjian 雲南年鑑 (Yunnan yearbook). 1997. Kunming: Yunnan Nianjian Zazhishe.

Yunnan Sheng Cehuiju 雲南省測繪局. 1980. *Lijiang Naxizu Zizhixian* 麗江納西族自治縣 (Lijiang Naxi Autonomous County). Yunnan Sheng Dituji 雲南省地圖集 (Yunnan Province maps).

Yunnan Sheng Chuxiong Xianzhi 雲南省楚雄縣志 (Gazetteer of Chuxiong County, Yunnan Province). 1910. Reprinted by Chengwen Chubanshe, Taipei, 1967.

Yunnan Sheng Jingdong Xianzhi Gao 雲南省景東縣志稿 (Draft gazetteer of Jingdong County, Yunnan Province). 1923. Reprinted by Chengwen Chubanshe, Taipei, n.d.

Yunnan Sheng Luquan Xianzhi 雲南省祿勸縣志 (Gazetteer of Luquan County, Yunnan Province). 1925. Reprinted by Chengwen Chubanshe, Taipei, n.d.

Yunnan Sheng Renmin Zhengfu Waishi Ban'gongshi 雲南省人民政府外事辦公室 (The Foreign Affairs Office of Yunnan Provincial People's Government), ed. n.d. (1992 or before). *Yunnan Minzu Caifeng Ji* 雲南民族采風集 / *Highlights of Minority Nationalities in Yunnan*. Bilingual pictorial. Kunming: Yunnan Sheng Renmin Zhengfu Waishi Ban'gongshi.

Yunnan Sheng Zhaotong Xianzhi Gao 雲南省昭通縣志稿 (Draft gazetteer of Zhaotong County, Yunnan Province). 1936. Reprinted by Chengwen Chubanshe, Taipei, 1967.

Yunnan Sheng Zhennan Zhou Zhilüe 雲南省鎮南州志略 (Gazetteer of Zhennan Prefecture, Yunnan Province). 1892. Reprinted by Chengwen Chubanshe, Taipei, n.d.

Zemtsovsky, Izaly, and Alma Kunanbaeva. 1997. "Communism and Folklore." In *Folklore and Traditional Music in the Former Soviet Union and Eastern Europe*, edited by James Porter, 3–23. Los Angeles: Department of Ethnomusicology, UCLA.

Zha, Jianying. 1995. *China Pop: How Soap Operas, Tabloids, and Bestsellers Are Transforming a Culture*. New York: New Press.

Zhal Xiweiq (Zhang Xingwen 張興文), Hoq Miqdaf (He Minda 和民達), and Hoq Yuaiqqil (He Yuanqing 和元慶), eds. 1987. *Naqxi Miqgo Xuai* (*Naxi Min'ge Xuan* 納西民歌選) (Anthology of Naxi folk songs). Kunming: YNMZCBS.

Zhang, Guangrui. "China's Tourist Development Since 1978: Policies, Experiences, and Lessons Learned." In *Tourism in China: Geographic, Political, and Economic Perspectives*, edited by Alan A. Lew and Lawrence Yu, 3–18. Boulder, CO: Westview Press.

Zhang Jiaxun 張家訓. 1987. "'Tonghai dongjing' jianshu" '通海洞經' 簡述 (Brief description of "Tonghai dongjing"). *Tonghai Wenshi Ziliao* 通海文史資料 (Tonghai cultural and historical records) 1: 124–134.

Zhang Xingrong 張興榮, ed. 1990. *Yunnan Minzu Qiyue Huicui* 雲南民族器樂薈萃 (Cream of Yunnan national instrumental music). Kunming: YNRMCBS.

———. 1998. *Yunnan Dongjing Wenhua—Ru Dao Shi Sanjiao de Fuhexing Wenhua* 雲南洞經文化—儒道釋三教的複合性文化 (Dongjing culture in Yunnan—a cultural crossroads of Confucianism, Taoism, and Buddhism). Kunming: Yunnan Jiaoyu Chubanshe.

Zhang Yunqing 張雲卿. 1983. "Naxizu wenyi diaocha" 納西族文藝調查 (Investigation of Naxi literature and art). In *Naxizu Shehui Lishi Diaocha* 納西族社會歷史調查 (Investigation of Naxi social history), 33–55. Kunming: YNMZCBS.

Zhao Jingxiu 趙淨修. 1995. "Lijiang dongjing yinyue de chengchuan ren" 麗江洞經音樂的承傳人 (The tradition bearers of Lijiang's Dongjing music). *LJWSZL* 13: 34–37.

Zhao Jishun 趙紀舜. 1951. "Lijiang Naxizu de min'ge" 麗江拿西族的民歌 (Folk songs of the Lijiang Naxi). *RMYY* 3.3: 31–32.

Zhao Kuanren 趙寬仁. 1989. "Naxizu de 'sugudu' yu Mengguzu de 'huobusi'" 納西族的 '蘇古杜' 與蒙古族的 '火不思' (The Naxi "sugudu" and the Mongol "huobusi"). In *Yunnan Minzu Yinyue Lunji* 雲南民族音樂論集 (Essays on ethnic music of Yunnan), edited by Yunnan Sheng Minzu Yishu Yanjiusuo 雲南省民族藝術研究所, 127–128. Kunming: YNRMCBS.

Zhao Yintang 趙銀棠. 1984. *Yulong Jiuhua Xinbian* 玉龍舊話新編 (New version of the Old Tales of Yulong). Kunming: YNRMCBS. Original edition published in 1948.

———, ed. 1985. *Naxizu Shixuan* 納西族詩選 (Anthology of poetry by Naxi). Kunming: YNMZCBS.

Zhongguo 1990 Nian Renkou Pucha Ziliao 中國1990年人口普查資料 / *Tabulation on the 1990 Population Census of the People's Republic of China*. 1993. Beijing: Zhongguo Tongji Chubanshe.

Zhongguo Lijiang Dayan Naxi Guyuehui 中國麗江大研納西古樂會. n.d. Chinese-language publicity leaflet.

Zhongguo Yinyuejia Xiehui 中國音樂家協會, Zhongyang Yinyue Xueyuan 中央音樂學院, Zhongguo Yinyue Xueyuan 中國音樂學院, Zhongguo Yishu Yanjiuyuan Yinyue Yanjiusuo 中國藝術研究院音樂研究所, Zhongyang Minzu Xueyuan 中央民族學院, Zhongguo Shaoshu Minzu Yinyue Xuehui 中國少數民族音樂學會, Zhongguo Chuantong Yinyue Xuehui 中國傳統音樂學會, Zhongguo Changpian Zong Gongsi 中國唱片總

公司, and *Renmin Yinyue* Bianjibu《人民音樂》編輯部. 1993. Invitation to Dayan Ancient Music Association to perform in Beijing.

Zhongguo Yishu Yanjiuyuan Yinyue Yanjiusuo 中國藝術研究院音樂研究所, ed. 1983. *Xinjiang Yili Weiwu'er Min'ge* 新疆伊犁維吾爾民歌 (Uighur folk songs of Yili, Xinjiang). Beijing: Renmin Yinyue Chubanshe.

Zhongyang Yinyue Xueyuan Minzu Yinyue Yanjiusuo 中央音樂學院民族音樂研究所, ed. 1956. *Kunju Chuida Qupai* 崑劇吹打曲牌 (Wind and percussion melodies in Kunju). Beijing: Yinyue Chubanshe.

Zhou Shanfu 周善甫. 1990. "Naxizu huajia Zhou Lin zhuanlüe" 納西族畫家周霖傳略 (Biographical sketch of the Naxi artist Zhou Lin). *Lijiang Zhiyuan* 麗江志苑 (Selections from Lijiang records) 7: 26–28. (First published in *Yunnan Wenshi Congkan* 雲南文史叢刊 [Yunnan literature and history collection].)

Zhou Yongxian 周咏先 and Huang Lin 黃林. 1983. "Dongjing yinyue diaocha ji" 洞經音樂調查記 (Report on an investigation into Dongjing music). *MZYY* 2: 78–96. Report prepared in 1962.

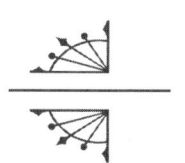

Discography

Commercially Available

Sound Recordings

Bilingual Chinese/English titles are given with a slash between them. English translations in parentheses are mine.

Baishibai: Songs of the Minority Nationalities of Yunnan. Pan 2038CD, 1995. CD.
Dongjing Music in Yunnan, China. King Record Co. KICC 5189, 5190, 1995. Two-CD set.
Dongjing Music: Where Confucian, Taoist and Buddhist Culture Meet. Pan 2058CD, 1998. CD.
A Happy Miao Family. Pan 2023CD, 1994. CD.
Hong Taiyang 紅太陽 (Red Sun). China Record Company, Shanghai Branch, L-133, L-138, L-152, 1992. Three-cassette set.
Lijiang Dongjing Yinyue 麗江洞經音樂 (Dongjing music of Lijiang). Yunnan Yinxiang Chubanshe H-427, n.d. (1993). Cassette.
Naxi Guyue 納西古樂 / *Classical Music of Naxi Minority.* Zhuhai Tequ Yinxiang Chubanshe ZAX-9103, n.d. (?1990). Cassette.
Naxi Guyue 納西古樂 / *Na-khi Music.* Yunnan Yinxiang Chubanshe H-427 and H-428, n.d. (1994 or after). Two-cassette set.
Naxi Guyue 納西古樂 / *Na-xi Music.* Bai Tian'e Yinxiang Chubanshe WS 92101, n.d. (1992). Cassette.
Naxi Music from Lijiang: The Dayan Ancient Music Association. Nimbus Records NI 5510, 1997. CD.
Sizhu Silk Bamboo: Chamber Music of South China. Pan 2030CD, 1994. CD.
Taiwan, Republic of China: The Confucius Temple Ceremony. Music of Man Archive/Jecklin-Disco JD 652-2, 1991. CD.
Yulong Shan—Yunnan Dongjing Yinyue 玉龍山一雲南洞經音樂 / *Yulong Mountain—Yannan Folk Songs* [sic]. *Dashi Yijingji zhi shiqi* 大師意境集之十七 / *Vision of the Maestros XVII.* Wave-Motion 74321-34762-2, 1995.

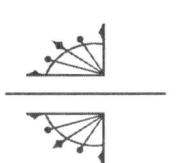

Videography
Commercially Available
Videos and VCD

China: Beyond the Clouds. National Geographic Society, 1994. Video.
JVC Video Anthology of World Music and Dance. East Asia Tape 4. Victor Company of Japan, 1990. Video.
Naxi Guyue 納西古樂 / *Naxi Ancient Music*. Zhongguo Guoji Dianshi Zong Gongsi/China International TV Corporation CT97-59, n.d. (?1997). VCD.
Tufeng Yueyun–Yunnan Shaoshu Minzu Qiyue 土風樂韻—雲南少數民族器樂 / *Local Customs and Music–Ethnic Music in Yunnan*. Vol. 2. Yunnan Yinxiang Chubanshe/Yunnan Sound and Vision Publishing House YX-128, n.d. Video.
Yunnan Yueqi Wangguo Kaocha Ji 雲南樂器王國考察記 / *The Instrument Kingdom in Yunnan, China*. UNESCO/IMC series "Universe of Music: A History," China, Video 1-2. Zhongguo Yinyuejia Yinxiang Chubanshe/China Musicians' Audio-Video Publishing House, 1994. Video.

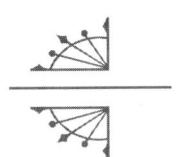

Recordings on Accompanying CD

Tracks 16 and 24 were recorded using a Sony PCM-M1 Digital Audio Recorder and an Audio-Technica 822 stereo microphone. All other tracks were recorded using a Sony Walkman D6C and a Sony ECM-909 stereo microphone. The CD was digitally restored and mastered by Pantelis Vassilakis using Sonic Foundry Sound Forge 4.1 at the Ethnomusicology Laboratory of the University of California, Los Angeles.

Some musicians gave me their date of birth, some their age at time of recording. Because Chinese calculation of age differs from Western custom, I have not converted the latter to birthdates. Ages given are accurate for the year of recording. Age or date of birth is only given for the first recording in which each musician appears.

1. He Yucai (a.k.a. He Shicheng) (b. 1909) chanting the opening of the *dongba* scripture *Lv Bber Lv Raq*. Recorded under interview conditions at the house of Xuan Ke, Dayan Town, 9 May 1989.
2. He Fengxiang (b. 1942) singing the folksong "Bbai neiq bbaq jji huil" (The Meeting of Bees and Flowers) to the melody *Gguq qil*. Recorded under interview conditions at the house of Zhang Kuiguang, Dayan Town, 20 May 1992.
3. Unidentified singers and dancers performing the dance song *A li li*. Recorded in the main square in the new part of Dayan Town during festivities celebrating the New Year on the evening of 1 January 1992.
4. Unidentified musician performing a dance tune on the mouth organ. Recorded in the main square in the new part of Dayan Town during festivities celebrating May Day on the evening of 1 May 1992.
5. Wang Chaoxin (b. 1954) performing a seven-beat dance tune on the fipple flute. Recorded under interview conditions at his house, Longquan Village, Baisha Township, 13 May 1992.
6. He Heng (age 74) performing the Jew's harp melody *Jiul bbu jjiq diu* (Water Dripping in a Copper Basin), expressing words indicating pleasure at my visit. Recorded under interview conditions at her home in Dayan Town, 11 May 1992.

7. Yang Houkun (age 51) performing the folk song melody *Salua bba xiuq bbaq* (Flowers Bloom in the Third Month) on a tree leaf. Recorded under interview conditions at his house, Dayan Town, 24 May 1992.
8. Yang Houkun performing a call between lovers on a tree leaf. Recorded under interview conditions at his house, Dayan Town, 24 May 1992.
9. He Maogen (age 52) playing the Baisha Xiyue flute solo *Me mil ngu* (The Princess Weeps). Recorded at a rehearsal of the Baisha Ancient Music Orchestra in the Dongba Art Exhibition Center in Baisha, 17 July 1996.
10. Baisha Ancient Music Orchestra playing the Baisha Xiyue ensemble piece *Ai lil li jji perq* (Beautiful White Clouds) (minus the words). Recorded at a rehearsal of the Baisha Ancient Music Orchestra in the Dongba Art Exhibition Center in Baisha, 17 July 1996.
11. Dayan Town Ancient Music Association. Zhang Longhan announces *Qigu Santong* (opening drumroll); the drumroll is played on the large drum *dagu* by Chen Qiuyuan; and the entire ensemble then performs the accompanied song (*dadiao*) *Bagua* (Eight Trigrams) (short version [*Bagua Tou*]). The percussion interlude and coda are the pattern *Bagua Wei* (Eight Trigrams Coda), played the first time on small gong *habagou* and small cymbals *xiaocha*, and the second time on large cymbals *nao* and *bo*; the final coda is extended and finished by the pattern *Da Xia* (Beating through to the End). Recorded at a tourist concert in Dayan Town Cultural Center, 14 July 1996. The Chinese-character text sung is given in Appendix C, No. 1.
12. Baihua Ancient Music Orchestra playing the instrumental piece (*xiaodiao*) *Yi Jiang Feng* (Wind on the River). The important large drum *dagu* part is played by Mu Zhu. Recorded at an informal Sunday afternoon gathering at the house of He Guowei, Baihua Village, Huangshan Township, 31 October 1991.
13. Dayan Town Ancient Music Association playing the instrumental piece (*xiaodiao*) *Shanpo Yang* (Sheep on the Hill). Recorded at a tourist concert in Dayan Town Cultural Center, 8 May 1989.
14. Specially assembled group of older musicians playing the instrumental piece (*xiaodiao*) *Dao Chun Lai* (Spring Has Come). He Yi'an (b. 1908) leads on high-pitch two-string bowed lute *erhuang*; the other musicians are

Wang Dejiu (b. ca. 1911)	*yunluo* (cloud gong) and *tongling* (bell)
He Wenxuan (b. ca. 1912)	*sanxian* (three-string plucked lute)
Zhang Kuiguang (b. ca. 1912)	*sugudu* (four-string plucked lute)
Sun Ziming (b. 1913)	*pipa* (four-string plucked lute)
Zhao Yingxian (b. 1916)	*dihu* (low-pitch two-string bowed lute)
Zhang Longhan (b. 1923)	*erhu* (mid-pitch two-string bowed lute)
Yang Zenglie (b. 1939)	*bobo* (double-reed pipe)

Recorded privately at Dayan Town Cultural Center, 24 May 1992.
15. Jinshan Ancient Music Orchestra playing the instrumental piece (*xiaodiao*) *Wannian Hua* (Eternal Flowers, also known as *Wannian Huan* [Eternal Joy]). Recorded at an informal Sunday afternoon gathering at the house of He Zegan, Kaiyuan Village, Jinshan Township, 17 November 1991.
16. Dayan Town Ancient Music Association. Sun Ziming announces *Shoujing Jie* (Closing Ode); then the entire group performs the piece. Recorded at a tourist concert in the

Naxi Ancient Music Palace, Dayan Town, 27 July 1998. The Chinese-character text sung is given in Appendix C, No. 2.

17. He Yi'an chanting (*song*) two incantations, *xilü zhenyan* (true words on clearing the mind) and *tiaoqi zhenyan* (true words on harmonizing the breath), from the beginning of the *Kaitan Yiwen* (Rite of Opening the Altar) volume of the *Yuqing Wuji Zongzhen Wenchang Dadong Xianjing* (Transcendent Scripture of the Great Grotto of Wenchang). He accompanies himself on the *muyu* (wood block shaped like a fish). Recorded under interview conditions at his home, Dayan Town, 7 May 1992. The Chinese-character text is given in Appendix C, No. 3.

18. He Yi'an demonstrating *du biaowen* (reading a memorial). Recorded under interview conditions at his house, Dayan Town, 11 June 1992. The Chinese-character text is given in Appendix C, No. 4.

19. He Yi'an demonstrating heightened speech style of *jiang xuan* (explication of mysteries). Recorded under interview conditions at his house, Dayan Town, 8 May 1992. The Chinese-character text is given in Appendix C, No. 5.

20. Zhang Longhan playing the tuning piece for the four-string plucked lute *pipa*. Recorded under interview conditions at the Dayan Town Cultural Center, 14 May 1992.

21. Zhang Longhan singing the *gongchepu* (Chinese solfège) to the instrumental piece (*xiaodiao*) *Shanpo Yang* (Sheep on the Hill). The recording fades out as he begins the repeat of the main body of the piece. Recorded under interview conditions at the house of Li Cheng'gan, Dayan Town, 17 June 1993.

22. Zhang Longhan on two-string bowed lute *erhu* and Li Cheng'gan (age 69) on four-string plucked lute *sugudu* playing the instrumental piece (*xiaodiao*) *Shanpo Yang* (Sheep on the Hill). The recording fades out as they begin the repeat of the main body of the piece. Recorded under interview conditions at the Dayan Town Cultural Center, 14 May 1992.

23. He Yi'an reciting the mnemonic syllables to the percussion interlude pattern of *Shoujing Jie* (Closing Ode). Recorded under interview conditions at his house in Dayan Town, 7 May 1992.

24. Dayan Town Xi'an Street Dianju Club performing "Qiang Yusan" (Vying for the Umbrella), a segment of the opera *Hutou Zhai* (Tiger Head Encampment). The performers (all male except for Zhao Guimei) are:

Tang Shulin, age 62	male singer
Zhao Guimei, age 58	female singer
Li Bin, age 68	*jinghu* (*dianhu*) (high-pitch two-string fiddle)
Sha Yuchun, age 65	*erhu* (mid-pitch two-string fiddle)
Li Linshu, age 70	*sanxian* (three-string plucked lute)
Zhou Kewu, age 65	*luo* (gong) and *bo* (cymbals)
Yang Guosheng, age 72	*xiaoluo* (small gong)
Li Zhenpeng, age 68	*ergu* (large drum)
Xi Hongyi, age 71	*xiaogu* (small drum) and *tishou* (clappers)

Instrument names are as listed by Xi Hongyi; they vary slightly in different sources on Dianju. The Chinese-character text is given in Appendix C, No. 6.

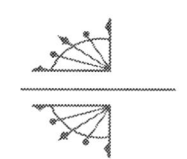

Index

Abing, 170–171, 222 n. 7
accompanied songs. *See dadiao*
aesthetics
   of conservatory-style Chinese music, 22, 157–158, 223 n. 11, 233–234 n. 5
   of Dayan Ancient Music Association's tourist concerts, 152–157, 183
   and domestic tourists, 157
   and foreign preferences, 154–158, 183
   of song and dance troupes, 137–139
   of traditional Dongjing musicians, 115, 138, 157–158
A li li (Naxi folk dance), 58–59, 128
Anlong Diantu Jing (Dragon Pacification and Earth Settling Scripture), 46
anti-Japanese war (1937–1945), 119–120
Anti-Rightist Campaign, 16, 33
Asian Music Circuit, 6, 160

Bai (ethnic group), 18, 25
   Dongjing associations of, 40
   in Lijiang, 30, 94, 150
Baihua Ancient Music Orchestra. *See* Baihua Dongjing music group
Baihua Dongjing music group (post-Cultural Revolution), 69 fig. 4.5, 142, 143, 144, 145, 167
   name of, 172
   and performance for birthdays, 146
   and performance at a funeral, 145–146
   and performance at a wedding, 147
   and tourists, 163–164, 183
Baihua's Dongjing music activities 1949–1966, 126

Baihua Guyuedui (Baihua Ancient Music Orchestra). *See* Baihua Dongjing music group
Baima Dongjing association, 102, 106, 114, 126, 142
Baisha Ancient Music Orchestra. *See* Baisha Dongjing music group
Baisha Dongjing association, 50, 105, 106, 107, 112, 113, 114
   festivals of, 51
   importance of education for members, 52
Baisha Dongjing music group (post–Cultural Revolution), 142, 143, 146, 167, 172
Baisha Guyuedui (Baisha Ancient Music Orchestra). *See* Baisha Dongjing music group
Baisha murals, 163, 167
Baisha Xiyue, 65–67, 77, 127, 132, 133, 140, 167
   fieldwork on, 65–66, 130–131
   mentioned in pre-twentieth-century documents, 67, 174
   origins of, 66–67
   performance of in Kunming (1957), 127, 133
   performers of, 65–66, 95
   recordings of, 67, 133, 157, 172, 179
ban'gu (small drum), 71, 77, 102
banhu (two-string bowed lute), 70
barley-stalk pipe (or barley pipe). *See wowo*
bberq ko (*dongba* yak horn), 56
Bbesheeq Xilli. *See* Baisha Xiyue

biliq (Naxi flute), 59–61, 61 fig. 4.2, 67, 68
bo (cymbals), 75, 75 fig. 4.7, 77, 143
bobo (Naxi double-reed pipe), 74 fig. 4.6
　in Baisha Xiyue, 67, 68
　in Dongjing music, 69–70, 76, 153, 188
boling. See jizi
Bolton, Michael, 136
boom boxes in Lijiang. *See* cassette culture
Buddhism in Lijiang, 168
　anti-Japanese war activities connected to, 119
　Chinese, 35, 119, 132
　lay organizations espousing, 36
　Tibetan, 35–36, 37, 119, 132
Buddhist music in Lijiang
　Chinese, 93, 97, 116, 132
　Tibetan, 94, 97, 132
Bulgarian music, 195

Cantonese instrumental ensembles, 83
Casals, Pablo, 136
cassette culture, 134–136, 140
Central Broadcasting Station (Central Radio Station), 131, 133
Central Conservatory of Music (Beijing), 156, 158, 161, 181
Central Nationalities University (formerly Institute) (Beijing), 17, 22, 158
Changshui Dongjing music group (post-Cultural Revolution), 142, 143, 144, 145, 146
chanting. *See du; song*
Chen Hongmou, 12
China: Beyond the Clouds (documentary film), 149, 160
China Conservatory of Music (Beijing), 156, 158
China Record Company, 158
Chinese Ethnic Culture Park (Beijing), 24–25
Christianity in Lijiang, 36, 37, 97
Christian music, 94, 97, 121
Chrysanthemum Festival (1933), 52, 126, 175
Chuanju (Sichuan Opera), 92
civil war (1945–1949), 120–121
commoditization of culture, 166

Confucian sacrifice, 37, 46, 171
　in Lijiang, 36, 51, 93, 101, 110, 126
　as tourist attraction, 150
constitutions
　and provision for minority citizens in Republican era, 13
　and provision for minority citizens in Communist era, 15–16, 20
cultural relativism, appeal for in musicology, 26–27
Cultural Revolution, 16, 21, 173, 194
　in Lijiang, 33, 37, 127, 129–130, 133
Cultured Music Association. *See Wenming Yuehui*

daba, 55
da bbe leq (*dongba* drum), 56
Dacheng Miaofa Lianhua Jing (Lotus Sutra), 46
dadiao (accompanied songs), 52, 77–78, 82, 91, 126
Dadong Xianjing (Transcendent Scripture of the Great Grotto of Wenchang), 41, 45, 51, 107, 110, 199, 200–202
　musical performance of in Lijiang, 81–82
dagu (large drum), 71
dahao (long trumpet), 93
Dai (ethnic group), 22, 26
daji yue (percussion music), 78
Daju Dongjing association, 107
Daju Dongjing music group (late 1990s), 167
daluo (large gong), 75, 75 fig. 4.7
datongtong. See dihu
Dayan Ancient Music Association. *See* Dayan Town Dongjing music group
Dayan Guyuehui. See Dayan Town Dongjing music group
Dayan Town Dongjing association, 101, 102, 104, 105–106, 107, 111, 142
　and accusations of "superstition" in 1912, 119
　and anti-Japanese war activities, 119–120
　disbandment of (1949), 121
　documents of, 48–49
　festivals of, 50–52
　funding of, 113–114
　history of, 49–50

officers of, 112
respectability and social prestige of, 52–53, 104, 175
Dayan Town Dongjing music group (post–Cultural Revolution), 142, 143, 144, 145, 165
and academy and training classes for young people, 144, 159, 167, 173, 185, 187
and the Ancient Music Palace (*Guyue Gong*) (1996), 167, 168 fig. 7.2
and commoditization, 165–166
and concert tour to Britain (1995), 160–161, 186, 193
and concert tour to Hong Kong (1997), 161, 187, 193
and concert tour to Norway (1998), 161, 193
and concert tour to Switzerland, Italy, Germany, and France (1998), 161, 193
and concert tour to Taiwan (1999), 161, 193
and domestic concert tours, 157–159, 180, 185–186, 193
featured in tour guides, newspapers, magazines, and on the Internet, 152, 160, 161–162, 163, 183
financial arrangements of, 163, 185
goals of, 185
and "Hundred Marvels of China" exhibition performance, 146, 157
name of, 173
officers of, 164
and performance at birthdays, 146
and performance at funerals, 146
and performance at government request, 146
and performance at weddings, 147
recordings by, 160, 172
tourist concerts by, 75 fig. 4.7, 147, 151–157, 183, 185
and transmission of repertoire to Daju, 167
dda keq (*dongba* drum), 56
declamation. See *jiang, xuan*
Deng Lijun (Teresa Teng), 135
Deng Xiaoping, 135
dialogue songs. See *duige*
dianhu (two-string bowed lute), 91

Dianju (Yunnan opera), 91–92, 92 fig. 4.9, 95, 96, 97, 115, 189
activities in Lijiang 1949–1966, 129, 133
activities in Lijiang after Cultural Revolution, 134, 139–140
and anti-Japanese war activities in Lijiang, 120
in celebration of liberation in Lijiang, 121
cassettes of, 134
dihu (two-string bowed lute, a.k.a. *datongtong*), 70
disco, 25, 136, 187
dizi (Han transverse flute)
in Chinese Buddhist ritual, 93
at Confucian sacrifice, 94
in Dianju, 91
in Dongjing music, 68–69, 76
in wedding music, 94
dongba, 35, 37, 132, 134, 146, 168, 174, 189
choreographic notation of, 57
music of, 55–57, 94, 96–97, 98, 132, 134
"*dongba* culture," 150, 163, 167
Dongba Culture Performance Troupe, 146–147, 189
Dongba Culture Research Institute, 150
"*dongba* dance," 22, 129, 132, 140
Dongba Palace, 163
dongba scripts, 35
Dongjing associations (*dongjinghui*) in Lijiang, 4, 48–53, 99–114, 175
exclusivity of, 52–53, 112, 189
festivals of, 50–51, 110
funding of, 113–114
internal relationships of, 102
membership of, 52
origins of, 48–50
relationships among, 101–102
and relationship with county government, 101
and relationship with the gods, 102–103
and relationship with nonmembers, 100–101
scriptures of, 51
and transmission of the Dongjing tradition, 104–112

Dongjing associations in Yunnan, 39–48
  Confucian affiliation of, 44–45, 48
  in Dali, 41
  derivation of term *dongjinghui*, 41
  distribution of, 39–40
  among ethnic minorities, 40
  festivals of, 45–46
  funding of, 44, 46–47
  history of, 41–43
  in Kunming, 41–42
  membership of, 43–44, 47
  music of, 76, 81, 82–83, 140
  performance of rituals by, 47–48
  post-1949 suppression of, 40
  post–Cultural Revolution revival of, 40, 46–47
  and Taoist priests, 44
dongjinghui. See Dongjing associations (*dongjinghui*) in Lijiang; Dongjing associations in Yunnan
Dongjing music in Lijiang, 4, 7, 68–91, 140, 141–169
  as ambassador for Lijiang and the Naxi, 165, 186, 188–189, 191, 192, 196
  and anti-Japanese war, 120–121
  and civil war, 120–121
  and Cultural Revolution, 127, 133
  and dangers of commercialization, 181, 182
  at Dongba Palace, 163, 164
  economic benefits of in the 1990s, 162–164, 186, 189, 191, 192, 195–196
  foreign instruments introduced into, 121
  at government events, 125–126, 133, 165
  at Guanfang Hotel, 163, 164
  international fame of, 140, 181, 191, 196
  intonation-checking pieces of, 82
  and local officials, 186–187
  melodic instruments in, 68–71, 76–77
  musical structure of, 76–77
  musical types in, 77–82
  Naxi affiliation and characteristics of, 174, 179, 181, 182, 183, 184, 185, 188, 189, 190, 191, 192, 193, 196, 235 n. 9
  notation of, 83–88
  percussion instruments in, 71–75, 75 fig. 4.7, 77, 78
  percussion mnemonic syllables in, 88, 90 table 4.3
  and performance in Canton (1991–1992), 146–147
  and performance in Kunming (1954), 127
  preservation of as ancient relic, 179–180, 181, 182, 183, 184, 185, 186, 187, 188, 192
  recordings of, 118, 131, 133, 153, 157–158, 160, 165, 172, 179, 187
  and recruitment crisis of early 1990s, 140, 143–144
  and recruitment success of mid and late 1990s, 166–167, 192
  refinement of, 95–96, 115, 189, 191
  as reinterpreted by Lijiang Naxi Autonomous County Song and Dance Troupe, 138
  revival of after the Cultural Revolution, 134, 139–140, 141–143
  in ritual performance and social communication, 99–104, 164–165
  scholarly study of, 131, 133, 184
  secularization of after 1949, 121–122, 126, 133, 167–169, 190
  and secular performance 1949–1966, 126–127, 133,
  and secular performance after the Cultural Revolution, 144–147, 151–169, 184–187
  and secular performance groups before 1949, 88–91, 114–116
  transmission of, 86–88, 109, 115–116, 167, 185
  tune titles in, 82–83
  and women, 97–98, 144, 169
  See also music as medicine
dongxiao (Han endblown flute), 70
Dragon Pacification and Earth Settling Scripture. *See Anlong Diantu Jing*
du (chanting/reading), 48, 79
duige, 57

erhu (two-string bowed lute), 70
erhuang (two-string bowed lute)
  in Baisha Xiyue, 67, 68
  in Chinese Buddhist ritual, 93
  in Dongjing music, 70

INDEX

Ershisi Xiaojing (Twenty-Four Exemplars of Filial Piety), 51, 108, 146
ethnic minorities in Bulgaria, 195
ethnic minorities in China
  and benefits of minority status, 18, 190
  and class, 19
  Communist policy towards, 7, 15–19, 178–179, 190–191, 194
  and definition of *minzu*, 15
  and domestic orientalism, 24–27
  and ethnic classification, 17–19, 182
  in film and on TV, 25–26
  and gender, 19
  prejudices against, 16
  Republican policy towards, 7, 13–15
  and rural-urban divide, 19
  as tourist attraction, 148–149
  See also constitutions; minority performing arts
ethnic minorities in the Soviet Union, 194, 195

folk dance (Naxi), 58–61, 60 fig. 4.1, 61 fig. 4.2, 129, 134, 138, 139, 174, 178, 189, 190
  area-specificity of, 59
  interethnic influence in, 59
  performance in Canton (1991–1992), 147
  presentation at national festival (1964), 128, 129
folk song (Naxi), 56, 57–58, 96, 133, 134, 139, 174, 177, 178, 190
  collection of and studies on, 130
  and propaganda, 127–129
funeral laments, 58
funerals in Lijiang, 36, 38, 58, 102, 114
  Dongjing music at, 51, 82, 89, 115, 140, 145–146, 166
fu shanzhang (Dongjing association second ritual officiant), 102, 112
Fu Youde, 42, 50
fvl sse (*dongba* conch shell), 56

gaitu guiliu (replacing the local and reverting to the mainstream), 12, 32
Gao Jianming, 106
Gaoshang Yuhuang Benhang Jijing (Jade Emperor Scripture), 46, 107

Gezi Dongjing association, 102, 105–106, 109
Gguq qil (Naxi folk song), 57–58, 127
gongchepu (solfège), 83–88, 85 fig. 4.2, 86 fig. 4.8, 89, 172, 228–229 nn. 25–26
Good Friends Music Association. *See Yiyou Yinyuehui*
Goullart, Peter, 122, 147, 154, 162, 175–176, 187, 192
Great Leap Forward, 16, 33
guan (double-reed pipe), 69, 70
Guandi (Chinese deity), 39, 45–46, 102–103
Guandi Enlightenment Scripture. *See Guansheng Dijun Jueshi Zhenjing*
Guanfang Hotel (Lijiang), 163, 167
Guansheng Dijun Jueshi Zhenjing (*Guandi Enlightenment Scripture*), 45–46, 51, 108, 201–202
Guan Xuexuan, 32, 38, 54, 174, 178
Guanyin (Chinese deity), 46
gue gueq. *See* Jew's harp
guyu (ancient music) (term for Dongjing music in Lijiang), 172, 173, 189

habagou (small gong, a.k.a. *nao lizi*), 75, 77
Han chauvinism, 16
He Changlin, 180, 182, 183, 184, 187
He Fengxiang, 57–58
He Gengji, 49, 65, 112, 119, 171, 175, 176
He Guowei, 145
He Heng, 63–64
He Hongzhang, 76, 86, 115–116
He Huihan, 50, 106
heightened speech. *See jiang*; *xuan*
He Ji'an, 106
He Jiaxiu, 186–187
Her La Leeq Keel (*dongba* ceremony), 55–56
He Linghan, 96, 172
He Minda, 142, 144
He Shicheng. *See* He Yucai
He Shiwei, 93, 116
He Wenxuan (musician), 76
He Wenxuan (official), 175, 176
He Xidian, 66–67, 127, 128, 142

He Yi'an, 43–44, 50, 52, 53, 103, 104, 105, 108, 121, 142, 169
  and funding for Dayan Town Dongjing association, 113–114
  as icon of Dongjing music tradition in tourist concert era, 153
  recording by, 118
  as teacher of Jinshan Dongjing association, 102, 108–109, 111
He Yucai (a.k.a. He Shicheng), 55
He Zhong (Dongjing musician from Fuhui Village), 86, 115–116
He Zhong (member of county song and dance troupe), 157
Hong Taiyang (Red Sun) cassette set, 135
Huadeng opera, 129, 134
Huangjing association (*huangjinghui*), 107–108, 111, 114, 175
Huang Limei, 144
Huangshan Commune Ancient Music Orchestra. *See Huangshan Gongshe Guyuedui*
Huangshan Gongshe Guyuedui (Huangshan Commune Ancient Music Orchestra), 142
Huang Zhen, 22
hubo. *See sugudu*
Hui (ethnic group) 19, 25, 30
huizhang (Dongjing association head), 102, 112
hulusheng (gourd mouth organ), 59, 60 fig. 4.1, 168, 174, 226–227 n. 7
huqin (two-string bowed lute), 74 fig. 4.6
  in Baisha Xiyue, 67, 68
  in Chinese Buddhist ritual, 93
  in Dongjing music, 70

the individual in music, 8, 9, 110, 111, 141–142, 162, 195, 196
Inner Mongolian Song and Dance Troupe, 67
instrumental pieces (in Lijiang's Dongjing music). *See xiaodiao*
"internal" and "external" audiences, 191
international music competitions, 161
iuqqil duel (Naxi term for playing music), 172, 173

Jade Dragon (Snow) Mountain, 34, 120, 149, 163, 186

Jade Emperor Scripture. *See Gaoshang Yuhuang Benhang Jijing*
Jew's harp, 61–64, 63 fig. 4.3, 96, 97, 134, 139, 227 n. 10
jiang (heightened speech), 48, 79–81
Jiangnan Sizhu, 76, 77, 88, 179
Jinshan Dongjing association, 102, 108–109, 112, 115
  funding of, 114
  officers of, 113
Jinshan Dongjing music group (post–Cultural Revolution), 142, 143, 144, 145, 145 fig. 7.1, 163, 167, 172
Jinshan Guyuedui (Jinshan Ancient Music Orchestra). *See* Jinshan Dongjing music group
jizi (small cymbals, a.k.a. *boling*), 75
Judian Dongjing association, 110
Judian Dongjing music group (post–Cultural Revolution), 140, 142, 146

karaoke, 25, 136
Kashgar Song and Dance Troupe, 150
Kazakh music, 22
Kou Bangping, 178, 179
Kublai Khan, 32, 50, 66, 175
Kunju, 83

L.A. Boyz, 136
Lake of Blood Scripture. *See Xuehu Jing*
Lasha Dongjing association, 105, 106, 112, 114, 142
  importance of education for members, 52
  officers of, 113
  secret revolutionaries in, 121–122
Lashi Dongjing associations, 106, 109, 113
Lashi Dongjing music group (post–Cultural Revolution), 140, 142, 143
leaf (as musical instrument), 64, 64 fig. 4.4, 227 n. 11
Lei Feng, 138
Li Baozhang, 106–107, 142
Liberation in Lijiang, 121–122
Li Chengzhen, 126
Lijiang County
  author's first visit to, 3–6
  film in, 125, 134
  geography of, 30–32
  history of, 32–34

INDEX

music and age in, 97–98, 197
music education in schools of, 136
music and ethnicity in, 96, 197
music and gender in, 97–98, 197
music and professional status in, 93–94, 95, 132
music and religious affiliation in, 96–97
music and rural or urban environment in, 96, 197
music and social standing in, 95–96, 190, 197
pianos in, 136
population of, 30
radio in, 125, 134, 136
television in, 125, 134, 136, 140
tourism in, 34, 149–151, 162–164, 186, 190
Lijiang County Cultural Office (*wenhua guan*), 125
Lijiang County Library, 121
Lijiang County Trade Union, 173
Lijiang guyue (Lijiang Ancient Music) (term for Dongjing music), 172
Lijiang Prefecture Archive, 121
Lijiang Prefecture Dianju Troupe, 91, 129, 130, 133, 136–137, 151, 232 n. 18
Lisu (ethnic group), 30, 94, 138
Liu Chao, 130, 177
Liu Tieshan, 21
Li Yunqing, 66, 67
Long Yun, 14
Lotus Sutra. *See* Dacheng Miaofa Lianhua Jing
Lou, Mrs. Rita. *See* Yang Dan'gui
Ludian Dongjing association, 110
Lu Dingyi, 124, 131–132
Lu Han, 14
Lv Bber Lv Raq (*dongba* scripture), 55–56

Mahler, 136
Mama hui, 36, 37, 97
Mao Jizeng, 65, 67, 130–131, 172
Mao Zedong, 21
and encouragement of introduction of foreign principles into Chinese music, 123
and the "Talks at the Yan'an Conference on Literature and Art," 20, 122–124, 131, 136, 156

Mao Zedong Thought Art Propaganda Troupe in Lijiang, 129–130
Miao (ethnic group), 12, 16, 18, 22
in Lijiang, 30
and "Miao albums," 26
in Splendid China theme park brochure, 25
minority performing arts in China
and arts festivals, 21, 22–23, 124, 128, 132, 137
Communist policy toward, 10, 19–23, 124–125, 131–132, 138–139, 178, 182, 190, 194
professionalization of, 21–22, 137–139
and tourism, 137, 139, 186
miscellaneous pieces (in Lijiang's Dongjing music). *See zaqu*
Mongolian oral epics, 195
Mongolia's approach to ethnic difference, 195
Morganian paradigm. *See* social evolutionary theory
Moshi Bu Wang (Never to Be Forgotten), 48–49
Moslem rebellion (a.k.a. Moslem uprising) in Yunnan (1856–1873), 12, 42, 91
and its effect on Lijiang, 49, 119
Mosuo (ethnic group), 12, 18, 19, 28–30, 170
"motif of the music-making African," 24
"motif of the music-making minority," 24–27, 177, 179
mouth organ. *See hulusheng*
Mu Gong, 50, 185
music as active cultural phenomenon, 9, 99–100, 116–117, 162, 195–196
music and history, 8–9, 98, 116–117, 118–119, 162, 170–171, 191, 196–197
music and meaning, 165, 169, 193
music as medicine, 180, 181, 182, 184
Music Research Institute (Beijing), 131, 158
Mu Tai, 38
Mu Wenyu, 106
muyu (fish-shaped woodblock)
in Chinese Buddhist rituals, 93
in Dongjing music, 48, 71–74, 79, 81, 102, 164
Mu Zhu, 106

muzi (mother-son) relationships (among Lijiang's Dongjing associations), 101–102, 106, 109, 164

nanhu (two-string bowed lute), 70
nao (cymbals), 75, 75 fig. 4.7, 77, 143
nao lizi. See habagou
nationalities. *See* ethnic minorities
Naxi (ethnic group)
    Chinese-language literacy and education of, 12–13, 37–38, 134, 190–191
    definition of, 28–30
    ethnicity and self-identity, 188–191
    folk dance. *See* folk dance (Naxi)
    folk song. *See* folk song (Naxi)
    as "good at singing and dancing," 24, 25, 177, 178, 179, 181, 191
    language, 28
    openness to Han culture, 16, 37–39
    origins of, 28
    participation in 1964 national arts festival, 128, 129
    population, 28
    women, 39
Naxi Ancient Music (*Naxi guyue*) (modern term for Lijiang's Dongjing music), 4, 6, 162, 164, 172, 181, 185, 186, 187, 188, 189, 191, 194, 197
Naxi guyue. See Naxi Ancient Music
Naxi Theater Troupe (*Naxi Jutuan*), 129
neng'ge shanwu (good at singing and dancing) (stock phrase for ethnic minorities), 25, 177
ngail mo. See hulusheng
Niu Tao, 65, 174

Oldfield, Mike, 136
oral history, 105, 111, 142, 196
O ssei sseil. See Worere

paq, 35
Pavarotti, Luciano, 136
Peking Opera, 92–93, 120, 129, 130, 134
pianos in Lijiang, 136
Pineflower Orchestra. *See Songhua Yuedui*
pipa (four-string plucked lute), 70, 74 fig. 4.6, 76, 138, 175
pop music, 134, 135–136, 144, 187
Pumi (ethnic group), 30, 67, 94

qin (bridgeless zither), 71, 173
qing (chime), 75

Red Sun. *See Hong Taiyang* (Red Sun) cassette set
reflexivity in ethnomusicology, 159
Remeicuo. See Worere
Renmin Yinyue (People's Music), 21, 127–128, 130, 158, 159, 172, 177, 180
representation in ethnography and music scholarship, 170–171, 181, 191–192
Rock, Joseph, 147, 149

sainii, 35, 37, 132
    music of, 57, 97, 132
Sakai, Noriko, 136
Sanduo (Naxi god), 51, 57
Sani (ethnic group), 150, 155
sanxian (three-string plucked lute), 70, 71, 76
scholarship on Naxi music, 65–66, 130–131, 133, 140
se (bridged zither), 71
Shanghai Chinese Orchestra, 156
Shanghai Conservatory of Music, 22, 138, 156
Shanying (Mountain Eagle) (Yi pop group), 136
shanzhang (Dongjing association chief ritual officiant), 102, 112
Shen Qia, 181, 182, 183
Shigu Dongjing association, 106, 108–110, 112, 113, 115
Shigu Dongjing music group (post–Cultural Revolution), 140, 142, 143, 145, 146
Shi Wang Jing (Ten Kings Scripture), 46
Shuhe Dongjing association, 52, 105, 106–107, 114
silk and bamboo (*sizhu*) music, 4, 155, 179
sizhu. See silk and bamboo (*sizhu*) music
solfège. *See gongchepu*
social evolutionary theory, 17–18, 30, 170
song (chanting), 48, 78–79, 93, 107
song and dance troupes, 20, 130, 131
    aesthetics of, 137–139
    in Lijiang, 129, 130, 131, 133–134, 136–139, 146, 151, 232 n. 18
    and tourism, 137, 150, 151
Songhua Yuedui (Pineflower Orchestra), 171

southwest China
  public education in, 12
  Han migration to, 11
  military campaigns in, 11–12
Soviet influence on and parallels with music and minority arts in China, 20, 22, 123, 131, 132, 194, 222 n. 10, 231 nn. 6–7
Splendid China theme park (Shenzhen), 25
Stalin's definition of nation, 17, 222 n. 4
sugudu (four-string plucked lute, a.k.a. *hubo*), 74 fig. 4.6
  in Baisha Xiyue, 67–68
  construction and performance technique of, 70–71
  in Dongjing music, 70–71, 76, 138, 153, 175
Sun Yat-sen, 13
Sun Ziming, 172
suona (shawm)
  at Confucian sacrifice, 94
  in Dianju, 91
  used by Ljiang Naxi Autonomous County Song and Dance Troupe, 138
  at weddings and funerals, 93–94

Tang Jiyao, 14
tanjing (discuss scriptures), 172
tanjingban (scripture discussion groups, term for Lijiang's Dongjing associations), 171
Taoist music, 179
  of Lijiang, 93, 97
  of Wudang Mountain, 83, 84–85
Taoist priests, 44, 48
  in Lijiang, 36, 37, 109, 116, 168
Tchaikovsky, 136
Teng, Teresa. See Deng Lijun
Ten Kings Scripture. See *Shi Wang Jing*
Ten Offerings (*Shi Gongyang*) (Dongjing ceremony), 79 table 4.1, 82, 102, 168–169
Third China Art Festival (1992), 23, 137, 185
Tibetans
  in Lijiang, 30, 94, 138
  in other parts of China, 13, 19
tishou (clappers), 71–74, 77, 102
Titanic soundtrack, 136
tongling (bell), 75

tourism
  in China, 147–148
  and handicrafts, 149–150
  in Lijiang, 34, 149–157, 162–164
  and performing arts, 137, 149–150, 151–157
  in Yunnan, 148–149
Transcendent Scripture of the Great Grotto of Wenchang. See *Dadong Xianjing*
tusi (native official) system, 11–12, 14
Twenty-Four Exemplars of Filial Piety. See *Ershisi Xiaojing*

UNESCO recognition of Dayan Town, 34, 149, 161, 162
uo uoq. See *wowo*
Uzbek music, 22

Wang Dejiu, 107, 111
Wang Liang, 110
wedding music in Lijiang, 93–94, 132, 147
Wenchang (Chinese deity), 39, 45, 49, 102–103, 119, 180–181
Wenming Yuehui (Cultured Music Association), 171
wenrenhui (literati association), 171
Western art/classical music, 22, 135, 136, 156, 170, 194, 234 n. 8
Worere (Naxi folk dance), 59
wowo (barley-stalk pipe), 64–65, 134, 174

Xiangyun Dongjing music group (1993 on), 143
xiao (Han endblown flute), 52, 175
xiaocha (small cymbals), 75, 77
xiaodiao (instrumental pieces), 52, 78, 91, 126
xuan (declamation), 48
Xuan Ke, 67, 157, 168 fig. 7.2, 183, 184
  and concert tour to England, 159–160
  international celebrity of, 188
  and lectures in Beijing (1993), 158
  at Oxford (1995), 160, 162
  and tourist concerts, 151, 152, 153–154, 155, 182, 187–188, 191–192
Xuehu Jing (Lake of Blood Scripture), 46

Yang Dan'gui, 143, 146
Yang Derun, 107, 115–116, 126

Yangge, 129
Yang Houkun, 64, 64 fig. 4.4, 126, 142
Yang Jian, 109, 111
Yang Jingren, 23
yangqin (hammered dulcimer), 121, 138
Yang Xizhen, 110
Yang Zenglie, 110, 159, 184
Yi (ethnic group)
  in Lijiang, 30, 94, 96
  in other parts of southwest China, 14, 18
Yiyou Yinyuehui (Good Friends Music Association), 90–91, 96, 114–115, 171
Yongbao Ping'an (Eternal Assurance of Well-Being), 41, 49–50, 112, 119, 171, 175
Yuan Bingchang, 181
Yueju (opera form from Shanghai/Shaoxing area), 134–135
yunluo (cloud gong), 69 fig. 4.5, 74–75, 75 fig. 4.7, 76, 78, 102, 138
Yunnan Art Institute, 22, 138, 158
Yunnan Ethnic Cultural Arts Exchange Company, 158, 186
Yunnan Nationalities Institute, 17, 183

Yunnan Normal University, 158
Yunnan Province Propaganda Department, 158, 186
Yunnan Province Revolutionary Modern Opera Festival (1964), 129
Yunnan Province Song and Dance Troupe, 130, 131
Yunnan University, 158

zai laiq (*dongba* bell), 56
zaqu (miscellaneous pieces), 82, 91
Zeng Guocai, 107
Zhang Kuiguang, 116
Zhang Longhan, 44, 88
Zhao Yintang, 41, 49, 171, 175, 176
Zhao Yuxian, 106, 109, 111
zheng (bridged zither), 173
  in Baisha Xiyue, 67, 68
  in Dongjing music, 71
zhong (bell), 75
zhonghu (two-string bowed lute), 70
Zhou Enlai, 17, 21
Zhou Fan, 121, 230 n. 3
Zhou Lin, 120, 121, 129, 130, 230 n. 3